Lecture Notes in Computer

Edited by G. Goos, J. Hartmanis, and .

T0230191

Springer
Berlin
Heidelberg
New York
Barcelona
Hong Kong
London
Milan
Paris
Tokyo

Graham N.C. Kirby   Alan Dearle
Dag I.K. Sjøberg (Eds.)

Persistent Object Systems

Design, Implementation, and Use

9th International Workshop, POS-9
Lillehammer, Norway, September 6-8, 2000
Revised Papers

 Springer

Series Editors

Gerhard Goos, Karlsruhe University, Germany
Juris Hartmanis, Cornell University, NY, USA
Jan van Leeuwen, Utrecht University, The Netherlands

Volume Editors

Graham N.C. Kirby
Alan Dearle
University of St. Andrews, School of Computer Science
North Haugh, St. Andrews, Fife KY16 9SS, UK
E-mail: {graham/al}@dcs.st-and.ac.uk
Dag I.K. Sjøberg
Simula Research Laboratory
P.O. Box 1080 Blindern, 0316 Oslo, Norway
E-mail: Dag.Sjoberg@ifi.uio.no

Cataloging-in-Publication Data applied for

Die Deutsche Bibliothek - CIP-Einheitsaufnahme

Persistent object systems : design, implementation, and use ; 9th
international workshop ; revised papers / POS-9, Lillehammer, Norway,
September 6 - 8, 2000. Graham N. C. Kirby ... (ed.). - Berlin ; Heidelberg ;
New York ; Barcelona ; Hong Kong ; London ; Milan ; Paris ; Tokyo :
Springer, 2001
    (Lecture notes in computer science ; 2135)
    ISBN 3-540-42735-X

CR Subject Classification (1998): C.2.4, D.2, D.3, D.4, H.2, H.4, F.3

ISSN 0302-9743
ISBN 3-540-42735-X Springer-Verlag Berlin Heidelberg New York

Springer-Verlag Berlin Heidelberg New York
a member of BertelsmannSpringer Science+Business Media GmbH

http://www.springer.de

© Springer-Verlag Berlin Heidelberg 2001

Typesetting: Camera-ready by author, data conversion by PTP-Berlin, Stefan Sossna
Printed on acid-free paper   SPIN: 10840119   06/3142   5 4 3 2 1 0

Preface

The Ninth International Workshop on Persistent Object Systems (POS-9) took place at the SAS Radisson Hotel in Lillehammer, Norway, from 6th to 8th September 2000. Previous workshops in the series have been held in Scotland (1 and 2), Australia (3), the USA (4), Italy (5), France (6), and the USA (7 and 8). In keeping with those workshops, POS-9 was short but intensive, fitting 28 papers and panel sessions, a boat excursion, and some memorable meals into two and a half days.[1] The participants' concentration was no doubt helped by the Northern European weather that prevailed for most of the workshop.

Continuing a trend experienced over the previous few workshops, POS-9 had difficulty attracting a high number of papers. Of course it is hard to tell whether this is a problem with the field of persistent systems itself, or merely a consequence of the increasing number of workshops, conferences, and journals competing for submissions. In his Epilogue to the proceedings, Ron Morrison makes some interesting suggestions for possible improvements to future POS workshops.

Out of a total of 26 submitted papers, 19 were accepted for presentation at the workshop. Breaking down by region, 6 1/2 came from the USA[2], 1 from Africa, 3 1/2 from Australia, and 8 from Europe. In a new development for POS, an equal number of papers came from England and from Scotland.

All submissions were reviewed by at least three members of the Program Committee. Several generated significant disagreement among their reviewers; these papers were accepted on the basis that substantial changes would be needed if they were to be included in the final proceedings. All such papers were updated successfully; our thanks go to the PC members who acted as shepherds to oversee the revisions. Indeed, as usual, the entire process relied on the dedication and hard work of the PC, and we thank them sincerely.

In full, the Program Committee was:

Ole Anfindsen	Atsushi Ohori
Malcolm Atkinson	Tamer Özsu
Jean Bacon	Fausto Rabitti
Sonia Berman	John Rosenberg
Steve Blackburn	Peter Schwarz
Richard Connor	Liuba Shrira
Laurent Daynès	Santosh Shrivastava
Giorgio Ghelli	Paul Wilson
Tony Hosking	Alex Wolf
Alfons Kemper	Stan Zdonik
Eliot Moss	Ben Zorn
Dave Munro	

---

[1] Photos from the workshop are on the POS-9 web site at http://www-ppg.dcs.st-and.ac.uk/Conferences/POS9/.

[2] Fractional numbers arise from trans-continental collaborations.

During the workshop, presentations were organized into short sessions of (loosely) related papers, each concluding with a panel during which the various authors had an opportunity to expand on deeper or more general issues. These proceedings include reports by the session chairs summarizing these discussions.

It is customary, in reporting on POS workshops, to note any current trends in areas of interest. The main broad research area addressed at POS-9 remained that of object stores, accounting for around half of the papers. The remaining papers covered a rich mixture of system architecture, middleware, and applications. A previously observed trend of diminishing interest in language design and type systems continued, with the almost complete dominance of Java as a language platform.

Finally, we acknowledge the generous support for POS-9 provided by the Research Council of Norway. We thank Ragnfrid Sjøberg and Helle Frøyseth for their excellent support with the local arrangements, and Helen Bremner for transcribing various session tapes.

June 2001

Graham Kirby
Alan Dearle
Dag Sjøberg

Table of Contents

Session 1: Overview

Graham N.C. Kirby

School of Computer Science, University of St Andrews,
North Haugh, St Andrews, Fife, KY16 9SS, Scotland
graham@dcs.st-and.ac.uk

The first session of the Workshop contained two papers addressing the implementation of persistence at the abstract machine level. „A Framework for Persistence-Enabled Optimization of Java Applications" by David Whitlock [DW] and Antony Hosking [AH] describes a number of techniques for optimizing Java programs by byte code transformation. Rather than treating persistence as a problem, the work exploits the presence of byte code in a persistent store to allow certain cross-class optimizations that are not viable in non-persistent Java implementations.

The second paper, „Architecture of the PEVM: A High-Performance Orthogonally Persistent Java™ Virtual Machine" by Brian Lewis [BL], Bernd Mathiske [BM] and Neal Gafter, describes the PEVM, a new implementation of orthogonal persistence for Java. PEVM runs significantly faster than previous implementations. It can also handle larger data sets and has a simpler structure.

During questions, Steve Blackburn [SB] asked Whitlock and Hosking how far their optimizations depended on orthogonal persistence. The response was that it was not always intrinsically necessary, but that it made certain optimizations economically viable where they might not be otherwise.

Alan Dearle [AD] asked whether the optimization costs varied linearly with program length, to which Whitlock replied that the relationship was in fact n^2. Then asked whether this meant that optimization was tractable in practice, he said that it was, since the programs in question were likely to be of the long-lived server type, in which the costs of optimization would be amortized over a relatively long time frame.

Ron Morrison [RM] asked Lewis and Mathiske to justify their design assumptions that direct pointers and explicit read barriers would lead to high performance. He also questioned the emphasis on scalability, observing that if a user only wanted to run small applications then it was more important for the system to run fast than for it to scale.

The authors acknowledged that efficiency at the small scale should not be sacrificed for scalability, for a general-purpose system. On the design decisions, Tony Printezis [TP] said that the big advantage of using direct pointers rather than fault blocks was that allocation was faster. Lewis and Mathiske stated that they had avoided using fault blocks or handles because of experience with PJama Classic, in which the cost of managing handles was significant compared with the cost of managing objects.

Malcolm Atkinson [MPA] followed up on the issue of using operating system traps versus explicit read barriers. Mathiske said that he had measured the cost of traps in Solaris, and they cost in the order of 10^5 cycles, which was clearly too slow.

Liuba Shrira [LS] asked why they had not been able to run the T2b benchmark on PJama Classic—Lewis answered that they just could not find any combination of system parameters that made it work. Mathiske added that an advantage of the PEVM

G.N.C. Kirby, A. Dearle, and D.I.K. Sjøberg (Eds.): POS-9, LNCS 2135, pp. 1-3, 2001.
© Springer-Verlag Berlin Heidelberg 2001

was that it didn't have so many parameters to tune. Shrira also asked about their experience with log structured stores, and making Swing and AWT persistent. Mathiske replied that he had implemented a simple log structured experiment along the lines of Lumberjack, but that its size was limited by its use of memory mapped files, and so it was not really comparable with the PEVM store. On making Swing/AWT persistent, Lewis and Mathiske said that a number of techniques had been needed to make them restartable after a stabilization. One problem was that C space allocated for GUI elements needed to be recreated on restart. This was tackled by a mechanism allowing callbacks to be assigned to particular objects; these could be invoked either at restart time, or when the object was first faulted during a run. These hooks were incorporated without changing the Swing/AWT APIs. When asked how many places in the code had been affected in this way, Mathiske replied that it was a couple of dozen callbacks—which was hastily amended to about 200 within the same sentence! Lewis remarked that an unfortunate aspect of JDK 1.2 was that more things had been implemented in C than in previous versions.

Dearle asked for clarification of one set of performance figures, comparing the PEVM and the original Research VM running a non-persistent application that generated purely transient objects. Lewis responded that the figures showed the cost of persistence support in PEVM: read and write barriers were always emitted whether they were necessary or not. He also pointed out PEVM's poor performance on the T6 benchmark, which he said was due to a higher number of garbage collections, since all objects were made slightly larger by the greater header overhead.

The general panel session started with a question from Morrison, who asked the panel to consider how systems could be built to allow optimization for various different applications with widely differing requirements. He gave the example of a query that touched every object only once, in which case many of the mechanisms described earlier would be redundant and introduce unnecessary overhead.

Mathiske responded that it was a straight trade-off between specific and general mechanisms. It would always be possible to build a faster specific mechanism for a particular application, but if the goal was to provide general purpose support then it was less important to be the fastest, or even fast, than to not be devastatingly slow!

Hosking replied that the key was to come up with a core set of abstractions to make the programmer's life easier, that could be implemented efficiently.

Whitlock agreed more with Ron, saying that we needed some way to characterise the nature of various applications so that specific persistence support products, such as orthogonally persistent languages and object databases, could be geared towards appropriate applications. Mathiske responded to this, saying that their persistent languages were optimized towards random access—and that for applications exhibiting a significant amount of linear behaviour, a relational database might well perform better.

Atkinson then observed that the two papers in the session went well together, in that the Purdue optimizations could be profitably combined with the Sun technology. However, this had not happened. He thought this was down to a fundamental trade-off with how well programmers could perform, given that they were more expensive than CPUs. Atkinson said that both groups had obviously needed to do a huge amount of work on the VM source code, and asked how future experiments could be made easier. Lewis replied that starting with a simpler VM would have made things a lot easier. Mathiske followed up with a comment that a fully bootstrapped VM, without a C runtime, would be beneficial.

Olivier Gruber [OG] said that recent experience at IBM indicated that the idea of a general purpose VM was perhaps not flexible enough. This considered both the spectrum of application behaviour and the capabilities of the host hardware—which ranged down to PDAs or smaller. He argued for greater modularity in application software and in persistence support, so that it might become easier to embed the same persistence runtime in an ORB, in a database, or in a web server as appropriate. Hosking agreed with this sentiment, saying that there was benefit in providing clean internal interfaces for persistence inside VMs, and also for other services such as garbage collection. Gruber added that we should stop thinking of persistent systems as standalone, whereas more and more they need to be embedded within other software that cannot be thrown away, such as ORBs. Whitlock agreed, saying that Gemstone implemented an ORB, and CORBA and JDBC services, on top of an underlying persistent system that was largely transparent to the user.

Hosking then turned the original question around, asking Morrison whether he had an answer. Morrison replied that the real difficulty was capturing the nature of the current and emerging applications. We don't know how to do this satisfactorily yet, but if we did then it might be possible to tailor persistence support appropriately for individual applications. Currently object stores were being built against some prejudices about how applications behaved, but these prejudices were not well supported by observations. To achieve high performance, it would be necessary to use a multitude of different implementation techniques, together with an effective framework for mapping techniques to applications appropriately.

Mathiske said that he had performed some experiments to test one of those prejudices: that using direct pointers, gains through reduced impact on mutator speed outweigh the costs of faulting in extra objects that are never used. Such „futile faulting" occurs for example when a reference is pushed on the stack only to be compared with another reference and not dereferenced; the object is faulted anyway. Mathiske measured the degree of futile faulting in a number of applications and found that it never rose above 10% of the total number of objects faulted.

Eliot Moss [EM] concluded the session, raising the issue of reflection and describing some of his current work using the Java-based Jalapeño VM from IBM. He said that the Java interface mechanism was useful in, for example, providing multiple garbage collector implementations that could be selected when a particular system was built.

A Framework for Persistence-Enabled Optimization of Java Object Stores

David Whitlock and Antony L. Hosking

Department of Computer Sciences
Purdue University
West Lafayette, IN 47907-1398
USA
hosking@cs.purdue.edu
davidw@gemstone.com
http://www.cs.purdue.edu/~hosking

Abstract. Aggressive optimization of programs often relies on analysis and transformation that cuts across the natural abstraction boundaries of the source programming language, such as procedures in procedural languages, or classes in class-based object-oriented languages like Java. Unfortunately, execution environments for languages such as Java dynamically link code into the application as it executes, precluding cross-cutting analyses and optimizations that are too expensive to apply on-line.

Fortunately, persistent object systems usually treat the code base as an integral part of the persistent store. This code base approximates the notion of "whole-program" that has been exploited in other optimization frameworks. This paper describes an analysis and optimization framework for Java that operates against the persistent code base, and couples the results of analysis and optimization with the run-time system to ensure continued correctness of the resulting code. The framework performs extensive analysis over the code in the store, supporting optimizations that cut across class boundaries in ways that are not safe to perform off-line on stand-alone Java classes.

1 Introduction

Techniques for aggressive optimization of programs often rely on analyses and transformations that cut across the natural abstraction boundaries that allow for separate compilation of the source programming language. These atomic compilation units typically correspond to natural encapsulation boundaries, such as procedures in procedural languages, or classes in class-based object-oriented languages like Java. Such aggressive analyses and optimizations then take into account the particular combination of units that make up a given application program, and specialize the code from each unit to that particular combination. For statically-linked languages such as C and Modula-3, where the units that make up a given program are known statically, aggressive (and possibly expensive) analysis and optimization can be performed off-line. Unfortunately, execution environments for more dynamic languages such as Java link code into the application as it executes, precluding analyses and optimizations that may prove too expensive to apply

G.N.C. Kirby, A. Dearle, and D.I.K. Sjøberg (Eds.): POS-9, LNCS 2135, pp. 4–17, 2001.
© Springer-Verlag Berlin Heidelberg 2001

on-line. Moreover, even for analyses that are not too expensive to apply on-line, some candidate optimizing transformations that are safe to apply at one time may subsequently become invalid if the code base evolves in a way that violates their safety.

Fortunately, persistent object systems usually treat the code base as an integral part of the persistent store. For example, the PJama prototype of orthogonal persistence for Java captures all classes loaded by a persistent application and stores them in the persistent store. This code base approximates the notion of "whole-program" that has been exploited in other optimization frameworks. We describe an analysis and optimization framework that operates against the code base of the PJama persistent store, and which couples the results of analysis and optimization with PJama's run-time system to ensure continued correctness of the resulting code. Our framework performs extensive analysis over the code in the persistent store, supporting optimizations that cut across class boundaries in ways that could not be safely achieved with stand-alone Java classes off-line.

The object-oriented programming paradigm aims to provide modular and reusable programs and libraries by encouraging the use of polymorphism and numerous small methods. However, the same qualities that make object-oriented programming attractive also make it difficult to optimize. Optimization techniques for procedural languages rely on potentially expensive static analysis of large portions of code. In contrast, object-oriented programs tend to be dynamic in nature and to have many short methods, so inlining is often employed to increase the size of the code regions for optimization.

We have implemented a number of analyses that attempt to reduce the dynamic nature of Java programs and, through method inlining, increase method size so that traditional optimizations may have a greater effect. The Java Language Specification [Gosling et al. 1996] requires that changes made to Java classes are *binary compatible* with pre-existing class binaries. However our optimizations break Java's data encapsulation model by allowing caller methods to access the private data of classes whose methods are inlined. For example, consider a method m_1 declared in class A and a method m_2 declared in class B that accesses one of B's private fields. Inlining a call in m_1 to m_2 would result in m_1 accessing one of B's private fields. This violates encapsulation as well as Java's static rules that ensure binary compatibility. Thus, our optimizations must be performed on classes in a safe environment in which the restrictions placed on transformations to ensure binary compatibility can be lifted. Code could be optimized at runtime when the virtual machine has complete control over the classes. However, our optimizations require extensive program analysis whose runtime cost would most likely outweigh any benefit gained by optimization.

Some implementations of orthogonal persistence for Java maintain a representation of classes, as well as instantiated objects, in the persistent store. Such a store provides a good approximation of the closed-world environment in which a Java program may actually run. The classes in a persistent store are verified to be binary compatible upon their entry to the virtual machine, so there is no need to "reverify" classes in the persistent store. Moreover, a program executing within a persistent store has an unusual concept of "runtime". Because data persists between executions in its runtime format, the execution of the program can be thought of in terms of the lifetime of its data. The program runs, pauses (no code executes, but the runtime data persists), then resumes. When the program is "paused" classes within the store may be modified without regard to binary compatibility. It is during these "pauses" that we perform our optimizations on classes residing with an persistent store.

Because our optimizations are static they cannot account for new classes that are introduced via class reflection or native methods. The introduction of new classes may invalidate some of our optimizations. To handle this, the virtual machine notifies the optimizer at runtime of changes in the class hierarchy. The optimizer, in turn, may revert certain methods to their unoptimized form, de-optimizing them based on the information provided by the virtual machine. We use a property known as *pre-existence* (discussed below) to avoid the need to de-optimize active methods (i.e., to avoid on-stack replacement).

Here we explore performing extensive *off-line* optimization of Java classes that reside in a persistent store. By off-line, we do not necessarily mean that the persistent system is inactive – transformations may be performed concurrently with the persistent application – but rather that the type analyses necessary for the optimizing transformations must not be invalidated by the concurrent execution through dynamic class loading. Thus, one might envision the optimizer running in a background thread, taking advantage of quiescent periods in the store. For now, however, our implementation operates against the persistent store as a separate, privileged application. This is unavoidable since we use the PJama prototype of orthogonal persistence for Java [Atkinson et al. 1996], which currently has no support for controlled concurrent access to a store by multiple applications. We use our Bytecode-Level Optimizer and Analysis Tool (BLOAT) [Hosking et al. 1999; Hosking et al. 2000] to model, analyze, and optimize Java programs, with method inlining to expose additional optimization opportunities to our intra-procedural optimizations.

2   Type Analysis

A *callee* method is invoked by a *caller* method at a *call-site*. There are two kinds of call-sites. A *dynamically bound* call-site invokes an *instance method* and requires a run-time *dynamic method lookup* to determine the exact method to be invoked based on the type of its *receiver* object. A *statically bound* call-site invokes a *class method* or a *constructor method* and does not require such a lookup. Type analysis computes the possible types of a receiver object and thus computes a set of methods that could be invoked at a call-site. If only one method can be invoked at a call-site, the call-site is said to be *monomorphic*. Otherwise, it is *polymorphic*.

Class hierarchy analysis [Dean et al. 1995; Fernandez 1995; Diwan et al. 1996] uses the class inheritance hierarchy in conjunction with static type information about a call-site to compute the possible methods that may be invoked. We use the class hierarchy given in Figure 1 to demonstrate our analyses and optimizations. Consider the getArea method in Figure 2 which contains a dynamically bound call to the area method. Without considering type and flow analysis (i.e., ignoring the context of the call), then the call to area might resolve to the implementation of the area method in any of the Triangle, Circle, or Rectangle classes. Observe that if the compile-time type of the receiver of the invocation of area is Rectangle or its subclass Square, the only method that could

```
abstract class Shape {
  abstract float area();
  float getPI() { return 3.14579F; }
  static float square(float f) {
    return f * f;
  }
}

class Triangle extends Shape {
  float b, h;
  Triangle(float b, float h) {
    this.b = b; this.h = h;
  }
  float area() { return b * h / 2; }
}

class Circle extends Shape {
  float r;
  Circle(float r) { this.r = r; }
  float area() {
    return getPI() * Shape.square(r);
  }
}

class Rectangle extends Shape {
  float s1, s2;
  Rectangle(float s1, float s2) {
    this.s1 = s1; this.s2 = s2;
  }
  float area() { return s1 * s2; }
}

class Square extends Rectangle {
  Square(float s) { super(s, s); }
}
```

Fig. 1. Example class hierarchy

possible be invoked is the **area** implementation in **Rectangle** because no subclass of **Rectangle** overrides **area**. This observation is key to class hierarchy analysis.

Rapid type analysis (RTA) [Bacon and Sweeney 1996] extends class hierarchy analysis by using class instantiation information to reduce the set of potential receiver types at a call-site. Consider the program in Figure 2. Class hierarchy analysis stated that the call to **area** could invoke the **area** method of **Triangle**, **Circle**, or **Rectangle**. However, a quick glance at the program reveals that it is impossible for the **area** method implemented in **Triangle** to be invoked because neither **Triangle** nor any of its subclasses is instantiated. Classes that are instantiated are said to be *live*.

RTA must be careful in the way that it marks a class as being instantiated. Invoking a class's constructor does not necessarily mean that the class is instantiated. Consider an invocation of the one-argument constructor of **Square**. Calling this constructor indicates that class **Square** is instantiated. However, **Square**'s constructor invokes the constructor of its superclass, **Rectangle**. This invocation of **Rectangle**'s constructor does not indicate that **Rectangle** is instantiated.

```
float getArea(boolean b) {
  Shape s;
  if(b)
    s = new Circle(2);
  else
    s = new Square(3);
  float area = s.area();
  return area;
}
```

Fig. 2. Calling method area

Rapid type analysis examines a program's methods starting at its entry point (e.g., main method). One following operations occurs at an invocation of method m.

- If the call-site is statically bound, then m is marked as being live and is examined further.
- If the call-site is dynamically bound, then the set of potential receiver types is calculated using class hierarchy analysis. For each potential receiver type that has been instantiated, T, the implementation of m that would be invoked with receiver type T is made live and is examined further. The implementations of m in the uninstantiated classes are "blocked" on each uninstantiated type T.
- If m is a constructor of class T and the caller is not a constructor of a subclass of T, the class T is instantiated and m becomes live and is examined. Additionally, any methods that were blocked on T are unblocked and examined.

In our running example, classes Circle and Square are live. The constructors for Circle and Square, the area methods of Circle and Rectangle, and the getPI and square methods are all live. The area method of Triangle is blocked on Triangle.

3   Call-Site Customization

The compiler for the SELF language introduced the notion of call-site *customization* [Chambers et al. 1989]. Customization optimizes a dynamically bound call-site based on the type of the receiver. If the type of the receiver can be precisely determined during compilation, then the call-site can be statically bound.

The call to area in Figure 2 can be customized in the following manner. Rapid type analysis concluded that the the area method of either Circle or Rectangle will be invoked. Customization replaces the dynamically bound call-site with two type tests and corresponding statically bound invocations (in the form of a call to a class method) as show in Figure 3. If the call-site is monomorphic, no type test is necessary. Two class methods, $area in Circle and $area in Rectangle have been created containing the same code as the instance method versions of area. In the case that the receiver type is none of the expected types, the virtual method is executed.

Once a call to an instance method has been converted into a call to a class method, the call may be *inlined*. Inlining consists of copying the code from the callee method into the caller method. Thus, inlining completely eliminates any overhead associated with invoking the method.

```
float getArea(boolean b) {
  Shape s;
  if (b)
    s = new Circle(2);
  else
    s = new Square(3);
  float area;
  if (s instanceof Circle) {
    Circle c = (Circle) s;
    area = Circle.$area(c);
  } else if(s instanceof Rectangle) {
    Rectangle r = (Rectangle) s;
    area = Rectangle.$area(r);
  } else
    area = s.area();
  return area;
}
```

Fig. 3. Customized call to area

Our optimization framework performs intra-procedural data-flow analysis that in some cases precisely determines the types of receiver objects. For instance, if the receiver object is created within the caller method by a constructor call, we know the receiver's type.

Our analyses have resulted in an increased number of statically bound call-sites whose callee methods are precisely known and may be *inlined*. Inlining involves copying the callee's code into the caller method. By inlining methods, we not only eliminate the overhead of invoking a method, but we also give our intra-procedural optimizer a large code context in which to perform its optimizations.

4 Pre-existence

When customizing call-sites certain assumptions are made about the classes in the program. For instance, the analysis may determine that a call-site is monomorphic and inlines the invocation. However, additional classes may enter the system that invalidate assumptions made during the analysis. In this case the optimized code must be de-optimized.

This situation is further exacerbated by the fact that optimized code may need to be de-optimized while it is executing. Consider the program in Figure 4a. The method getSomeShape may potentially load a subclass of Shape that is unknown at analysis time. getSomeShape could be a native method or, in the worst case, could ask the user for the name of a class to load. In any case, the call to area cannot be inlined without the possibility of later adjustment.

The SELF system [Hölzle et al. 1992] solved this problem by using a run-time mechanism called *on-stack replacement* to modify executing code. SELF maintains a significant amount of debugging information that allows for quick de-optimization of optimized code. When an optimization is invalidated, SELF recovers the original source code and re-optimizes it taking the invalidating information into account. Maintaining the amount of information necessary to perform these kinds of optimizations requires a noticeable

```
float getSomeArea() {              float getSomeArea(Shape s) {
   Shape s = getSomeShape();          float area = s.area();
   float area = s.area();             return area;
   return area;                    }
}
```

(a) Receiver does not pre-exist   (b) Receiver pre-exists

Fig. 4. Pre-existence of receiver objects

space and time overhead, increases the complexity of the optimizer, and places certain constraints on the kinds of optimizations that can be performed.

Detlefs and Agesen [1999] introduced the concept of *pre-existence* to eliminate the need for on-stack replacement. Consider a method foo containing an invocation of method bar with receiver object o. o is said to *pre-exist* if it is created before foo is called. The type of any pre-existent object must have been introduced before the method foo is called. Any invalidation of assumptions made about the type of o this introduction may cause will not affect the method foo while it is executing. Therefore, on-stack replacement on method foo will never occur and it is safe to inline the call to bar.

Consider the version of getSomeArea presented in Figure 4b. In this method the call-site's receiver is one of the method's arguments. If any previously unknown sub-class of Shape were to enter the system, it would have to do so before the call to getSomeArea. At the time that the new class enters the system, the as-yet-uncalled getSomeArea method would be appropriately re-optimized to account for the new class.

A technique called *invariant argument analysis* is used to determine whether or not a call-site's receiver pre-exists. Invariant argument analysis traces the uses of the caller's arguments. If an argument is used as receiver, then it pre-exists. Additionally, receivers that result solely from allocations operations pre-exist.

5   Implementation

We analyze and optimize *class files*, a binary representation of Java classes that are suitable for execution on a Java virtual machine, and are able to take advantage of the semantics of some of the machine's instructions. When performing rapid type analysis, instead of analyzing calls to constructors, we use occurrences of the new instruction to denote a class instantiation. When customizing call-sites we transform invokevirtual instructions which call an instance bound method to invokespecial instructions that invoke an instance method, but do not perform a dynamic method lookup.

To accommodate our optimizations several changes were made to the PJama virtual machine. By allowing caller methods access to the private data of their inlined methods, our optimizations break encapsulation. Once a class is loaded into the virtual machine, it is no longer necessary to enforce encapsulation. Thus, we disable data access checks for loaded classes. Also, for security reasons, the Java Virtual Machine Specification [Lindholm and Yellin 1999] allows the invokespecial instruction to only invoke super-class and private methods. We have relaxed this rule and allow invokespecial to call any instance method.

6   De-optimization

Pre-existence ensured that classes entering the system could never invalidate executing code. However, other optimized code may need to be de-optimized in the face of such changes to the type system. Consider a caller method foo that contains a call to the area method. Suppose that rapid type analysis has determined that the call-site will only invoke the area method of Triangle and that its receiver object pre-exists because it is a method parameter. Customization will transform this call into a non-virtual call to the area method of Triangle. Suppose further that at runtime the program, using Java's reflection mechanism, loads the EquilateralTriangle class, a subclass of Triangle that overrides the area method. During customization we assumed that no subclass of Triangle overrode the area method. However, the introduction of the EquilateralTriangle invalidates this assumption and the customized invocation of the area method of Triangle is incorrect because the receiver object may be an instance of EquilateralTriangle in addition to Triangle. Thus, we must de-optimize foo at runtime by undoing the effects of customization. In an attempt to make de-optimization as fast as possible, foo is simply reverted to its unoptimized form.

In the above example, we say that method foo *depends* on the area method of Triangle because if the area method of Triangle is overridden, then foo must be de-optimized. The optimizer maintains a series of dependencies [Chambers et al. 1995] among methods resulting from call-site customization. As a result of the customization shown in Figure 3 the getArea method would depend on the area method of Circle and the area method of Rectangle. Note that if our analysis can precisely determine the type(s) of a receiver object (e.g., the object is created inside the caller method), then no dependence is necessary. The dependencies are represented as Java objects and reside in the persistent store.

The PJama virtual machine was modified to communicate with the optimizer at runtime to determine when methods should be de-optimized. When a class is loaded into the virtual machine, the optimizer is notified. If the newly-loaded class invalidates any assumptions made about the class hierarchy during optimization, the optimizer consults the method dependencies and de-optimizes the appropriate methods. To account for any degradation in performance that de-optimization may produce, it may be desirable to re-optimize a Java program multiple times during its lifetime. Subsequent re-optimizations will account for classes that are introduced by reflection.

A persistent store provides a closed-world model of a Java program, allows us to disregard the restriction of binary compatibility, and provides a repository in which the optimizer can store data necessary for de-optimization to ensure correct program behavior when classes are introduced into the system at runtime. Thus, persistence enables us to safely perform our inter-procedural optimizations on Java programs.

It is important to note that the general cross-class optimizations we support cannot be performed outside the virtual machine by modifying the bytecode at load time, since the modified bytecode would violate Java's structural constraints and fail bytecode verification.

Table 1. Benchmarks

Name	Description
crypt	Java implementation of the Unix crypt utility
db	Operations on memory-resident database
huffman	Huffman encoding
idea	File encryption tool
jack	Parser generator
jess	Expert system
jlex	Scanner generator
jtb	Abstract syntax tree builder
lzw	Lempel-Ziv-Welch file compression utility
mpegaudio	MPEG Layer-3 decoder
neural	Neural network simulation

7 Results

To evaluate the impact of inter-procedural optimizations on Java programs, we optimized several Java benchmark applications and compared their performance using static and dynamic performance metrics. To obtain the measurements we used a software library that allows user-level access to the UltraSPARC hardware execution counters,[1] permitting us to gain accurate counts of hardware clock cycles, cache misses such as instruction fetch stalls and data read misses. Benchmarks were run with the operating system in single-user mode to avoid spurious interference from unrelated processes.

The experiments were performed on a Sun Ultra 5 with a 333 MHz UltraSPARC-IIi processor with a 2MB external (L2) cache and 128MB of RAM. The UltraSPARC-IIi has a 16-KB write-through, non-allocating, direct mapped primary data cache that is virtually-indexed and virtually-tagged. The 16-KB primary instruction cache is two-way set associative, physically indexed and tagged, and performs in-cache 2-bit branch prediction with single cycle branch following.

We used eleven benchmarks programs as described in Table 1 to measure the impact of inter-procedural optimizations. Several of the benchmarks were taken from the SpecJVM [SPEC 1998] suite of benchmarks. Table 2 gives some static statistics about the benchmarks: the number of live classes and methods, the number of virtual call-sites, the percentage of those call-sites that pre-exist, and the percentage of pre-existent call-sites that are monomorphic and duomorphic (only two methods could be invoked). It is interesting to note that for most benchmarks the majority of virtual call-sites are precluded from inlining because they do not pre-exist. Note also that nearly all (89.8–95.7%) of pre-existent call-sites are monomorphic or duomorphic. Thus, from a static point of view, extensive customization of polymorphic call-sites seems unnecessary.

Table 3 summarizes the time spent optimizing each benchmark and supports our claim that our inter-procedural optimizations are too expensive to perform during program execution. The optimizer spends the vast majority of its time constructing the call

---

[1] See http://www.cs.msu.edu/~enbody/

Table 2. Inlining statistics (static)

Benchmark	live classes	live methods	virtual calls	% preexist	% mono	% duo
crypt	134	853	1005	38.9	87.0	3.1
db	151	1010	1373	36.7	87.7	4.2
huffman	141	875	1071	38.6	87.7	2.9
jack	184	1170	2305	31.5	86.1	8.3
jess	245	1430	2563	35.0	92.2	3.0
jlex	154	1008	1315	35.4	88.8	2.6
jtb	273	2111	3965	32.8	87.7	8.0
lzw	142	905	1031	38.3	86.8	3.0
mpegaudio	173	1146	1594	31.6	87.1	5.2
neural	139	883	1024	39.1	87.2	3.0

Table 3. Optimization times

Benchmark	Total (sec)		% Call Graph		% Customize		% Inline		% Commit	
	User	System	User	System	User	System	User	System	User	System
crypt	75.40	17.63	56.84	81.79	7.88	0.62	19.58	0.51	15.70	17.07
db	317.97	61.30	74.68	84.34	5.99	0.20	7.30	1.55	12.03	13.92
huffman	78.59	18.29	58.65	82.23	7.79	0.55	18.59	0.71	14.98	16.51
jack	333.69	65.56	71.34	81.18	6.54	0.23	9.85	5.54	12.27	13.06
jess	394.01	72.26	66.50	75.63	9.17	0.26	12.17	10.64	12.16	13.47
jlex	90.11	19.03	55.03	81.87	7.70	0.84	22.02	0.68	15.25	16.61
jtb	258.14	23.26	31.05	75.71	7.53	0.47	46.82	3.83	14.60	19.99
lzw	75.43	18.43	56.81	82.69	7.93	0.38	19.58	0.65	15.68	16.28
mpegaudio	351.02	64.04	74.09	85.81	7.17	0.27	7.69	0.50	11.04	13.43
neural	74.52	18.63	58.99	81.59	8.24	0.27	17.35	1.13	15.42	17.02

graph and committing the optimized classes back to class-files. Call-site customization and inlining is comparatively inexpensive to perform.

Each benchmark was optimized in five configurations: no optimization, (nop), only intra-procedural optimizations (intra), call-site customization (cust), inlining of non-virtual calls (inline), and intra-procedural optimizations on top of inlining (both). Our intra-procedural optimizations include dead code elimination, constant/copy propagation, partial redundancy elimination, and register allocation of Java virtual machine local variables. Through analysis of empirical data, several conditions on the inter-procedural optimizations were arrived at: only monomorphic call-sites were customized, no callee method that is larger than 50 instructions is inlined and no caller method is allowed to exceed 1000 instructions because of inlining.

Examining the number of bytecodes executed provides insight into the effectiveness of our inter-procedural optimizations. Figures 5 and 6 summarize bytecode counts for the five optimization levels: nop, intra, cust, inline, and both. As Figure 5 demonstrates

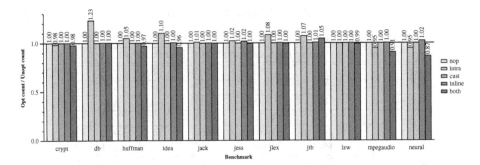

Fig. 5. Total bytecodes executed

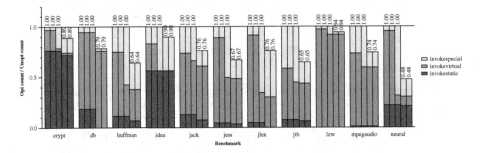

Fig. 6. Method invocations

the inter-procedural optimizations, cust and inline, do not have a significant effect on the total number of bytecodes executed. However, combining inter-procedural and intra-procedural optimizations (both) results in up to 8% fewer bytecodes being executed than with the intra-procedural optimizations alone (intra).

The effects of call-site customization and method inlining can be seen by examining the number and kind of methods executed. Figure 6 reports the number of invokespecial, invokevirtual[2], and invokestatic instructions. Call-site customization (cust) results in an often drastic reduction in the number of invokevirtual instructions. Likewise, method inlining removes as many as 52% of method invocations. For several benchmarks (crypt, idea, and neural) very few static method invocations are inlined. This is most likely due to the fact that the bodies of these methods exceed the 50 instruction limit placed on inlined methods.

Figure 7 compares the execution times (number of cycles executed) of our benchmarks. The benchmarks were executed on the Sun Java 2 SDK Solaris[TM] Production Release Virtual Machine with Just-In-Time compilation disabled[3]. Our optimizations cause a -2–22% decrease in the number of machine cycles. For several benchmarks, our optimizations cause an increase in the number of instruction fetch stalls and data read misses leading to an increase in the number of cycles.

---

[2] There were a negligible number of invokeinterface instructions executed.

[3] For some benchmarks, our optimizations expose a bug in the JIT.

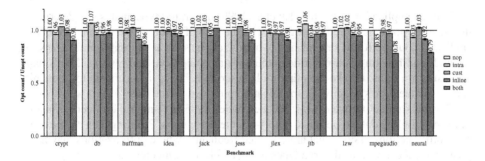

Fig. 7. Execution times (cycles)

For most benchmarks customizing monomorphic call-sites has little effect on the number of cycles executed. This leads us to believe that the interpreter's **invokevirtual** instruction has been optimized for maximum efficiency since it appears to have the same cost as the non-virtual **invokespecial** instruction. However, the increase in speed provided by method inlining demonstrates that the method invocation sequence is still costly. In most cases inlining enabled the intra-procedural optimizations to increase performance further.

8 Related Work

Much work has been done in the area of type analysis of object-oriented programming languages, particularly in type prediction and type inferencing. Palsberg and Schwartzbach [1991] present a constraint-based algorithm for inter-procedural type inferencing that operates in $O(n^3)$ time where n is the size of the program. Agesen [Agesen 1994] presents a survey of various improvements to the $O(n^3)$ algorithm. Several strategies create copies of methods called "templates" whose type information is specialized with respect to the type of the parameters. Agesen also describes the "Cartesian Product Algorithm" [Agesen 1995] that creates a template for every receiver and argument tuple per call-site. Several of the above algorithms were considered for our type analysis. However, as implementation began it became obvious that none of them is practical using our modeling framework for the numerous classes in JDK1.2.

Diwan et al. [1996] use class hierarchy analysis and an intra-procedural algorithm in addition to a context-insensitive type propagation algorithm to optimize Modula-3 programs. Budimlic and Kennedy present inter-procedural analyses and method inlining of Java programs [Budimlic and Kennedy 1997; Budimlic and Kennedy 1998]. They implement *code specialization* in which virtual methods contain a run-time type test to determine whether or not inlined code should be executed. In order to preserve Java's encapsulation mechanism, their analyses must operate on one class at a time. Thus, no method's from other classes may be inlined.

The Soot optimization framework [Sundaresan et al. 1999] performs similar analysis to ours. While they describe type analyses that are more aggressive than rapid type analysis, it is unclear as to the practicality of these analyses under JDK1.2.

The Jax application extractor [Tip et al. 1999] uses rapid type analysis to determine the essential portions of a Java program with the goal of reducing the overall size of the application. Jax performs several simple optimizations such as inlining certain accessor methods and marking non-overridden methods as being final and respects Java's data encapsulation rules. Unlike the other tools described above, Jax accounts for dynamic changes in the type system via a specification provided by the user.

Several studies [Grove et al. 1995; Fernandez 1995] examine the effects of using run-time profiling data to optimize object-oriented programs. Profiling data can be used to identify sections of code that are executed frequently where optimizations may have greater impact as well as the true types of the receivers of method calls.

More recently, the Jalepeño Java Virtual machine [Alpern et al. 1999] has taken a unique approach to optimizing Java program. Jalepeño is written almost entirely in Java and yet it executes without a bytecode interpreter. It employs several compilers that translate bytecode into native machine instructions. The compilers use both static techniques and profiling data, but differ in the number and kinds of optimizations they perform.

9   Conclusions

Java programs whose classes reside inside a persistent store give us a unique opportunity for whole-program optimization. We can relax certain constraints placed on stand-alone Java programs and safely perform expensive off-line optimizations. In order to ensure correct program execution in the face of an evolving system, certain optimizations are undone at runtime. Our results show that our optimizations are able to remove a significant portion of the dynamic call overhead associated with Java programs, and to inline methods for more effective optimization of the resulting regions of larger context.

Acknowledgements. This research is supported in part by the National Science Foundation under Grant No. CCR-9711673 and by gifts from Sun Microsystems and IBM.

References

AGESEN, O. 1994. *Constraint-Based Type Inference and Parametric Polymorphism.* lncs, vol. 864. 78–100.

AGESEN, O. 1995. The cartesian product algorithm: Simple and precise typing of parametric polymorphism. See ECOOP'95 [1995], 2–26.

ALPERN, B., ATTANASIO, C. R., BARTON, J. J., COCCHI, A., HUMMEL, S. F., LIEBER, D., NGO, T., MERGEN, M., SHEPHERD, J. C., AND SMITH, S. 1999. Implementing Jalepeño in Java. See OOPSLA'99 [1999], 314–324.

ATKINSON, M. P., DAYNÈS, L., JORDAN, M. J., PRINTEZIS, T., AND SPENCE, S. 1996. An orthogonally persistent Java. *ACM SIGMOD Record 25,* 4 (Dec.), 68–75.

BACON, D. F. AND SWEENEY, P. F. 1996. Fast static analysis of c++ virtual function calls. See OOPSLA'96 [1996], 324–341.

BUDIMLIC, Z. AND KENNEDY, K. 1997. Optimizing Java: Theory and practice. *Software—Practice and Experience 9,* 6 (June), 445–463.

BUDIMLIC, Z. AND KENNEDY, K. 1998. Static interprocedural optimizations in java. Tech. Rep. CRPC-TR98746, Rice University.

CHAMBERS, C., DEAN, J., AND GROVE, D. 1995. A framework for selective recompilation in the presence of complex intermodule dependencies. In *Proceedings of the International Conference on Software Engineering* (Seattle, Washington, Apr.). IEEE Computer Society, 221–230.

CHAMBERS, C., UNGAR, D., AND LEE, E. 1989. An efficient implementation of Self, a dynamically-typed object-oriented language based on prototypes. In Proceedings of the ACM Conference on Object-Oriented Programming Systems, Languages, and Applications (New Orleans, Louisiana, Oct.). *ACM SIGPLAN Notices 24*, 10 (Oct.), 49–70.

DEAN, J., GROVE, D., AND CHAMBERS, C. 1995. Optimization of object-oriented programs using static class hierarchy analysis. See ECOOP'95 [1995].

DETLEFS, D. AND AGESEN, O. 1999. Inlining of virtual methods. In *Proceedings of the European Conference on Object-Oriented Programming* (Lisbon, Portugal, June), R. Guerraoui, Ed. Lecture Notes in Computer Science, vol. 1628. Springer-Verlag, 258–278.

DIWAN, A., MOSS, J. E. B., AND MCKINLEY, K. S. 1996. Simple and effective analysis of statically-typed object-oriented programs. See OOPSLA'96 [1996], 292–305.

ECOOP'95 1995. *Proceedings of the European Conference on Object-Oriented Programming* (Åarhus, Denmark, Aug.). Lecture Notes in Computer Science, vol. 952. Springer-Verlag.

FERNANDEZ, M. F. 1995. Simple and effective link-time optimization of Modula-3 programs. In Proceedings of the ACM Conference on Programming Language Design and Implementation (La Jolla, California, June). *ACM SIGPLAN Notices 30*, 6 (June), 103–115.

GOSLING, J., JOY, B., AND STEELE, G. 1996. *The Java Language Specification.* Addison-Wesley.

GROVE, D., DEAN, J., GARRETT, C., AND CHAMBERS, C. 1995. Profile-guided receiver class prediction. In Proceedings of the ACM Conference on Object-Oriented Programming Systems, Languages, and Applications (Austin, Texas, Oct.). *ACM SIGPLAN Notices 30*, 10 (Oct.), 108–123.

HÖLZLE, U., CHAMBERS, C., AND UNGAR, D. 1992. Debugging optimized code with dynamic deoptimization. In Proceedings of the ACM Conference on Programming Language Design and Implementation (San Francisco, California, June). *ACM SIGPLAN Notices 27*, 7 (July), 32–43.

HOSKING, A. L., NYSTROM, N., WHITLOCK, D., CUTTS, Q., AND DIWAN, A. 1999. Partial redundancy elimination for access path expressions. In *Proceedings of the Intercontinental Workshop on Aliasing in Object Oriented Systems* (Lisbon, Portugal, June).

HOSKING, A. L., NYSTROM, N., WHITLOCK, D., CUTTS, Q., AND DIWAN, A. 2000. Partial redundancy elimination for access path expressions. *Software–Practice and Experience.* To appear in Special Issue on Aliasing in Object-Oriented Systems.

LINDHOLM, T. AND YELLIN, F. 1999. *The Java Virtual Machine Specification.* Addison-Wesley.

OOPSLA'96 1996. *Proceedings of the ACM Conference on Object-Oriented Programming Systems, Languages, and Applications* (San Jose, California, Oct.). *ACM SIGPLAN Notices 31*, 10 (Oct.).

OOPSLA'99 1999. *Proceedings of the ACM Conference on Object-Oriented Programming Systems, Languages, and Applications* (Denver, Colorado, Nov.). *ACM SIGPLAN Notices 34*, 10 (Oct.).

PALSBERG, J. AND SCHWARTZBACH, M. I. 1991. Object-oriented type inference. In Proceedings of the ACM Conference on Object-Oriented Programming Systems, Languages, and Applications (Phoenix, Arizona, Oct.). *ACM SIGPLAN Notices 26*, 11 (Nov.), 146–161.

SPEC. 1998. SPECjvm98 benchmarks. http://www.spec.org/osg/jvm98.

SUNDARESAN, V., RAZAFIMAHEFA, C., VALLÉE-RAI, R., AND HENDREN, L. 1999. Practical virtual method call resolution for java. Trusted objects, Centre Universitaire d'Informatique, University of Geneva. July.

TIP, F., LAFFRA, C., SWEENEY, P. F., AND STREETER, D. 1999. Practical experience with an application extractor for Java. See OOPSLA'99 [1999], 292–305.

Architecture of the PEVM: A High-Performance Orthogonally Persistent Java™Virtual Machine

Brian Lewis, Bernd Mathiske, and Neal Gafter

Sun Microsystems, Inc.*
901 San Antonio Road
Palo Alto, CA 94303-4900
{brian.lewis,bernd.mathiske,neal.gafter}@sun.com

Abstract. This paper describes the design and implementation of the *PEVM*, a new scalable, high-performance implementation of orthogonal persistence for the Java™platform (OPJ).

The PEVM is based on the Sun Microsystems Laboratories Virtual Machine for Research (ResearchVM), which features an optimizing Just-In-Time compiler, exact generational garbage collection, and fast thread synchronization. It also uses a new, scalable persistent object store designed to manage more than 80GB of objects. The PEVM is approximately ten times faster than previous OPJ implementations and can run significantly larger programs. It is faster than or comparable in performance to several commercial persistence solutions for the Java platform. Despite the PEVM's speed and scalability, its implementation is simpler than our previous OPJ implementation (e.g., it needs just 43% of the VM source patches previously required). Its speed and simplicity are largely due to our pointer swizzling strategy, the ResearchVM's exact memory management, and a few simple but effective mechanisms. For example, we implement some key data structures in the Java™programming language since this automatically makes them persistent.

1   Introduction

The Forest project at Sun Microsystems Laboratories and the Persistence and Distribution Group at Glasgow University are developing *orthogonal persistence* for the Java platform (OPJ) [3]. This gives programs, with only minor source file changes, the illusion of a very large object heap containing objects that are automatically saved to stable storage, typically on disk, and fetched from stable storage into virtual memory on demand [15].

The PEVM is our most recent OPJ implementation. Based on our experience with our previous PJama system ("PJama Classic") [6], we wanted an OPJ system with more performance, scalability, and maintainability to support our development of OPJ and a related project that is investigating controlled sharing and concurrency control through transactions [7]. The PEVM is based on the high performance Sun Microsystems Laboratories Virtual Machine for Research

---

* Copyright 2000 Sun Microsystems, Inc., All rights reserved.

G.N.C. Kirby, A. Dearle, and D.I.K. Sjøberg (Eds.): POS-9, LNCS 2135, pp. 18–33, 2001.
© Springer-Verlag Berlin Heidelberg 2001

("ResearchVM")[1], which includes an optimizing Just-In-Time (JIT) compiler [8], fast thread synchronization [1], and exact generational garbage collection. The PEVM is also based on the Sphere recoverable persistent object store from Glasgow University [21], [20]. Sphere is intended specifically to overcome the store-related limitations we experienced with PJama Classic. It can store up to 2^{31} objects, or about 80GB with 40 byte objects.

This paper describes the design and implementation of the PEVM. Our design goals are listed in Section 2. Section 3 outlines and describes in detail the PEVM's architecture. This is followed by a section that discusses the performance of the PEVM, another that describes related work, and then by a summary and conclusion section.

2   Design Goals

This section discusses our goals for the PEVM. Our primary goals were to provide high performance and scalability:

- Execution speed of persistent applications should be as high as possible. For example, while some other persistent systems (e.g., PJama Classic) use indirect pointers to objects to simplify their implementation of eviction, we wanted the PEVM to use direct pointers for speed.
- Object caching should be efficient and non-disruptive: the pauses it produces should be small. As an example, while some other systems such as PM3 [12] use virtual memory traps to retrieve objects, we wanted the PEVM to use explicit read barriers since these have lower cost.
- The PEVM must be able to operate with the same large number of objects as Sphere.
- The ResearchVM supports heaps of more than one gigabyte. The PEVM should be able to use such large heaps without significantly increasing the disruption caused by garbage collection.
- The ResearchVM supports server applications with hundreds of threads. The PEVM should not introduce bottlenecks that significantly reduce its multi-threading capabilities.

A secondary design goal was simplicity. We wanted to create a system that was easy to maintain and enhance. We deliberately chose simple initial solutions as long as they were easy to replace. This allowed us to build a running system quickly, which we used to gain experience and to discover where improvements were needed. For example, our first implementation of the Resident Object Table (ROT) (see Sect. 3.3) was a single-level hashtable that required long pauses during reorganization when it grew to hold a large number of objects. We subsequently replaced it with a more sophisticated implementation.

In addition, we also began with the goal of having the PEVM support persistent threads—to be able to store the state of all threads, and then later restart

---

[1] The ResearchVM is embedded in Sun's Java 2 SDK Production Release for the Solaris[TM] Operating Environment, available at http://www.sun.com/solaris/java/.

each thread at the machine instruction where it left off. However, we were unable to implement persistent threads because the thread support libraries used by the ResearchVM do not allow us to read and later restore the state of threads. As a result, we can only checkpoint the state of objects.

3   Architecture of the PEVM

The ResearchVM consists of an interpreter, a JIT compiler, runtime support functions, and a garbage collected heap. The PEVM extends the ResearchVM with an object cache and a persistent object store. Fig. 1 shows its main components and indicates where data transfers between them occur:

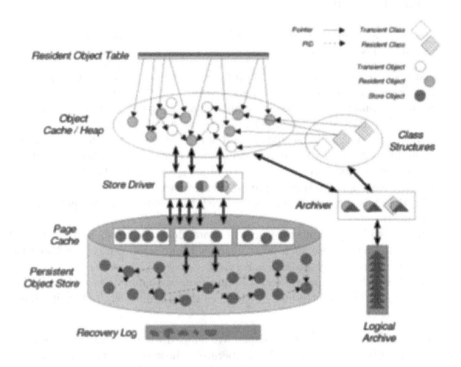

Fig. 1. Architectural Components

- The heap and the object cache are integrated and contain both transient and persistent objects (see Sect. 3.3). The PEVM uses the ResearchVM's default heap configuration with a nursery generation and a mark-compact old generation.
- The scalable resident object table (ROT) (see Sect. 3.3) translates references to objects in the store into virtual memory addresses in the object cache.

- The store driver (see Sect. 3.2) hides details of interacting with a store from the rest of the PEVM.
- The default persistent object store implementation used by the PEVM is Sphere, which includes an internal page cache and a recovery log. Other store architectures can be used by writing a new driver that implements the store driver interface.
- The logical archiver exports a store's objects to a file in a format that survives changes to the PEVM. It also supports reconstructing the "store" from an archive file. (see Sect. 3.5).
- The *evolution* facility supports application change while preserving the existing data in a store (see Sect. 3.6).

3.1   Representation of Objects and References

An object reference in the PEVM is either a direct pointer to an object in the heap or a persistent identifier (*PID*) that uniquely identifies the object in the store. A PID is allocated by the store the first time an object is written to it by a *checkpoint* operation. PIDs are distinguished from heap pointers by having a *1* in their low-order bit (heap objects are allocated on an eight byte boundary). We use direct pointers to heap objects to maximize the PEVM's CPU performance; see Sect. 3.3 for more detail.

The PEVM adds additional information to the header of each heap object. This includes an object's PID (if persistent) or 0. A flag indicates whether the object has been modified. Other flags support eviction and indicate, for example, whether the object can never be evicted because it is essential for the PEVM's operation. The modified flag actually indicates, when set, whether the object is "clean" (unmodified); this allows a single instruction to mark objects dirty.

To make checkpointing and object faulting as fast as possible, the PEVM uses representations for instance and array objects in the store that closely resemble those in memory, except that the object references they contain are replaced by the corresponding PIDs (*unswizzled*). It represents classes on disk using an architecture-neutral description that includes a PID for an array containing the class file's bytes, a PID for its class loader, the values of static fields, and a set of flag bits that indicate whether the class has been verified, linked, and initialized. This representation is much simpler than one that tries to mirror the in-memory representation of classes (as in PJama Classic). The PEVM reloads classes (without reinitializion or relinking) when it faults them in, and uses the flag bits and static field values to restore the class's state. We found that reloading classes from the store is not a significant runtime cost.

3.2   Store Driver

While Sphere is the default store used by the PEVM, we occasionally use a second, simpler store implementation to isolate problems. We are also beginning to experiment with a third store that is log-structured. A store driver insulates the PEVM from the details of a store. It implements a high-level interface of store operations used by the rest of the PEVM. It also performs all conversions between the heap and store representations of objects, and is the only system component that understands both representations. To adapt the PEVM to an additional store architecture, it is enough to implement a new store driver.

3.3   Object Cache Architecture

As described above, the heap and the persistent object cache are combined. Other persistent systems (including PJama Classic) sometimes use a separate object cache so that persistent objects can be managed differently from transient ones. Despite the potential advantages of this architecture, we chose a combined heap because it required fewer changes to the ResearchVM and because it uses storage more effectively: space not needed for transient objects can be used for persistent objects, and vice-versa. The remainder of this section describes other components of the object cache.

ROT (Resident Object Table). The ROT is a lookup table holding pointers to every persistent object in the object cache. It can be queried with a PID to determine whether the corresponding persistent object is already cache-resident and, if so, its address (see the description of object faulting in Sect. 2). The ROT also serves as a GC root, which prevents (reachable) persistent objects from being discarded by a garbage collection. The PEVM uses a separate ROT for each heap generation to speed up young generation garbage collections.

Since the size of the ResearchVM's heap can be more than one gigabyte, the ROT must be capable of holding references to hundreds of millions of objects. To scale well, the ROT is organized as two tiers. A large fixed-size "high" table points to a number of small, fixed-size "low" tables. The high-order bits of the PID are used to index the high table to get the appropriate low table, then the low-order PID bits are used to search that low table. The small low tables allow fast reorganization and fine-grained locking. The PEVM must lock a low table when entering a new persistent object to prevent another thread from also entering an object and possibly reorganizing the table.

The PCD and the String Intern Table. The PEVM uses two other key data structures, the Persistent Class Dictionary (PCD) and the String intern table. These are metadata that are maintained in the store. Both data structures are implemented in the Java programming language because their performance is not critical and persistence is automatic. PJama Classic implemented these in C and we found the code that translated between the memory and store representations error prone. However, implementing them in the Java programming language does complicate the PEVM's bootstrap initialization somewhat because they cannot be used until enough of the VM is running to support programs.

To ensure type safety, the store must include the class for each object and it uses the PCD to hold that class information. The PCD is searched whenever a class is loaded: if the class is in the store, it is loaded using the PCD's information. Like the ROT, the PCD is organized as a two-level hashtable.

The String intern table manages String literals, which the Java programming language requires be unique (and shared) within a program's execution. The PEVM uses the String intern table to ensure that a literal String is unique across the entire lifetime (that is, repeated executions) of a persistent program.

Swizzling strategy. *Pointer swizzling* speeds up programs by translating PIDs into normal virtual memory addresses in the object cache. The PEVM swizzles a reference when it is first pushed onto a thread stack: if it is a PID, it faults the object in if necessary (it may already be in the object cache), then replaces the PID on the stack and in memory with the object's address. References are pushed when a value is accessed in an object: an instance (including a class) or an array. The primitive language operations that access object references from other objects are listed in Table 1. Thus, references on the stack are always direct

Table 1. Language operations that are sources of object references

Operation	Example
instance field access	*instance.field*
static field access	*Clazz.field*
array element access	*array[index]*

pointers; this includes all references in local variables, temporaries, and method invocation parameters.

Using the terminology of [23], our swizzling strategy is lazy and direct. It is lazy at the granularity of a single reference: references in resident objects stay unswizzled until they are accessed.[2] This has the advantage that only the references that are actually used are swizzled. Our strategy is direct because we replace a PID by the in-memory address of the referenced object. Other persistent systems often use indirect pointers: in these, a swizzled reference points to an intermediate data object (*fault block*) that itself points to the object when it is in memory. Indirect swizzling provides more flexibility in deciding what objects to evict from the cache and when to evict them [6]. We chose a direct strategy because it requires fewer source changes: only the implementations of the *getfield/putfield*, *getstatic/putstatic*, and array access bytecodes need to be changed. It also has less CPU overhead since it avoids an extra level of indirection. More detail about our swizzling strategy appears in [18].

Persistence Read and Write Barriers. *Barriers* [11] are actions performed during certain object access operations (e.g., reads, writes) to support object

---

[2] Another term for this lazy swizzling strategy is "swizzling on discovery."

caching and checkpointing. The PEVM's persistence read barrier is responsible for swizzling object references and, when necessary, faulting in persistent objects. Because of its swizzling strategy, the PEVM only needs to add read barriers where the three operations in Table 3.3 are performed and where the result is known to be a reference. As a result, stack operations (the majority of operations) do not require read barriers.

The PEVM's persistence write barrier marks updated objects so that on a later checkpoint (if they are reachable from a persistent root), they will be propagated to the store. Since writes occur much less frequently than reads, we can afford to use a relatively expensive but simple mechanism for marking objects dirty: the PEVM's write barrier marks an object dirty by resetting the "isClean" flag in its header. At checkpoint time, we must scan all resident objects in order to discover which ones have been updated. This scheme is adequate today, but when the number of resident objects becomes large (several million), a more sophisticated technique will be needed to keep checkpointing non-disruptive.

The JIT can implement the persistence write barrier using a single instruction since it already holds the reference in a machine register. Similarly, the JIT implements the read barrier by seven inline instructions. Three instructions are executed in the common case (already swizzled), while all seven and a procedure call are executed if a PID is encountered:

1. Check if the reference is a PID or an address. If an address (fast path), skip the rest of the barrier.
2. (Slow path) Pass the PID to a procedure that tests whether the PID's object is resident in memory and, if not, faults it in. In any case, the procedure returns the object's heap address. The PID in memory is replaced by this address to avoid re-executing the barrier's slow path if a future access is made with the same reference

Except for JIT-generated code and a few support routines in assembly language, the ResearchVM uniformly uses its *memsys* software interface to access runtime values such as objects, classes, arrays, and primitive values [24]. This meant we could easily get nearly total coverage of all access operations in non-JITed code by adding our barriers to the implementation of *memsys*.

Checkpointing. The checkpoint method first invokes any *checkpoint listeners* and then *stabilizes* the state of the program. Special actions that must occur when a checkpoint happens are supported by the event listener interface, *OPCheckpointListener*. A checkpoint listener is an object whose class implements this interface and which is registered using *OPRuntime.addListener()*. Its *checkpoint* method will be called at the start of each checkpoint.

Stabilization writes all changed and newly persistent objects to the store. The PEVM does not currently checkpoint threads: it cannot write the state of each thread and cannot restore the state of each thread after a restart. It starts a checkpoint by stopping all other threads to ensure that it writes a consistent set of objects. It then makes two passes: a gather pass to identify and allocate

PIDs for the objects to stabilize, and a save pass to write objects to the store. It does not need to do a garbage collection, which is crucial to keep latency down. Objects are written using a breadth-first traversal. They are unswizzled in the store's buffer pool so that they are left intact in the heap and are immediately usable after a checkpoint, which also minimizes latency.

Object and Class Faulting. When the PEVM's read barrier faults in an object, it ensures that the object's class is in memory (faulting it in if necessary) and swizzles the object's reference to it. This allows the PEVM to use the ResearchVM's existing procedures without change. It allocates space for the object in the heap and then enters the object into the ROT. Class faulting uses information recorded in the PCD. The class is loaded using the PID found there for its class file. To use the ResearchVM's standard class loading code, the PEVM first ensures that the class loader for the class is resident and swizzles its reference.

Eviction. The PEVM frees up space in the object cache by *evicting* some persistent objects. We do eviction during garbage collection since that allows us to use the collector's mechanisms to update all references to each object. More specifically, we do eviction during full garbage collections (those that collect all heap generations), since at that time it is essential to free space. Because of the complexity required, we do not currently evict dirty objects or objects directly referenced from a thread stack.

We support multiple eviction strategies:

1. Total eviction. This discards all possible persistent objects. Only those objects necessary for the PEVM's operation are kept.
2. Random eviction. This randomly selects objects to evict until it has evicted a percentage of objects that was specified on the PEVM's command line.
3. Second chance eviction. In this strategy, an object marked for eviction is kept if it is referenced before the next old space collection. Second chance eviction keeps the most recently used objects in the hope that they will be used again.

The default eviction strategy we use is second chance since it proved to be the most effective strategy among those we tried. It allows the highest application throughput with reasonably large heaps, which is the normal case. Our second chance eviction strategy is relatively aggressive since it evicts *all* unreferenced objects, including some that might be referenced again in the future. It typically evicts more objects than the second chance strategy of PJama Classic, which evicts no more than a portion of the object cache. As a result, we are investigating modifications of our scheme that will retain more objects.

3.4   Store Garbage Collection

Like the heap, the store can accumulate objects that are no longer reachable. Sphere includes a compacting store ("disk") garbage collector to reclaim space

[21]. This collector deals with the large size of stores. It also deals with the slow access time of disks by minimizing the number of disk accesses it does. The store garbage collector operates concurrently with programs and allows concurrent access to the objects it is collecting. It is also fault-tolerant: if a collection crashes, either all updates will be reflected in the store or none will.

3.5 Archiving

A store depends on the version of the PEVM that created it. It may no longer be usable if a change is made to the store format or to a class in the store, even if that class is purely internal to the PEVM's implementation.[3] To avoid this problem, we created a portable archive file format that represents the user-visible state of the program.

Creating an archive resembles checkpointing except that objects are written in a portable format. Each object is assigned a unique index and references to it are replaced by that index. The archive format for each object includes its identity hash value. The format for a class instance has its class and the values of all fields, and the format of a class includes its name, class loader, and a list of the names and types of its non-static fields. We record the values of static variables and the class file for *user-defined classes*: those loaded into the application class loader or a user-defined class loader. By only recording such data for these classes, the archive is isolated from most changes to classes implementing the PEVM.

Restoring from an archive recreates the application's state. Classes are loaded and set to the state in the original program (linked, initialized, etc.) without running static initializers. Instances are created without running a constructor, then their identity hash value and field values are set from the archive.

The logical archive and restore utilities are written almost entirely in the Java programming language. To allow this, the PEVM includes reflection-like native methods to read and write private fields, create instances without running constructors, mark a class as already initialized without running a static initializer, and assign identity hash values to objects.

3.6 Evolution

Traditionally, applications are separated from their data: a program loads its data from a file or database, does its work, then writes its results back. Changes to a program, including changes to its internal data structures, do not affect the on-disk data unless the on-disk representation is changed.

Orthogonal persistence saves application developers the difficulty and cost of explicitly managing the persistence of their data. Unfortunately, it breaks the traditional program development model: changing a class can make its instances

---

[3] However, the PEVM's stores depend much less on the specific version of the PEVM than those of PJama Classic. The store format for PJama Classic was much more intricate and changed more frequently.

in a store invalid. To deal with this, we implemented a *program evolution* facility [4] that allows programmers to simultaneously change programs and their data. The evolution facility determines how each class is being changed and, for many changes, automatically converts its instances. Complex changes that modify the representation of data structures (e.g., changing a point's representation from Cartesian to polar coordinates) may require help from the programmer.

4   The PEVM's Performance

Table 2 shows average "warm" execution time results for several OO7 queries and traversals [5] when PJama Classic, the PEVM, and the ResearchVM (labeled "ResVM") are run transiently. OO7 is a standard benchmark that simulates the

Table 2. Transient OO7 operations: warm runs

	Small			Medium			Large		
	Classic	*PEVM*	*ResVM*	*Classic*	*PEVM*	*ResVM*	*Classic*	*PEVM*	*ResVM*
Q1	1.00	1	1.00	1.00	1	1.00		1	1.00
Q4	2.00	1	1.00	2.00	1	1.00		1	1.00
T1	15.87	372	0.80	12.49	3389	0.86		3332	0.87
T2a	15.84	373	0.78	13.14	3288	0.88		3371	0.86
T2b	15.78	378	0.78	13.00	3289	0.89		3322	0.88
T2c	16.56	388	0.81	13.78	3441	0.89		3499	0.86
T6	22.41	73	0.40	19.56	75	0.40		79	0.44
mean	4656	273	187	22237	1567	1180		1595	1211

behavior of a CAD system traversing graphs of engineering objects. Times for the PEVM are given in milliseconds while the other times are expressed as ratios with respect to the PEVM's time for the same OO7 configuration. We repeated each operation five times during one execution of the virtual machine. After each operation a transaction commit (in our case a *checkpoint()* call) was performed, and its time was included in the operation's total time. For these "warm" times, we computed the average time for the final four operations (ignoring the initial "cold" operation). The operations were run on a Sun Enterprise 3500 with four 400MHz UltraSPARC-II[TM]CPUs and 4GB of memory. The OO7 benchmark is single-threaded so the additional CPUs had little effect. Each run was made with a heap large enough to hold the entire OO7 database. The geometric means of the run times in milliseconds of the traversal operations T1-T6 (only) are given at the bottom of the table for each combination of virtual machine and OO7 configuration; the query operations run too fast to give meaningful means. PJama Classic cannot run the large OO7 database, so that column is blank.

These results demonstrate how much faster the PEVM and ResearchVM are compared to PJama Classic. For the medium database, the PEVM and ResearchVM are faster by factors of 13.1 and 14.9, respectively. These results also show the low cost of the PEVM's persistence barriers: with the medium database, the PEVM's total runtimes for all operations is just 14% greater than the ResearchVM. One surprise in these results is how much faster the ResearchVM is on traversal T6 than the PEVM. This is due to the PEVM's more expensive garbage collections: these do additional work necessary for persistent programs even though these runs are transient.

Table 3. Transient OO7 operations: cold runs

	Small			Medium			Large		
	Classic	*PEVM*	*ResVM*	*Classic*	*PEVM*	*ResVM*	*Classic*	*PEVM*	*ResVM*
Q1	0.50	4	0.75	0.40	5	0.80		17	0.18
Q4	0.60	5	1.00	0.33	6	0.67		6	0.83
T1	10.85	557	0.58	12.71	3324	0.90		3315	0.89
T2a	15.76	375	0.79	12.63	3355	0.88		3314	0.88
T2b	15.98	374	0.79	12.96	3288	0.90		3348	0.86
T2c	16.51	390	0.77	14.73	3448	0.88		3420	0.88
T6	21.50	75	0.48	18.66	79	0.57		83	0.59
mean	4668	296	198	22462	1585	1287		1599	1296

Table 3 shows the average "cold" execution time results for the same operations. The results here are slower than those above but are otherwise similar.

Tables 4 and 5 show the average warm and cold execution time results for the same operations when PJama Classic and the PEVM are run persistently. The column for the ResearchVM is included but left blank to make it easier to

Table 4. Persistent OO7 operations: warm runs

	Small			Medium			Large		
	Classic	*PEVM*	*ResVM*	*Classic*	*PEVM*	*ResVM*	*Classic*	*PEVM*	*ResVM*
Q1	0.83	18		1.17	18			16	
Q4	1.53	19		1.94	17			25	
T1	13.62	411		11.71	3600			3581	
T2a	13.20	428		11.56	3652			3625	
T2b	10.16	606			6523			6508	
T2c	10.85	618			6633			6615	
T6	14.13	109		14.68	105			106	
mean	4578	373			2266			2262	

compare the two tables. Note that the warm runs of traversals T2a and T2b, which update every atomic part in the OO7 database, are much slower than either T1 (which just visits each atomic part) or T2a (which only updates one atomic part per composite part) since they cause more objects to be written during a checkpoint. We could not run PJama Classic on two update-intensive OO7 traversals (it crashed due to object cache problems) so we did not compute geometric means for those cases.

Table 5. Persistent OO7 operations: cold runs

	Small			Medium			Large		
	Classic	*PEVM*	*ResVM*	*Classic*	*PEVM*	*ResVM*	*Classic*	*PEVM*	*ResVM*
Q1	0.84	62		2.31	89			249	
Q4	1.27	49		1.34	50			72	
T1	1.16	6473		1.59	66831			66229	
T2a	1.16	6486		1.58	66962			65902	
T2b	1.19	6692			69405			68668	
T2c	1.30	6735			69652			68867	
T6	3.27	616		3.19	658			805	
mean	6024	4104			26957			27804	

Experience with several programs shows that the average overhead of the PEVM's persistence barriers is about 15%. The barrier cost in the interpreted PJama Classic is also about 15% [14] and we expected, when designing the PEVM, that the relative cost for the PEVM's barriers would be much higher because of the ResearchVM's greater speed. The execution time overhead for the *pBOB* benchmark [9] is just 9% compared to the standard ResearchVM. The SPECjvm98 [22] *db* and *javac* benchmarks are slowed down by 14% and 18%, respectively. Programs that do extensive array computation such as the SPECjvm98 *compress* benchmark are slowed down by up to 40%. This is because we needed to disable a ResearchVM optimization that reduces the cost of array bounds checks since it interacts badly with our read barrier.

The overall performance of the PEVM is good when running large persistent programs. As an example, pBOB run with the ResearchVM yields about 27000 pBOB "transactions" per minute when run with a single pBOB thread over a 100% populated "warehouse". When the PEVM runs that same configuration of pBOB persistently, the result is 23403. This is despite the fact that the PEVM must fault in more than 220MB of objects from the store for this benchmark.

The PEVM can scale to *very* large numbers of objects. It easily supports the large OO7 database. In additional, we ran an experiment where we added additional warehouses to pBOB (each containing about 212MB of objects) until it ran over 24 warehouses: a total of more than 5GB of objects. This is significantly more than will fit into our 32 bit virtual memory and made heavy use of the PEVM's cache management. Furthermore, we were able to run five threads per warehouse, each simulating a different client, for a total of 120 threads accessing those objects.

5   Related Work

Over the past two decades, orthogonal persistence has been implemented in a number of programming languages designed to support persistence. These persistent programming languages include PS-Algol [2] and Napier88 [19]. Orthogonal persistence has also been implemented as extensions to existing languages such as Smalltalk [16] and Modula-3 [12]. This remainder of this section discusses persistence solutions specifically for the Java platform. These systems differ in the extent of their orthogonality and their scalability.

Serialization: Java[TM]Object Serialization [13] encodes object graphs into byte streams, and it supports the corresponding reconstruction of those object graphs. It is the default persistence mechanism for the Java Platform. Serialization is easy to to use and, for many classes, automates the serialization/deserialization of their instances. However, it only serializes classes that implement the *java.io.Serializable* interface. Since many core classes do not implement this, Serialization does not support orthogonality and persistence by reachability. It also suffers from severe performance problems. Furthermore, an entire stream must be deserialized before any objects can be used.

ObjectStore PSE Pro: Excelon Corporation's ObjectStore PSE Pro for Java [17] is a single-user database implemented as a library. It provides automatic support for persistence but it requires that all class files be postprocessed to add annotations: additional calls to library methods to, e.g., fetch objects. This postprocessing complicates the management of class files since it results in two versions of each class file (one for transient and one for persistent use). It also makes it difficult to use dynamic class loading. The additional method calls are expensive and slow program execution significantly.

PJama Classic: Our previous implementation of orthogonal persistence for the Java platform, PJama Classic, is based on the "Classic" VM used in the Java[TM]2 SDK, Standard Edition, v 1.2, which is significantly slower than the ResearchVM, primarily because of its slower garbage collection and thread synchronization. The Classic VM uses a conservative garbage collector and objects are accessed indirectly though handles, which adds a cost to every object access. It also has a JIT, but PJama Classic does not support it. As a result, PJama Classic is approximately 10 times slower than the PEVM. PJama Classic is also more complex than the PEVM (requires more software patches to the underlying VM) because the Classic VM has no memory access interface that corresponds to the ResearchVM's *memsys*: PJama Classic needs 2.3 times more patches, 1156 versus 501. The object cache in PJama Classic is separate from the heap, which made it possible to manage persistent objects separately from transient objects at the cost of a more complex implementation. Like the PEVM, PJama Classic implements second chance eviction but since the garbage collector in the Classic VM is conservative, it lacks exact information about the location of objects, which significantly complicates eviction and checkpointing, both of which may move objects referenced from a *C* stack. Another limitation of PJama Classic is that its store is directly addressed (a PID is the offset of an object), which makes it nearly impossible to implement store garbage collection or reclustering that operate concurrently with a persistent program.

Gemstone/J: Gemstone/J [10] is a commercial application server that supports E-commerce components, process automation, and J2EE^{TM}services. It includes a high-performance implementation of persistence for the Java platform that approaches orthogonality more closely than most other systems. However, it requires use of a transactional API and does not have complete support for core classes. Gemstone/J uses a modified version of the Java HotSpot^{TM}performance engine. It implements a shared object cache that allows multiple Gemstone/J VMs to concurrently access objects in the cache. When transactions commit, changed objects are visible to other VMs. It does not store the values of static fields persistently since Gemstone felt that this would cause too many third-party libraries to fail. Interestingly, while the PJama system moved towards using a unified heap and object cache, Gemstone/J moved towards using a separate cache. Their most recent version, 3.2.1, includes a separate "Pom" region that holds (most) resident persistent objects. Gemstone found that garbage collections in a unified heap shortened the lifetime of persistent objects and so reduced throughput. Since our experience with a unified heap has been positive, we believe more study is needed to understand the advantages and disadvantages of using unified heaps.

6   Conclusions

We set out to build a new OPJ implementation with better performance, scalability, and maintainability than PJama Classic. The PEVM's overall performance is good: it is about 10 times faster than PJama Classic with an overhead (compared to an unchanged ResearchVM) of about 15%. This is largely because of our swizzling strategy, which made it simple to modify its optimizing JIT while preserving almost all of the speed of the code it generates. Also, our use of direct object pointers minimizes CPU overhead. It ties eviction to garbage collection, but we have still been able to implement a variety of different eviction schemes. In addition, the PEVM's checkpointing is much faster than that of PJama Classic. We compared the PEVM's performance to several commercial persistence solutions for the Java platform, and found it as fast or faster; however, we are unable to quote specific numbers due to licensing restrictions.

We have shown that the PEVM can scale to large numbers of objects. We do not yet know how well it scales with many hundreds of threads. We have tried a moderate number of threads (e.g., the 120 mentioned above), but we need to do further experiments. The PEVM has longer pause times than the ResearchVM, and we expect to work on improving responsiveness in the future. Responsiveness will become even more important as the scale of our programs and data increase.

We made a first internal release of the PEVM in only half the time needed for PJama Classic. This was due to a combination of factors: our swizzling strategy, the ResearchVM's *memsys* memory interface, our decision to build a relatively simple system, and the quality of the system we started with (the ResearchVM). The PEVM's relative simplicity compared to PJama Classic (501 VM source patches versus 1156) has made it easier for us to maintain.

We have demonstrated that an implementation of orthogonal persistence for the Java platform can be straightforward, can perform well, and can preserve most of the performance of the fast virtual machine upon which it was built.

Acknowledgments. We want to thank the other members of the Forest team for their numerous ideas and contributions. Grzegorz Czajkowski, Laurent Daynès, Mick Jordan, Cristina Cifuentes, Jeanie Treichel, and the anonymous referees helped us by reviewing earlier drafts of this paper.

References

1. Agesen, O., Detlefs, D., Garthwaite, A., Knippel, R., and White, D.: An Efficient Meta-Lock for Implementing Ubiquitous Synchronization. Proceedings of OOP-SLA, Denver, Colorado, USA, November 1999.
2. Atkinson, M., Chisolm, K., and Cockshott, P.: PS-Algol: an Algol with a persistent heap. ACM SIGPLAN Notices **17**(7), July 1982.
3. Atkinson, M. and Morrison, R.: Orthogonally Persistent Object Systems. VLDB Journal, **4**(3), 1995.
4. Atkinson, M., Dmitriev, M., Hamilton, C., and Printezis, T.: Scalable and Recoverable Implementation of Object Evolution for the PJama Platform. Proceedings of the Ninth International Workshop on Persistent Object Systems: Design, Implementation and Use, Lillehammer, Norway, September 2000.
5. Carey, M., DeWitt, D., and Naughton, J.: The OO7 Benchmark. ACM SIGMOD Record, **22**(2), June 1993.
6. Daynès, L. and Atkinson, M.: Main-Memory Management to Support Orthogonal Persistence for Java. Proceedings of the 2nd International Workshop on Persistence and Java (PJW2), Half Moon Bay, CA, USA, August 1997.
7. Daynès, L.: Implementation of Automated Fine-Granularity Locking in a Persistent Programming Language. Special Issue on Persistent Object Systems, Software–Practice and Experience, **30**(4), April 2000.
8. Detlefs, D. and Agesen, O.: Inlining of Virtual Methods. Proceedings of ECOOP 1999, Lisbon, Portugal, June 1999.
9. Dimpsey, R., Arora, R., and Kuiper, K.: Java Server Performance: A Case Study of Building Efficient, Scalable JVMs. IBM Systems Journal, **39**(1), 2000.
10. Gemstone Systems, Inc.: Gemstone/J Programming Guide, Version 1.1, March 1998.
11. Hosking, A. and Moss, J. E.: Protection Traps and Alternatives for Memory Management of an Object-Oriented Language. Proceedings of the 14th Symposium on Operating Systems Principles, Asheville, NC, USA, December 1993.
12. Hosking, A. and Chen, J.: PM3: An Orthogonally Persistent Systems Programming Language – Design, Implementation, Performance. Proceedings of the 25th VLDB Conference, Edinburgh, Scotland, 1999.
13. Java^{TM}Object Serialization Specification, Revision 1.43. Sun Microsystems Inc., 901 San Antonio Road, Palo Alto, CA, 94303, USA, November 1998. http://java.sun.com/products/jdk/1.2/docs/guide/serialization/index.html.

14. Jordan, M.: Early Experiences with Persistent Java. Proceedings of the First International Workshop on Persistence and Java (PJ1), Glasgow, Scotland, September 1996.

15. Jordan, M. and Atkinson, M.: Orthogonal Persistence for the Java Platform–Specification and Rationale. Sun Labs Technical Report TR-2000-94, Sun Microsystems Laboratories, Sun Microsystems Inc., 901 San Antonio Road, Palo Alto, CA, 94303, USA, 2000.

16. Kaehler, T. and Krasner, G.: LOOM–large object-oriented memory for Smalltalk-80 systems. Smalltalk-80: Bits of History, Words of Advice, G. Krasner, Ed., Addison-Wesley, Chapter 14, 1983.

17. Landis, G., Lamb, C., Blackman, T., Haradhvala, S., Noyes, M., and Weinreb, D.: ObjectStore PSE: a Persistent Storage Engine for Java. Proceedings of the 2nd International Workshop on Persistence and Java (PJW2), Half Moon Bay, CA, USA, August 1997.

18. Lewis, B. and Mathiske, B.: Efficient Barriers for Persistent Object Caching in a High-Performance Java Virtual Machine. Technical Report TR-99-81, Sun Microsystems Laboratories, Sun Microsystems Inc., 901 San Antonio Road, Palo Alto, CA, 94303, USA, 1999.

19. Morrison, R., Brown, A., Carrick, R., Connor, R., Dearle, A., and Atkinson, M.: The Napier type system. Proceedings of the Third International Workshop on Persistent Object Systems (Newcastle, New South Wales, Australia, Jan. 1989), J. Rosenberg and D. Koch, Eds., Workshops in Computing. Springer-Verlag, 1990.

20. Printezis, T., Atkinson, M., Daynès, L., Spence, S., and Bailey, P.: The Design of a Scalable, Flexible, and Extensible Persistent Object Store for PJama. Proceedings of the 2nd International Workshop on Persistence and Java (PJW2), Half Moon Bay, CA, USA, August 1997.

21. Printezis, T.: Management of Long-Running High-Performance Persistent Object Stores. Ph.D. thesis, University of Glasgow, May 2000.

22. The SPECjvm98 Benchmarks. http://www.spec.org/osg/jvm98, August 1998.

23. White, S.: Pointer Swizzling Techniques for Object-Oriented Database Systems. Ph.D. thesis, Department of Computing Science, University of Wisconsin–Madison, Madison, Wisconsin, 1994.

24. White, D. and Garthwaite, A.: The GC Interface in the EVM. Technical Report TR-98-67, Sun Microsystems Laboratories, Sun Microsystems Inc., 901 San Antonio Road, Palo Alto, CA, 94303, USA, 1998.

Session 2: Overview

Stephen M. Blackburn

Department of Computer Science, University of Massachusetts,
Amherst, MA 01003, USA
steveb@cs.umass.edu

The three papers in this session each address different aspects of the provision of rich environments for persistent application development. The first, which was presented by Erik Voges [EV], looks at the provision of high level tools for spatiotemporal querying. The second, presented by Nicolas Richer [NR], addresses support for distributed persistent applications. The third, presented by Alan Kaplan [AK], looks at heterolingual persistent programming.

In his talk Voges motivated the need for spatiotemporal querying with the example of a GIS used for fisheries research. He explained that spatiotemporal query classes written in Java, layered over PJama (an orthogonally persistent Java), provided a suitable infrastructure for the construction of a spatiotemporal GIS. He argued that this approach was better than building the GIS directly over either PJama or a relational GIS—the encapsulation provided by the spatiotemporal class greatly aided construction of the GIS, and the abstraction over persistence provided by PJama in turn substantially simplified construction of the spatiotemporal class.

Olivier Gruber [OG] asked for more details about the performance analysis, in particular, what size the systems were. Voges explained that they had not yet performed rigorous analysis but that the largest system was about 1GB. Ole Anfindsen [OA] asked about the role of PJama in the system, and what the differences might be from the standpoint of the application developer if the underlying system had been a relational database with support for Java. Voges responded by saying that he thought that relational query languages and the object-oriented design approach were somewhat at odds. Anfindsen then asked whether a query example presented in the talk could have been implemented using a relational query. Voges said he thought it could have been, but went on to say that some more complex queries might have been hard to implement using a relational query language.

In the second talk, Richer described PerDIS as a new technology for sharing over the internet—a Persistent Distributed Store. PerDIS is targeted at applications such as distributed GIS, and was motivated through an example based on an internationally-distributed building project involving architecture, engineering, etc. The focus was on constructing a system that allowed sharing in such an environment. Central to the approach was the use of 'domains' as a means of limiting the scope of coherency operations. Intra-domain coherency is maintained transactionally (either 'pessimistically' or 'optimistically'), but inter-domain coherency is manually mediated using a simple check-in, check-out model. Caching is performed at various grains adaptively. The PerDIS model is one of a network-wide persistent shared memory, and so is amenable to both distributed application construction, and the hosting of legacy applications. The persistent shared memory space is garbage collected.

G.N.C. Kirby, A. Dearle, and D.I.K. Sjøberg (Eds.): POS-9, LNCS 2135, pp. 34-35, 2001.
© Springer-Verlag Berlin Heidelberg 2001

Richard Jones [RJ] asked whether the inability of Larchant (the garbage collector used by PerDIS) to collect cycles had proved to be a problem. Richer said that it was indeed a problem and that in fact he was presenting a paper later in the proceedings that addressed that issue. Anfindsen asked whether failures that arise due to optimistic transaction commit conflicts or the need for manual intervention during check-in amounted to a serious problem for PerDIS. Richer explained that the problem was not negligible, and pointed out that the semantics of reconciliation in the check-out model necessarily involved manual intervention.

During the panel session Anfindsen asked whether the lack of support for distributed transactions was a serious restriction. Richer replied that for the applications they were targeting, most concurrency issues occurred intra-site (for example between cooperating engineers), rather than inter-site (an architect might only require read only access to the engineers' work). He said that although inter-site transactions would enrich PerDIS, such an addition would be a major undertaking.

In his presentation, Kaplan explained pure polylingual persistence by contrasting it with homogeneous (monolingual) persistent systems, segregated heterolingual systems, polylingual persistent systems where object closures must be monolingual (such as that provided by PolySPIN) and pure polylingual systems, where object closures may be heterolingual. He then presented P^3, a general framework for pure polylingual persistence. P^3 assumes reachability-based orthogonal persistence, where each language is responsible for the persistence of objects it instantiates. He explained how heterolingual objects (objects that contain pointers to objects from different languages) are implemented through the use of proxies. In support of the case that pure polylingual persistence is viable, performance results were presented for a Java/C++ polylingual implementation of OO7.

Antony Hosking [AH] asked how P^3 might be applied to languages which are significantly different. Kaplan said that while the application of P^3 to languages with similar type systems such as C++, Java, Ada95 or Eiffel was fairly clear, he was not sure how it would be applied to languages with very different type systems, such as ML and Java. Graham Kirby [GK] then asked whether consideration had been given to mixing languages at the class rather than instance level. The response was yes, but there were a number of interesting issues that needed to be addressed, particularly with respect to inter-lingual inheritance. Alan Dearle [AD] then asked where in the system the proxy mechanisms were manifest. Kaplan explained that the proxy mechanisms did have to be written into the code, but that their system tried to make the insertion of this code transparent to the application programmer. Ewa Bem [EB] asked whether a language-neutral storage format had been considered. Kaplan said that they felt that any universal representation is unlikely to be optimal for any language and that the cost of transformation would have to be weighed against the overhead of proxies used for inter-lingual accesses.

During the panel session that followed the talks Malcolm Atkinson [MPA] asked all of the speakers how they might measure the utility of what each of their systems added to persistent environments (spatiotemporal querying, distribution, polylingual capabilities). All of the speakers agreed that this was an important issue, but one that is particularly hard to quantify. In particular, it is hard to calibrate the tradeoff between usability and programmability enhancements (development) and any performance impact (runtime).

A Spatiotemporal Model as the Basis for a Persistent GIS

Erik Voges and Sonia Berman

University of Cape Town, South Africa

Abstract. Most spatiotemporal systems are implemented on relational DBMSs, and are limited in terms of the types of data and queries they support. We present a persistent environment based on an abstract model of space and time, that can be used for faster development of better quality GIS (Geographical Information Systems).
The architecture we propose is flexible, dynamic, and easy to use; implemented in PJama (a persistent Java), it exploits the benefits of object-orientation and orthogonal persistence and extends this with a framework of classes for effectively modeling and accessing spatiotemporal data sets. This paper gives an overview of the underlying model and its realisation in a PJama object architecture, and outlines the benefits we perceived in experiments building prototype marine biology applications.

Keywords: Persistence, Java, spatiotemporal data, indexing.

1   Introduction

Persistent languages are primarily targeted at complex applications such as CASE and GIS (Geographic Information Systems) [KM97], yet comparatively little work has been done in building such software using orthogonal persistence. This paper attempts to answer the following questions:

- is it possible to build persistent store libraries that make the creation of GIS systems significantly easier?
- how should such a persistent library be structured and what should it comprise?
- how would using this library affect the quality and quantity of code in GIS applications?
- is orthogonally persistent Java a suitable platform for this?
- how would a GIS application using such a system compare with one built on conventional technology ?

The main use of GIS (Geographic Information Systems) [KM97] is to answer complex queries based on the *spatial* properties of data. Until very recently, the *temporal* aspects of geographic data have been neglected [Yua95]. During the past decade spatiotemporal data management has been approached from two main angles. Some researchers suggest ways of incorporating temporal attributes

G.N.C. Kirby, A. Dearle, and D.I.K. Sjøberg (Eds.): POS-9, LNCS 2135, pp. 36–54, 2001.

into existing spatial systems [SN97], [SB97]; others designed new spatiotemporal models for systems to be built from the ground up [TH97], [GBE+98], [Wor98]. Very few spatiotemporal models have been implemented [FMN98], although some have emerged in the last two years (e.g. [PSZ99]).

As a result of the immaturity of spatiotemporal data management technology, developing such an application is far from a simple task. Even if an appropriate model is found, the task of implementing it and setting up a database is highly time-consuming.

To address this problem we propose a GIS environment based on an orthogonally persistent Java [JA98] realisation of an abstract spatio-temporal model [GBE+98]. To discover its relative benefits and disadvantages, we built GIS software for the Sea Fisheries Research Institute (SFRI) using this approach as well as two other technologies: the relational GIS system ArcView 3, and a PJama implementation based only on a GiST [HNP95] (index) library [SVZB98].

The Java language is ideal for the fast development of applications because it is known to increase programmer productivity [Eck98]. It has strong type checking and solid exception handling – leading to robust and highly reusable code. The time saved in writing and maintaining Java code makes up for the fact that it still performs slower than languages like C++. Apart from not having to manage memory (done through garbage collection in Java), using persistence relieves the programmer of having to write code for data storage and retrieval, and avoids the well-known impedance mismatch problem.

The rest of the paper is divided as follows: in the next section we introduce the abstract model along with our mapping of this onto a discrete representation in PJama. In section 3 some issues in indexing the spatiotemporal data are discussed. Section 4 presents a few queries for an experimental marine biology system, and summarises our experience of the usability and benefits provided by the model in practical applications. Our conclusion summarises the work done and lessons learnt, and makes some suggestions for further development.

2 Implementing a Spatiotemporal Model

This section outlines the model our system is based on, describing the classes we used for it at the same time. For the sake of brevity we have not described the abstract continuous model and its mapping onto a discrete model, the two steps which precede implementation of the model in a programming language [GBE+98].

2.1 The Underlying Model

We used the model of Güting et al since its types and operations are clearly and simply defined, and lend themselves to an object oriented language. A full description of the model can be found in [GBE+98]. Its basic design objectives are:–

1. orthogonality in the type system (that constructors can be uniformly applied).
2. genericity of operations (operations can be applied to as many types as possible and behave consistently).
3. closure and consistency between behaviour of operations on temporal and non-temporal types.

As a result of the second and third objectives, a significant number of operations have been defined. They have been divided into two main categories: operations on non-temporal and on temporal types (in tables 1 and 2 respectively).

Table 1. Classes of Operations on Non-Temporal types

Category	Operations
Predicates	**isempty** **equals,not_equals,intersects,inside** **less_than,greater_than,le,ge,before** **touches,attached,overlaps,on_border,in_interior**
Set Operations	**intersection,union,minus** **crossings,touchpoints,common_border**
Aggregation	**min,max,avg,centre,single**
Numeric	**no_components,size,perimeter,duration,length,area**
Distance and Direction	**distance,direction**
Base Type Specific	**and,or,not**

Table 2. Classes of Operations on Temporal types

Category	Operations
Projection to Domain/Range	**deftime,rangevalues,locations,trajectory** **routes,traversed,inst,val**
Interaction with Domain/Range	**atinstant,atperiods,initial,final,present** **at,atmin,atmax,passes**
When	**when**
Lifting	(inferred operations)
Rate of Change	**derivative,speed,turn,velocity**

In table 2 the category "Lifting" refers to all operations on non-temporal types that could also be applied to temporal types. For example, considering **distance** when applied to a *line* and a *point* is

$line \times point \rightarrow real$

it is "lifted" to also include temporal points/lines, i.e. the signatures

$$movingline \times point \rightarrow movingreal$$
$$line \times movingpoint \rightarrow movingreal$$
$$movingline \times movingpoint \rightarrow movingreal$$

We took the abstract model from [GBE+98] and developed Java classes and algorithms to implement all its types and operations. The following sections introduce these classes, with some of the issues that arose in mapping the model to a discrete representation in PJama.

2.2 *Spatial* Types

In our discrete representation of spatial types each spatial object is represented by a set of vertices and a set of edges. Points, lines and regions are represented as simplexes of dimension 0, 1 and 2 respectively (see Fig. 1).

The most primitive spatial type is `Point`, which currently holds two coordinates. A `Point` contains exactly one "vertex" and no edges. The `Points` data type is a set of zero or more vertices, but no edges.[1]

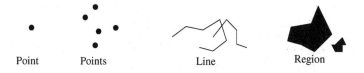

| Point | Points | Line | Region |

Fig. 1. Spatial objects

A `Line` is a set of vertices that are connected by edges. It inherits its vertices from `Points`(Fig. 4). Each edge is an object referencing the two vertices that are its endpoints. The `addVertex()` method is overridden in the `Line` class to ensure that vertices are connected to the line (Fig. 2). An example of a `Line` method is `intersect`, which returns the `Points` at which it intersects a given spatial object.

New vertex

Fig. 2. Adding new vertices to a `Line`

`Region` is a subclass of `Line` as it has the same features, with the added characteristic that its `Edges` form a closed polygon. It has additional methods such as `contains()` which tests whether the `Region` contains a given spatial object.

---

[1] Since `Points` is nothing more than a set of `Point` objects it does not add much to the expressive power of the model, however it does improve ease of use.

There are several benefits of this inheritance hierarchy for spatial types. For example the `intersect()` method is declared only once, but can be used to test intersection between any combination of lines and regions. (see Fig. 3). Also, since `Region` inherits the `intersect()` method, it can call `intersect()` inside its `contains()` method.

Fig. 3. The `intersect()` method of `Line` can check for intersection between `Line` and `Region` objects.

All spatial classes inherit from a parent class `SpatialObject` (see figure 4). This enables the user to form heterogeneous groups of spatial objects (e.g. geometrical sets comprising `Points` and `Lines`). `SpatialObject` methods are common spatial operations such as interactive capture(drawing) and display.

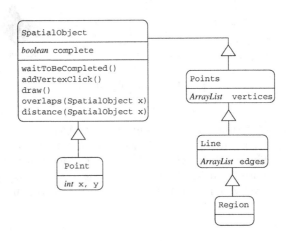

Fig. 4. The inheritance structure of spatial objects.

An example of where multiple inheritance would have been useful is with the `Point` class. If we could inherit from both `SpatialObject` and `Point` in the Java AWT, then we would not have needed to create our own `Point` class. However the `Point` class is fortunately very simple and did not take a lot of work to design.

Representing spatial objects using vertices and edges is very flexible. Constraints can be relaxed by further subclassing, for example to allow holes inside a `Region`, or disjoint `Edges` in a `Line`.

Our spatial objects can easily be extended to 3 dimensions. Only a few changes would have to be made:

- add a third coordinate to `Point`
- update some methods to handle the 3rd co-ordinate
- overload some methods to handle 3–D
- add a new spatial type for a 3-simplex or polyhedron.

2.3 *Temporal* Types

This section outlines the structures where time is bound to any (spatial or non-spatial) class.

The `InTime` class (Fig. 5) has two object references, the one referencing a `Period` instance, and the other referencing *any* type of object. The `Period` object in turn holds two references to `Date` objects, the valid time for which the object is defined. An `InTime` can be seen as a single value at certain interval or instant in time (a $< time, value >$ pair). To handle *transaction time* as well, an extra `Period` could be added to this class.

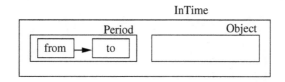

Fig. 5. An `InTime` object contains a `Period` and another object

The class `Moving` contains a *Collection* of `InTime` objects (Fig. 6). Each time the object moves, a new `InTime` is created containing the new state of the object and its associated time `Period`. A subclass of `Moving` was created for each of the *spatial* types, e.g. `mPoint` ("moving point") and `mRegion` ("moving region").

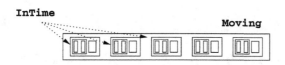

Fig. 6. A `Moving` object consist of a number of "replicated" `InTime`-s

A `Moving` object can change position (e.g. an aeroplane) or position and state (e.g. a scientific cruise) over time. Adding an `InTime` object to a `Moving` object therefore cannot simply alias its component object; a new component object is needed to reflect the new position (and new state if applicable). The model is well suited to both cases. For the former example, by having `Aeroplane` extend `mPoint`, the static properties of the aeroplane (e.g. model number) are stored once only, while `InTime` movements contain only `Point`-s (i.e. record its changing location). In the latter case, `Cruise` extends `mPoint` but scientific readings are stored in the `Measurements` object of its `InTime` component, where `Measurements` *extends* `Point`. In this way the changing position and oceanographic properties are recorded separately for each point along the cruise.

The `move()` method of a `Moving` object can be overloaded to simplify creation of such spatiotemporal histories by taking into account the semantics of the application domain. Methods automatically preserving the shape, size and orientation of a moving object proved useful for the SFRI, since fishing boat location is recorded using a regular rectangular grid over the ocean.

2.4 A Core Spatiotemporal GUI

The ability to construct user interface objects quickly and easily is a major advantage of Java. A `TestArea` object permits easy testing of new code by allowing interactive rendering of spatial objects using a mouse.

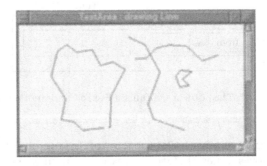

Fig. 7. Spatial objects are interactively drawn in a `TestArea` window.

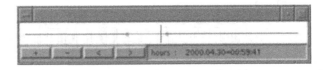

Fig. 8. A `Slider` was easily created to make spatiotemporal queries simpler to specify.

To define time intervals there is a `Slider` object, with the ability to select different time granularities. The `TestArea` proved to be a very useful development tool, and is designed to form the basis of a generic query tool being built for spatiotemporal applications.

3 Building Spatiotemporal Indices into the Model

Index structures can greatly improve access times, but present a tradeoff in terms of store size and insertion time (GIS applications rarely edit or delete data). A dataset must be large enough to justify an index, otherwise a simple structure such as a linked list suffices. Since a moving object has the ability to grow indefinitely over time, some could need to index their history. And since queries can involve multiple objects, there is also a need for indices over sets of spatiotemporal objects. The next two subsections look at each of these issues in turn.

3.1 Indices Inside Moving Objects

Many of the operations defined in spatial and moving classes operate on sets of objects (sets of vertices, edges, InTimes or Periods). We have dealt with them using Collection objects, so as to use this standard Java interface throughout.

In the case of Moving classes, an index can be used to speed up queries on highly mobile objects. The index can be built using time or space as keys in the internal nodes.

A simple interface was designed as a general 'template' for indexing structures. Any structure which implements this interface can then be used to index the history of a moving object. Two indices previously built using the GiST structure [VO97] implement this interface and are included in the library. An index can be added through a built-in method of the Moving class, and updates to the data are then applied to the indices transparently.

```
anyMoving.addIndex(Index next);
```
This adds any index passed in the argument to the moving object.

```
anyMoving.addTemporalIndex();
```
This adds a B^+-tree temporal index to any moving object.

```
anyMovingSpatial.addSpatialObject();
```
This adds a R*-tree spatial index to a moving spatial object.

The Moving class keeps track of all the indices built over its history, and every time the object moves, all indices are updated accordingly. Moving classes can also be tuned to automatically "upgrade" to an index when the size of the InTimes history passes some threshold.

3.2 Indices over Multiple Objects

It is essential to also have efficient querying of collections of objects occupying the same interval of space and time (e.g. the South African coastal waters over the last 4 decades). The mechanism (and interface) described above for creating and managing indices over the histories of moving objects is also used for indices over multiple objects in a shared global space and time.

The most popular spatiotemporal indices are based on the R-Tree, a spatial indexing structure ([Gut84], [BKSS90]). Some of these are the TPR-tree [SJLL99], the GR-tree [BSJS98], and the HR-tree [NST98]; an evaluation of these appears in [NST99].

The most intuitive extension of the R-Tree is to add an extra dimension for time. There are two problems with this approach.

The first problem is that the current/latest situation is not directly represented, and yet many queries are likely to deal only with this [CDI+97]. A proposed solution is the 2+3R-tree of [NST99] where the history is stored in a 3D R-Tree and the *current* state is stored separately in a 2D R-Tree (excluding the time dimension).

The second problem is that the minimum bounding region (MBR) of a moving object is often hard to determine, causing a lot of "dead space" in the R-Tree structure, which makes it less efficient. In our system, if `InTime` objects are indexed *individually*, dead space can be drastically reduced (Fig. 9). Although this increases the index size, it brings about improvement in access times.

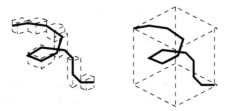

Fig. 9. The Minimum Bounding Region of a `Moving` object can be significantly larger than the sum of the MBRs of its individual `InTime` components, thus having potentially greater overlap with other objects in the index, which is not desirable.

4   An Experimental System for Sea Fisheries

In earlier work we built a spatiotemporal index library for PJama and used this to create a prototype GIS for the South African Sea Fisheries Research Institute (SFRI); a comparison was made between this and an ArcView 3 (relational GIS) implementation [SVZB98]. The PJama application ("VIBES") performed queries faster than the relational system, but was slower on insertions. Of more concern than insertion speed however, was the fact that both prototypes were too difficult and time-consuming to develop. The index library offered too few reusable classes and no guidelines to aid designers; while ArcView provided too many isolated low-level procedures which were hard to compose into applications.

We have rebuilt our VIBES prototype from scratch using the spatiotemporal classes described in this paper, in order to see the impact on development effort. To assess the benefits of the model, we also had three groups of senior students design and implement a reduced version of the SFRI application. Group A used

PJama without the GIS library, group B used the model and group C did each
in turn. Performance measurement is also underway and we are experimenting
with changes to the structures and methods of our class library, using VIBES
to assess effects and direct subsequent tuning. Some performance results are
given in the next section. Here, we illustrate how the class library can be used
for spatio-temporal queries and then present some observations on the utility
of the model, based on our own experience and that of the students in the 3
experiments.

4.1   Query Examples

This sections shows how queries are done using methods inherited from the ST
classes.

A typical query of interest to Sea Fisheries is:

```
Return the incident light readings during a specified
time period, within a specified region.
```

where space and time granularities differ for different queries.

The `Cruise` class extends `mPoint`, with its `InTime` components referencing `Measurements` objects. `Measurements` extends `Point` with values such as
`salinity`, `incidentLight`, etc.

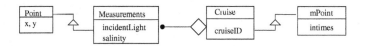

Fig. 10. A `Cruise` class in our prototype system.

Using classes inherited from the new ST classes, the query above can be
answered using a statement such as:

```
result = aCruise.atPeriod(aTime).at(aRegion).rangeValues();
```

`atPeriod()` in `mPoint` returns another `mPoint` (a subset of the original, with
its history during `Period` *aTime*). `at()` restricts this subset further, to those
`InTimes` within the given `Region`. A collection containing all the **value** parts of
a moving object (in this case `Measurements`) is returned by the `rangeValues()`
method. Figure 11(b) shows the result of such a query over the dataset in 11(a).

In the original VIBES implementation, this query was done using a single
method which accepts longitude, latitude, starting time and ending time values,
and looks up objects in a 4-D R*-tree index.

Another query relates to fishing trips, where the position of a boat is given
in terms of a rectangular grid over the ocean. `FishingTrip` extends `mRegion`
("moving region") and has `InTime` components that reference `Catch` objects.
`Catch` extends `Region`, with data on fish caught and where the net was thrown.
A query asking which `Cruise Measurements` co-incided in time and space with
a particular `FishingTrip` can be done using the following statement:

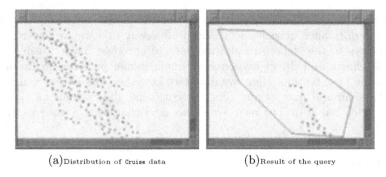

(a)Distribution of Cruise data   (b)Result of the query

Fig. 11. A spatiotemporal query for a given time and region.

```
result = aFishingTrip.containsWhere(aCruise);
```

ContainsWhere() accepts an mPoint as parameter and returns Region and Point values wherever the mPoint was within the mRegion (at the same time) (Fig. 12).

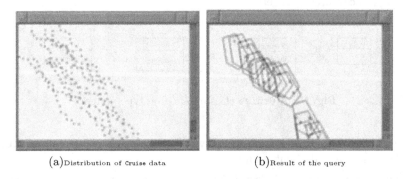

(a)Distribution of Cruise data   (b)Result of the query

Fig. 12. A query returning all positions where a moving point was inside a moving region.

4.2   Experiments Using the Spatiotemporal Model

In this section we review the impact of the model on programmers designing spatio-temporal application systems in PJama, and then compare this with our earlier experiment implementing the same application using the ArcView (relational) GIS system.

Effect of the model on PJama applications. Building a spatiotemporal model would be approached by most people in the following manner. They understand that a timestamp has to be included with every new "value" of an object that changes over time. Therefore, ultimately most class designers would come up with a design where data values and timestamps are encapsulated together, and grouped under larger structures representing the moving object. This larger structure can also contain non-changing data. For example, a moving ship can have its name and registration stored together with a series of time-position pairs which describe where the ship was at any given time. It was indeed a structure similar to this that was originally designed for the VIBES project. There was a `Cruise` class containing non-changing data about a research vessel, and it related to a number of `Station` objects that had timestamps and values of numerous changing oceanographic properties. From a high-level point of view, this design was similar to that obtained with our spatiotemporal (ST) classes which group time-value pairs (`InTime` objects) together under single moving objects. It turned out that all the students, whether or not they used the model, also ended up with this same overall approach to structuring the data. This is encouraging because it means that the classes produced using the model aren't counter-intuitive, and are easy and natural for developers to work with.

There are however a number of important differences between systems built using the model and those that don't. The original VIBES design was based on existing relational database and spreadsheet structures, as there was no other starting point available. Unfortunately it is not necessarily a good idea to retain this organisation in PJama, because one may lose some of the benefits of object orientation. The final VIBES classes still reflect the 3NF decomposition that was used to design the original data organisation. In some instances this meant that the one-to-one mapping between program object and real-world entity has been lost. In our experiment with student programmers, this problem was again evident.

Another important distinction is that query methods were separate from the objects that contain the data. From the outset most students saw query tasks as distinct classes unrelated to ships, measurements, etc. A few tried to encapsulate them as behaviours of classes like Ships, but abandoned this after much effort continually adjusting them to accommodate new queries. Now if query methods and data objects are separate, then in order to reuse the code in another similar application, the code has to be modified in both places. Furthermore, large amounts of code ended up being duplicated. Designers not using the model aimed at some *specific* tasks of interest to the client, and because of this were unable to find a generic solution to the problem (despite attempts by some of the good students). This is not really surprising, because it is very difficult to design a specific application by seeing it as an instance of a general spatio-temporal problem - one reason why a model is badly needed. By failing to build a set of common underlying types and operators, unanticipated queries are really hard to handle well. The idea behind the model on the other hand is that spatio-temporal methods are generic, and can be inherited without having to be modified. The moving types have methods that perform seemingly simple functions, but can be used to construct powerful queries.

In our approach, the query methods of moving types often return other moving objects. For example the `distance()` method of a moving `Point` can measure the distance to another moving `Point`. Since the distance is not constant, the method returns a moving real number (`mReal`). The `mReal` is an object that can then have its own (inherited) methods invoked, such as `lessThan()` or `average()`. In contrast, the query methods of VIBES - and of the student systems built without the model - return lists of values, and there are no methods available on such results. It is very difficult for the application designer to foresee this kind of implication early on in the design. If the designer has an existing framework such as the ST model which can be specialised through inheritance, this not only ensures that method signatures are appropriate but also provides ready-made methods for spatio-temporal operators (many of which involve fairly complex algorithms).

Our experiments indicate that the model is organised in such a way that the types and operators are quickly assimilated. The students had only a brief introduction to the model (short talk and handout), and found it easy to understand and use. A student typically took 5 hours to learn the model, compared with 4 hours to learn PJama (in fact all experienced a little difficulty with PJama initially, since the use of configuration files for the store is unfamiliar, and the fact that static members are persistent roots is not simple to understand at first). The only design difficulty experienced by some of the students was uncertainty over integration of spatial data with other time-varying attributes. For example: should there be a class Ship containing an `mPoint` attribute giving its spatial variation over time and a separate `mReal` attribute having its changing salinity over time, or should these be combined into a single spatio-temporal attribute `salinity`? In the latter case `salinity` would be of type `Measurement` (say) which extends `mPoint` with a salinity value.

Generally, our experiments show that the model enhances productivity and results in code that is shorter, simpler and more reusable. Our own re-implementation of the SFRI system was completed in approximately half the time of the VIBES work (done without the model). The students' productivity was improved likewise - those using the model required just over half the time of those tackling the task without the model.

Comparison with the ArcView GIS System. A commercial GIS system such as ArcView also presents its users with a data model and set of methods for spatiotemporal operations, but there are major differences in their underlying approach. Relational GIS systems typically offer a subset of our spatial types as their data model: point, line and polygon. There is no possibility of a single object comprising e.g. several lines or several (disjoint) polygons, nor is there any special representation of time (other than as a regular attribute). Realworld entities are generally represented with their spatial data separate from their other properties, and with the latter further decomposed into 3NF relations. This is a lower-level model than the one presented here, and the productivity benefits of object-orientation are totally lacking as a result.

GIS systems such as ArcView are primarily end-user tools, and the programming language they provide for customised applications is inferior to modern languages like Java. The available data types are very limited, there is no inheritance, the statements and operators are very low-level, and the vast amount of built-in functionality is difficult to work with because it is spread over a huge number of separate routines in a vast number of built-in "objects". Temporal queries are performed using relational selection (predicates on temporal attributes).

Generally the ArcView programming language is hard to learn, and we found that since programmers struggled to obtain working solutions, they often failed to pursue more efficient alternatives. Compared to the PJama implementations, it took the ArcView programmers a great deal longer to reach the stage where the database and query methods were well understood. At this stage, they progressed more rapidly than programmers using PJama without the class library - this being more evident with moderately difficult queries, where the availability of a suite of spatial operations was critical. The introduction of the model with its built-in spatio-temporal methods has alleviated this situation but, in the context of spatial operators, systems such as ArcView still offer a great deal more sophisticated primitives. On the other hand, if the end-user requires functionality which is not provided by the (admittedly extensive) ArcView libraries, then it is far harder to provide this oneself compared to having to code one's own functions in PJama - because PJama is a higher-level language and the data types and class structure are far easier to work with.

In a commercial GIS there is no need (or possibility) for code to translate between "store" and "local" data structures because persistence is by type not by reachability. There are hardly any non-persistent items (typically just user inputs and the like), as bulk operations work only on files/relations. As a result of this, programmers are very aware of underlying physical data storage, in stark contrast to PJama where the use of a disk is transparent and does not introduce any additional complexity for the developer to grapple with.

The advantages of a system such as ArcView over our current PJama system are that end users find the simplicity and familiarity of the relational data model easier to relate to, being so similar to the spreadsheets which they often use, while its mapping facilities are clearly superior to those currently available for Java (such as the JShape package).

5   Performance Measurements

An experiment was conducted using a number of spatiotemporal objects of varying complexity and different history sizes. Objects consisting of 10, 50, and 250 vertices were given histories of 200, 1000, and 5000 *intime* components each. The resulting nine combinations were used in queries to test whether the indexing schema described above brings down query times significantly.

In two queries the spatial and temporal indices were tested separately. The first requests a subset of some moving object based on a given time interval by calling the atPeriod() method. The results are shown in Fig. 13.

Another query requests a subset of a moving object's history while it was inside a given region by calling the at() method (Fig. 14).

Store growth was measured and found to be proportional to the total number of InTime objects added. This was not the case with the Napier88 GIS system in [TBB95] where the store growth increased more as more data was added [TBB95].

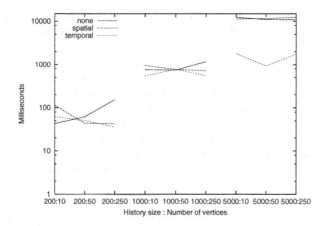

Fig. 13. Results of a query requesting moving objects at a specific time interval.

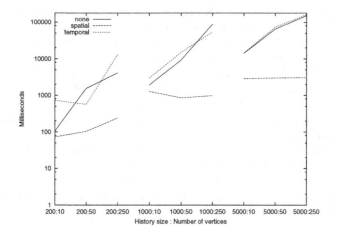

Fig. 14. Results of a query requesting moving objects inside a specific region.

With insertion, we discovered that adding many objects with relatively small histories takes significantly less time than inserting a few objects with large histories. For example 5 objects with a history size of 10000 `InTime` objects takes approx. 5000 seconds to insert, while 50 objects of size 1000 took less than 1000 seconds.

6   Conclusion

This paper has described a persistent Java class library for GIS applications based on an abstract spatiotemporal model [GBE+98]. We aimed to see how this could be mapped onto a discrete representation and implemented in a persistent object-oriented system, and how it would affect the development time and quality of PJama GIS applications. The model has been created, with classes containing a representative sample of spatiotemporal operations, and a proto-type GIS for the (SFRI) Sea Fisheries Research Institute has been built using the environment. This was compared with SFRI applications built in PJama that did not use the model, as well as with an earlier [SVZB98] ArcView3 implementation. We also conducted experiments with three groups of students to verify the usability of our library. Further operations are currently being added to the model and the range of SFRI queries extended.

In conclusion, we return to the questions posed in the introduction.

Is orthogonally persistent Java a suitable platform for implementing a spatio-temporal model?

Overall, we found persistence relatively easy to use and very valuable in terms of decreased development times and better quality solutions. If serialisability or a relational database had to be used instead, we would have achieved a great deal less in the same amount of time. We could focus purely on the spatiotem-poral and index classes without being concerned about the use of a disk at all. Programs could be written on any Java platform and by only adding a few extra lines of code, they could run on a persistent store. The tradeoff here is that working persistent solutions are simple to obtain, but tuning for performance is more difficult through lack of knowledge of storage details - parameters such as the number of values per index node are more difficult to optimise, and the performance impact of data structure changes (e.g. adding inverse references) are more time-consuming to assess.

Java was a good choice of language, with only one instance where single inher-itance proved slightly inconvenient (Point could not inherit from both the AWT Point class and also our SpatialObject class). The object-oriented paradigm was very beneficial because of abstract classes, encapsulation and inheritance. Com-mon functionality between Moving classes could be kept in the parent class, and spatial classes could share methods and add functionality down the hierarchy. Behaviours could also be imposed on certain objects through the use of inter-faces and abstract classes. For instance if 3-dimensional spatial types are added to the model, they will be forced to implement methods that allow them to be used in place of 2-D equivalents anywhere in the model.

The GIS environment and the code and data of our SFRI application are tightly integrated and totally contained within a single store, instead of in many separate files and databases. The ability to create GUI objects effortlessly in Java, and the rapidly-expanding population of Java packages (like JShape which we use for displaying results as maps) makes PJama even more attractive.

Is it possible to build persistent store libraries that make the creation of GIS systems significantly easier?

How would using this library affect the quality and quantity of code in GIS applications?

The SFRI prototype built using the model took about half the development time of our original PJama prototype; a similar reduction in programming time was also found with the students in our case study. This is because the spa-tiotemporal model provides so much infrastructure that both design and coding are greatly simplified. The model is easy to understand and the mapping of real-world entities onto spatial and moving objects is straight-forward; while the many built-in methods considerably reduce the amount of programming required. The resulting data is also better structured – in the original PJama implementation the objects were too similar to the records formerly used in SFRI files and spreadsheets, and methods were badly placed (in query classes instead of using inheritance in the data classes), causing code duplication and little opportunity for reuse. Systems built using the model contain less code and are easier to maintain because they have a better underlying organisation of data into classes.

Having completed and evaluated the model, performance optimisation is now underway. Initial results show performance is acceptable, with no discernible delays between query specification and graphical display of results, while our initial measurements for inserting moving objects into the persistent store indicate that speed and store growth are reasonable.

How would a GIS application using this model compare with one built on conventional technology ?

The provision of a spatio-temporal model has eliminated the major problems we observed when comparing PJama GIS work with that using a commercial product (ArcView3) based on a relational data model [SVZB98]. Foremost among these was the absence of design guidelines and frameworks which made it difficult to know whether one's class structure was appropriate or was more likely to provide some nasty surprises later on. Additionally, the range of queries which were easier to satisfy using PJama than using ArcView was extended because of the spatio-temporal operations provided as methods with the model. The major tradeoffs between using commercial GIS and PJama remain the following: PJama improves productivity by keeping underlying disk storage concerns totally transparent to programmers and enabling them to work with objects and inheritance rather than low-level data items; on the other hand end-users relate more easily to the relational model, and products such as ArcView provide a far larger and more sophisticated set of spatial (though not temporal) operations and mapping functions. Only time and sufficient effort spent extending libraries such as ours will be able to address these issues.

We conclude that PJama is a suitable platform for spatio-temporal application systems, and that class libraries such as that described in this paper are necessary to make persistent GIS a viable alternative to current technology, which fails to support space and time adequately. Future experiments will study the effect of different combinations of intra- and inter-object index, investigate optimisation of internal structures and methods, etc. We will also be using our GIS environment in a land-based application as part of an agricultural research project.

References

[BKSS90] Norbert Beckmann, Hans-Peter Kriegal, Ralf Schneider, and Bernhard Seeger. The R*-tree: An Efficient and Robust Access Method for Points and Rectangles. *Proc. ACM SIGMOD International Conf. on Management of Data*, pages 325–331, 1990.

[BSJS98]   Rasa Bliujute, Simonas Saltenis, Christian Jensen, and Giedrius Slivinskas. R-Tree Based Indexing of Now-Relative Bitemporal Data. In *Proceedings of the 24th VLDB Conference*, 1998.

[CDI⁺97]   James Clifford, Curtis E. Dyreson, Tomás Isakowitz, Christian S. Jensen, and Richard T. Snodgrass. On the Semantics of "Now" in Databases. *TODS*, 22(2):171–214, 1997.

[Eck98]   Bruce Eckel. *Thinking in Java*. Prentice Hall, 1998.

[FMN98]   Claucia Faria, Claudia Bauzer Medeiros, and Mario A. Nascimento. An Extensible Framework for Spatio-temporal Database Applications. Technical report, TimeCenter, 1998.

[GBE⁺98]   R. H. Güting, M. H. Boehlen, M. Erwig, C. S. Jensen, N. A. Lorentzos, M. Schneider, and M. Vazirgiannis. A Foundation for Representing and Querying Moving Objects. Technical report, FernUniversität Hagen, September 1998.

[Gut84]   Antonin Guttman. R-Trees: A Dynamic Index Structure for Spatial Searching. pages 47–52, 1984.

[HNP95]   Joseph M. Hellerstein, Jeffrey F. Naughton, and Avi Pfeffer. Generalised Search Trees for Database Systems. Technical report, University of Berkeley, California, June 1995.

[JA98]   Mick Jordan and Malcolm Atkinson. Orthogonal Persistence for Java - a Mid-term Report. In *Third International Workshop on Persistence and Java*, 1998.

[KM97]   M.J. Kraak and M. Molenaar. *Advances in GIS Research II*. Taylor & Francis, 1997.

[NST98]   Mario Nascimento, Jefferson Silva, and Yannis Theodoridis. Towards Historical R-Trees. In *Proceedings of the 1998 ACM Symposium on Applied Computing*, pages 235 – 240, February 1998.

[NST99]   Mario Nascimento, Jefferson Silva, and Yannis Theodoris. Evaluation of Access Structures for Discretely Moving Points. In *International Workshop on Spatio-Temporal Database Management*, 1999.

[PSZ99]   Christine Parent, Stefano Spaccapietra, and Esteban Zimanyi. Spatio-Temporal Conceptual Models: Data Structures + Space + Time, 1999.

[SB97]   B. Skellaug and A. J. Berre. Mulit-Dimensional Time Support for Spatial Data Models. Technical Report 253, Institutt for Informatikk, Universitet i Oslo, May 1997.

[SJLL99]   Simonas Saltenis, Christian Jensen, Scott Leutenegger, and Mario Lopez. Indexing the Positions of Continuously Moving Objects. Technical report, Chorochronos, 1999.

[SN97]   Andreas Steiner and Moira C. Norrie. Implementing Temporal Databases in Object Oriented Systems. Technical report, TimeCenter, 1997.

[SVZB98]   Richard Southern, Aisling Vasey, Daniel Ziskind, and Sonia Berman. Spatiotemporal Access in Persistent Java, 1998.

[TBB95]   Hogan Thring, Simon Buffler, and Jessica Burger. Accessing Spatial Data. Technical report, University of Cape Town, 1995.

[TH97]   N. Tryfona and T. Hadzilacos. Logical Data Modelling of Spatio-Temporal Applications: Definitions and a Model. Technical report, Chorochronos, 1997.

[VO97]   Erik Voges and James Owen. A Generic Indexing Mechanism for Persistent Java, 1997.

[Wor98]   Michael F. Worboys. A Generic Model for Spatio-Bitemporal Geographic Information. In Max J.Egenhofer and Reginald G. Gollegde, editors, *Spatial and Temporal Reasoning in Geographic Information Systems*, chapter 2. Oxford University Press, 1998.

[Yua95]   May Yuan. Temporal GIS and Spatio-Temporal Modeling, 1995.

Experience with the PerDiS Large-Scale Data-Sharing Middleware*

Marc Shapiro[1,2], Paulo Ferreira[3], and Nicolas Richer[2]

[1] Microsoft Research Ltd., St. George House, 1 Guildhall St., Cambridge CB2 3NH, United Kingdom; mailto:marc.shapiro@acm.org, http://www-sor.inria.fr/~shapiro/
[2] INRIA projet SOR, Domaine de Voluceau, B.P. 105, Rocquencourt, 78153 Le Chesnay Cedex, France; mailto:nicolas.richer@inria.fr, http://www-sor.inria.fr/~richer/
[3] INESC, Rua Alves Redol 9 - 6, 1000 Lisboa Cedex, Portugal; mailto:paulo.ferreira@inesc.pt, http://www.gsd.inesc.pt/

Abstract. PerDiS is a distributed persistent middleware platform, intended to ease the distributed sharing of long-term data. Its users belong to geographically-distant and non-trusting entreprises. It targets CAD applications for the building industry: data sets are large and pointer-rich; simultaneous reads and updates are supported; there is no central database; migrating legacy applications is accessible to unskilled programmers. A number of real applications have been either ported or written specifically for PerDiS.

The following design decisions were essential to the scalability and to the useability of PerDiS. Isolation (transactions) decouples users from one another. The system design provides different granularities. The programming abstraction is a fine-grain, persistent, isolated shared memory, with objects, invocations and URLs. The system mechanisms are coarse-grained, loosely-coupled and optimistic. Fine-grain application entities are encapsulated into coarse-grain system entities, respectively clusters, domains, transactions, and projects.

1 Introduction

PerDiS provides a new technology for sharing over the Internet, the Persistent Distributed Store. PerDiS enables application programmers to use shared, complex objects in a distributed environment. PerDiS is a middleware layer, designed for use in cooperative CAD applications across long distances and across organisational boundaries. Some of the requirements are to ease the porting of a legacy application by programmers unskilled in distributed systems; to support large and pointer-rich data sets; to support simultaneous reads and updates; and support multiple, geographically-distant storage sites. Interfacing to PerDiS is easy

---

* Published in Ninth International Workshop on Persistent Object Systems, Lillehammer (Norway), 5–7 September 2000.
http://www-ppg.dcs.st-and.ac.uk/Conferences/POS9/

G.N.C. Kirby, A. Dearle, and D.I.K. Sjøberg (Eds.): POS-9, LNCS 2135, pp. 55–69, 2001.
© Springer-Verlag Berlin Heidelberg 2001

and natural: an application allocates its data in (the PerDiS-managed) memory. Since the major PerDiS abstraction is just memory, sharing some object is just a matter of setting a pointer to it.

Objects automatically become persistent and shared over the network. Transactions isolate applications from one another. Caching and replication techniques ensure that data is accessed efficiently and rapidly. Automatic persistence and garbage collection take away many of the headaches of sharing. Objects are protected from unwanted access or tampering by distributed access control and encryption.

Although our primary target is the building and construction industry, the technology should be applicable to other application domains where distributed access to complex, mutable data is needed.

All the results of PerDiS are available on our Web site http://www.perdis. esprit.ec.org/, in accordance with our open source policy.

2   Requirements

2.1   Cooperative Work in Building and Construction

A Building and Construction (B&C) project is represented by an object for each wall, window, door, fitting, etc. The size of an object is of the order of 1–10 Kbytes. Objects are connected by pointers (e.g., a wall points to all its windows, doors, adjacent walls, floor and ceiling; and vice-versa). All told the data size of a reasonable building is in the order of tens of megabytes.

A B&C project often involves a "Virtual Entreprise" (VE), a temporary alliance between specialists of different domains (such as architects, structural engineers, heating or electricity specialists) from geographically-distant and mutually untrusting companies.

Previous attempts at cooperative CAD tools by our partners [2] were based on remote object invocation [8]: a client application running on a workstation invokes objects, stored in a remote server, through remote references. With fine-grain CAD objects this architecture results in abysmal performance[1] (especially over a WAN in a VE) unless applications are completely re-engineered.

Other attempts have used object-oriented databases, whose interface is appropriate to this application area. However OODBs are are not designed to be used across slow connections or across trust boundaries. Furthermore, each company in the VE is likely to have their own storage system; therefore a central database cannot be assumed.

2.2   B&C Requirements

The foremost requirement is for a middleware layer that insulates application programmers from the complexities of distributed programming. However some

---

[1] See Section 5.1 for a performance comparison between remote invocation and PerDiS on CAD data.

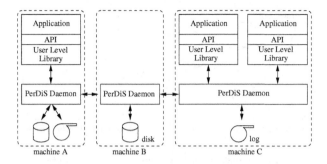

Fig. 1. PerDiS platform design

network imperfections cannot be totally masked; much of our design effort has been to make sure they only appear at clear, intuitive and coarse-grain boundaries.

This middleware should make it easy to share the common data of a building project. PerDiS fulfills these requirements by offering the simplest, most familiar API: a network-wide, persistent shared memory.

In B&C, collaboration follows an essentially sequential workflow between workgroups. People within a workgroup exchange a high volume of data with each other. There is a high degree of temporal and spatial locality within a workgroup. There is also some real concurrency, including write conflicts, which cannot be ignored; for instance working on alternative designs in parallel is common practice. Each of the workgroups is small, trusting, and typically located connected by a fast LAN. In contrast, different workgroups often belong to geographically-distant and mutually-distrusting companies, connected by slow, unreliable and sometimes intermittent WANs. These considerations justify the concept of a *domain*, explained in Section 3.1.

The data stored in the platform should inter-operate with different applications on different platforms. This requirement was satisfied in the PerDiS project by implementing an industry standard interface called SDAI. Implementing SDAI was made very easy thanks to the shared memory abstraction [13].

3   PerDiS Basics

The PerDiS architecture is illustrated in Figure 1. The different processes isolate crucial platform functions from applications, and applications from one another. It uses peer-to-peer cooperative caching for best performance.

A node runs a single *PerDiS Dæmon* (PD), and any number of application processes. Applications interact with PerDiS through an API layer, which interfaces to the *User Level Library* (ULL).

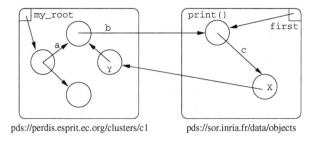

pds://perdis.esprit.ec.org/clusters/c1   pds://sor.inria.fr/data/objects

Fig. 2. Clusters, objects and remote references.

3.1   Domains

We make an essential distinction between two modes of operation: in-domain (i.e., within a workgroup, on a LAN) and inter-domain (e.g., between workgroups, or over a WAN).

A domain is a set of well-connected and mutually-trusting workstations. They share data using coherent caching and strong transactional semantics. A domain is designed for a fast LAN connection.

In contrast, the protocols between domains are designed for loosely-coupled interaction. Workgroups that distrust each other, those that interact infrequently, or those separated by a poor WAN connection, should be in separate domains.

Each domain has a *gateway* node responsible for interacting with off-domain servers. This gateway caches remote clusters and provides access to local clusters to remote domains.

3.2   Objects and Clusters

A PerDiS object is a sequence of bytes representing some data structure. Objects are opaque to the PerDiS platform, although the system stores a type descriptor for every object, and although its garbage collector is capable of following pointers in an object.

The memory is partitioned into coarse-grain structures called clusters. A cluster is a physical grouping of logically related objects. A cluster has a variable and unlimited size; clusters are disjoint.

When any object in a cluster is accessed at some site, the whole cluster is cached, supporting very fast, local access to all the objects of the cluster. A cluster is cached and possibly stored at all sites where it is in use, but each cluster has a designated *home site* storing its authoritative version. This was an application requirement for legal reasons.

An object in some cluster may point to some other object, either in the same cluster or in another one. The application program navigates the object graph from a root. See for instance Figure 2. A program might navigate from the root point in the leftmost cluster, executing for instance my_root->a->b->print(). This implicitly loads the corresponding cluster.

3.3   Caching and Replication

A PerDiS application always accesses the objects it needs in its local memory. This makes it easy for programmers unskilled in distributed systems to share information. Since furthermore data is cached in large chunks, this eliminates the remote access bottleneck. The system caches data lazily, i.e., only when an application accesses it. Caches at different sites cooperate to fetch the data that an application needs while minimising input-output operations.

The PerDiS API allows access at whatever granularity is most appropriate. (The default is to fetch a whole page into application memory on a page fault.) The application programmer may choose to access a small object at a time for greatest concurrency, or to access a whole range of adjacent objects in one go, for consistency. However the system mechanisms are coarse-grain: when an application requests access to a single byte, the whole enclosing cluster is opened and brought into the cache of the corresponding PD.

3.4   Transactions

PerDiS supports a broad range of transactional facilities, motivated by the application domain of cooperative engineering.

PerDiS provides different flavours of transactions: (i) classical pessimistic ACID (Atomic, Consistent, Isolated, and Durable); (ii) optimistic ACID; and (iii) check-out/check-in. Pessimistic concurrency control locks data while accessed, and holds on to a lock until the transaction terminates. Optimistic concurrency control will access data concurrently without locking; conflicts are detected through data versioning.

Check-out/check-in transactions control inter-domain sharing. (Domains were defined in Section 3.1.) When domain A needs data whose home site is in domain B, a *gateway* in domain A takes copies of the data for faster service and availability. The unit of inter-domain sharing is a *project*, a predefined set of clusters to be accessed together. A check-out transaction brings a project from its remote domain(s) into the current domain; it is cached on the local gateway. The clusters of the project can be manipulated and shared within the domain using the usual pessimistic or optimistic transactions. Finally a check-out transaction stores the updated clusters of the project in their respective home domains. The system detects at this point any potential conflicts. Currently it is up to the application to repair such conflicts.

3.5   Security

Protecting data in VEs is important, since partners in one project may be in competition for another one. Our security mechanisms [7] provide both access control and secure communication. Each cluster has an access control list indicating the access rights assigned a to a user's role within a task. Secure communication uses public key schemes for signed data access requests, shared keys for encryption and a combination of the two for authentication of message originators.

4   Distributed Memory Management

4.1   Distributed Memory Management

The memory management (MM) state is recorded in data structures such as free lists, object tables, roots, etc., collectively called the MM *meta-data*. Meta-data constitutes a shared resource, which in a distributed system faces concurrency and consistency issues.

To avoid locking meta-data, we propose a new transaction model, called *system transactions*.

A system transaction is a sub-transaction (of a user transaction) that takes into account the semantics of its operation. The operation can either be applied immediately and undone if the transaction aborts, or delayed and redone when the transaction commits.

Consider for instance a top-level (application) transaction that creates a new cluster. This operation is executed in its local addressing space and within a system transaction. Only at commit time is the cluster is inserted in the global cluster list, under a short-term exclusive lock. If the transaction aborts, the cluster is never inserted in the list, and never becomes visible to other transactions. This delayed operation is safe because the order in the list is immaterial to the semantics of clusters. Note that this technique still works in a disconnected environment, where the insertions can safely be delayed until the network is reconnected.

In contrast, segment reservation cannot be delayed because two different segments must not have the same address. Creating a new segment reserves its address immediately (under a short locks to avoid blocking other transactions) and records it in an undo log. If the transaction aborts, the undo log cancels its reservations.

In both cases, the semantics of the operations in the system transaction is well-known; this technique cannot be generalised to arbitrary objects.

4.2   Distributed Garbage Collection (DGC)

Persistence in PerDiS is based on reachability [3]. To decide whether an object is reachable is a difficult problem in a distributed and replicated environment. We use the Larchant distributed GC model and algorithm [9,14]. A DGC is modeled as a per-site constructive component, which identifies new pointers, a per-site destructive component, which identifies unreachable objects, and a distribution component, which ensures consistency of GC meta-data. Larchant posits five ordering rules that enforce a safe global ordering between mutation, data coherence, and GC components, such that a destructive GC never misses a reachable object. These rules are general enough to ensure safety of any distributed GC, whatever consistency model is used.

PerDiS uses a novel algorithm for its distribution component [5,6], based on Goldberg's hierarchical weighted reference counting [1]. This is a variation on

Weighted Reference Counting [4,16] where each node in the diffusion tree keeps an independent count of its children so to avoid weight underflow.

The Larchant rules impose that the constructive GC run before events that act on mutator updates. The simplest way to enforce this is to run it at transaction commit. However scanning the updates is expensive and introduces a bottleneck into the commit path. To diminish the impact on performance, we are currently moving the constructive GC out of the commit path, at the expense of more complex scheduling. It does not slow down the transaction commit anymore, and can run in parallel with local mutators, which are allowed to access the newly-committed data.

However, the constructive GC must finish before either the destructive GC or the coherence engine can access the newly-committed data. This impacts mutators on remote sites, which cannot access committed data immediately. In effect we have moved the (unavoidable) constructive-GC bottleneck from the transaction commit path to the remote communication path. The advantage is that local applications are not slowed down by it any more.

5   Application Experience

Porting an application to the PerDiS platform requires data and code conversions, which are both relatively straightforward.

Code conversion can be done in several ways. The simplest is the following: (i) embed the application in a pessimistic transaction that uses default data access (see Section 3.3), (ii) open persistent roots, (iii) replace writes into a file with commit.

These simple modifications bring many gains. In particular, there is no more need for flattening data structures, explicit disk I/O, or explicit memory management. In addition, data distribution, transactions and persistence come for free. However concurrency is limited; more concurrency can be achieved, at the cost of a bigger programming effort, using explicit data access primitives, the different transaction types, non-serialisable access, etc.

Table 1. Rendering application. For each test set, we provide: (a) Name of dataset; size of SPF file (KB); number of SPF objects and of polyloop objects. (b) Execution times in seconds: original stand-alone version; PerDiS and Corba port, 1 and 2 nodes.

Test	Dataset	size	SPF objects	Poly-Loops
1	cstb_1	293	5 200	530
2	cstb0rdc	633	12 080	1 024
3	cstb0fon	725	12 930	1 212
4	demo225	2 031	40 780	4 091

(a) Test applications

Test	Orig	Pds1	Pds2	Cba1	Cba2
1	0.03	1.62	2.08	54.52	59.00
2	0.06	4.04	4.27	115.60	123.82
3	0.07	4.04	5.73	146.95	181.96
4	0.16	13.90	271.50	843.94	1452.11

(b) Test application execution times (s)

5.1   CAD Rendering Application

This section presents our experience with a CAD rendering application. This application is relatively simple, yet representative of the main loop of a CAD tool. We compare the original, stand-alone version, with a Corba and a PerDiS version.

The stand-alone version has two modules. The *read module* parses an ASCII file and instantiates the corresponding objects in memory. The *mapping module* traverses the object graph to generate a VRML view, according to object geometry (polygons) and semantics (for instance, a load-bearing wall is colored differently from a partition). The object graph contains a hierarchy of high-level objects representing projects, buildings, storeys and staircases. A storey contains rooms, walls, openings and floors; these are represented by low-level geometric objects such as polyloops, polygons and points.

In the Corba port, the read module is located in a server which then retains the graph in memory. The mapping module is a client that accesses objects remotely at the server. To reduce the porting effort, only four geometric classes were enabled for remote access. The port took two days. The code to access objects in the mapping module had to be completely rewritten. The functionality of this version is reduced with respect to the original since only geometric information is transmitted and the architectural semantics is lost.

In the PerDiS port, the read module runs as a transaction in one process and stores the graph in a cluster. The mapping module runs in another process and opens that cluster. The port took half a day.

The stand-alone version is approximately 4,000 lines of C++, in about 100 classes and 20 files. In the Corba version, only 5 of the classes were made remotely accessible, but 500 lines needed to be changed. In the PerDiS version, only 100 lines were changed.

Table 1 compares the three versions for various test sets and in various configurations. Compared to the stand-alone version, performance is low, but this is not surprising for a proof-of-concept platform. Compared to a remote-object system, even a mature industrial product, such as Orbix, the PerDiS approach yields much better performance.

The one-machine configuration is a Pentium Pro at 200 MHz running Windows-NT 4.0. It has 128 Mbytes of RAM and 100 Mbytes of swap space. In the two-machine configuration for Corba, the server runs on the same machine as above. The client runs on a portable with a Pentium 230 MHz processor, 64 Mbytes RAM and 75 Mbytes swap space, running Windows-NT 4.0. In the two-machine configuration for PerDiS, both processes run on the first machine, whereas its home site is on the second one.

This experience confirms our intuition that the persistent distributed store paradigm performs better than an industry-standard remote-invocation system, for data sets and algorithms that are typical of distributed VE applications. It also confirms that porting existing code to PerDiS is straightforward and provides the benefits of sharing, distribution and persistence with very little effort.

5.2   Standard Data Access Interface in PerDiS

The Standard Data Access Interface (SDAI) is an ISO standard API that allows CAD applications to access to a common store.[2] The standard does not cover data distribution, multi-user access or security issues. In PerDiS we developed a late-binding implementation of the SDAI in C++. The code is about 50 000 lines written with Microsoft Visual C++ environment and using the MFC (Microsoft Foundation Classes) containers.

This reader part of this module loads a SPF file and populates a SDAI model. The writer exports a SDAI model in a SPF file.

The first step was to port the container classes of MFC (Clist, Cstring, Cvector, Carray, Cmap, and all the template containers). This porting took about 2 weeks, most of which was spent in understanding how MFC classes are implemented. The Cstring class was the must difficult: all its operators are overloaded to avoid duplicating the string array. To differentiate between a transient and persistent container, every element of a container is allocated in the same cluster as the container itself.

We then linked the SDAI layer with the persistent containers, with some minor modifications.

The SDAI implementation was a very positive experience. The PerDiS SDAI extends the standard, making it distributed and guaranteeing security. It showed that relatively complex, widely-used libraries such as MFC and SDAI can be ported with ease, once the original source code and the PerDiS model have been well understood. This vindicates our previous experience in porting the C++ Standard Template Library (STL). Any single-process application that uses either the STL or the MFC containers, or the SDAI, can be converted to a distributed, multi-user, persistent one simply by linking in our libraries.

5.3   Atlantis

Porting a real application to PerDiS is not always an easy task. The major difficulty occurs in legacy applications that contain their own implementation of the PerDiS facilities, such as persistence. We provide here some examples, that we discovered when porting Atlantis (a CAD tool provided by the PerDiS partner IEZ).

When an application is conceived without support for automatic persistence the programmer explicitly saves objects to disk. Later, when those objects are read from disk in order to be accessed again, new instances are created and initialized with the values read from disk. With this mechanism, the constructor is invoked each time an object is read from disk. Note that this constructor invocation does not occur in PerDiS; it is invoked only when the object is created and not when mapped into memory from disk.

In legacy applications with no automatic persistence support programers usually split objects into persistent and temporary, i.e. those that do not have to be saved on disk when the application ends. In PerDiS it is not necessary to make such a distinction. An object is saved to disk if it is reachable from

---

[2] See http://www.perdis.esprit.ec.org/apf/sdai/ for more detail.

the persistent root. So, if you have an application with "temporary objects", you will have to ensure that they are not reachable from the persistent root; otherwise, they will be saved to disk. This leads to decreased performance and to unnecessary disk occupation.

6   Platform Assessment

A detailed assessment of the platform has been produced [12]. The main conclusions are reproduced hereafter.

6.1   Qualitative Assessment

The distributed shared memory model of PerDiS is a simple paradigm that appeals to application developers. For the targeted application domain, it is much more intuitive than alternatives such as relational database or remote invocation. It frees users from explicit decisions about object persistence, and simplifies considerably the porting of legacy applications.

The distribution model of PerDiS makes it easy to distribute data. Furthermore the granularity of distribution is selectable, which makes it superior to fine-grain systems such as DCOM or Corba. At first access, a large granule is cached locally; further accesses are local, which improves execution time over Corba by a factor of 5 (for 40K objects), of memory by a factor of 15 (for 10K objects). The drawback is that currently the application must specify object groupings manually.

The current implementation has known limitations. Currently the system is very homogeneous, lacking a data translation layer, object relocation ("pointer swizzling" [10]), and support for the evolution of shared classes. In order to correct these shortcomings, a system for extracting type information from binary files was developed [11] but was never integrated in the platform for lack of time.

6.2   Quantitative Assessment

We have done quantitative assessments of several aspects of the PerDiS platform. Some were documented in earlier sections of this paper; here we focus only on general performance.

The experimental conditions are the following: PerDiS platform version 6.1, compiled in release mode (i.e., compiler optimisations on, debugging information off). We used workstations with a Pentium II 300 MHz CPU, 128 MB of memory, and running NT 4.0. We measured and profiled the the most commonly-used API calls. We include here the numbers for the transaction creation primitive new_transaction, the commit and abort primitive end_transaction and an end-to-end benchmark that allocates 1000 objects within a transaction. (All transactions measured are pessimistic.) For brevity we comment only on the first set of numbers.

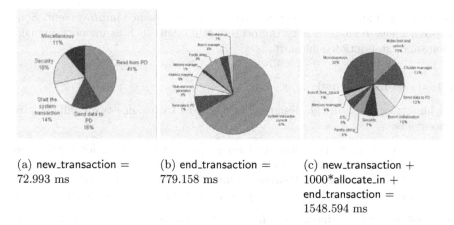

(a) new_transaction = 72.993 ms

(b) end_transaction = 779.158 ms

(c) new_transaction + 1000*allocate_in + end_transaction = 1548.594 ms

Fig. 3. Execution time breakdowns.

Figure 3 (a) shows the execution time breakdown to start a new transaction. 57% of the time, marked "Read from PD & Send data to PD," is spent communicating with the PD through TCP/IP sockets (on the same machine). The amount of data sent is small, and sending data involves no wait for the ULL.

When the ULL reads data from the PD, it can either be actually reading data from the socket, or waiting for the PD to complete an operation before returning a value. In this latter case, it blocks in a function called wait_for_reply, whereas reading functions – the former case – do not block but actually read data from the socket. So, the time spent by the PD to perform its tasks is almost equal to the time spent by the ULL in wait_for_reply.

In all the tests we performed, the ULL spent only a few more milliseconds in wait_for_reply than in the function reading from the socket. This shows that reading from the socket accounts for half of the communication time induced by a new_transaction call. Consequently, the tasks taking most of the execution time are the ones heavily communicating with the PD.

The basic security checks and the start of the system transaction are the most expensive tasks performed in the ULL for the start of a new transaction. A glance at the code shows that these two tasks are not overwhelmingly complex; hence, most of the time is spent in communication and, more generally, in system calls.

11% of the total execution time of this primitive is spent in miscellaneous such as internal data handling (e.g. constructors and destructors, list handling...), that account for less than 1% each. These calls are almost inherent to C++ programming, and are unavoidable.

In summary, the PerDiS platform must be evaluated for what it is, i.e., a research platform. Its main focus is testing a novel approach to sharing data in the Internet: testing new paradigms, assessing feasibility, and evaluating their cost. Performance was not the primary focus, but having demonstrated feasibility of our ideas, performance becomes essential to their acceptability. The PerDiS model is feasible, but there is much room for performance improvement. Some research issues related to performance are still open, such as memory management, and transactional support.

6.3   Lessons Learned

An important issue in the design of PerDiS was to balance two conflicting requirements:

1. A simple, transparent, uniform interface, to make it easier for applications to use distribution and persistence.
2. Powerful control of, and feedback from, the distributed architecture, in order to handle the complexities and imperfections of a large distributed system.

It is not possible to maintain complete transparency in a large-scale system: failures, latency, and locality cannot (and should not) be masked. A major design issue is where such problems are made visible to the application. In a fine-grain system, the answer is "anywhere": when accessing any object, when making any call.

In contrast, a major result of PerDiS is its dual-granularity design. A PerDiS application is written in terms of the application's native, fine-grain objects, which are simply mapped into the PerDiS memory, where they can be invoked. Fine-grain entities are grouped into coarser-grain ones, which the application can control. For instance objects are grouped into clusters; an application will never encounter a problem when accessing an individual object, although it might get one when first opening its cluster. Similarly, invocations are grouped into transactions; problems occur only at the well-defined transaction boundary. Two more coarse-granularity entities are of interest to the programmer, the domain (Section 3.1) and the project (Section 3.4).

The PerDiS architecture distinguishes between local (within a domain) and inter-domain operation. As argued earlier, this answers both application requirements (tighter coupling within a work group) and system constraints: latency, security, availability, administrative are all different on a WAN. It would be a simple to extend this architecture to more hierarchy levels if there was a need.

To summarise, whereas an application deals mostly with fine-grain entities, the PerDiS platform deals with large granularities. This dual fine-grain/coarse-grain model is essential to the success and scalability of PerDiS and has a number of advantages:

1. Accessing a cluster provides implicit data pre-fetch, making future accesses much faster.
2. Expensive system calls are made infrequently.
3. A relatively small number of clusters is more manageable than an immense sea of objects.
4. Optimisation opportunities such as sharing pages between processes.
5. Adapting mechanisms to needs and costs: protocols within a domain are cheaper than across domain boundaries.
6. The failure model is simplified, because failure can occur only at coarse-grain, well-understood boundaries.

Experience confirms that our transactional design effectively combines isolation and co-operation in a wide-area loosely coupled environment. PerDiS transactions have the flexibility to adapt to a more strict and connected environment or to a typical Internet environment. Many of the transactional features introduced in PerDiS were aimed at that goal: combining optimistic and pessimistic transactions, allowing multiple locking modes, using a multi-version store which ensures data availability for remote clients and providing notifications of important transactional events.

We conclude that the main design choices have been validated. All the aspects of sharing data are combined into a uniform and simple API, including data access transparency, persistence and distribution. The approach eases the port of existing applications (within the limits of the targeted domain) and makes writing new distributed applications very easy. Some limitations remain, some that can be solved with better engineering, some that remain open research issues.

7   Conclusion

The PerDiS platform is fully functional and freely available on our Web site. It supports a number of representative applications. Our experience is that porting to PerDiS, or writing an application for PerDiS, is a relatively easy and painless way to get persistence and distribution. The current version is a research prototype; its main purpose was to demonstrate the viability of the approach. It embodies 18 man-years of research and development. Although it has a number of limitations, using it can save your own project that amount of work. Furthermore the source is freely available for others to re-use and improve.

PerDiS has a number of distinct advantages over competing approaches. It has a familiar memory interface. Its dual-granularity approach combines the best features of an intuitive, object-oriented access at the application programming language level, and simple, efficient, coarse-grain system mechanisms. In a large-scale distributed system, where network problems cannot be totally masked, one major advantage of coarse granularity is the simplified failure model: an application can be exposed to a failure only at a cluster or a transaction boundary.

Domains are another important PerDiS coarse-grain structure. They provide a mechanism for limiting the scope of expensive network operations such as cache coherence or two-phase commit. Coupled with projects they provide a way to quickly set up a new VE.

Another key factor in scalability of PerDiS is the widespread use of optimistic techniques such as optimistic and check-out/check-in transactions. Optimistic techniques are also used in other areas such as caching, security and garbage collection algorithms.

Our experience points out some interesting open issues. The direct mapping of objects into application memory is a considerable simplification, but the current model is too restrictive. Users (although happy with the shared memory abstraction) have asked us to provide different views of the same data. This would be useful for sharing data between very different applications, languages, or storage systems; it also integrates into a single coherent framework some of the needs from swizzling, security, versioning, and schema evolution. In the near future we will integrate pointer swizzling, but more general, application-specific transformations are needed, such as masking information to some users, changing measurement units, presenting the same information in different formats, or evolving class definitions. This is an area of active future research.

Another fundamental research problem is reconciliation. In a large-scale network divergence of replicas is a fact of life. Currently PerDiS detects diverging replicas and lets applications repair after the fact. Although reconciliation depends on data semantics (and indeed is not even always possible) we are trying to have the system take some of the burden and simplify the application's task [15].

Acknowledgments. We warmly thank the following members of the PerDiS project for their contribution to this paper: Xavier Blondel, George Coulouris, Jean Dollimore, Olivier Fambon, João Garcia, Sacha Krakowiak, Fadi Sandakly, and Ngoc-Khoi Tô. We also thank all those who worked on PerDiS and contributed to its success, in particular Sytse Kloosterman, Thomas Lehman, and Marcus Roberts.

References

1. Saleh E. Abdullahi and Graem A. Ringwood. Garbage collecting the Internet: a survey of distributed garbage collection. *ACM Computing Surveys*, 30(3):330–373, September 1998.
2. Virginie Amar. *Intégration des standards STEP et CORBA pour le processus d'ingénierie dans l'entreprise virtuelle*. PhD thesis, Université de Nice Sophia-Antipolis, September 1998.
3. M. P. Atkinson, P. J. Bailey, K. J. Chisholm, P. W. Cockshott, and R. Morrison. An approach to persistent programming. *The Computer Journal*, 26(4):360–365, 1983.
4. D. I. Bevan. Distributed garbage collection using reference counting. In *Parallel Arch. and Lang. Europe*, pages 117–187, Eindhoven, The Netherlands, June 1987. Spring-Verlag Lecture Notes in Computer Science 259.
5. Xavier Blondel. Report on the scalability of garbage collection. Deliverable TC.1.3-B, PerDiS project, November 1999.
   http://www.perdis.esprit.ec.org/deliverables/docs/wpC/tc13b/.
6. Xavier Blondel. *Gestion des méta-données de la mémoire dans un environnement réparti persistant transactionnel à grande échelle : l'exemple de PerDiS*. PhD thesis, Conservatoire National des Arts et Métiers, To appear, September 2000.
7. George Coulouris, Jean Dollimore, and Marcus Roberts. Role and task-based access control in the PerDiS groupware platform. In *W. on Role-Based Access Control*, Washington DC (USA), October 1998. http://www.dcs.qmw.ac.uk/research/distrib/perdis/papers/Coulouris-RBAC9\%8-final.ps.gz.
8. Digital Equipment Corporation, Hewlett-Packard Company, HyperDesk Corporation, NCR Coporation, Object Design, Inc., and SunSoft, Inc. The Common Object Request Broker: Architecture and specification. Technical Report 91-12-1, Object Management Group, Framingham MA (USA), December 1991.

9. Paulo Ferreira and Marc Shapiro. Modelling a distributed cached store for garbage collection. In *12th Euro. Conf. on Object-Oriented Prog. (ECOOP)*, Brussels (Belgium), July 1998. http://www-sor.inria.fr/publi/MDCSGC_ecoop98.html.

10. J. Eliot B. Moss. Working with persistent objects: To swizzle or not to swizzle. *IEEE Transactions on Software Engineering*, 18(8):657–673, August 1992.

11. Alexandru Salcianu. Extraction et utilisation des informations de type pour le support des objets répartis. Mémoire de dea, École Normale Supérieure de Lyon, July 1999. http://www-sor.inria.fr/publi/EUITSOR_dea-salcianu-1999-07.html.

12. F. Sandakly, O. Fambon, M. Roberts, X. Blondel, and N. Tô. Final report on assessment of the platform and proposed improvements. Deliverable TA.3-A, PerDiS project, March 2000. http://www.perdis.esprit.ec.org/deliverables/docs/wpA/ta3a/.

13. Fadi Sandakly, Marcus Roberts, and Thomas Lehmann. Report on experience programming over IPF. Deliverable TA.2.2-D, PerDiS Project, March 2000. http://www.perdis.esprit.ec.org/deliverables/docs/wpA/ta22d/.

14. Marc Shapiro, Fabrice Le Fessant, and Paulo Ferreira. Recent advances in distributed garbage collection. In S. Krakowiak and S. K. Shrivastava, editors, *Recent Advances in Distributed Systems*, volume 1752 of *Lecture Notes in Computer Science*, chapter 5, pages 104–126. Springer-Verlag, February 2000. http://www-sor.inria.fr/publi/RAIDGC_lncs1752.html.

15. Marc Shapiro, Antony Rowstron, and Anne-Marie Kermarrec. Application-independent reconciliation for nomadic applications. In *Proc. SIGOPS European Workshop: "Beyond the PC: New Challenges for the Operating System"*, Kolding (Denmark), September 2000. ACM SIGOPS. http://www-sor.inria.fr/~shapiro/papers/ew2000-logmerge.html.

16. P. Watson and I. Watson. An efficient garbage collection scheme for parallel computer architectures. In *PARLE'87—Parallel Architectures and Languages Europe*, number 259 in Lecture Notes in Computer Science, Eindhoven (the Netherlands), June 1987. Springer-Verlag.

Toward Pure Polylingual Persistence

Alan Kaplan[1], John V.E. Ridgway[2], Bradley R. Schmerl[1],
Krishnan Sridhar[1], and Jack C. Wileden[2]

[1] Dept. of Computer Science, Clemson University, Clemson, SC 29634, USA
{kaplan,schmerl,krish}@cs.clemson.edu
[2] Dept. of Computer Science, University of Massachusetts, Amherst, MA 01003, USA
{wileden,ridgway}@cs.umass.edu

Abstract. A heterogeneous persistent object system provides multiple programming language interfaces. This gives rise to the polylingual interoperability problem, namely, how can an application uniformly process data objects that have been defined, created and persistently stored using distinct programming language type models. At POS-7, we reported on the PolySPIN approach (polylingual support for persistence, interoperability and naming). A prototype based on PolySPIN, which was built as an extension to the TI/Darpa Open Object-Oriented Database, supports transparent polylingual access for persistent C++ and CLOS objects. The approach, however, assumes that objects in the persistent store are monolingual structures. That is, while a C++ application using the PolySPIN approach may access and manipulate a persistent CLOS object as if it were implemented in C++, that CLOS object must be entirely implemented in CLOS. In this paper, we report on our recent efforts toward extending PolySPIN with *pure polylingual persistence* capabilities. Our new approach supports transparent construction and manipulation of *heterolingual* persistent data objects. This means that a persistent object may have in its closure objects that are defined using different languages. The pure polylingual persistence mechanism transparently manages heterolingual persistent objects. We illustrate the pure polylingual approach by applying it to a Java-C++ realization of the 007 benchmark as implemented using the TI/Darpa Open Object-Oriented Database.

1 Introduction

The typical, *homogeneous* persistent object system (POS) assumes a homogeneous data model. In such a homogeneous POS a single type model provided by a single programming language, either one designed specifically for persistence or one created by extending an existing language, serves as the basis for defining persistent data. While issues related to individual language type models and/or constructs in POSs have received a great deal of attention, few research activities have addressed the problems inherent in heterogeneous POSs.

A *heterogeneous* POS provides two or more application programming interfaces based on two or more different programming languages. This means that a

G.N.C. Kirby, A. Dearle, and D.I.K. Sjøberg (Eds.): POS-9, LNCS 2135, pp. 70–83, 2001.

given heterogeneous POS may contain persistent objects that have been defined and created using different programming language type models. The TI/Darpa Open Object-Oriented Database [11] is one example of a heterogeneous POS. Unfortunately, heterogeneous POSs do not necessarily provide support for *interoperability*, but instead keep persistent objects segregated based on the programming language that was used to define and create them. Even those heterogeneous POSs that do support some aspects of interoperability do not generally support *polylingual* interoperability, by which we mean that an application can uniformly and transparently access and process persistent data that was defined and created using different programming language type models[7].

We believe that the lack of support for interoperability, and particularly polylingual interoperability, has unduly limited the potential utility of POSs. In particular, there are a host of potential applications of POS technology, such as genetic research, chemical and pharmaceutical research, engineering design automation or electronic commerce, that fundamentally depend upon the ability to combine existing, and often massive, quantities of persistent data. Moreover, all of these applications involve synthesizing new data (e.g., new chemical compounds, new designs, new products or marketing data) comprising various pieces of the preexisting persistent data. Unless it can offer support for transparently creating and processing heterolingual persistent objects, POS technology is unlikely to penetrate this potentially vast and important class of applications.

At POS-7, we presented our work on PolySPIN – polylingual support for persistence, interoperability and naming [7]. PolySPIN attempts to desegregate heterogeneous persistent repositories through provision of a uniform name management mechanism. By extending the uniform naming mechanism to a name-based persistence mechanism, our PolySPIN approach allows objects defined and created using different programming languages to effectively reside in the same store. Moreover, the polylingual interoperability capabilities in PolySPIN permit applications to uniformly and transparently access and update persistent objects independently of the programming language used in their original definition and creation.

One significant limitation of PolySPIN is that it does not support the concept of *pure polylingual persistence*. Pure polylingual persistence allows persistent objects to be composed from other objects that have been defined in different languages. That is, the transitive closure of an object defined in language A may contain objects defined not just in language A but also in languages B, C, etc. We call such an object a *heterolingual object*. Since it represents an extension to polylingual persistence, pure polylingual persistence retains and extends the property that the programming language(s) used to define and create persistent objects (and their components) is completely transparent to applications. Thus, an application written in language A should be able to access and update a persistent object and all the objects (including heterolingual objects) in its closure as if they were defined in language A. We believe that POSs supporting pure polylingual persistence maximize the potential utility of POS technology.

In this paper we describe our recent efforts toward developing a general framework for pure polylingual persistence that we call P^3. We also report on an initial prototype version of P^3 and some preliminary experimentation with its use. Our development, experimentation and evaluation were performed using the TI/Darpa Open Object-Oriented Database (Open OODB). Our initial P^3 prototype provides pure polylingual persistence between C++ and Java objects. Our preliminary experimentation illustrates the viability of our approach by applying it to a pure polylingual version of the 007 benchmark [3]. The results of this preliminary experimentation show that our approach incurs minimal overhead while providing enhanced functionality.

The remainder of this paper is organized as follows. In Section 2 we provide an overview of issues related to heterogeneous POSs and a review of related work. We then outline our P^3 framework for pure polylingual persistence in Section 3. We present experimental results in Section 4. We conclude with a summary and plans for future work in Section 5.

2   Heterogeneous Persistent Object Systems

In this section we provide a categorization of alternative levels of support for accessing and manipulating data in heterogeneous POSs. We then outline related work in this area.

2.1   Three Levels of Interoperability

To help illustrate some of the issues that arise in heterogeneous POSs and in supporting pure polylingual persistence, we consider an example representing (a highly simplified version of) the persistent data storage and manipulation that might be involved in chemical or pharmaceutical research. Figure 1 contains (portions of) C++ and Java class definitions for molecules and atoms that might exist for a chemical compound database. Although the two versions of the Molecule and the Atom classes, respectively, are remarkably similar, their existence makes possible several alternative levels of interoperability for applications needing to access chemical data in a heterogeneous C++/Java POS. To help illustrate these alternatives, as well as our approach, we use the class definitions in Figure 1 throughout the remainder of this paper.

Alternative One – Segregated Persistence. Figure 2(a) shows a heterogeneous POS that contains both persistent C++ and Java chemical data objects. In a *segregated* heterogeneous POS, C++ applications are restricted to accessing C++-defined Molecule and Atom objects, while Java applications may only access Java-defined Molecule and Atom objects. As a result, a C++ application needing to access Java-defined data is faced with the difficult and tedious task of translating the Java-defined data into appropriate C++-defined data.

Java Classes	C++ Classes
| ```
class Atom {
    public Atom (StringBuffer name,
                 double weight) {...}
    public double weightOf () {...};
    private StringBuffer name;
    private double weight;
    ...
}
``` | ```
class Atom {
    public: Atom (char *name,
                  double weight) {...};
            double weightOf () {...};
    private: char* name;
             double weight;
    ...
}
``` |
| ```
class Molecule {
    public Molecule (StringBuffer name)
                 {...}
    public void insert (int count,
                 Atom atom) {...}
    public double weightOf () {...}
    private StringBuffer name;
    private Atom[];
    ...
}
``` | ```
class Molecule {
    public: Molecule (char* name)
                 {...}
            void insert (int count,
                 Atom atom) {...}
            double weightOf () {...}
    private: char* name;
             Atom *atoms;
    ...
}
``` |

Fig. 1. Java and C++ Classes for Molecules and Atoms

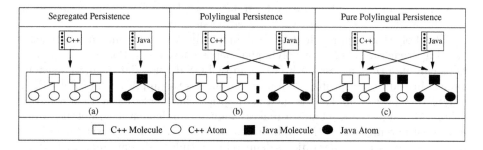

Fig. 2. Three Alternatives for Heterogeneous POSs

Alternative Two – Polylingual Persistence. Figure 2(b) shows a heterogeneous POS with polylingual persistence capabilities. This level of interoperability in heterogeneous POSs supports uniform access to compatible data that has been defined in different languages. Thus, a C++ application that processes Molecule data can access and update both C++- and Java-defined Molecule objects. However, in a polylingual POS, persistent objects are homogeneous structures. In other words, a Java application can access C++ Molecule and Atom objects as long as the entire chemical compound is implemented in C++. This also means that an existing C++ Molecule, for example, cannot be extended with a Java Atom.

Alternative Three - Pure Polylingual Persistence. A third alternative is shown in Figure 2(c), which shows a heterogeneous POS that supports *pure polylingual persistence*. Similarly to a polylingual POS, a pure polylingual POS allows applications to simultaneously access compatible data that has been defined in different languages. Moreover, a pure polylingual POS allows heterogeneous persistent structures, or heterolingual objects, to be formed. Thus, a C++ Molecule may be composed of both C++-defined and Java-defined Atom objects. From a C++ application's perspective, however, the object and the objects in its transitive closure, all appear to be implemented in C++. In addition, the C++ application could potentially create new Java Atom objects (although they will be viewed as C++ objects) and insert these new objects into a C++ Molecule. When the root C++ Molecule is made to persist, all the objects in its transitive closure will also persist, despite their being implemented in multiple languages.

2.2   Related Work

The Object Data Management Group has defined a standard for object-oriented databases [4]. The ODMG standard is based on an intermediary language called the Object Definition Language (or ODL), which is used to define database schemas. A schema can then be translated to a particular language according to the ODMG ODL language binding for that language. Although seemingly sensible, intermediary-based approaches introduce an impedance mismatch between the language used to define data and the language used to manipulate it. Moreover, despite defining a uniform data model, the ODMG approaches, at least in practice, are limited to segregated persistence.

The PolySPIN approach described in [7] describes a name management-based approach for achieving polylingual persistence. Using PolySPIN, applications can uniformly access both C++- and CLOS-defined data using persistent names. In addition, a prototype toolset automates the application of PolySPIN. PolySPIN, however, makes the tacit assumption that persistent data is homogeneous. Although the mechanism makes language implementation details of objects transparent, PolySPIN applications cannot create new persistent objects that are composed of other objects defined in multiple, different languages. Thus, PolySPIN can be classified as a polylingual persistence mechanism. It is worth noting, however, that the name management structure underlying PolySPIN is a pure polylingual structure since it is composed of heterolingual objects.

Another approach to polylingual persistence has been proposed in [8]. Their approach utilizes a canonical type system for persistent data, which then serves as a basis for allowing applications written in multiple languages to access persistent data that may also have been defined using multiple languages. Since the canonical type system is not object-oriented, their approach does not address, and would not directly extend to, pure polylingual persistence.

Various commercial object-oriented databases provide varying degrees of interoperability between languages. Versant, Objectivity and POET, for example, implement the ODMG standard, and provide language bindings for various languages (e.g., C++, Java and Smalltalk). Some of these vendors claim that applications can access heterolingual objects. However, it is not clear if either polylingual or pure polylingual persistence capabilities are provided in these databases. In addition, ongoing efforts are being directed toward using XML as an interoperability substrate. XML approaches do not require an intermediary, but they do require that all data be translated into XML. This not only incurs a performance penalty, but also results in redundant, and possibly, due to language type model mismatches, inaccurate data. In summary, ODMG object-oriented databases support limited aspects of polylingual and pure polylingual persistence. Unfortunately, these mechanisms are highly specialized and vendor specific.

3   A General Framework for Pure Polylingual Persistence

In this section, we describe P^3, a general framework for pure polylingual persistence. The organization of P^3 is designed to minimize its impact on existing heterogeneous POSs by making use of some common basic persistence abstractions and constructs. The result is a robust pure polylingual persistence mechanism that is independent of any particular heterogeneous POS.

There are two major components to P^3. One component involves the use of some specially defined classes, called proxies, and an underlying language interoperability substrate in order to support transparent polylingual access and update to persistent objects. This part of P^3 is largely based on our PolySPIN approach [7]. The other component employs a multi-language persistence algorithm that allows heterolingual objects to be created, as well as saved to, and retrieved from, a persistent store.

We begin with a brief overview of common POS abstractions that P^3 requires. We then describe the two components of P^3 in greater detail.

3.1   Common POS Abstractions

P^3 attempts to minimize the impact on an existing POS by relying on abstractions found in most modern POSs. First, the framework assumes that persistence is an orthogonal and transparent property of types. No special keywords, declarations or constructs are required to make objects persist and an object may be made to persist at any point during its lifetime. Second, a reachability-based model of persistence is assumed. When a root object is made to persist, all objects that are reachable from the root are also made to persist. Third, each programming language (or application programming interface) is responsible for managing persistent objects in its own language space. This means that for heterolingual objects, the persistence algorithm must dispatch persistence-related operations to the appropriate language. (This is explained in Section 3.3.) Fourth, each language must provide the following operations (or methods):

$PID \leftarrow object.persist()$ – When invoked, the *persist* operation marks the *object* (and implicitly the objects in its transitive closure) for persistence. The returned PID is a persistence identifier, which is assumed to be in a format that can easily be transferred between languages.

object ← *fetch*(*PID*) – Given a value for a *PID*, the *fetch* operation returns
   the associated persistent object. Note that an *object* is more precisely an L-
   value. Since L-values are language dependent and can be volatile, additional
   mappings are needed to support polylingual access. (This is explained in
   Section 3.2.)

commit() – The *commit* operation performs two tasks. Any object marked for
   persistence is actually saved to the persistent store, while any changes to
   existing persistent objects are made permanent.

These basic abstractions are not novel to the P^3 framework. However, their
presence in POSs facilitates pure polylingual persistence capabilities.

3.2   Proxy Classes and Interoperability Substrates

An important feature of P^3 is its support for heterolingual objects. As shown
in Figure 3(a), it should be possible to create a C++ Molecule, which refers
to both C++ and Java Atom objects. Allowing for such structures raises the
issue of *cross-language type compatibility*. Although we have claimed that the
Atom classes (as well as the Molecule classes) are compatible, in general such
determinations require a deeper understanding of type interoperability theory.
Since this research issue is beyond the scope of this paper, we assume cross-
language compatibility between types. (See [1] for a more detailed discussion.)

Assuming two types are cross-language compatible, a goal of the P^3 framework is to make their differences in language definition transparent to programs,
that is, to support polylingual access. For example, from the perspective of the
C++ Molecule, each Atom should be viewed and manipulated as a C++ Atom.
Moreover, if the C++ Molecule needs to manipulate its Atom constituents (e.g.,
to compute its total molecular weight), invoking methods on the individual objects should be dispatched to the appropriate language run-time space.

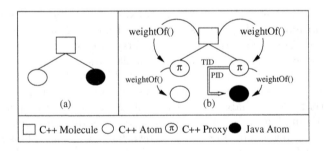

Fig. 3. A Polylingual C++ Molecule

The P^3 framework defines a special class called a *proxy* class. The proxy
class plays a similar role to the NameableObject and UOR classes employed in
PolySPIN[7]. Figure 4 shows the abstract interface for a proxy, which can be

realized using various techniques, such as inheritance or interface implementation. A proxy serves four important purposes. First, a proxy makes the implementation language of an object transparent to referring objects. For example, in Figure 3(b), a proxy is used to access both C++ and Java Atom objects. From the perspective of the C++ Molecule, both objects appear and behave as C++ Atoms. Second, a proxy encapsulates language-dependent and persistence-related information about implementation objects. Specifically, a proxy encodes the language, a transient identifier (TID), and a persistent identifier (PID) for an implementation object. The TID is a non-volatile reference or pointer to an implementation object, while a PID is a unique identifier generated by a language's persistence mechanism. Third, proxies enable the composition of heterolingual objects. By decoupling a proxy from its implementation object, other objects that are defined in the same language as the proxy can hold references (or pointers as the case may be) to a proxy object. The proxy object, in turn, holds language-independent references to the implementation object. In Figure 3(b), the C++ Molecule is actually composed of two C++ proxies (which in turn refer to their appropriate implementation objects). Finally, a proxy is responsible for dispatching operations to the implementation object. Thus, the proxy determines the implementation language of the object, and using the non-volatile reference and/or persistent identifier, locates the implementation object and invokes the actual operation. For example, in Figure 3(b), computing the molecular weight of a Molecule requires invoking the weightOf operation, which is defined by the Atom classes. If an object is implemented in C++, the proxy dispatches the method call to the C++ Atom object. However, if an object is implemented in Java, the proxy dispatches across language spaces to the Java Atom object.

```
class Proxy {
public:
    void setLanguage (LANG): // sets the implemention language
    LANG getLanguage (): // gets the implemention language
    void setPID (PID): // sets the PID for an object
    PID getPid (): // gets the TID for an object
    void setTID (TID): // sets the PID for an object
    TID getTid (): // gets the TID for an object
}
```

Fig. 4. Abstract Proxy Class

While a proxy hides the language of an implementation object, method invocations on a proxy must eventually be passed to the actual object. An interoperability substrate allows methods to be invoked across language spaces. Single address space-based substrates, such as the Java Native Interface [9], generally use C as an underlying conduit for communication, where modules for the interoperating languages are (logically) linked together into a single executable. In contrast, many distributed address space-based mechanisms use language-neutral type models called *interface description languages* [10,5]. These approaches are based on distributed client-server architectures, where clients and servers can be written in different languages. The P^3 framework is independent of any particular interoperability substrate. The selected substrate, however, must permit both TIDs and PIDs to be transmitted across language spaces. It must also, of course, allow for method invocations between languages.

3.3   A Multi-language Persistence Algorithm

The multi-language persistence algorithm in P^3 is a reachability-based model of persistence, which accounts for heterolingual objects, i.e., objects that are implemented in a language that is different than the controlling application. The P^3 persistence mechanism is designed as an extension to existing reachability-based persistence mechanisms. The extensions involve: creating a heterolingual object, committing a root of a heterolingual object to a persistent store, and retrieving a root of a heterolingual object from a persistent store. Each of the extensions is described in greater detail below.

Heterolingual Object Creation. As shown in Figure 3, an object in some application may refer, via a proxy, to a heterolingual object. There are two primary ways a heterolingual object can be created. First, an application may issue a request to retrieve a heterolingual object from the persistent store using a persistent name. This assumes, as in PolySPIN, that there is a uniform name management mechanism that permits access to heterolingual objects. To hide the fact that the object is heterolingual, the persistence mechanism in P^3:

1. Dispatches the request to the heterolingual object's language persistence mechanism;
2. Retrieves the object from the store in the heterolingual object's language address space;
3. Generates a proxy for the calling application, where the proxy includes the implementation object's language, PID and TID, as described in Section 3.2.

Second, an application might create a transient heterolingual object which may later become persistent. In the chemical compound POS, for instance, new Atom objects may need to be created using Java, rather than C++. This can be accomplished by directing the constructor for the C++ proxy to invoke the Java constructor. In this case, if an application creates an object that turns out to be heterolingual, P^3:

1. Creates a proxy in the application's language;
2. Instantiates the heterolingual object in the heterolingual objects' implementation language;
3. Marks the heterolingual object for persistence, by obtaining a PID for it;
4. Obtains a TID for the implementation object;
5. Generates a proxy for the calling application, where the proxy includes the implementation object's language, PID and TID, as described in Section 3.2.

One potential drawback of this component of the P^3 persistence mechanism is that it is overly aggressive, since it assumes that all heterolingual objects are persistent. Although not practical in all settings, this policy greatly simplifies the multi-language persistence mechanism. As we discuss in Section 5, we are currently investigating more sophisticated approaches.

Commit. Invoking a persist operation in a POS marks a root object for persistence. Objects are not actually saved to the store until a commit operation is called, which subsequently traverses the transitive closure for all marked objects, saves each object to the store and translates pointers to PIDs. The commit operation in P^3 works in a similar fashion, with the following extensions:

1. The commit operation in each language, other than the application's language, is invoked. Any objects that have been marked for persistence are saved to the store. In addition, any objects that were already persistent, but were updated as a result of invoking an operation (via a proxy), are also saved to the store.
2. The commit operation of the application's language is invoked. All objects defined in the language of the application that have been marked for persistence are made to persist. This includes proxy objects, which contain the PIDs of their implementation objects.

Note that it is also possible for a heterolingual object to contain references to proxies to objects defined in other languages. Since such objects have already been marked for persistence (as described in the discussion on heterolingual object creation), their proxies must contain valid PIDs. Therefore, a commit operation will ensure that their implementation objects are saved to the store.

Retrieve. An application retrieves an object from the persistent store when it either uses a (persistent) name for an object or follows a reference to a persistent object. The retrieve operation is extended as follows:

1. After an object is retrieved, determine if the object is heterolingual. This is determined by comparing the referring object's language to the retrieved object's language. If it is not heterolingual, then no additional processing is required;
2. If the object is heterolingual, then the retrieved object is actually a proxy for its implementation object. The proxy object contains a valid PID for the implementation object. Using this PID, the retrieve operation is invoked in the implementation object's language;
3. After retrieving the implementation object (in its language's run-time address space), the TID for the object is returned and recorded in its corresponding proxy.

We observe that the current retrieve algorithm is based on a relatively simple "an object at a time policy." Although we have not investigated the merits of other policies, it should be possible to accommodate more sophisticated prefetching methods into P^3.

4   Evaluation

In this section, we report on several preliminary performance experiments involving the P^3 approach. The primary objective of these experiments is to determine the overhead of checking a persistent object's implementation language and dispatching method invocations across persistent language address spaces. The cost of additional processing in the pure polylingual POS is compared to access costs in a homogeneous, segregated POS.

Our experimental testbed is the TI/DARPA Open Object-Oriented Database [11], using its Sun 4.2 C++ application programming interface. We also used our persistent Java extension to the Open OODB (called jSPIN) [6]. Both the C++ and Java APIs were extended with a realization of the P^3 framework. This involved defining appropriate proxy classes, augmenting classes with cross-language dispatching logic and extending the create, persist and retrieve operations as defined by the P^3 framework.

Our experiments involved constructing databases using the 007 benchmark [3]. This benchmark provides a variety of objects for modeling a "complex design," where composite parts are composed of atomic parts and other documents, and complex assemblies are composed of base assemblies. Each part or document has a set of attributes and may contain links to other objects. The construction of examples in this benchmark results in a large number of objects and is meant to represent a real world example of object relationships in an object-oriented database.

To gain an understanding of the performance overhead associated with our pure polylingual instantiation of the 007 benchmark, we first created six different databases:

100% C++: A homogeneous C++ implementation of 007 using the default Open OODB C++ API.

100% Java: A homogeneous Java implementation of 007 using the jSpin Open OODB Java API.

C++ Application/100% C++ Objects/P^3: A P^3 implementation of 007. The application is written in C++ and all of the objects in the 007 transitive closure are implemented in C++.

Java Application/100% C++ Objects/P^3: A P^3 implementation of 007. The application is written in Java and all of the objects in the 007 transitive closure are implemented in C++.

C++ Application/100% Java Objects/P^3: A P^3 implementation of 007. The application is written in C++ and all of the objects in the 007 transitive closure are implemented in Java.

Java Application/100% Java Objects/P^3: A P^3 implementation of 007. The application is written in Java and all of the objects in the 007 transitive closure are implemented in Java.

C++ Application/50% C++–50% Java Object/P^3: A P^3 implementation of 007. The application is written in C++. The 007 hierarchy is composed of 50% C++ and 50% Java objects, randomly dispersed throughout the hierarchy.

Java Application/50% C++-50% Java Object/P^3: A P^3 implementation of 007. The application is written in Java. The 007 hierarchy is composed of 50% Java and 50% C++ objects, randomly dispersed throughout the hierarchy.

Next, we applied eight different traversals on each database. Several of these traversals are based on the 007 benchmark traversals. However, since we were more interested in the performance of the P^3 approach relative to homogeneous POSs, we found it unnecessary to implement all of the 007 benchmark traversals. For example, since the Open OODB does not support indexing, traversals requiring indexes were not implemented. The following traversals were implemented:

Traversal 1: Traverses the 007 object hierarchy using depth-first search (DFS), visiting each AtomicPart. This traversal returns the number of AtomicPart objects visited.

Traversal 2: Visit each AtomicPart using a DFS and swap each of its x and y attributes.

Traversal 3: Randomly select a BaseAssembly object and visit each of its CompositeParts updating one AtomicPart per CompositePart.

Traversal 4: Randomly selects a BaseAssembly object and visits each of its AtomicParts, swapping their x and y attributes.

Traversal 5: Visits each AtomicPart using a DFS and updates its date attribute.

Traversal 6: Randomly selects a BaseAssembly object and visits each of its AtomicParts, updating the date attribute.

Each experiment was conducted on a SPARC Ultra 10 with 128Mb of memory running Solaris 2.6. Although these experiments were conducted when the machine was lightly loaded, we could not isolate the machine from the local network. Thus, we conducted each experiment ten times to ameliorate outlying results. The results reported in this paper are the average real times, in seconds, for each of the traversals. We report real times since the database's storage manager (Exodus [2]) runs as a separate server process (on the same machine).

Our results are given in Table 1. Each row indicates one of the databases. Each column represents the times for each traversal, labeled T1, T2, etc.

These preliminary results indicate that the P^3 approach does not incur a prohibitive cost. There is still a cost overhead with using P^3, as would be expected since the language implementation of each object must be checked before dispatching method calls. We consider this a reasonable penalty to pay for the added functionality of pure polylingual persistence.

Of course, other overhead is due to the underlying interoperability mechanism. For example, the Java application that accesses C++ objects typically runs faster than the corresponding C++ application that accesses Java objects. In fact, we have already isolated some areas that can be optimized to improve The overall performance of P^3. For example, the current code that allows a C++ proxy to invoke a Java implementation object is somewhat naive, and may account for the excessive overhead. Specifically, each time a Java method is invoked

Table 1. Performance Results

Database	T1	T2	T3	T4	T5	T6
100% C++	1.46	1.60	2.38	2.65	1.60	2.60
100% Java	9.10	7.72	8.20	8.32	7.78	8.35
C++ App/100% C++/P^3	2.92	2.30	6.47	6.42	2.28	6.42
Java App/100% C++/P^3	2.35	2.09	5.18	5.21	2.06	5.21
C++ App/100% Java/P^3	11.62	9.37	11.55	11.62	9.34	11.55
Java App/100% Java/P^3	9.58	8.68	9.75	10.06	8.71	9.93
C++ App/50%C++–50% Java/P^3	7.05	5.33	9.10	9.97	5.18	6.40
Java App/50%C++–50% Java/P^3	7.03	6.34	6.73	7.03	6.27	7.08

from C++, we perform a class and method search in the Java language space. This is a costly operation, which will be avoided in future implementations by caching the results of these lookups. We anticipate better performance results from this improvement alone.

These experiments report some preliminary results using the P^3 methodology. We find the results encouraging, and more thorough experimentation and analysis will involve implementation of additional traversals and databases.

5 Conclusion

In this paper, we have described a new approach to interoperability in POSs called pure polylingual persistence, or P^3. P^3 establishes of a new computational artifact that illustrates the viability and potential of polylingual persistent environments. The approach builds on our previous PolySPIN work [7]. We have described the P^3 framework, which allows for the transparent creation, storage and retrieval of heterolingual objects. We have discussed a realization of P^3 in the TI/Darpa Open OODB, supporting pure polylingual persistence for C++ and Java objects. Our preliminary experimental data, which is based on the 007 benchmark classes and traversals, indicates that the P^3 approach incurs minimal overhead, while providing pure polylingual capabilities.

The work reported in this paper represents an important extension to POS technology and its support of interoperability in heterogeneous POSs. There are, however, several research directions we intend to continue to pursue. Clearly, cross language type compatibility is a critical area of research. As noted earlier, determining the compatibility between two classes in different language is an area we plan to explore. Another related issue concerns subclassing accross language type systems. Our current framework does not, for example, allow a Java (sub)class to be derived from a C++ (super)class. We intend to explore extensions to our framework that would support this. While the traversal experiments are very positive so far, we intend to develop and analyze additional traversal experiments. This will allow us to further confirm the viability of our approach. It should also help suggest various optimizations. We also plan to experiment with other interoperability substrates, such as CORBA. To validate the generality of P^3, we also plan to instantiate the framework in other heterogeneous POSs and compare its performance to related polylingual persistence mechanisms.

References

[1] Barrett, D. J., Kaplan, A., and Wileden, J. C. Automated support for seamless interoperability in polylingual software systems. In *The Fourth Symposium on the Foundations of Software Engineering*, San Francisco, CA, Oct. 1996.

[2] Carey, M. J., DeWitt, D. J., and Vandenberg, S. L. A data model and query language for EXODUS. *SIGMOD Record (ACM Special Interest Group on Management of Data)*, 17(3):413–423, Sept. 1988.

[3] Carey, M. J., J.DeWitt, D., and Naughton, J. F. The OO7 benchmark. In *Proceedings of the ACM SIGMOD Conference*, pages 12–21, Washington, D.C., May 1993.

[4] Cattell, R. G. G., Barry, D. K., Berler, M., Jeff Eastman, D. J., Russell, C., Schadow, O., Stanienda, T., and Velez, F., editors. *The Object Data Standard: ODMG 3.0*. Morgan Kaufmann, Jan. 2000.

[5] Janssen, B. and Spreitzer, M. ILU: Inter-language unification via object modules. In *Workshop on Multi-Language Object Models*, Portland, OR, Aug. 1994. (in conjunction with OOPSLA'94).

[6] Kaplan, A., Myrestrand, G., Ridgway, J. V., , and Wileden, J. C. Our spin on persistent Java: The JavaSPIN approach. In *First International Workshop on Persistence and Java*, Drymen, Scotland, Sept. 1996.

[7] Kaplan, A. and Wileden, J. C. Toward painless polylingual persistence. In Connor, R. and Nettles, S., editors, *Proceedings Seventh International Workshop on Persistent Object Systems*, pages 11–22, Cape May, NJ, May 1996.

[8] Kato, K. and Ohori, A. An approach to multilanguage persistent type system. In *25th Hawaii International Conference on System Sciences*, Jan. 1992.

[9] Liang, S. *The Java[tm] Native Interface: Programmer's Guide and Specification*. Addison Wesley, Jan. 1999.

[10] Object Management Group. *The Common Object Request Broker: Architecture and Specification*, Aug. 1997. Revision 2.1.

[11] Wells, D. L., Blakely, J. A., and Thompson, C. W. Architecture of an open object-oriented database management system. *IEEE Computer*, 25(10):74–82, Oct. 1992.

Session 3: Overview

Richard Jones

Computing Laboratory, University of Kent at Canterbury, UK
R.E.Jones@ukc.ac.uk

This session contained four papers, three of which focussed on the implementation of persistent object stores and one, the first of the session, on caching in distributed, transactional, persistent systems.

In this paper, Magnus Bjornsson and Liuba Shrira [LS] describe SiteCache, a cache coherence architecture for persistent object systems designed to reduce transaction latency. Despite improvements in network bandwidth, distributed systems suffer the high latencies of wide area networks, such as the Internet. Although co-operative web caching is common solution for HTTP systems, the challenge for SiteCache is to support transactional objects.

In a similar fashion, SiteCache places a proxy agent between a group of clients and the servers. Unlike web-caches, a proxy agent does not store pages but redirects fetch requests to the caches of other clients in its group. Fetch misses and commits are forwarded to servers and replies are propagated back to clients. Bjornsson and Shrira assume that the network connections between clients and proxy agent are fast, with low latency, in comparison with the connection between proxy and servers. They also assume that clients have large caches and that there is substantial sharing of objects between clients: a plausible scenario might be a conference of co-workers connected by a LAN but accessing data from a persistent object repository at their remote home site. In such a scenario, not only does SiteCache reduce the latency of fetches but also avoids repeating outstanding fetches, and can abort commits early where it is known that they would fail.

There was some discussion of SiteCache's context. Alexander Wolf [AW] believed that there were WAN issues of distance and latency, but that the WWW introduced factors such as size, number of users, number of servers, and so on that SiteCache could not address. Alan Dearle [AD] disagreed, highlighting needs of companies like Reuters, the existence of smart clients retrieving data from caches across the net and the need for transactional systems for applications such as on-line trading.

In the second paper, Zhen He, Stephen Blackburn [SB], Luke Kirby and John Zigman [JZ] describe Platypus, a flexible, high performance object store. Platypus attempts to bridge the gap between the strong transactional semantics and good transaction throughput of mainstream data management systems and the demands made of orthogonally persistent systems by tightly coupled language clients. Abstraction is at the heart of the Platypus design, and provides a flexible framework for prototyping and analysing components of its design. By dividing responsibility for the visibility of transactions between a local and a global visibility manager, Platypus manages transactional visibility between distributed nodes without compromising on efficiency when distribution is not required. High- and low-level stability managers allow low-level changes (such as object location) to be isolated from high-level object

G.N.C. Kirby, A. Dearle, and D.I.K. Sjøberg (Eds.): POS-9, LNCS 2135, pp. 84-86, 2001.
© Springer-Verlag Berlin Heidelberg 2001

store behaviour and also help reduce concurrency conflicts. Availability managers manage store pages, log pages and shared meta-data.

The paper offers three particular innovations. Performance is enhanced by allowing the store client direct access to the mapped memory rather than requiring objects to be copied from store to run-time (and back again). Platypus uses write-ahead logging (in order to minimise I/O) but avoids the cost of log sequence numbers by using rolling checksums to identify pages; a further benefit of write-ahead logging is its support for store clients' direct access to memory described above. Thirdly, the authors describe a new hash-splay data structure, a hash table that implements buckets with splay trees rather than the usual buckets. By matching hash table size with working set size, hash-splays yield near optimal access to items.

In comparison with the SHORE object system, Platypus demonstrated substantial performance gains. In discussion, the authors considered that the main factor in Platypus' performance edge was the use of memory mapping to reduce copying; Platypus' object faulting mechanism. Careful design of data structures with a view to concurrency was also important—for example, splay-trees were used throughout Platypus.

The last two papers in this session focussed on garbage collection for persistent object stores. Persistence by reachability, and hence garbage collection, is fundamental to orthogonal persistence. The collection of large object stores requires algorithms to be scalable: a common solution is to partition the store and process partitions separately. However, although it is straightforward to identify garbage local to a particular partition, identification of garbage cycles that cross partitions is a less tractable problem. One family of solutions, Mature Object Space (MOS) collectors, partitions the address space into 'cars' that are grouped into 'trains'. Train collectors achieve scalability by collecting one car at a time, and completeness (reclamation of all garbage) by moving cycles into a single train: this train can be reclaimed entirely once there are no remaining references to objects in that train from outside the train.

David Munro [DM] and Alfred Brown report on their experiments with partition selection policy[1] using the PMOS collector. In part, they aimed to repeat the work done by Cook, Wolf and Zorn for object databases, but they also introduced two further selection policies specific to the PMOS algorithm. Not only do Munro's and Brown's results differ markedly from the earlier study, but they also show that the train collector collected relatively little garbage under any partition policy.

Considerable discussion of these results followed. Munro agreed with Wolf's suggestion that one cause for the difference between the two studies was that the applications had generated garbage in different ways. The Chair [RJ] suggested that at least one of the synthetic benchmarks appeared to encourage the creation of cross-car cycles: the worst case for train collectors, which benefit from clustering. Blackburn observed that the benchmarks were comparatively short-lived and may not have given the train collector sufficient time to round up garbage cycles into a single train: a prerequisite for their collection. There was some consensus that programs do not behave randomly: real applications running real work-loads are needed before we can get reliable results.

In the last paper in this session, John Zigman, Stephen Blackburn and Eliot Moss [EM] introduced TMOS, a design for a transactional garbage collector. Transactional storage systems present a particular problem for garbage collection. As Zigman *et al*

---

[1] Which car to collect next.

observe, transactions break the common garbage collection assumption that being garbage is a stable property: transaction aborts may undo changes to the object graph[2]. A naïve solution would be to encapsulate the identification of garbage into a single transaction accepting the performance penalty that this would incur. The goal of the TMOS design is a collector that is both safe and efficient.

Zigman *et al* start from the premise that cost factors differ substantially for heap and disk collection. In the first part of their paper, they describe an abstract approach to the design of transactional collectors. Their abstract system comprises three independent components: a mutator, a store that supports transactional semantics, and a collection algorithm. Their approach to garbage collection separates identification of garbage from its subsequent reclamation. In partitioned systems, both of these activities have a local (intra-partition) and a global (cross-partition) component[3]. The paper concludes with a description of how this abstraction is mapped onto an efficient MOS collector through a mechanism that provides the collector with a coherent snapshot of the car to be collected, through indirection between mutator and store level addressing, and by allowing the movement of objects by the collector to be deferred.

---

[2] Distributed garbage collection systems face an analogous scenario: locally unreachable data may be made locally reachable again by the action of a remote mutator (and only by the action of a remote mutator).

[3] Again, this distinction of identification and reclamation, local and global is also key to distributed garbage collection techniques.

Transactional Remote Group Caching in Distributed Object Systems

Magnus E. Bjornsson and Liuba Shrira

Department of Computer Science, Brandeis University,
415 South Street, Waltham MA 02454-9110
{magnus, liuba}@cs.brandeis.edu

Abstract. Peer group computing is an increasingly popular class of distributed applications enabled by universal access to global networks. The applications allow collaborating peers to share cached data, but up to now only read-only applications were supported. This paper describes BuddyCache, a caching architecture for peer group applications updating shared data. Earlier group caching approaches only worked in local area networks or did not support fine-grain coherence and transactions. BuddyCache coherence protocol is the first transactional fine-grain group coherence protocol for object repositories in high-latency networks. The main challenge in BuddyCache is how to provide low-latency access to consistent shared objects cached by peers when consistency management requires high-latency coordination with remote servers accessed over wide-area networks.

1 Introduction

Peer group computing is an increasingly popular class of distributed applications enabled by universal access to global networks. The applications allow collaborating clients to share cached data, but up to now only read-only applications were supported. This paper describes BuddyCache, a cache coherence architecture that deals with the network latency problem in peer group applications updating shared data in transactional object repositories. The main challenge is how to provide consistent low-latency access to shared objects cached by peers when consistency management requires high-latency coordination with remote servers.

Modern repositories provide clients located on a global network with access to distributed data. To improve access latency, clients fetch objects from repository servers and cache and access them locally. Coherence protocols insure that client caches remain consistent when objects are modified.

Consider a group of co-worker clients in a hotel conference room accessing data in a transactional object repository at a remote home site. In a traditional repository architecture, when an object access misses in one member cache, the missing object is fetched from the remote server even when the object is available in the cache of a nearby group member. BuddyCache allows to directly

G.N.C. Kirby, A. Dearle, and D.I.K. Sjøberg (Eds.): POS-9, LNCS 2135, pp. 87–99, 2001.

fetch consistent objects from group members caches avoiding the high-latency round trip to the server.

To insure that client caches remain consistent, a coherence protocol keeps track of pages cached by clients to identify where to send update information when objects are modified. Since pages can be fetched into BuddyCache client cache without server intervention, the coherence protocol is hierarchical; a group directory tracks page coherence for individual group members, server directory propagates updates and collect acknowledgements for groups, treating pages cached in a group as a single cache. This creates a problem if some clients in a group run on slower machines, since a co-worker, slow in acknowledging updates, delays a group acknowledgement, which can delay a subsequent commit by a fast group member.

BuddyCache uses a new fine-grained hierarchical coherence protocol that allows fast clients with up-to-date objects to commit independently of slower group members. To support fine-grain coherence the protocol manages a small recently modified object cache at the client combined with page-level directories avoiding large object-level directories.

When one of the co-workers in the group creates or modifies data shared with other group members, the new data is often likely to be of potential interest to all group members. BuddyCache provides group members with fast consistent access to the new data committed within the group without imposing extra overhead on other parts of the global caching system. This is achieved by combining efficient propagation of updates committed by BuddyCache members to other group member caches, with a light-weight lazy invalidation-based coherence protocol for clients outside the group.

BuddyCache coherence protocol is the first fine-grain group coherence protocol for distributed transactional object repositories in high-latency networks. Earlier group caching approaches only worked in fast local area networks [1,9] or did not support fine-grain coherence [4,3] and transactions.

BuddyCache architecture has been incorporated into Thor distributed object storage system [2]. Thor is a client/server system based on optimistic concurrency control in which servers provide persistent storage for objects and applications run at client machines using cached copies of persistent objects. BuddyCache protocols assume an optimistic concurrency control scheme but are otherwise independent of Thor architecture.

We are currently working on the implementation of the BuddyCache. The paper presents the BuddyCache protocol in the fault-free operation, and the BuddyCache failover protocol that deals with client crashes and network failures.

The rest of the paper is organized as follows. Section 2 discusses related work, Section 3 describes the basic Thor architecture that provides the framework for our work. Section 4 describes BuddyCache protocols, Section 5 describes BuddyCache failover, Section 6 discusses BuddyCache performance, and section 7 presents the conclusion.

2   Related Work

Our work builds on earlier work in scalable wide-area coherence protocols, transactional caching and techniques for fine-grained sharing.

Yin, Alvisi, Dahlin and Lin [4,3] present a hierarchical WAN cache coherence scheme. The protocol uses leases to provide fault-tolerant call-backs and takes advantage of nearby caches to reduce the cost of lease extensions. The study addresses latency and fault tolerance issues similar to ones we address in BuddyCache in the context of a pessimistic concurrency control scheme but does not consider issues of consistent access to objects in group caches.

Chase, Gadde and Rabinovich's approach in [7] is similar to BuddyCache in limiting fetches to "close by" caches to improve fetch latency. Their protocol maintains a directory of objects cached in selected close by proxies, and runs a distributed directory updates protocol for tracking cache changes. The study does not consider issues of fine-grain coherence or transactional updates.

Anderson, Eastham and Vahdat in WebFS [14] present a global file system coherence protocol that allows clients to choose on per file basis between receiving updates or invalidations. Updates and invalidations are multicasted on separate channels and clients subscribe to one of the channels. The protocol is limited to file systems exploiting application specific methods to deal with concurrent updates, e.g. last-writer-wins policy for broadcast applications. This approach works when entire file is overwritten but does not support fine-grain modifications and multiple operation transactions.

Concurrent with our work, Cheriton and Li proposed MMO [8] a hybrid web coherence protocol that combines invalidations with updates using multicast delivery channels and receiver-reliable protocol, exploiting locality in a way similar to BuddyCache. Their multicast transport level solution is geared to the single writer semantics of web objects. In contrast, BuddyCache uses "application level" multicast and a sender-reliable coherence protocol to provide similar access latency improvements for transactional objects.

Our earlier work on the cooperative cache coherence scheme called *fragment reconstruction* [1] deals with high disk latency in an environment where servers and clients run on a fast local area network. BuddyCache extends the earlier work in several important ways. It addresses new object coherence issues facing transactional peer caching in high-latency networks: avoiding commit delays caused by slow peers, and accelerating peer group access to shared objects modified by a peer, and it introduces new efficient implementation techniques: version number cache at the client, and modified object cache in the redirector.

3   Base System

To allow a concrete description of BuddyCache protocols, we introduce the base storage system. We choose to incorporate BuddyCache into Thor client/server object-oriented database [2] because Thor already supports high performance access to distributed objects [11] and therefore provides a challenging test platform to investigate BuddyCache performance. This section describes the base

Thor cache architecture before we have extended it to incorporate BuddyCache protocols.

Thor servers provide persistent storage for objects and clients cache copies of these objects. Applications run at the clients and interact with the system by making calls on methods of cached objects. All method calls occur within atomic transactions. Clients communicate with servers to fetch pages or to commit a transaction.

The servers have a disk for storing persistent objects, a stable transaction log, and volatile memory. The disk is organized as a collection of pages which are the units of disk access. The stable log holds commit information and object modifications for committed transactions. The server memory contains cache directory and a recoverable modified object cache called *mcache*. The directory keeps track of which pages are cached by which clients. The mcache holds recently modified objects that have not yet been written back to their pages on disk. As mcache fills up, a background process propagates modified objects to the disk [10, 13].

3.1   Transactional Cache Coherence

Transactions are serialized using optimistic concurrency control [2]. The client keeps track of objects that are read and modified by its transaction; it sends this information, along with new copies of modified objects, to the servers when it tries to commit the transaction. The servers determine whether the commit is possible, using a two-phase commit protocol if the transaction used objects at multiple servers. If the transaction commits, the new copies of modified objects are appended to the log and also inserted in the mcache. The mcache is recoverable, i.e. if the server crashes, the mcache is reconstructed at recovery by scanning the log.

Since objects are not locked before being used, a transaction commit can cause caches to contain obsolete objects. Servers will abort a transaction that used obsolete objects. However, to reduce the probability of aborts, servers notify clients when their objects become obsolete by sending them *invalidation messages*; a server uses its directory and the information about the committing transaction to determine what invalidation messages to send. Invalidation messages are small because they simply identify obsolete objects. Furthermore, they are sent in the background, batched and piggybacked on other messages.

When a client receives an invalidation message, it removes obsolete objects from its cache and aborts the current transaction if it used them. The client continues to retain pages containing invalidated objects; these pages are now *incomplete* with "holes" in place of the invalidated objects. Performing invalidation on an object basis means that false sharing does not cause unnecessary aborts; keeping incomplete pages in the client cache means that false sharing does not lead to unnecessary cache misses. Invalidation messages prevent some aborts, and accelerate those that must happen — thus wasting less work and offloading detection of aborts from servers to clients.

Clients acknowledge invalidations. The transaction validation protocol relies on these acknowledgements to insure that transaction has not read stale data. Like invalidations, acknowledgements are sent in the background, batched and piggybacked on other messages.

When a transaction aborts, its client restores the cached copies of modified objects to the state they had before the transaction started; this is possible because a client makes a copy of an object the first time it is modified by a transaction.

4   The BuddyCache

High network latency imposes significant performance penalties for applications accessing transactional data over wide-area networks. The problem is likely to persist in foreseeable future in spite the advances in network technology. In this section we describe BuddyCache architecture for reducing the high network latency penalty in peer group applications accessing shared objects in transactional repositories. The challenge in BuddyCache is how to provide consistent low-latency access to shared objects cached by peers when consistency management requires high-latency coordination with remote servers.

We consider the following environment to be common for BuddyCache systems. A distributed transactional repository stores company data in highly reliable servers outsourced in data-centers located on a global network. Collaborating peers at a remote site connect via high-latency, possibly satellite, links to the servers at the data-centers to access shared company data. The peer group site has excellent low-latency high-bandwidth peer-to-peer connectivity such as short-range wireless or fast Ethernet. In addition, ample CPU cycles may be available within the site infrastructure for the temporary use by the visiting peer group. The performance problem facing the collaborating peer group is the high network latency of accessing the shared data at the remote home sites.

BuddyCache addresses the network latency problem by introducing new cache coherence techniques for fetches, transaction commits, and cache updates. *Peer fetch* allows to fetch objects cached in the peer group, *hybrid coherence* accelerates the access to modified objects of interest to the peer group without imposing overhead on the other parts of the caching system, and *solo commit* reduces the transaction commit latency for fast clients with slow peers.

BuddyCache uses a simple *redirector* component to support the peer fetch. The redirector runs on the same local network as the peer group, in one of the peer nodes, or in a special node within the infrastructure. It maintains a directory of pages available in the peer group and provides fast centralized fetch redirection between the peer caches. To improve performance, clients inform the redirector when they evict pages or objects by piggybacking that information on messages sent to the redirector.

To insure up-to-date objects are fetched from the group cache the redirector tracks the status of the pages. The protocol for maintaining page status when pages are updated and invalidated is described in Section 4.1.

When a client request has to be processed at the servers, e.g., a complete requested page is unavailable in the peer group or a peer needs to commit a transaction, the redirector acts as a server proxy: it forwards the request to the server, and then forwards the reply back to the client. Redirector also distributes page update information sent by a server, to clients caching the modified page and, after all clients acknowledge the update, propagates the group acknowledgement back to the server. (see figure 1). The redirector-server protocol is, in effect, the client-server protocol used in the base Thor system, where the combined peer group cache is playing the role of a single client cache in the base system.

The BuddyCache architecture supports multiple concurrent peer groups. Potentially, it may be faster to access data cached in another peer group then to access a remote server. In such case extending BuddyCache protocols to support multi-level peer caching could be worthwhile. We have not pursued this possibility for several reasons.

Unlike in web caching workloads, where just increasing the population of clients in a proxy cache often increases the overal cache hit rate, we expect the sharing patters in BuddyCache applications to result mainly from explicit client interaction and collaboration, limiting the benefits of inter-group fetching. Moreover, measurements from multi-level web caching systems such as Harvest indicate that a multi-level system may not be advantageous unless the network connection between the peer groups is very fast. Since we are primarily interested in environments where closely collaborating peers have fast close range connectivity but the connection between peer groups can span wide-area network, we decided not to support inter-group fetching in BuddyCache at this time.

To support heterogenous resource-rich and resource-poor peers, the BuddyCache redirector can be configured to run either in one of the peer nodes or, when available, in a separate node within the site infrastructure. Moreover, in a resource-rich infrastructure node, the redirector can be configured as a stand-by peer cache to receive pages fetched by other peers, emulating a central cache somewhat similar to a regional web proxy cache. From the BuddyCache cache coherence protocol point of view, however, such a stand-by peer cache is equivalent to a regular peer cache and therefore we do not consider this case separately in the discussion in this paper.

4.1   Invalidations and Updates

Our experience in Thor system, and work by other researchers [6] show that invalidation-based coherence protocols are efficient since invalidations are small, batched and piggybacked on other messages. Moreover, they match well the current hardware trend for increasing cache size, making it more likely that client caches contain much more data then is actively used. Propagating updates to low interest objects in a wide-area network would be wasteful.

Nevertheless, in high-latency networks invalidation-based coherence can cause high delays when invalidated objects are accessed [8]. When one of the co-workers in a collaborating client group creates or modifies objects shared among

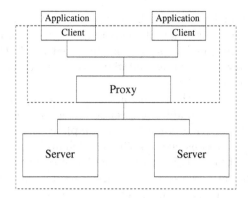

Fig. 1. Thor setup with BuddyCache

group members, this new data is often likely to be of interest to another group member. With invalidation-based protocol, after one member updates an object, the next member access to this object will cause a high latency fetch of the new value from the server.

To avoid this latency in peer groups with shared objects, BuddyCache redirector retains and propagates updates committed by a client to other clients within the BuddyCache group. Invalidations are used to maintain the coherence of client caches outside the committing BuddyCache. This "application-level multicast" of shared object updates provides BuddyCache group members with fast transactional access to the modified and new shared data created within the group without imposing extra overhead on other parts of the global caching system.

The scheme works as follows. When a transaction commit request arrives at the redirector, it retains the updates until a commit reply. When a transaction commits, using a two phase commit if needed, the coordinator server sends a commit reply to the redirector of the committing client group. The redirector forwards the reply to the committing client, and also propagates the retained committed updates to clients caching the modified pages and collects client acknowledgements.

When a transaction accesses objects in multiple servers, a participant server that is not a coordinator and is a home to a modified object, generates corresponding invalidations for each cache group that caches the modified object (including the committing group). The invalidations are sent lazily to the redirectors to insure that all the clients in the groups caching the modified objects get rid of the stale data.

In a cache group other then the committing group, the redirector propagates the invalidations to all the clients caching the modified pages, collects the client acknowledgements and after completing the collection, propagates an acknowledgement back to the server. Therefore, a redirector acknowledgement indicates to the participant server that no stale objects are present at the client group.

Within the committing client cache group, the arriving invalidations are not propagated since the propagation of the committed updates replaces the propagation of invalidations for the transactions initiated within the group. Instead, the redirector acknowledges the invalidations using the corresponding collected update acknowledgements.

An invalidation changes the status of a *complete* page p into an *incomplete* rendering the page p unavailable for peer fetching. In the committing group, an update of a *complete* page preserves the complete page status. As shown by studies of the fragment reconstruction scheme, such update propagation allows to avoid the penalties of false sharing. I.e., when clients in the same group modify different objects on the same complete page, such a page retains its *complete* status and remains available for fetching.

4.2   Solo Commit

The cache coherence protocol manages at the server a directory of pages cached by clients to identify where to send update information when objects are modified. Since pages can be fetched into BuddyCache client cache without server intervention, the protocol is hierarchical; the redirector maintains page coherence for individual group members, the server treats pages cached in the entire group as a single cache, propagates updates and collects acknowledgements for entire groups. The hierarchical acknowledgement collection creates a potential performance problem if some clients in a group run on slower machines because a slow client can delay a group acknowledgement potentially delaying subsequent commit by a fast group member.

The *solo* commit protocol allows fast clients with up-to-date objects to commit independently of slower group members. The protocol supports fine-grain coherence without resorting to object-level directories. Consider a situation where a client in a peer group P issues a commit request for a transaction T that reads the latest version of a recently modified object x. If the commit request reaches the server before the collective acknowledgement from group P for the last modification of x arrives at the server, the base fine-grain validation protocol [2] considers x to be stale in the group cache P and aborts T. To avoid the abort when clients read valid objects, the solo commit protocol allows T to pass validation if additional coherence information supplied by the client with the transaction's read object set indicates that transaction T has read up-to-date objects.

The additional coherence information exploits page version numbers. A server increments a page version number each time a transaction commits modifications to the page. Since a unique page version number corresponds to each committed object update, the version numbers can be used by the validation procedure in the solo commit protocol to check if the transaction has read up-to-date objects. I.e. client includes the page version number corresponding to the current object value in the transaction read object set sent in the commit request to the server. If an unacknowledged invalidation is pending for an object x read by a transaction T, the validation procedure checks if the version number for x in T's read set matches the version number for highest pending invalidation for x, in which case the object value is current, otherwise T fails validation.

Note, that the page version number based checks, and the invalidation acknowledgement based checks are complimentary in the validation procedure and both required. I.e. page version check in itself is not sufficient to support fine-grain coherence without the invalidation acknowledgements and the later is insufficient to distinguish between stale object values cached in different client caches within the group.

A client stores a version number for each page it caches. The protocol insures that if a cached page P has a version number v, then the value of an object o on a cached page P is either invalid or reflects at least the modifications committed by transactions preceding the transaction that set P's version number to v.

New object values and page version numbers arrive when a client fetches a page or when a commit reply or invalidations arrive for this page. The invalidations or updates and their corresponding page version numbers can arrive at the client out of sequence. E.g. a commit reply for a transaction that updates object x on page P in server $S1$, and object y on page Q in server $S2$, can deliver a new version number for P from the transaction coordinator $S2$ before an invalidation generated for an earlier transaction that has modified object y on page P arrives from $S1$. The protocol insures that the value of an object o on a cached page P reflects the update or invalidation with the highest observed version number. I.e. obsolete updates or invalidations received out of sequence do not affect the value of an object.

To maintain the correct mapping from the current object value to its corresponding page version number, the client manages a small version number cache $vcache$ that holds the mapping from an object into its corresponding page version number for all re-ordered version number updates until a complete page version number sequence is assembled.

The vcache is used at transaction commit time to provide version numbers for the read object set. If the read object has an entry in the vcache, its version number is equal to the highest version number in the vcache for this object. If the object is not present in the vcache, its version number is equal the version number of its containing cached page.

An in-sequence page version number arriving at the client in a commit or invalidation message advances the version number for the entire cached page, but an out-of-sequence version number does not. When the missing version numbers for the page arrive and complete a sequence, the version number for the entire page is advanced to the highest received contiguous version number, and all the vcache entries for this page are removed from the vcache.

We expect version number reordering to be uncommon and therefore expect the vcache to be very small.

4.3 Preprocessing in the Redirector: Pre-aborts and Stalls

Since the redirector has the information about all the outstanding requests in a cache group, we can take advantage of this information to avoid unnecessary processing at the servers. We can avoid forwarding multiple fetch requests for a page p when a fetch to this page is outstanding. We can also avoid forwarding a commit request that is known to result in an abort. Consider the case where a redirector distributes an invalidation of an object o and receives a commit request for a transaction T that has object o in its read set. We can prevent the unnecessary abort processing of T at the server. Since T must have read stale data the redirector can abort T locally.

For simplicity reasons, current BuddyCache design does not support preprocessing except in the simple case of fetches.

5   BuddyCache Failover

To accommodate heterogeneous clients including resource-poor hand-helds we do not require the availability of persistent storage in the BuddyCache peer group. BuddyCache design assumes that client caches and redirector data structures do not survive node failures.

A failure of a client or a redirector is detected by a membership protocol that exchanges periodic "I am alive messages" between group members and initiates a failover protocol. The failover determines the active group participants, re-elects a redirector if needed, reinitializes the BuddyCache data structures in the new configuration and restarts the protocol. The group reconfiguration protocol is similar to the one presented in [12]. Here we describe how the failover manages BuddyCache state.

To restart BuddyCache protocol, the failover needs to resynchronize the redirector page directory and client-server request forwarding so that active clients can continue running transactions using their caches. In the case of a client failure, the failover removes the crashed client pages from the directory. Any response to an earlier request initiated by the failed client is ignored except a commit reply, in which case the redirector distributes the retained committed updates to active clients caching the modified pages.

In the case of the redirector failure, the failover protocol reinitializes sessions with the servers and clients, and rebuilds the page directory using a protocol similar to one in [5]. The newly restarted redirector asks the active group members for the list of pages they are caching and the status of these pages, i.e. whether the pages are *complete* or *incomplete.*

Requests outstanding at the redirector at the time of the crash may be lost. A lost fetch request will time out at the client and will be retransmitted. A transaction running at the client during a failover and committing after the failover is treated as a regular transaction, a transaction trying to commit during a failover is be aborted by the failover protocol. A client will restart the transaction and the commit request will be retransmitted after the failover. Invalidations, updates or collected update acknowledgement lost at the crashed redirector could prevent the garbage collection of pending invalidations at the servers or the vcache in the clients. Therefore, servers detecting a redirector crash retransmit recent unacknowledged invalidations and commit replies. Unique version numbers in invalidations and updates insure that duplicate retransmitted requests are detected and discarded.

Since the transaction validation procedure depends on the cache coherence protocol to insure that transactions do not read stale data, we now need to argue that BuddyCache failover protocol does not compromise the correctness of the validation procedure. Recall that BuddyCache transaction validation uses two complementary mechanisms, page version numbers and invalidation acknowledgements from the clients, to check that a transaction has read up-to-date data.

The redirector-based invalidation (and update) acknowledgement propagation insures the following invariant. When a server receives an acknowledgement for an object o modification (invalidation or update) from a client group, any client in the group caching the object o has either installed the latest value of object o, or has invalidated o. Therefore, if a server receives a commit request from a client for a transaction T reading an object o after a failover in the client group, and the server has no unacknowledged invalidation for o pending for this group, the version of the object read by the transaction T is up-to-date independently of client or redirector failures.

Now consider the validation using version numbers. The transaction commit record contains a version number for each object read by the transaction. The version number protocol insures the invariant that the value of object o read by the transaction corresponds to the highest version number for o received by the client. The invariant holds since the client never applies an earlier modification after a later modification has been received. Retransmition of invalidations and updates maintains this invariant. The validation procedure checks that the version number in the commit record matches the version number in the unacknowledged outstanding invalidation. It is straightforward to see that since this check is an end-to-end client-server check it is unaffected by client or redirector failure.

6   Performance and Tradeoffs

We expect BuddyCache to provide significant object access latency improvements for common workloads in wide-area network environments. Specifically, we expect peer fetching to result in significant latency improvements for collaborating client cold cache startup. Solo commit should improve commit latency for fast peers for workloads containing repeatedly modified objects, a common access pattern observed in file system traces. The update propagation within a peer group should improve the latency of access to frequently modified shared objects avoiding the extra round-trip delay to due to invalidation triggered misses, and provide an advantage over either invalidation-only and update-only coherence scheme for workloads containing objects cached in multiple peer groups. In addition, we expect the fine-grain updates in the peer group to achieve similar benefits to ones observed in the fragment reconstruction system [1] i.e. alleviating the performance penalty introduced by false-sharing on poorly clustered pages.

Nevertheless, since the redirector serves as an intermediary for all the client-server communication, we need to insure in the implementation that the extra time it takes the redirector to forward and process requests does not outweigh the aggregate performance benefits of peer fetching.

After completing BuddyCache implementation we plan to conduct a comprehensive performance study to evaluate the performance advantages that Buddy-Cache delivers in practice.

7   Conclusion

BuddyCache is a new cache coherence architecture that deals with the network latency problem facing peer group applications accessing shared data in transactional object repositories in wide-area network environment. The main challenge in BuddyCache is how to provide consistent low-latency access to shared objects cached by peers when consistency management requires high-latency coordination with remote servers.

BuddyCache addresses the network latency problem by introducing new cache coherence techniques for fetches, transaction commits, and cache updates. *Peer fetch* allows to fetch objects cached in the peer group, *solo* commit reduces the transaction commit latency for fast clients with slow peers, and *hybrid coherence* accelerates the access to modified objects of interest to the peer group without imposing overhead on the other parts of the caching system.

BuddyCache coherence protocol is the first fine-grain group coherence protocol for distributed transactional object repositories in high-latency networks. Earlier group caching approaches only worked in fast local area networks [1,9] or did not support fine-grain coherence [4,3,9] and transactions.

In the paper we have described the design of the new BuddyCache protocols and its main architectural components, redirector and version cache. Paper discussed both failure-free BuddyCache operation and BuddyCache operation in the presence of failures, and outlined a correctness argument for how the failover protocol insures that failures do not compromise the consistency of persistent objects.

Technology trends indicate that with processor speeds improving and memory sizes increasing, the latency penalty for remote access to consistent shared data will continue to present a challenge for storage system performance. Buddy-Cache design has addressed this challenge by supporting faster access to shared objects by trading fast close range access to objects for slow remote access. Nevertheless, since the redirector components act as an intermediary between the clients and the servers, and all communication goes through the redirector, BuddyCache implementation needs to insure that the performance benefits from using BuddyCache outweigh the extra time it takes to forward requests.

We are currently working on the BuddyCache implementation and conducting an extensive study to evaluate its performance.

References

1. A. Adya, M. Castro, B. Liskov, U. Maheshwari, and L. Shrira. Fragment reconstruction: Providing global cache coherence in a transactional storage system. *Proceedings of the International Conference on Distributed Computing Systems*, May 1997.
2. A. Adya, R. Gruber, B. Liskov, and U. Maheshwari. Efficient optimistic concurrency control using loosely synchronized clocks. In *Proceedings of the ACM SIGMOD International Conference on Management of Data*, 1995.
3. L. Alvisi, M. Dahlin, C. Lin, and J. Yin. Hierarchical cache consistency in a WAN. In *The 1999 USENIX Symposium on Internet Technologies and Systems (USITS99)*, October 1999.
4. L. Alvisi, M. Dahlin, C. Lin, and J. Yin. Volume leases for consistency in large-scale systems. *IEEE Transactions on Knowledge and Data Engineering*, 1999.
5. M. Baker. *Fast Crash Recovery in Distributed File Systems*. PhD thesis, University of California at Berkeley, 1994.
6. P. Cao and C. Liu. Maintaining strong cache consistency in the world wide web. In *17th International Conference on Distributed Computing Systems.*, volume 47 of *IEEE Transactions on Computers*, pages 445–57, April 1998.
7. J. Chase, S. Gadde, and M. Rabinovich. Not all hits are created equal: Cooperative proxy caching over a wide-area network. In *Third International WWW Caching Workshop*, June 1998.
8. D. R. Cheriton and D. Li. Scalable web caching of frequently updated objects using reliable multicast. *2nd USENIX Symposium on Internet Technologies and Systems*, October 1999.
9. Michael Franklin, Michael Carey, and Miron Livny. Global memory management for client-server dbms architectures. In *Proceedings of the 19th Intl. Conference on Very Large Data Bases (VLDB)*, 1992.
10. S. Ghemawat. *The Modified Object Buffer: A Storage Management Technique for Object-Oriented Databases*. PhD thesis, Massachusetts Institute of Technology, 1997.
11. B. Liskov, M. Castro, L. Shrira, and A. Adya. Providing persistent objects in distributed systems. In *Proceedings of the 13th European Conference on Object-Oriented Programming (ECOOP '99)*, June 1999.
12. B. Oki and B. Liskov. Viewstamped Replication: A New Primary Copy Method to Support Highly-Available Distributed Systems. In *Proc. of ACM Symposium on Principles of Distributed Computing*, 1988.
13. J. O'Toole and L. Shrira. Opportunistic log: Efficient installation reads in a reliable object server. In *OSDI*, 1994.
14. A. M. Vahdat, P. C. Eastham, and T. E Anderson. Webfs: A global cache coherent file system. Technical report, University of California, Berkeley, 1996.

Platypus: Design and Implementation of a Flexible High Performance Object Store

Zhen He[1], Stephen M. Blackburn[2], Luke Kirby[1], and John Zigman[1]

[1] Department of Computer Science
Australian National University
Canberra ACT 0200, Australia
{Zhen.He, Luke.Kirby, John.Zigman}@cs.anu.edu.au
[2] Department of Computer Science
University of Massachusetts
Amherst, MA, 01003, USA
steveb@cs.umass.edu

Abstract. This paper reports the design and implementation of Platypus, a transactional object store. The twin goals of flexibility and performance dominate the design of Platypus. The design includes: support for SMP concurrency; standalone, client-server and client-peer distribution configurations; configurable logging and recovery; and object management which can accommodate garbage collection and clustering mechanisms. The first implementation of Platypus incorporates a number of innovations. (1) A new recovery algorithm derived from ARIES that removes the need for log sequence numbers to be present in store pages. (2) A zero-copy memory-mapped buffer manager with controlled write-back behavior. (3) A data structure for highly concurrent map querying. We present performance results comparing Platypus with SSM, the storage layer of the SHORE object store. For both medium and small OO7 workloads Platypus outperforms SHORE across a wide range of benchmark operations in both 'hot' and 'cold' settings.

1 Introduction

This paper describes the design and implementation of an object store with a flexible architecture, good performance characteristics, and a number of interesting implementation features such as a new recovery algorithm, an efficient zero-copy buffer manager, and scalable data structures. Furthermore, this work represents a step towards our goal of both meeting the demands of database systems and efficiently supporting orthogonally persistent run-time systems.

The key to orthogonal persistence lies in the power of *abstraction over persistence*, the value of which is being recognized by a wider and wider audience. The potential for orthogonal persistence in mainstream data management appears to be massive and yet largely unrealized. As appealing as orthogonal persistence is, it must be applicable to the hard-edged data management environment in which the mainstream operates before it will see uptake in that world. Traditionally, object stores for orthogonally persistent languages have not strongly targeted this domain, so strong transactional semantics and good transaction throughput have not normally been goals or features of such stores. On the other hand, relational, object relational, and object oriented databases have not

G.N.C. Kirby, A. Dearle, and D.I.K. Sjøberg (Eds.): POS-9, LNCS 2135, pp. 100–124, 2001.

focused strongly on the demands of a tightly coupled language client and so tend to provide a particularly inefficient foundation for orthogonally persistent systems. One result is a lack of systems that can effectively bridge that gap. We have developed Platypus in an attempt to address that gap.

The backdrop to the design of Platypus is the *transactional object cache* architecture which strongly separates storage and language concerns [Blackburn 1998]. Central to the architecture is the concept of both store and runtime sharing *direct access* to an object cache, where access is moderated by a protocol manifest in a transactional interface. This architecture provides a layer of abstraction over storage while removing impedance between the store and the language runtime implementations.

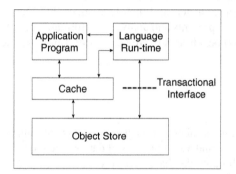

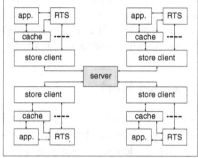

(a) The transactional object cache architecture. The cache is directly accessible shared memory.

(b) Underlying store architectures are transparent to the client runtime (RTS).

Fig. 1. The transactional object cache tightly couples the store and runtime/application through *direct access* to a cache, while abstracting over the store architecture.

A focus on abstraction is reflected in the design of Platypus, which has the flexibility to support a range of storage layer topologies (such as stand-alone, client-server, and client-peer). The design also includes replaceable modular components, such as the object manager, which is responsible for providing a mapping between the underlying *byte store*[1] and the *object store* projected to the client. This flexibility is critical to the utility of Platypus as it provides a single solid framework for prototyping and analyzing most aspects of store design.

The focus on minimizing store/runtime impedance impacts strongly on the implementation of Platypus and led directly to the development of a zero-copy buffer cache implementation. The zero-copy buffer cache presents a number of technical hurdles, notably with respect to the recovery algorithm and controlling page write-back.

---

[1] We use the term *byte store* to describe untyped, unstructured data.

The construction of a flexible, robust, high performance transactional store is a major undertaking, and in our experience is one filled with problems and puzzles. In this paper we touch on just a few aspects of the construction of Platypus. We address the architecture of the system because we believe that it embodies decisions that were key to delivering both flexibility and performance. We also address some major performance issues that arose in the course of implementation, as we believe that the solutions we have developed are novel and are likely to find application in other systems. For other details of the construction of Platypus which are not novel, such as the intricate workings of the ARIES [Mohan 1999; Mohan et al. 1992] recovery algorithm and the choice of buffer cache eviction policies, the reader is referred to the substantial literature on database and store design and implementation.

In section 2 Platypus is related to existing work. Section 3 describes the architecture of Platypus. Sections 4 and 5 focus on implementation issues, first with respect to the realization of an efficient zero-copy buffer manager, and then techniques that greatly enhance the scalability of Platypus. Section 6 presents and analyzes performance results for Platypus and SHORE using both the OO7 benchmark [Carey et al. 1993] and a simple synthetic workload. Section 7 concludes.

2   Related Work

This paper is written in the context of a large number of object store design and implementation papers in the POS workshop series and a vast number of database and OODB design and implementation papers in the broader database literature.

Architecture. A number of papers have reported on the design of object stores targeted specifically at orthogonally persistent programming languages. Brown and Morrison [1992] describe a layered architecture that was used as the basis of a number of persistent programming languages, including Napier and Galileo. Central to the architecture is an abstract *stable heap* (also a feature of the Tycoon architecture [Matthes et al. 1996]). This model offered a clean abstraction over persistence in the store architecture, and the architectures were sufficiently general to admit a wide range of concurrency control policies. However the stable heap interface is fine grained both temporally and spatially (*read_word, write_word*, etc.) and so incurs substantially more traversals of the interface than a transactional object cache, which is coarse grained spatially (per object *c.f.* per word) and temporally (per transaction *c.f.* per access).

Of the many store architectures in the literature that do not directly target orthogonal persistence, most address specific optimizations and improvements with respect to OODB design. The THOR architecture from MIT [Liskov et al. 1999] has been the context for OODB research in the areas of buffer management, recovery algorithms, cache coherency and garbage collection. Other projects have supported a similar breadth of work in the context of an OODB architecture. The system that comes closest to the architectural goals of Platypus is SHORE [Carey et al. 1994], a successor to EXODUS and E [Carey et al. 1988], which set out to be flexible (with respect to distribution, for example), focussed on performance, and supported a persistent programming language. SHORE is publicly available and has been used as the point of comparison in our performance analysis of Platypus (section 6).

By contrast to the systems built on the stable heap [Brown and Morrison 1992; Matthes et al. 1996], Platypus is built around the transactional object cache abstraction [Blackburn and Stanton 1998], which allows direct access to a cache shared by storage and language runtime layers (although it limits the language-side client to *transactional* concurrency control). Platypus is thus closer to orthodox OODBs than such systems. One notable distinction is that while many OODBMs focus on scalability of client-server (and in the case of SHORE, client-peer) architecture, Platypus's approach to scalability extends towards SMP nodes—either stand-alone, or in client-server or client-peer configurations.

Buffer Cache Implementation. Most recent work on buffer management has focused on efficient use of buffers in a client-server context. Kemper and Kossmann [1994] explored adaptive use of both object and page grain buffering—object buffering incurs a copy cost, but may be substantially more space-efficient when objects are not well clustered. The THOR project [Liskov et al. 1999] has included a lot of work on buffer management in client-server databases, mostly focusing on efficiently managing client, server, and peer memory in the face of object updates at the clients. Platypus's buffer cache is in most respects orthodox (implementing a STEAL/NO-FORCE [Franklin 1997] buffer management policy), and is amenable to such techniques for managing data cached via a network. The novelty in our buffer manager lies in its use of memory mapping to address efficiency with respect to access of data resident on *disk*. We address the problem of controlling write-back of mapped pages which have become dirty (any such write-back must be strictly controlled to ensure recoverability). We also outline an extension to the ARIES [Mohan et al. 1992] recovery algorithm which obviates the need for log sequence numbers (LSNs) to be included on every page.

Scalable Data Structures. There exists an enormous literature on data structures and scalability. Knuth [1997] provides an excellent discussion of sorting and searching that proved to be very helpful in our implementation efforts. Kleiman, Smalders, and Shah [1995] give an excellent treatment of issues relating to threads and concurrency in an SMP context, describing numerous techniques for maximizing scalability which were relevant to our store implementation. One of the scalability problems we faced was in the efficiency of map structures. After exploring splay trees [Sleator and Tarjan 1985], and hashes (including dynamic hashes [Larson 1988]) and their various limitations, we developed a new data structure which is a simple hybrid, the *hash-splay*. The hash-splay data structure is explained in full in section 5.1.

3   Architecture

At the core of the Platypus architecture are three major separable abstractions: *visibility*, which governs the inter-transactional visibility of intra-transactional change, *stability*, which is concerned with coherent stability and durability of data, and *availability* which controls the availability of data (i.e., its presence or absence in a user-accessible cache) [Blackburn 1998]. Each of these corresponds to one or more major functional units (called 'managers') in the Platypus architecture. On top of these three concerns there exists an *object* manager, which projects an object store from an underlying 'byte store', and a *transaction* manager, which orchestrates visibility, stability and availability concerns on account of user requests across the transactional interface. This architecture is illustrated schematically in figure 2.

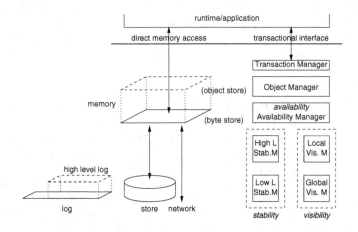

Fig. 2. Platypus architecture schematic. Managers (right) oversee the structure and movement of data between memory, a store, a log, and remote stores (left). Through the transactional interface the client runtime gains direct access to the memory it shares with the store.

3.1 Visibility

Isolation is a fundamental property of transactions [Härder and Reuter 1983]. While changes made by an uncommitted transaction must be isolated from other transactions to ensure serializability, serializability also demands that those changes be fully exposed once the transaction is successfully committed. Visibility is concerned with controlling that exposure in the face of particular transactional semantics. Visibility becomes some-what more complex in the face of distribution, where a range of different strategies can be employed in an effort to minimize the impact of *latency* [Franklin 1996]. Since these strategies are concerned solely with efficiently maintaining coherent visibility in the face of distribution-induced latency, they are not relevant to purely local visibility issues. We thus carefully separate visibility into two distinct architectural units: a *local visibility manager* (LVM), and a *global visibility manager* (GVM).

The LVM is concerned with the mediation of transactional visibility *locally* (i.e., within a single uniformly addressable memory space, or 'node'). In the absence of network latency, optimism serves little purpose, so the LVM can be implemented using an orthodox lock manager (as found in most centralized database systems).[2] The LVM

---

[2] Optimism is a computational device for hiding latencies associated with the in-availability of information on which a decision must be made (typically due to physical dislocation or dependencies on incomplete concurrent computations). In a context where the information is

operates with respect to *transactions* and abstract *visibility entities*, which the transaction manager would typically map directly to objects but which could map to any other entity over which visibility control were required. Through the transaction manager, transactions acquire locks from the LVM, which ensures that appropriate transactional visibility semantics are preserved and detects and reacts to deadlocks when necessary.

The GVM manages transactional visibility *between* the LVMs at distributed nodes (i.e., nodes which do not share a uniformly addressable memory). The GVM may implement any of the considerable range of transactional cache coherency algorithms [Franklin 1996]. The GVM operates between distributed LVMs and works with respect to *transactions*, *visibility entities*, and *sets of visibility entities*. By introducing *sets of visibility entities*, interactions can occur at a coarser grain. Just as visibility entities may be mapped to objects, sets of visibility entities may be mapped to pages, allowing global visibility to operate at either page or object grain (or both [Voruganti et al. 1999]). The GVM allows access rights over visibility entities (objects) and sets of visibility entities (pages) to be cached at nodes. Once rights are cached at a node, intra-node, inter-transaction visibility is managed by the LVM at that node. The GVM exists only to support transactional visibility between *distributed* LVMs, so is only necessary in the case where support for distribution is required.

3.2   Stability

Durability is another fundamental property of transactions. Härder and Reuter [1983] define durability in terms of *irrevocable stability*, that is, the effects of a transaction cannot be undone once made durable. An ACID transaction can only be undone logically, through the issue of another transaction (or transactions) which counters the first transaction. There are other important aspects to managing stability, including crash recovery, faulting of data into memory and the writing of both committed (durable) and uncommitted data back to disk. Given the pervasiveness and generality of the write ahead logging (WAL) approach to recovery [Mohan 1999], we model stability in terms of a store and a stable log of events (changes to the store)[3]. This model allows uncommitted store data to be safely stabilized, as the log always maintains sufficient information to bring the store data to a state that coherently reflects all committed changes to the store. Stability functionality is divided into two abstract layers managed respectively by the *high level stability manager* (HSM) and the *low level stability manager* (LSM).

The HSM is responsible for maintaining and ensuring the recoverability of 'high level' logs which stably reflect changes to the store induced by user actions (as opposed to actions internal to Platypus's management). For example a user's update to an object, O, is recorded by the HSM in relatively abstract terms: 'transaction T mutated object O thus: $O' = O + \Delta$'. The HSM's log of changes is robust to lower level events such as the movement of an object by a garbage collector operating within the store because the HSM log does not record the physical location of bytes changed, but rather records deltas to abstractly addressed objects. Another role of the HSM is that it manages 'before-images'

---

available—such is the case with shared memory concurrency control—optimism is unnecessary and in fact deleterious (there is no point in computing 'optimistically' when information indicating the futility of that computation is immediately available).

[3] There were other important reasons for choosing WAL, not least of these is that unlike shadowing, WAL admits the possibility of a zero-copy buffer cache (see section 4.1).

of objects which the user has stated an intention to update. Before images serve two important roles. They are necessary for the calculation of change deltas ($\Delta = O' \oplus O$), and they allow updates to the store to be undone. The latter is made necessary by our desire for a zero copy object cache and the possibility of implementing a STEAL policy in the buffer cache (i.e., that uncommitted mutated pages might be written to the store [Franklin 1997]). The HSM ensures that deltas are made stable at transaction commit time, and that before-images are made stable prior to any page being 'stolen' from the buffer cache.

The LSM has two roles. It maintains and ensures the recoverability of 'low level' logs which stably reflect changes to store meta-data and store structure (such as the movement of an object from one disk page to another or the update to some user-transparent index structure). The LSM also encapsulates HSM logs. Recovery is primarily the responsibility of the LSM. When the LSM finds a log record containing a HSM log record, it passes responsibility for that update to the HSM. This separation has two major benefits. First, it allows any low-level activities such as changes to object allocation meta-data to be completely separated from the high level object store behavior, which allows modular, independent implementation. Second, it opens the way for a two-level transaction system which can reduce or remove concurrency conflicts between low-level activities and high level activities (this is essential to minimizing conflicts between concurrent user transactions and garbage collection). For example a high-level transaction maybe updating an object while it is being moved by a low-level transaction. The two-level system allows both transactions to proceed concurrently.

3.3   Availability

The *availability manager* (AM) has a number of roles, all of which relate to the task of making data available (to the user and the store infrastructure). The centerpiece of the AM is thus the buffer cache—the (bounded) set of memory pages in which the store operates. For each node there exists one AM.[4] The AM manages three categories of pages: *store pages* which are mapped from secondary storage (through the LSM) or from a remote node (through the GVM), *log pages* which are mapped from secondary storage (through the LSM) and *shared meta-data* which is common to all processes executing at that node. Whenever there is demand for a new page, a frame is allocated in the buffer cache (possibly causing the eviction of a resident page). In the case of a store page, the LSM or GVM then faults the page into the new frame. Evicted pages are either swapped to their corresponding store page (a page STEAL), or to a special swap area on disk (for non-store pages).[5]

The AM operates at two grains: *available regions*, which are typically mapped to objects, and *pages*, which is the operating system's unit of memory management. Through the transaction manager, the AM keeps track of which memory regions are in use (pinned) by the user, and which regions are dirty, information which is used when making decisions about which pages to evict.

---

[4] The AM is managed cooperatively by all store processes executing concurrently on the node.

[5] This is simply achieved by 'mmap'ing non-store pages to a swap file.

3.4 Objects

An *object manager* (OM) is responsible for establishing (and maintaining) a mapping between an underlying 'byte store' (unstructured data) and the object store projected to the user. The nature of this mapping and the sophistication of the OM is implementation dependent and may vary enormously, from a system that treats objects as untyped byte arrays and simply maps object identifiers to physical addresses, to a system that has a strong notion of object type and includes garbage collection and perhaps a level of indirection in its object addressing. The strength of this design is that while the object manager is a relatively small component of the store in implementation terms, it largely *defines* the store from the user perspective. Thus making this a modular, separable component greatly extends the utility of the remainder of the store.

3.5 Transactions

The *transaction manager* is a relatively simple architectural component that sits between the transactional interface and the remainder of the architecture. It executes user transactions by taking user requests (such as readIntention, writeIntention, new, commit, and abort), and orchestrating the appropriate transactional semantics through the OM (creating new objects, looking up OIDs), AM (ensuring that the object is in cache), LVM (ensuring that transactional visibility semantics are observed), and HSM (maintaining the persistent state of the object).

Having described the Platypus architecture, we now discuss aspects of its implementation.

4 Implementing a Zero-Copy Buffer Cache

At the heart of the transactional object cache architecture is the concept of both store and runtime sharing *direct access* to an object cache, where access is moderated by a protocol manifest in a transactional interface (see figure 1). This contrasts with interfaces that require that objects be *copied* from the store to the runtime and back again. In our recent experience with a commercial database product and the SHORE [Carey et al. 1994] object database, neither would allow direct ('in-place') updates to objects.[6] Such a requirement is understandable in the face of normal user access to an object database. If direct, unprotected, access is given to a cached database page the grave possibility exists of the user *breaking* the protocol with an update that (inadvertently) occurrs outside an object's bounds and overwrites critical metadata or an object for which the transaction had not declared a write intention. Furthermore, the efficient implementation of a direct access interface presents some challenges.

In pursuit of performance, Platypus is implemented with a zero-copy buffer cache. By zero-copy we mean that disk pages are memory mapped (avoiding copying that occurs in `stdio` routines), and that the store client (language runtime) is given direct access to the mapped memory, client updates being written directly into the mapped

---

[6] We were able to circumvent this limitation in SHORE—*at the expense of recoverability* (this is described in section 6).

file. Of course a particular language runtime may well choose to copy objects before updating them (this happens in our orthogonally persistent Java implementation, where each object must be copied into the Java heap before it can be used). However, we have nonetheless removed one level of copying from the store's critical path.

Unfortunately the implementation of a zero-copy buffer cache in the context of a standard Unix operating system presents two significant hurdles: controlling the movement of data between memory and disk, and dealing with log sequence numbers (LSNs) in multi-page objects.

4.1   Controlled Write-Back in a Memory Mapped Buffer under POSIX/UNIX

While the mmap system call provides a means of accessing the filesystem without copying, mmap does not allow re-mapping (i.e. once data is mapped from disk address d to virtual address v it can only be written to some other disk address d' via a copy). Furthermore, while msync can be used to *force* a mapped page to be written back to disk, the only means of *stopping* data from being written back in a conventional user-level Unix process is through mlock, which is a privileged command that binds physical memory to a particular mapping. This presents a serious hurdle. Without using mlock, any direct updates to an mmapped file could at any time be written back to disk, destroying the coherency of the disk copy of the page.

We see Platypus's primary role as the back-end to a persistent language runtime system, and therefore do not think that it would be satisfactory for store processes to require root privileges. A standard solution in Unix to problems of this kind is to use a privileged *daemon process* to perform privileged functions as necessary. Using this approach, as soon as a *non-resident* page is faulted in, an *mlock daemon* could be triggered which would lock the page down, preventing any write-back of the page until the lock was released.[7] Control would then revert to the store process.

place request in mlock circular buffer		*blocked on condition variable*
call mmap		*blocked on condition variable*
signal mlock daemon		*condition variable unblocked*
trigger I/O	*– control →*	*inspect circular buffer*
blocked on I/O		for each non-empty entry in circular buffer
blocked on I/O		call mlock & set done flag
I/O completes	*← control–*	*finished [time slice consumed]*
check mlock done flag		*blocked on condition variable [sleep]*
[block on condition variable	*– control →*	*continue processing circular buffer]*
store process		**mlock daemon**

Fig. 3. Overlapping I/O with context switches to a daemon to efficiently use mlock in a non-privileged store process. Access to the mlock circular buffer is done in a mutually exclusive manner. Events in brackets (*[ ]*) depict scenario where daemon does not complete request.

---

[7] Through the use of mlock and mprotect, residency is under the control of Platypus.

The use of a daemon process comes at the cost of two context switches (context must move from the store process to the daemon and back). Given our focus on performance, this could present a significant problem. Fortunately, the context switch can be completely overlapped with the latency associated with faulting in the page which is to be locked. Thus `mlock` semantics are attained without requiring store processes to be privileged and without an appreciable performance penalty. The approach is sketched in figure 3. When a store process requests a page to be faulted into the store, it first signals a condition variable that the `mlock` daemon is waiting on, then it triggers the I/O. The I/O causes the store process to block and thus giving the `mlock` deamon (which is now no longer blocked on a condition variable) a chance to be switched in. A lock-protected circular buffer is used to deal with the possibility of multiple store processes simultaneously making requests to the mlock daemon, and a flag is used to allow the store process to ensure that the `mlock` did in fact take place while it was blocked on the I/O. If the daemon has not run and the mlock has thus not occurred, the store client blocks on a condition variable which is signalled by the daemon when it completes the `mlock`. The `mlock` daemon is central to the successful implementation of the zero-copy buffer cache in Platypus.

4.2 Avoiding LSNs in a Write-Ahead Logging Recovery Algorithm

Write-ahead logging (WAL) algorithms (such as ARIES [Mohan 1999; Mohan et al. 1992]) revolve around two key persistent entities, a *store* and a *log*. The log is used to record changes (deltas) to the store. This allows I/O to be minimized by only writing store pages back to disk opportunistically or when no other choice exists.[8] Abstractly, the WAL protocol depends on some means of providing linkage between the store and the log at recovery time. Such linkage provides the means of establishing which of the changes recorded in the log have been propagated to the store and so are essential to the recovery process. Concretely, this linkage is provided by log sequence numbers (LSNs), which are essentially pointers into the log [Mohan et al. 1992]. The natural way to implement LSNs is to include them in store pages—a store page can then be read upon recovery and its state with respect to the log quickly established by checking the LSN field of the page.

LSNs have the less desirable side-effect of punctuating the persistent storage space with low-level recovery-related information. This perturbation is particularly noticeable in the context of objects that are larger than a page because the object will have to be broken up to make way for an LSN on each of the pages that it spans (a coherent object image will thus only be constructible by copying each of the parts into a new contiguous space). More generally, this use of LSNs precludes zero-copy access to objects of any size that span pages. Motivated by our goal of a zero-copy object store and the possibility of an object space not interrupted by low-level recovery data, we now describe an alternative approach that avoids the need for explicit LSNs to be stored in store pages without loosing the semantics that LSNs bring to widely used WAL algorithms such as ARIES.

---

[8] Note that it is because WAL maintains only one store page copy (unlike shadow-paging) that a zero-copy buffer cache is possible. Shadow-paging essentially requires a remapping of the memory↔store relationship each time a page is committed, which precludes zero-copy use of `mmap` as described above.

Our approach follows an interesting remote file synchronization algorithm, *rsync* [Tridgell 1999; Tridgell and Mackerras 1998], which makes clever use of *rolling checksums* to minimize the amount of data required to synchronize two files. Checksums are used by rsync to identify which parts of the files differ (so that minimal deltas can be transmitted), and the *rolling* property of rsync's checksum algorithm allows checksums to be cheaply and incrementally calculated for a large number of offsets within one of the two files being compared.

At recovery time in WAL systems the log may contain many updates to a given store page. Thus there exists a many-to-one relationship between log records and store pages. A critical part of the recovery process is reducing this to a one-to-one relationship linking each store page with the log record corresponding to the last update to that page before it was flushed. An LSN stored in the first word of the store page provides a trivial solution to the problem—the LSN is a pointer to the relevant record. By associating a checksum with each log record, the problem is resolved by selecting the log record containing a checksum which matches the state of the store page. This amounts to a minor change to the recovery process and depends on only a small change to the generation of log records during normal processing. Each time a log record is produced, the checksums of all updated pages are calculated and included in the log record. Thus the use of checksums in place of LSNs is in principle very simple, yet it avoids the fragmentation effect that LSNs have on large objects (ones that span multiple pages). However this simple change to the WAL algorithm is made more complex by two issues: the cost of checksum calculation, and the problem that checksums may not *uniquely* identify page state. We now address these concerns in turn.

Cheap Checksum Calculation. The 32-bit Adler rolling checksum [Deutsch 1996] efficiently maintains the checksum (or '*signature*') for a window of k bytes as it is slid across a region of memory one byte at a time. The algorithm calculates each new checksum as a simple function of the checksum for the last window position, the byte that just entered the window, and the byte that just left the window. It is both cheap and incremental.

In an appendix to this paper, we generalize the Adler checksum to *partial checksums* (which indicate the contribution to the total checksum made by some sub-part of the checksummed region). We then show that in addition to its property of incrementality, the Adler checksum has a more general *associative* property that allows checksums to be calculated using *delta checksums*. A delta checksum is simply a partial checksum calculated with respect to the byte-wise difference between old and new values. The new checksum for a modified region is equal to its old checksum plus the delta checksum of the bytes that were modified.

Thus rather than recalculate the checksum for a whole page, it is only necessary to establish the delta checksums for any updated objects and add them to the page's old checksum. Furthermore, the calculation of the checksum is very cheap (involving only an add and a subtract for each byte), and can be folded into the calculation of the delta which must be generated from the before and after images of the changed object prior to being written to the log at commit time. A derivation of the incremental checksum and a pseudo-code description are included an appendix to this paper.

Dealing with Checksum Collisions. It is essential that at recovery time the state of a store page can be unambiguously related to exactly one and only one (of possibly many) log records describing changes to that page. Checksum collisions can arise from two sources. First, although any two consecutive changes must, by definition, leave the page in different states, a subsequent change could return the page to a previous state (i.e. $A \to B \to A$). Secondly, two store page states can produce the same checksum. The 32-bit Adler checksum used in Platypus has an *effective bit strength* of 27.1 [Taylor et al. 1998], which means that the probability of two differing regions sharing the same checksum is approximately $1/2^{27}$. So a checksum alone is inadequate.

To this end we introduce page flush log records (PFLR) to the basic WAL algorithm. Positive identification of a page's log state can be simplified if for each time a page is flushed to disk a PFLR is written to the log—each flush of a store page is followed by a log record recording that fact. The problem then reduces to one of determining which of *two* states the store page is in. Either both the flushed page and the associated PFLR which follows it are on disk or only the flushed page made it to disk before a failure occurred. If the PFLR contains the page's checksum, determining which state the system is in is trivial unless there is a checksum collision. However, a checksum collision can be trivially identified at the time that a PFLR is created by remembering the checksum used in the last PFLR for the page in question and identifying any occurrence of consecutive PFLRs which contain the same page checksum. As long as consecutive PFLRs for a given page hold unique checksums, the state of a store page can be unambiguously resolved.

If the page state is the same (i.e. the state of the page in consecutive flushes is unchanged), then the page need not actually be flushed and a flag can be set in the second PFLR indicating that the page has been logically flushed although its state has not changed since the last flush. When collisions do occur (i.e. same checksum but different store state), they can be disambiguated by appending the second (conflicting) PFLR with the full state of all regions of the page that have been modified since the last page flush. A conflict between the two PFLRs is then simply resolved by checking whether the store page state matches with the state appended to the second PFLR. While in the worst case this could involve including the entire page state in the log record (if the entire page were changed), checksum collisions occur so infrequently that any impact on overall I/O performance will be extremely small (on average only 1 in 2^{27} page flushes could be expected to generate any such overhead, and the WAL protocol already minimizes the occurance of any page flushes by using the log rather than page flushes to record each commit).

The common-case I/O effect of using checksums instead of in-page LSNs is negligable as the total number of bytes written to disk in both cases is similar. In the case of the checksum, store page utilization improves slightly because there is no space lost to LSNs, an effect that is compensated for by including the checksum in each log record.[9] The store page and PFLR flushes can be asynchronous so long as the PFLR is flushed from the log before the next flush of the same store page. This is guaranteed, however, because a subsequent page flush can only arise as a result of an update to that page, and under the WAL protocol any such update *must* be logged before the page is flushed, and

---

[9] LSNs are not normally explicitly included in log records because they are encoded as the *log offset* of the log record [Mohan et al. 1992].

the logging of such an update will force all outstanding PFLRs in the log to be written out. However, on the rare occasion when collisions occur, the PFLR *must* be written to the log and the log flushed *prior* to flushing the store page.

Although the checksum approach requires that checksums be recalculated upon recovery, the time taken to perform an Adler checksum of a page is dominated by memory bandwidth, and so will be small in comparison to the I/O cost associated with bringing the page into memory. The checksum technique will therefore not significantly effect performance on the rare occasion that recovery does have to be performed.

Page checksums and PFLRs can thus be used to replace intrusive LSNs for the purposes of synchronizing store and log state at *recovery time*. However, LSNs may be used for other purposes during *normal execution* such as reducing locking and latching [Mohan 1990]. The use of conventional LSNs during *normal execution* is not effected by the use of PFLRs because LSNs may still be associated with each page while the page resides in memory (in data structures which hold other volatile metadata maintained for each page). Thus algorithms like Commit_LSN [Mohan 1990] remain trivially applicable when checksums and PFLRs are used instead of in-page LSNs.

4.3   Checksum-Based Integrity Checks

A side effect of maintaining checksums for each page is that page integrity checks can be performed if desired. Such checks can be used for debugging purposes or simply to increase confidence in the store client's adherence to the transactional object cache protocol. The first of these goals is met by a function that checks pages on demand and ensures that only areas for which the client had stated a writeIntention were modified. Someone debugging a store client could then use this feature to identify any pages which had inadvertently been corrupted. The second goal is met by checking each page prior to flushing it to disk, checking that only those regions of the page with a declared writeIntention had been updated. The associative property of the Adler checksum (see above and the appendix to this paper), makes the efficient implementation of such partial checksums efficient and straightforward. Because of the checksum's probabilistic behavior, such checks can only be used to check integrity to a *very high level of confidence*, not as *absolute* checks of integrity.

5   Maximizing Scalability

Performance is a key motivator for Platypus, so it follows that scalability is a major implementation concern. After briefly outlining the approach we have taken to scalability, we describe in some detail two techniques that were significant in delivering good performance results for Platypus.

At the highest level, the store architecture must be able to exploit scalable hardware. For this reason the Platypus architecture supports different distributed hardware topologies including client server and client peer (figure 2 and section 3.3). The second of these has been demonstrated to scale extremely well on large scale multicomputers [Blackburn 1998]. In addition to distributed memory machines, the Platypus architecture is also targeted at SMP platforms, where memory coherency is not a problem but resource contention can be a major issue. Through the use of daemon processes all store processes on a node can share the common data and meta-data through a buffer cache that is mmaped to the same address in each process and cooperatively maintained.

At a lower level, we found two primary sources of in-scalability when building and testing Platypus, *data structures that would not scale well*, and *resource contention bottlenecks*. We successfully addressed all major resource contention bottle necks by using techniques such as *pools* of locks, which provide a way of balancing the considerable space overhead of a POSIX lock with the major contention problems that can arise if locks are applied to data structures at too coarse a grain [Kleiman et al. 1995]. We now describe the *hash-splay*, a specific solution to a key data structure scalability problem.

5.1   Hash-Splay: A Scalable Map Data Structure

Map data structures are very important to databases and object stores. Platypus implements a number of large map structures, most notably the LVM has a map relating object identifiers (OIDs) to per-object meta-data such as locks, update status, and location. Prior to the development of Platypus, we implemented a PSI-compliant object store based on the SHORE [Carey et al. 1994] object database, and found that map lookups were a bottleneck for SHORE. Consequently we spent time analyzing the scalability characteristics of common map structures, most notably hash tables and splay trees [Sleator and Tarjan 1985], each of which have some excellent properties. Knuth [1997] gives a detailed review of both hashes and binary search trees.

Primary features of the memory resident maps used by Platypus and other object stores are that access time is at a premium *and* they have key sets of unknown cardinality. The same map structure may need to efficiently map no more than a dozen unique keys in the case of a query with a running time in the order of a few hundred microseconds, and yet may need to map millions of keys for a large transaction that will take many seconds. The challenge therefore is to identify a data structure that can satisfy both the variability in cardinality and the demand for fast access. Another characteristic of these maps is that they will often exhibit a degree of locality in their access patterns, with a 'working set' of w keys which are accessed more frequently (such a working set corresponds to the locality properties inherent in the object store client's object access patterns).

While binary search trees are ideal for mapping key sets of unknown cardinality, their access time is $O(\log n)$ for n keys. On the other hand, hash tables can deliver access time performance of $O(1)$, *but* are not well suited to problems where the cardinality of the key set is unknown.

Our initial experiments were with splay trees, which are self-adjusting binary search trees. Splay trees re-adjust at every access, bringing the most recently accessed item to the root. While this provides excellent performance for access patterns of the type $\{aaaaabbbbbba...\}$, splay trees perform particularly poorly with an access pattern like $\{abababababab...\}$. We quickly found that by using 'sampling' (the tree is re-adjusted with some probability p), the re-adjusting overhead dropped appreciably with no appreciable degradation to access performance, providing a substantial overall performance improvement. This idea has been independently developed and analyzed by others [Fürer 1999].

Others have experimented with *linear hashing*[10] which adapts to the cardinality of the key set. This was originally developed for out-of-memory data [Litwin 1980;

---

[10] Not to be confused with the standard technique of *linear probing* in hash tables.

Larson 1980] and subsequently adapted to in-memory data [Larson 1988]. Aside from the question of key set cardinality, the reality of non-uniform hash functions means that a significant tradeoff must be made between space and time for any hash which takes the conventional approach of linear-probing on its buckets. Access time can be minimized by reducing collisions through a broad (and wasteful) hash space, *or* space efficiency can be maximized at the cost of relatively expensive linear searches through buckets when collisions do occur. Significantly, the impact of a *access locality* on the behavior of splays and hashes appears not to have been well examined in the literature, rather, performance analyses tend to address random access patterns only.

These observations lead us to the *hash-splay*, a simple data-structure which combines the $O(1)$ access time of a hash with the excellent caching properties and robustness to key sets of unknown cardinality that splay trees exhibit. The hash-splay consists of a hash where the hash targets are splay trees rather than other more traditional bucket structures.[11]

The hash-splay data structure has *excellent* caching properties. The combination of the re-adjusting property of the splay trees and the $O(1)$ access time for the hash means that for a working set of size w, average access times for items in the set is approximately $O(\log(w/k))$ where k represents the hash breadth. By contrast, for a simple splay it is approximately $O(\log w)$, and for a simple linear probing hash it is $O(n/k)$. If k is chosen to be greater than w, and a suitable hash function is chosen, working set elements should be at the roots of their respective buckets, yielding near-optimal access for these items. Significantly, k is selected as a function of w, not n, allowing k to be substantially smaller.

Platypus successfully implements the hash-splay to great effect. We find that our data structures perform very well for both huge transactions (where many locks and objects are accessed), as well as for small transactions (see section 6.2).

6   Performance Analysis of Platypus

We conducted a number of experiments to assess the performance of Platypus. For each of the experiments we use SHORE as a point of comparison. After describing the experimental setup, we compare the overall performance of the two stores. We then compare the performance of each store's logging system. The comparative read fault performance of the two stores was the next experiment conducted. Finally we compare the scalability of the data structures used by each store for reading and locking objects.

6.1   Experimental Setup

All experiments were conducted using Solaris 7 on an Intel machine with dual Celeron 433 Mhz processors, 512MB of memory and a 4GB hard disk.

Platypus. The system used in this evaluation was a first implementation of Platypus. The features it implements include: a simple object manager which features a direct mapping between logical and physical IDs; a local visibility manager; both low level and high level logging; and an availability manager. The page buffer implemented in the availability

---

[11] *c.f. hash-trees* [AGRAWAL AND SRIKANT 1994], which are trees with hashes at each node.

manager supports swapping of store and meta-data pages, and implements the NO-FORCE/STEAL recovery policy [Franklin 1997]. The features described in sections 4 and 5 have all been implemented with the exception of checksum-based integrity checks. The system is SMP re-entrant and supports multiple concurrent client threads per process as well as multiple concurrent client processes. Limitations of the implementation at the time of writing include: the failure-recovery process is untested (although logging *is* fully implemented); the availability manager does not recycle virtual address space; the store lacks a sophisticated object manager with support for garbage collection; no GVM has been implemented, precluding distributed store configurations.

SHORE. SHORE is a persistent object system designed to serve the needs of a wide variety of target applications, including persistent programming languages [Carey et al. 1994]. SHORE has a layered architecture that allows users to choose the level of support appropriate for a particular application. The lowest layer of SHORE is the SHORE Storage Manager (SSM), which provides basic object reading and writing primitives. Using the SSM we constructed PSI-SSM, a thin layer providing PSI [Blackburn 1998] compliance for SSM. By using the PSI interface, the same OO7 code could be used for both Platypus and SHORE. SSM comes as a library that is linked into an application either as a client stub (for client-server operation) or as a complete system—we linked it in to PSI-SSM as a complete system to avoid the rpc overhead associated with the client-server configuration. We also bypass the SSM's *logical* record identifiers, using *physical* identifiers instead in order to avoid expensive logical to physical lookups on each object access. This simple mode of object identification closely matches the simple object manager currently implemented in Platypus. We perform *in-place* updates and reads of objects[12] which further improves the SHORE results reported in this section. The PSI-SSM layer also has the effect of caching handles returned by SSM on a read request, reducing the number of heavy-weight read requests to SSM to one per-object per-transaction, as subsequent read requests for the same object are trapped by PSI-SSM. PSI-SSM uses the hash-splay data structure to implement its light-weight map. We used SHORE version 2.0 for all of the experiments reported in this paper.

OO7. The OO7 benchmark suite [Carey et al. 1993] is a comprehensive test of OODB performance. OO7 operations fall into three categories, traversals which navigate the object graph, queries like those typically found in a declarative query language and structural modifications which mutate the object graph by inserting and deleting objects. The OO7 schema is modeled around the components of a CAD application. A hierarchy of assembly objects (referred to as a module) sits at the top level of the hierarchy, while composite part objects lie at the bottom of the schema. Each composite part object in turn is linked to the root of a random graph of atomic part objects. The OO7 database is configurable, with three sizes of database commonly used—*small, medium,* and *large.* In our study we use small (11,000 objects) and medium (101,000 objects) databases. The results of OO7 benchmark runs are considered in terms of *hot* and *cold* results,

---

[12] SSM does not support *in-place* updates, so when a write intention is declared with respect to an object, PSI-SSM takes a before-image of the object to enable the undo of any updates if the transaction is aborted. While this is safe with respect to aborts, a STEAL of a page updated this way will lead to store corruption. This optimization therefore comes at the expense of recoverability in a context where swapping (STEALing) is occurring.

corresponding to transactions run on warm and cold caches respectively. Operations are run in batches and may be run with *many* transactions per batch (i.e., each iteration includes a transaction commit), or as *one* transaction (i.e., only the last iteration commits). All of the results reported here were run using the *many* configuration. For a detailed discussion of the benchmark schema and operations, the reader is referred to the paper and subsequent technical report describing OO7 [Carey et al. 1993]. We use the same implementation of the OO7 benchmark for both Platypus and SHORE. It is written in C++ and has explicit read and write barriers embedded in the code. This implementation does not depend on store support for indexes and maps, but instead implements all necessary maps explicitly.

While we acknowledge the limitations of using any benchmark as the basis for performance analysis, the operations included in the OO7 suite emphasize many different aspects of store performance, so the performance of a system across the entire suite of operations can give a reasonable indication of the general performance characteristics of that system.

6.2   Results

Overall Performance. Figure 4 shows the relative performance of Platypus with respect to SHORE for the twenty-four operations of the OO7 benchmark for both hot and cold transactions with small and medium databases. Of the 92^{13} results, Platypus performs significantly worse in only five 5 (5.4%), the results are marginal in 9 (9.8%), and Platypus performs significantly better in 78 (84.8%). The geometric means of the time ratios for the four sets of results range from 0.580 to 0.436, corresponding to Platypus offering average performance improvements over SHORE from 72% to 129%. The hot results spend proportionately more time in the application and performing simple OID to virtual address translations (corresponding to application reads). Since both systems execute the same application code and the PSI-SSM layer performs OID to virtual address translations using a hash-splay (saving SHORE from performing such lookups), there is appreciably less opportunity for the advantages of Platypus over SHORE to be seen in the hot results.

Logging Performance. Table 1 outlines the results of a comparison of logging performance between Platypus and SHORE. The results were generated by re-running the OO7 benchmark suite using both systems with logging turned off (i.e., without write I/O at commit time), and then subtracting these results from those with logging turned on. The difference between the results yields the logging (write I/O) cost for each system. The table reveals that Platypus performs logging far more efficiently than SHORE, which may be attributed to the zero copy nature of `mmap` (used to allocate memory for log records and used to flush log records to disk in Platypus). The better results for the small database suggests that logging in Platypus is particularly low latency (any latency effect will be diminished in the medium database results, where bandwidth may dominate).

---

[13] We were unable to use the large database configuration (and unable to get results for t3b and t3c on the medium configuration) because of failures in PSI-SSM and/or SSM once the database size exceeded the available physical memory. This behavior may well be related to our use of in-place updates which is unsafe in the face of page STEAL.

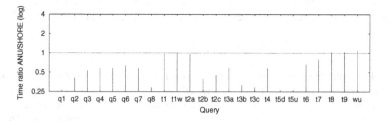

(a) Execution time ratios for *cold* benchmark runs over the OO7 *small* database (geometric mean = 0.495, with 0.0156 coefficient of variation).

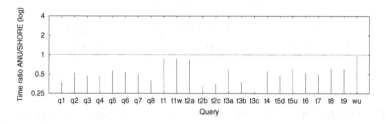

(b) Execution time ratios for *hot* benchmark runs over the OO7 *small* database (geometric mean = 0.517, with 0.0141 coefficient of variation).

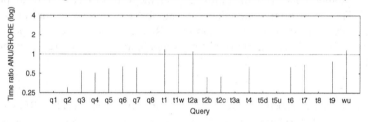

(c) Execution time ratios for *cold* benchmark runs over the OO7 *medium* database (geometric mean = 0.436, with 0.0142 coefficient of variation).

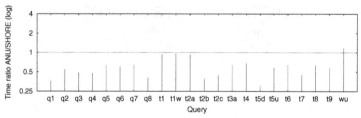

(d) Execution time ratios for *hot* benchmark runs over the OO7 *medium* database (geometric mean = 0.580, with 0.0176 coefficient of variation).

Fig. 4. Execution time comparison of Platypus and SHORE for the OO7 benchmark. Each impulse represents the ratio of average execution time for Platypus and the average execution time for SHORE for a particular operation in the OO7 suite. Average results are generated from 3 repetitions. A result less than 1 corresponds to Platypus executing faster than SHORE.

This result also supports the claim that the new recovery algorithm (including incremental checksum calculations) presented in section 4.2 is efficient in terms of logging costs.

Table 1. Performance comparison of logging between Platypus and SHORE, showing the geometric means of ratios of logging times for selected operations for each system. Only times for the benchmark operations where at least 1% of execution time was spent on logging were included in the results (8 operations for medium results and 15 operations for small results). The results shown are average results from 3 repetitions. The values in brackets () depict the coefficient of variation of the corresponding result.

Store Size	Time Ratio Platypus /SHORE	
	Hot	Cold
Small	0.290 (0.0141)	0.396 (0.0169)
Medium	0.362 (0.0225)	0.401 (0.0181)

Read Fault Performance. To compare how well the two systems perform read I/O, we subtracted the hot time from the cold time for each benchmark operation. This difference represents the cost of faulting pages into a cold cache, and any incidental per-transaction costs. The geometric means of the ratios between the results for each store are presented in table 2. The use of mmap both reduces the number of pages copied during page fault to zero and also reduces memory consumption. Reducing memory consumption has the secondary effect of deferring the need for swapping and so further reducing both read and write I/O.

Table 2. Performance comparison of read fault time between Platypus and SHORE, showing the geometric means of ratios of read fault times for each system. The results shown are average results from 3 repetitions. The values in brackets () depict the coefficient of variation of the corresponding result.

Store Size	Time Ratio Platypus /SHORE
Small	0.775 (0.0156)
Medium	0.338 (0.0176)

Data Structure Scalability. This experiment explores the scalability of map and locking data structures used in Platypus and SHORE. We did not use the OO7 benchmark, but constructed a trivial synthetic benchmark that involved no writes and did not read any object twice. These constraints allowed us to bypass the caching and before-image creation functionality of the PSI-SSM layer, and thereby get a direct comparison of the Platypus and SSM data structure performance. The synthetic benchmark operates over

a singly-linked list of 100,000 small objects.[14] Before each test, a single transaction
that reads all of the objects is run. This is done to bring all objects into memory and so
remove any I/O effects from the timing of the subsequent transactions. After the initial
transaction, many transactions of various sizes (traversing different numbers of objects)
are run. To measure the 'per-read' cost, we subtract from the time for each transaction
the time for an empty (zero reads) transaction, and divide the result by the number of
objects read. Figure 5 depicts a comparison of the data structure scalability for Platypus
and SHORE. As the number of objects read increases, the amount by which Platypus
outperform SHORE also increases, indicating the data structures used in Platypus are
substantially more scalable than those used in SHORE.

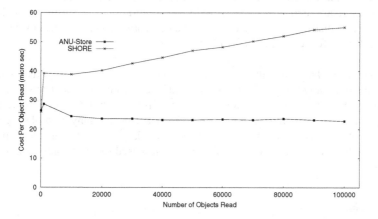

Fig. 5. Data structure scalability comparison between Platypus and SHORE. The results shown
are average results from 5 repetitions. The coefficient of variation for the results shown above
range from 0.0667 to 0.112.

7   Conclusions

The power of abstraction over persistence is slowly being recognized by the data management community. Platypus is an object store which is specifically designed to meet
the needs of tightly coupled persistent programming language clients and to deliver
the transactional support expected by conventional database applications. The design of
Platypus embraces the theme of abstraction, abstracting over store topology through a
flexible distribution architecture, and encapsulating the mechanisms by which the object
store abstraction is constructed from an untyped byte store. In addition to a high level
of flexibility, Platypus is extremely functional. It is multi-threaded and can support a

---

[14] The objects contain only a pointer to the next object. The smallest possible object size was used
to ensure that all objects would fit each store's cache and so avoid the possibility of swapping
effects impacting on the comparison.

high degree of concurrency, both intra and inter process and intra and inter processor on an SMP architecture. The implementation of Platypus resulted in the development of a simple extension to the ARIES recovery algorithm and a simple combination of existing data structures, both of which perform well and should have application in other object store implementations. Performance analysis shows that Platypus performs extremely well, suggesting that the combination of orthodoxy and innovation in its design and implementation has been a successful strategy.

The most obvious area for further work is to complete the construction of Platypus. The completed store would include a more sophisticated object manager that allows a garbage collector to be implemented, a fully tested failure-recovery process and a GVM (allowing for a distributed store configuration). Further experiments that may be conducted include assessing the performance of the store when the number of concurrent client processes are increased in a stand-alone configuration, measuring the scalability of the store in a distributed configuration and a comparative performance evaluation of using checksums for recovery versus LSN.

Acknowledgements. The authors wish to acknowledge that this work was carried out within the Cooperative Research Center for Advanced Computational Systems established under the Australian Government's Cooperative Research Centers Program.

We wish to thank Andrew Tridgell and Paul Mackerras for many helpful suggestions and comments on this work, and would like to particularly acknowledge the inspiration provided by their package 'rsync' for the checksum-based recovery algorithm used by Platypus.

References

[Agrawal and Srikant 1994] AGRAWAL, R. AND SRIKANT, R.   1994.   Fast algorithms for mining association rules in large databases. In J. B. BOCCA, M. JARKE, AND C. ZANIOLO Eds., *VLDB'94, Proceedings of 20th International Conference on Very Large Data Bases, September 12-15, 1994, Santiago de Chile, Chile* (1994), pp. 487–499. Morgan Kaufmann.

[Blackburn 1998] BLACKBURN, S. M.   1998.   *Persistent Store Interface: A foundation for scalable persistent system design*. PhD thesis, Australian National University, Canberra, Australia. http://cs.anu.edu.au/~Steve.Blackburn.

[Blackburn and Stanton 1998] BLACKBURN, S. M. AND STANTON, R. B.   1998.   The transactional object cache: A foundation for high performance persistent system construction. In R. MORRISON, M. JORDAN, AND M. ATKINSON Eds., *Advances in Persistent Object Systems: Proceedings of the Eighth International Workshop on Persistent Object Systems, Aug. 30–Sept. 1, 1998, Tiburon, CA, U.S.A.* (San Francisco, 1998), pp. 37–50. Morgan Kaufmann.

[Brown and Morrison 1992] BROWN, A. AND MORRISON, R.   1992.   A generic persistent object store. *Software Engineering Journal 7*, 2, 161–168.

[Carey et al. 1994] CAREY, M. J., DEWITT, D. J., FRANKLIN, M. J., HALL, N. E., MCAULIFFE, M. L., NAUGHTON, J. F., SCHUH, D. T., SOLOMON, M. H., TAN, C. K., TSATALOS, O. G., WHITE, S. J., AND ZWILLING, M. J.   1994.   Shoring up persistent applications. In R. T. SNODGRASS AND M. WINSLETT Eds., *Proceedings of the 1994 ACM SIGMOD International Conference on Management of Data, Minneapolis, Minnesota, May 24-27, 1994*, Volume 23 of *SIGMOD Record* (June 1994), pp. 383–394. ACM Press.

[Carey et al. 1993] CAREY ET AL., M. J., DEWITT, D. J., AND NAUGHTON, J. F.   1993.   The 007 benchmark. In P. BUNEMAN AND S. JAJODIA Eds., *Proceedings of the 1993 ACM SIGMOD International Conference on Management of Data, Washington, D.C., May 26-28, 1993* (1993), pp. 12–21. ACM Press.

[Carey et al. 1988] CAREY, M. J., DEWITT, D. J., AND VANDENBERG, S. L.   1988.   A data model and query language for exodus. In H. BORAL AND P.-Å. LARSON Eds., *Proceedings of the 1988 ACM SIGMOD International Conference on Management of Data, Chicago, Illinois, June 1-3, 1988* (1988), pp. 413–423. ACM Press.

[Deutsch 1996] DEUTSCH, P.   1996.   RCF 1950 ZLIB compressed data format specification version 3.3. Network Working Group Request for Comments: 1950. http://www.faqs.org/rfcs/rfc1950.html.

[Fletcher 1982] FLETCHER, J.   1982.   An arithmetic checksum for serial transmissions. *IEEE Transactions on Communications 30*, 1 (Jan.), 247–253.

[Franklin 1996] FRANKLIN, M. J.   1996.   *Client Data Caching: A Foundation for High Performance Object Database Systems*, Volume 354 of *The Kluwer International Series in Engineering and Computer Science*. Kluwer Academic Publishers, Boston, MA, U.S.A. This book is an updated and extended version of Franklin's PhD thesis.

[Franklin 1997] FRANKLIN, M. J.   1997.   Concurrency control and recovery. In A. B. TUCKER Ed., *The Computer Science and Engineering Handbook*, pp. 1058–1077. CRC Press.

[Fürer 1999] Fürer, M.   1999.   Randomized splay trees. In *Proceedings of the tenth annual ACM-SIAM Symposium on Discrete Algorithms, 17-19 January 1999, Baltimore, Maryland.* (1999), pp. 903–904. ACM/SIAM.

[Härder and Reuter 1983] HÄRDER, T. AND REUTER, A.   1983.   Principles of transaction-oriented database recovery. *ACM Computing Surveys 15*, 4 (Dec.), 287–317.

[Kemper and Kossmann 1994] KEMPER, A. AND KOSSMANN, D.   1994.   Dual-buffering strategies in object bases. In J. B. BOCCA, M. JARKE, AND C. ZANIOLO Eds., *VLDB'94, Proceedings of 20th International Conference on Very Large Data Bases, September 12-15, 1994, Santiago de Chile, Chile* (1994), pp. 427–438. Morgan Kaufmann.

[Kleiman et al. 1995] KLEIMAN, S., SMALDERS, B., AND SHAH, D.   1995.   *Programming with Threads*. Prentice Hall.

[Knuth 1997] KNUTH, D. E.   1997.   *The Art of Computer Programming* (second ed.), Volume 3. Addison Wesley.

[Larson 1980] LARSON, P.-Å.   1980.   Linear hashing with partial expansions. In *Sixth International Conference on Very Large Data Bases, October 1-3, 1980, Montreal, Quebec, Canada, Proceedings* (1980), pp. 224–232. IEEE Computer Society Press.

[Larson 1988] LARSON, P.-Å.   1988.   Dynamic hash tables. *Communications of the ACM 31*, 4 (April), 446 – 457.

[Liskov et al. 1999] LISKOV, B., CASTRO, M., SHRIRA, L., AND ADYA, A.   1999.   Providing persistent objects in distributed systems. In R. GUERRAOUI Ed., *ECCOP'99 - Object-Oriented Programming, 13th European Conference, Lisbon, Portugal, June 14-18, 1999, Proceedings*, Volume 1628 of *Lecture Notes in Computer Science* (1999), pp. 230–257.

[Litwin 1980] LITWIN, W.   1980.   Linear hashing: A new tool for file and table addressing. In *Sixth International Conference on Very Large Data Bases, October 1-3, 1980, Montreal, Quebec, Canada, Proceedings* (1980), pp. 212–223. IEEE Computer Society Press.

[Matthes et al. 1996] MATTHES, F., MÜLLER, R., AND SCHMIDT, J. W.   1996.   Towards a unified model of untyped object stores: Experiences with the Tycoon Store Protocol. In *Advances in Databases and Information Systems (ADBIS'96), Proceedings of the Third International Workshop of the Moscow ACM SIGMOD Chapter* (1996).

[Mohan 1990] MOHAN, C.   1990.   Commit_LSN: A novel and simple method for reducing locking and latching in transaction processing systems. In D. McLEOD, R. SACKS-DAVIS, AND H.-J. SCHEK Eds., *16th International Conference on Very Large Data Bases, August 13-16, 1990, Brisbane, Queensland, Australia, Proceedings* (1990), pp. 406–418. Morgan Kaufmann.

[Mohan 1999] MOHAN, C.   1999.   Repeating history beyond ARIES. In M. P. ATKINSON, M. E. ORLOWSKA, P. VALDURIEZ, S. B. ZDONIK, AND M. L. BRODIE Eds., *VLDB'99, Proceedings of 25th International Conference on Very Large Data Bases, September 7-10, 1999, Edinburgh, Scotland, UK* (1999), pp. 1–17. Morgan Kaufmann.

[Mohan et al. 1992] MOHAN, C., HADERLE, D. J., LINDSAY, B. G., PIRAHESH, H., AND SCHWARZ, P.   1992.   ARIES: A transaction recovery method supporting fine-granularity locking and partial rollbacks using write-ahead logging. *TODS 17*, 1, 94–162.

[Sleator and Tarjan 1985] SLEATOR, D. D. AND TARJAN, R. E.   1985.   Self-adjusting binary search trees. *Journal of the ACM 32*, 3, 652–686.

[Taylor et al. 1998] TAYLOR, R., JANA, R., AND GRIGG, M.   1998.   Checksum testing of remote synchronsation tool. Technical Report DSTO-TR-0627 (March), Defence Science and Technology Organisation, Canberra, Australia. http://www.dsto.defence.gov.au.

[Tridgell 1999] TRIDGELL, A.   1999.   *Efficient Algorithms for Sorting and Synchronization.* PhD thesis, Australian National University.

[Tridgell and Mackerras 1998] TRIDGELL, A. AND MACKERRAS, P.   1998.   The rsync algorithm. Technical report, Australian National University. http://rsync.samba.org.

[Voruganti et al. 1999] VORUGANTI, K., ÖZSU, M. T., AND UNRAU, R. C.   1999.   An adaptive hybrid server architecture for client caching ODBMSs. In M. P. ATKINSON, M. E. ORLOWSKA, P. VALDURIEZ, S. B. ZDONIK, AND M. L. BRODIE Eds., *VLDB'99, Proceedings of 25th International Conference on Very Large Data Bases, September 7-10, 1999, Edinburgh, Scotland, UK* (1999), pp. 150–161. Morgan Kaufmann.

Appendix: Calculation of Page Checksums Using Differences

We note the following definition of an 'Adler' signature $r(x, k)$ corresponding to a range of bytes $x_0, x_1, \ldots, x_{k-1}$, where M is an arbitrary modulus (usually 2^{16} for performance reasons) [Deutsch 1996]:[15]

$$r_1(x, k) = (\sum_{i=0}^{k-1} x_i) \bmod M$$

$$r_2(x, k) = (\sum_{i=0}^{k-1} (k-i)x_i) \bmod M$$

$$r(x, k) = r_1(x, k) + M r_2(x, k)$$

Calculating Partial Signatures. The *partial checksum*, $p(x, k, s, e)$, corresponding to the contribution to $r(x, k)$ made by some sub-range of bytes $x_s, x_{s+1}, \ldots, x_e$ ($0 \leq s < e \leq k - 1$) is then:

---

[15] Adler-32 is a 32-bit extension of the Fletcher checksum [Fletcher 1982].

$$p_1(x,s,e) = (\sum_{i=s}^{e} x_i) \bmod M$$

$$p_2(x,k,s,e) = (\sum_{i=s}^{e}(k-i)x_i) \bmod M$$

$$p(x,k,s,e) = p_1(x,s,e) + Mp_2(x,k,s,e)$$

Calculating Delta Signatures. Consider the Adler signature $r(x,k)$ for a range of bytes $x_0, x_1, \ldots, x_{k-1}$. If the bytes in the range $x_s \ldots x_e$ are changed $x'_s \ldots x'_e$ ($0 \le s \le e \le (k-1)$), the components $r_1(x',k)$ and $r_2(x',k)$ of the new checksum $r(x',k)$ are then:

$$r_1(x',k) = (r_1(x,k) - p_1(x,s,e) + p_1(x',s,e)) \bmod M$$

$$= (r_1(x,k) - (\sum_{i=s}^{e} x_i) \bmod M + (\sum_{i=s}^{e} x'_i) \bmod M) \bmod M$$

$$= (r_1(x,k) + (\sum_{i=s}^{e}(x'_i - x_i)) \bmod M) \bmod M$$

$$r_2(x',k) = (r_2(x,k) - p_2(x,k,s,e) + p_2(x',k,s,e)) \bmod M$$

$$= (r_2(x,k) - (\sum_{i=s}^{e}(k-i)x_i) \bmod M + (\sum_{i=s}^{e}(k-i)x'_i) \bmod M) \bmod M$$

$$= (r_2(x,k) - (\sum_{i=s}^{e}(k-i)(x'_i - x_i)) \bmod M) \bmod M$$

If we further consider a *delta image*, $\bar{x}$ such that $\bar{x}_i = x'_i - x_i$ for the range of bytes corresponding to $x_s \ldots x_e$, and a partial checksum $p(\bar{x}, k, s, e)$ with respect to $\bar{x}_s \ldots \bar{x}_e$, we note that the above can be further simplified:

$$r_1(x',k) = (r_1(x,k) + p_1(\bar{x},s,e)) \bmod M$$
$$r_2(x',k) = (r_2(x,k) + p_2(\bar{x},k,s,e)) \bmod M$$
$$r(x',k) = (r(x,k) + p(\bar{x},k,s,e)) \bmod M$$

Thus the checksum (signature) $r(x',k)$ for some modified page of size k can be calculated from its previous checksum $r(x,k)$, and the partial checksum of the delta image for the region of the page that was changed, where the delta image is a simple byte-wise subtraction of old from new values.

Simplifying Signature Calculation. A naive implementation of the signature calculation would see a multiply in the inner loop. The following analysis shows how the (partial) signature implementation can be done with just a load, an add and a subtract in the inner loop.

$$p_2(x,k,s,e) = (\sum_{i=s}^{e}(k-i)x_i) \bmod M$$

$$= (\sum_{i=0}^{e-s}(k-i-s)x_{s+i}) \bmod M$$

$$= ((k-s)\sum_{i=0}^{e-s}x_{s+i} - \sum_{i=0}^{e-s}ix_{s+i}) \bmod M$$

$$= ((k-s)\sum_{i=0}^{e-s}x_{s+i} - \sum_{i=0}^{e-s}\sum_{j=0}^{i-1}x_{s+i}) \bmod M$$

From the above, we note the following recurrence relations:

$$f_p(x,e,i) = \begin{cases} f_p(x,e,i-1)+x_{e-i} & \text{if } i>0 \\ x_e & \text{if } i=0 \\ \textit{undefined} & \text{otherwise} \end{cases}$$

$$f(x,e,i) = \begin{cases} f(x,e,i-1)+f_p(x,e,i-1) & \text{if } i>0 \\ 0 & \text{if } i=0 \\ \textit{undefined} & \text{otherwise} \end{cases}$$

We therefore note the following expressions for p_1, p_2 and p:

$$p_2(x,k,s,e) = ((k-s)f_p(x,e,e-s) - f(x,e,e-s)) \bmod M$$
$$p_1(x,s,e) = f_p(x,e,e-s) \bmod M$$
$$p(x,k,s,e) = f_p(x,e,e-s) \bmod M + M(((k-s)f_p(x,e,e-s) - f(x,e,e-s)) \bmod M)$$

which leads us to the following pseudo-code:

```
int signature(char *x,   /* start of block */
              int L,     /* block length */
              int s,     /* start index of signature region */
              int e      /* end index of signature region */
              )
{
    for (int i = c, p_1 = 0, p_2 = 0; i > s; i+-) {
        p_1 -= x[i];
        p_2  - p_1;
    ;
    p_1 += x[s];
    p_2 += (l.-s) * p_1;
    p_1 &= (1<<16)-1;   /* mod 2^16 */
    p_2 &- (1<<16) 1;   /* mod 2^16 */
    return p_1  (p_2 << 16);
}
```

Fig. 6. Pseudo code for partial Adler-32 signature calculation.

Evaluating Partition Selection Policies Using the PMOS Garbage Collector

David S. Munro and Alfred L. Brown

Department of Computer Science, University of Adelaide,
South Australia 5005, Australia
{dave, fred}@cs.adelaide.edu.au

Abstract. Implementors of garbage collection algorithms are, in general, faced with determining a number of policy decisions such as when to collect, how to collect space or how to interact with the running application. With main memory collectors such decisions are usually influenced by results and experiences from a wealth of previous work. However, with partitioned collection of persistent objects stores, the implementor has a much smaller base to draw from. This is due not just to the small number of existing incremental object store collector implementations but also because the tradeoffs are significantly different from main-memory collection.

This paper reports on investigations, using the PMOS collector, into policy choices determining which partition should be chosen for collection. A previous study on partition selection postulated that a flexible selection policy can significantly reduce I/O and increase the amount of space reclaimed. That study was based on simulations on a synthetic object database. Here we test these conclusions by repeating the experiments using real applications, a partitioned store collector and an implemented persistent object store.

1   Introduction

The benefit of automatic storage management techniques to programmers has long been appreciated. For over thirty years, numerous and diverse garbage collection algorithms for programming languages have been devised, implemented, analysed and tested (See Wilson [17] for an excellent survey). When building such systems the implementor is faced with many policy decisions such as when to collect, how to collect space or how to interact with the running application. Making good choices here can have a dramatic effect on the collector and application performance and requires a detailed understanding of the algorithm's behaviour, the application's access patterns and the underlying run-time system. Fortunately the designer can appeal to a wealth of existing work to guide policy choice, ranging from analytical studies, simulations to measured implementations [16, 20, 10, 5].

However, with automatic reclamation of secondary storage for object databases and persistent stores, the trade-offs are different. The potential size of such object stores, coupled with their atomicity and stability requirements and the need to consider the overhead of I/O costs mean that garbage collection algorithms developed for programming languages are inherently unsuitable. Whilst there is a growing

G.N.C. Kirby, A. Dearle, and D.I.K. Sjøberg (Eds.): POS-9, LNCS 2135, pp. 125–137, 2001.

research interest in this area [1, 19, 13] there are still only a limited number of algorithms targeted at persistent object stores, even fewer implementations and virtually nothing by way of measurement and analysis.

One notable exception is the work of Cook et al [7, 8] on object database garbage collection. This seminal study investigates policies for *partitioned* collection where the address space is divided into a number of areas that can be independently collected. The work analyses, compares and measures a number of policy choices for selecting which partition to collect. Their results, based on simulation runs over a synthetic database, show that a flexible policy choice could use less I/O and reclaim more storage than random selection.

Our interest in their research relates to work on the PMOS collector [14]. PMOS is an incremental garbage collection algorithm specifically designed for reclaiming persistent object storage. The collector extends the Mature Object Space algorithm (sometimes known as the *train* algorithm) to ensure incrementality in a persistent context, to achieve recoverability, and to impose minimum constraints on the order of collection of areas of the persistent address space. PMOS is able to collect partitions in arbitrary orders whilst eliminating cyclic garbage, guaranteeing progress and minimising the impact on the I/O.

The initial implementation of the PMOS collector [12], built into a layered persistent object store [2], demonstrated the efficacy of the algorithm but highlighted some architectural assumptions and performance drawbacks. A new implementation, incorporating numerous lessons learned, has been designed and constructed enabling a range of collector policies to be researched. Here we report on results and experiments into partition selection policy, effectively repeating Cook's work and testing the simulation results against a working implementation. The conclusions show that whilst simulations may be reasonable predictors of real behaviour and offer a useful guide to policy choice, they often miss a subtle or unaccounted for interaction that arises in actual implementations.

2 Related Work

It has been argued that, in general, garbage collection algorithms for persistent object stores should be incremental, bounded, complete and designed to minimise I/O [19, 14]. However, early work on collection of databases and object stores were either non-incremental [4] or concerned with schemes that work in conjunction with concurrency and atomicity [9, 11]

Partitioned collection was first proposed by Bishop [3]. He details a scheme that divides the heap into multiple areas in such a way that each area can be garbage collected individually so that the collections do not interfere with processes that do not use the area being collected. To effect independent collection, each area keeps track of pointers both into the area (commonly called remsets) and out of the area (outrefs). Amsaleg et al [1] investigate partitioned collection in a client-server environment where the collector runs concurrently with user transactions. They use a mark-sweep algorithm that includes techniques to reduce the amount of logging required and avoid rollbacks.

Maheshwari and Liskov [13] discuss a scheme that is specifically targeted for the collection of large object stores. Like PMOS, this collector attempts to minimise the collector's impact on disk I/O and normal processing. It takes the partitioning approach by dividing up the store address space into separate areas and collecting these in individual increments. There are essentially two separate collection phases. The first is concerned with the collection of acyclic garbage whilst the second uses an incremental global marking scheme for finding inter-partition cycles of garbage.

Yong et all [19] undertake a detailed evaluation of incremental, reference counting and partitioned collection algorithms over a client-server persistent store. They conclude that an incremental algorithm gives better performance when tested under scalability and locality metrics.

None of these schemes, however, investigate selection policy. The comprehensive study by Cook et al in this area has done a useful job in starting the investigation of suitable policies. Their evaluation of different policies is derived from experiments using trace-driven simulations. The next section summarises their work on partition selection and discusses some of the differences between their experimental architecture and the PMOS implementation.

3   Review of Cook's Partition Selection Policies

In order to understand our evaluation methods and comparisons with Cook's work (which we shall call *PSP-S* for partition selection policy under simulation) we give an overview here of their testbed and experiments.

The database used in PSP-S is a forest of binary trees where each tree root is a root of reachability in the database. The trees are not strictly binary in that a number of additional edges connect random nodes in the same tree. The size of the database objects is randomly distributed around an average of 100 bytes bounded between 50 and 150 bytes. In addition a few of the leaf nodes comprise large objects of around 64Kb. Object connectivity is varied to test the effect on selection policies by adjusting the average number of pointers per object. The overall database size varies from 3 to 40 megabytes. The database is partitioned by physically dividing the address space into contiguous areas. The partition size varies depending on the database size, ranging from 192Kb to 800Kb.

The principal metric in PSP-S by which the policies are measured and compared is to select the partition that contains the most garbage. Six different selection policies are tested namely: mutated-partition, updated-pointer, weighted-pointer, random, oracle and no-collection.

- The mutated-partition policy selects the partition in which the greatest number of pointer updates has occurred since the last collection. The reasoning here is that the partition with the greatest pointer mutation is a good indicator of where the greatest amount of garbage may be.
- The updated-pointer policy selects the partition that has the greatest number of over-written pointers into it. The rationale is that when a pointer is overwritten, the object that was pointed at may have become garbage.
- The weighted-pointer policy is an extension of updated-pointer policy. It tries to take advantage of the notion that an over-written pointer nearer the root of an object graph may produce more garbage than an over-written pointer nearer the leaves since the connectivity of the database is potentially greater nearer the root.

To effect this in PSP-S, each pointer is given a weight that approximates its distance from the root. An exponentially weighted sum of updated pointers is maintained and the policy selects the partition with the greatest value.

- The random policy chooses a partition at random giving a guide to the effectiveness of the heuristic-based policies.
- The oracle policy selects the partition with the greatest amount of reclaimable garbage. The policy traverses each partition and remset in the database and for each partition calculates the amount of garbage that could be if that partition is selected. In general this is likely to be an expensive operation to run on a real system and hence the oracle policy is probably only achievable in a simulation. It, however, gives a guide to the effectiveness of the other policies.
- The no-collection policy does not perform any garbage collection and gives an indication of the total amount of storage that the test applications require.

The simulations involve runs that invoke around 25 collections. Database accesses involve partial tree traversals. A visited edge has a 95% chance that it will be traversed. Visited trees are randomly picked and for each such tree there is a 30% chance that it won't be traversed, 20% odds of a depth-first traversal and a 50% chance of a breadth-first traversal. A visited object has a 1% chance of being modified. Garbage is created by randomly deleting tree edges. The PSP-S uses a simple copying collector technique that moves live objects from the selected partition to a newly allocated partition. Note that the policies tested only select one partition for collection and that only one partition is reclaimed at each invocation. The collection is performed after a set number of pointer updates.

In terms of throughput, the results of the simulations show that the updated-pointer policy is better overall. The mutated-partition policy performs very poorly and often worse than no-collection. The relative difference between policies varied little with database size. For space usage, the updated-pointer again dominates, performing close to the oracle policy. In addition, investigations into the effects of object connectivity tested the policies over databases with varying numbers of pointers per object. The results show that all of the policies suffer performance degradation due to the increasing number of inter-partition references. Because of the conservatism of partitioned collection, unreachable data may be treated as live until further invocations. More interestingly, Cook observes that the increase in connectivity uncovers a significant increase in cyclic garbage, i.e., interconnected garbage that spans more than one partition. The amount of cyclic garbage appears to be very sensitive to even small increases in connectivity. This challenges previous views that cyclic garbage is rare and unlikely to cause space problems [16, 19].

3.1   Comments on PSP-S

The work in PSP-S presents a sound set of experiments and results that can help guide selection policy in an implementation. Of course, as with all simulations, the accuracy of the PSP-S results in a real system is unknown. One notable example of accuracy of simulation studies comes from Wilson [18], He has shown that many of the implemented policies for main-memory allocation have been derived from simulation results and may be far from optimal since the access patterns are significantly different from real application behaviour. The same could be true of PSP-S where somewhat arbitrary choices of access and update patterns together with the random pruning of objects are unlikely to capture the behaviour and locality characteristics of real applications and may skew the results.

4 PMOS

PMOS is one of a family of garbage collectors derived from the Mature Object Space collector. PMOS is concerned with the collection of secondary memory space from a persistent object system. It is tailored to incrementally and completely reclaim all garbage from such stores with minimum impact on I/O. PMOS is a copying collector and naturally supports compaction and clustering without the need for semi-space techniques. It can be implemented on stock hardware and does not require special operating systems support such as pinning or external pager control.

In PMOS the persistent address space is divided into a number of disjoint partitions called *cars*. The car is the unit of I/O and collection and one (or more) cars are collected at each invocation. To collect cycles, cars are grouped together into *trains*. To guarantee completeness it is sufficient to order the trains in terms of the (logical) time they are created. The algorithm proceeds by copying the potentially reachable data from cars into other cars in younger trains in such a way a cycle of garbage ends up in a single train. Further, any live data in that train will be copied to other trains thus isolating an unreferenced train of garbage objects. To minimise the I/O induced by the collection algorithm, PMOS defines two sets, a Δref set and a Δloc set. The Δref set records information about cross-car references that have been created or deleted. This information is used to update the remset of a target car at some later time (for example when the target car is faulted in). The Δloc set plays a similar role to the Δref set. As a copying collector, PMOS moves potentially reachable objects from one car to another. Since pointers are actual object addresses, any pointers, which reference an object that has been moved, need to be updated. The Δloc set records information about objects that have moved and enables pointer updates to cars on disk to be done lazily. When a car is fetched into memory it scans the Δloc set and applies any relevant pointer updates. In essence then the effect of pointer update and object movement are constrained to the object itself and these two sets. The reader can find a more detailed description of the algorithm in [14].

In [12] we describe PMOS#1, the first implementation of the algorithm, and present the lessons learned from this prototype. In the light of this, a new implementation, PMOS#2, has been designed and built to meet all the design goals of the original PMOS algorithm. In particular it allows any car to be selected for collection at each collector invocation. The PMOS#2 architecture can be divided into three layers, an object cache with which applications interact, a stable persistent heap of objects managed by PMOS#2 and an explicitly buffered stable store. PMOS#2 has been implemented in the stable heap layer of the Napier88 layered architecture [2]. The key differences between this architecture and the prototype implementation are the use of an object cache and tracking of pointer updates.

All persistent objects referenced are faulted into the object cache. Objects are written back to the persistent store either on a checkpoint operation or if the cache overflows. The object cache has its own independent collector that works effectively like a first generation collector. As a result of using the object cache only a small fraction of the pointer updates are ever seen by PMOS#2. The pointer updates that are seen by PMOS#2 are immediately recorded in the Δref set or appropriate car remembered set rather than being deferred. The underlying stable storage is buffered rather than memory-mapped.

These changes enhance the performance noticeably over PMOS#1 and also afford significant flexibility in implementing differing policies.

5   Pointer Selection in PMOS

One of the obvious appeals of PSP-S is the similarity between PMOS and the model used in the simulations. In particular, PMOS, like PSP-S, is an incremental, partitioned collector that uses a copying technique. This similarity aids the implementation of the same selection policies and adds some credence to comparisons with the PSP-S results. However, there are a number of differences that affect the extent to which the same policies can be replicated identically.

PMOS is complete. The algorithm will, after a finite number of invocations, reclaim all garbage, including cyclic garbage the spans more than one car. One of the criteria to effect completeness is the rule that every car must be selected eventually. In PMOS#2 this constraint is achieved by selecting cars in a round-robin fashion, using a configurable ordering of either youngest to oldest train or vice versa. To work in conjunction with the particular selection policy under test (e.g., updated pointer), a balance is struck between the tested policy and the completeness constraint so that on every nth invocation, the collector will choose a car from the round-robin set. The frequency of this is a configurable parameter that can be selected at run-time.

PMOS#2 has been built, populated and tested using a standard release Napier88 system. Using this configuration, a number of selection policies have been implemented and analysed. The policies tested include Updated-Pointer, Mutated-Partition, Weighted-Pointer, Random, No-Collection, Cyclic and Reverse-Cyclic. The Updated-Pointer and Mutated-Partition policies are identical to those defined in PSP-S. Because of the way that remsets are maintained in PMOS#2, these policies are easily implemented. Like PSP-S, the Weighted-Pointer policy is an extension of Updated-Pointer policy. However, the weighting is not calculated as an object depth from the tree root. Instead the weighting is calculated as the inverse depth (in terms of trains) that the object's car is from the youngest train. Thus, a higher weighting is given to updated cars that were nearer the roots when these cars were created. The premise being that updates to cars nearer the roots gives an indication of where the greatest garbage may be. This policy is chosen in preference to the PSP-S weighted-pointer definition since the weighting is much more easily calculated.

The cyclic and reverse cyclic policies use a simple round robin method. These polices are devised primarily to ensure that every car is selected eventually. At the start of a cycle, a snapshot is taken of which cars are in which trains, effectively producing an ordering of cars in trains. Using this snapshot, the cyclic policy selects the cars in order starting with the first car in the youngest train through to the last car of the oldest train. The reverse-cyclic policy is similar but starts with the first car of the oldest train through to the last car of the youngest train.

The experiments were carried out on a Sparc Ultra-10/440 with 128MB RAM and a 7200RPM 9Gbyte IDE disk and measurements taken from three consecutive phases, namely store setup, OO1 and Trees. Each set of experiments is repeated for car sizes of 64Kbytes and 256Kbytes. The store setup phase involves initialising a new store with objects from the Napier88 standard release. The OO1 phase involves running a version of the OO1 benchmark [6] written in Napier88 over a newly initialised store for each of the policies under test. The third phase runs a Trees program over a newly initialised store. The program effectively creates numerous trees of objects in the store, randomly selects a node and then replaces that node with a new tree.[1]

5.1   Store Setup

The store setup involves populating the object store with the Napier88 standard release system. This system includes the Napier88 programming environment with persistent browsers, editors, compilers and window managers and a collection of libraries (arithmetical, concurrency, graphical etc). A summary of the store after Setup under the No-Collection policy is given in Table 1 with totals on the left column and averages on the right. Cross-car references are pointers from one car to another and cross-train references are pointers from cars in one train to cars in another train. The management space is made up of the size of the remsets for the cars and the other related data structures such as train and car tables (see [13] for a description of these tables).

Table 1. Store summary after Setup if No Collections

Allocated space	36.853 MB	Bytes/Object	46.90
Management space	3.63 MB	Pointers /Object	2.59
Car size in bytes	65,536	Cross-Car Refs/Object	1.77
# of objects	823,962	Cross-Train Refs /Object	0.56
# of pointers	2,137,758	Objects/Car	1,256.04
# of cross-train references	177,796	Pointers /Car	3,258.78
# of cross-car references	802,069	Cross-Car Refs /Car	2,218.73
# of pointer updates	189,290	Cross-Train Refs /Car	700.49
# of data cars	680	# of Remset entries /Car	1,223.09

Table 2 gives an analysis of the object size spread and connectivity. Each table entry indicates the number of objects in the store whose size and numbers of pointer fields falls within a particular range. So for example there are 511 objects whose size is between 17 and 32 words and that have between 9 and 16 pointers. From these tables it is clear that the distribution in the store is far from even with several clusters of particular sizes and particular numbers of pointers.

---

[1] We hope to include additional results from OO7 runs as well as some interactive and other Napier88 applications in the near future

Table 2. Object Size vs Number of pointers using No-Collection policy

							Numbers of Pointers						
		0	**1**	**2**	**4**	**8**	**16**	**32**	**64**	**128**	**256**	**512**	**1024**	**1024+**
	2	419												
	4	19123	51659	147335										
	8	18596		537578	24205	1317								
	16	4410		1156	881	4754	3408							
	32	285		965	202	7	511	1248						
	64	2298	1	344	127	93	48	82	233					
	128	1500		184	90	38	136	14	5	28				
	256	97		55	48	41	16	89	29		45			
	512	17		8	6	19	7	11	40	16	1			
	1024	35		1		5	6	4	1	16	4	50		
	024+	11					3			1		1	1	

Table 3 summarises the cross-car pointers for the No-Collection policy showing that for both 64Kb and 256Kb cars there are again clusters and a number of popular cars. It also shows that cars are fairly dense with objects and that there is a fairly high cross-linking between cars, reflecting the high inter-connectivity of the Napier88 programming environment. The unusual entry in the first column of Table 3 indicates a car with up to 512 objects and no remset entries. As explained in [13], Napier88 defines a number of objects that are heavily referenced such as the abstract machine root object, nil, nullstring etc. These objects are essentially *immortal* since they will never become unreachable and will also incur large remsets because of their popularity. To avoid this, we define a root train whose cars contain objects that form the roots for collection. The cars of this train are never collected and since the objects in these cars never move, there is no need to maintain their remsets.

5.2 Comparing Selection Policies

Table 4 illustrates the measured results from testing different selection policies of a sequence of Napier88 programs. Each test run begins with the setup program, as explained above, to initialise the store with the standard Napier88 environment, followed by a full run of the OO1 benchmark program and finally a run of the Trees program. The table shows the number of bytes collected by each of the selection policies for each of the program runs with results for both car sizes.

The OO1 benchmark run involves creating a 20MB database containing 20,000 interconnected parts on which the following queries are performed:

insert: 10 transactions are executed. Each transaction enters 100 new parts into the database and commits. Each new part is connected to 3 other (randomly selected) parts.

lookup: A set of 1,000 random part identifiers is generated. 10 transactions are then executed, each of which fetches the set of parts from the database.

traverse: 10 transactions are executed. Each transaction selects a part at random and recursively traverses the connected parts, down to a depth of 7 (a total of 3,280 parts, with possible duplicates). A null procedure is called for each part traversed.

scan: All parts in the database are fetched once in index order.

insert100: Generates the same workload as insert, except that 100 transactions are executed.

update: 500 update transactions are executed. Each transaction reads and updates 10 parts chosen at random from a contiguous range of 10% of the database

The queries are carried out in the order insert, lookup, traverse, scan, insert100, lookup, traverse, scan, update, lookup, traverse and scan.

Table 3. Objects per car vs Number of remset entries in No-Collection

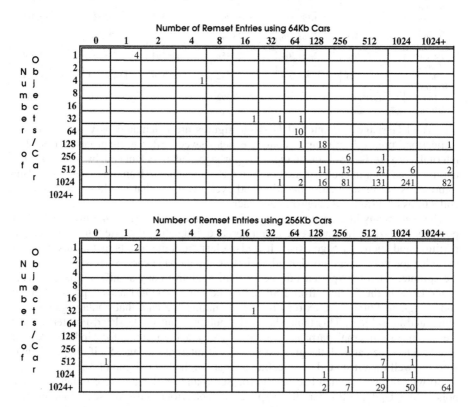

Number of Remset Entries using 64Kb Cars

Number of objects per Car	0	1	2	4	8	16	32	64	128	256	512	1024	1024+
1		4											
2													
4				1									
8													
16													
32							1	1	1				
64									10				
128									1	18			1
256											6	1	
512	1								11	13	21	6	2
1024							1	2	16	81	131	241	82
1024+													

Number of Remset Entries using 256Kb Cars

Number of objects per Car	0	1	2	4	8	16	32	64	128	256	512	1024	1024+
1		2											
2													
4													
8													
16													
32						1							
64													
128													
256											1		
512	1											7	1
1024									1			1	1
1024+									2	7	29	50	64

The Trees program is an artificial program written specifically to generate store garbage and is not dissimilar to the test programs used in PSP-S. It creates tree of objects with a fixed depth and breadth. An arbitrary node of the given tree is chosen randomly and replaced with a new tree. This is repeated 1,000 times thus creating a significant amount of garbage.

The same sets of experiments are carried out over a store based on 64KB and 256KB car sizes. The incremental collector is called once for every 400 pointer updates to the store. Every 100th collector invocation a car is chosen from the cyclic list of cars to guarantee completeness as explained above. The train policy is fixed in these runs whereby a new train is created once the youngest train is found to have 16 cars on completion of a checkpoint of garbage collection

Table 4. Bytes of garbage collected per selection policy

Policy / Car Size	Setup		OO1		Trees	
	64KB	256KB	64KB	256KB	64KB	256Kb
No collections	0	0	0	0	0	0
Updated pointer	185,632	699,140	317,360	851,224	186,552	828,076
Weighted pointer	194,120	364,180	217,572	540,372	220,420	508,132
Mutated partition	431,520	1,059,732	585,180	1,184,424	471,516	1,263,068
Random	429,976	1,195,932	461,700	1,338,552	463,836	1,195,932
Cyclic	523,548	2,363,976	523,548	2,613,468	523,548	2,365,432
Reverse Cyclic	792,080	2,431,304	872,468	2,633,504	793,264	2,431,304
Internal Garbage	558,244	768,800	663,332	876,136	12,474,080	16,519,624
Total Garbage	11,046,034	11,046,034	11,157,392	11,157,392	29,053,260	29,053,260

The Total Garbage and Internal Garbage figures are calculated only under the No Collections policy by taking a complete heap sweep after each program run. The internal garbage is a subset of the total garbage and is calculated by summing the unreferenced data in each car, i.e., data in cars unreachable from a remset entry. This figure does not include cross-partition and cyclic garbage that would be uncovered if collections occurred in an appropriate order.

There are many inferences one can make from the data in Table 4. One of the clear points is the size of internal versus total garbage, indicating the extent to which cross-partition and cyclic garbage exists. It is also clear from the results that almost none of the selection policies are good at all at finding the garbage cars. Surprisingly, none of the „pointer-counting" policies do better than random to any significant degree. This is at odds with the findings from PSP-S. For the setup and OO1 tests, Updated-Pointer and Weighted-Pointer are extremely bad at finding the cars that contain garbage as illustrated in Table 5. This table shows the policy count for Updated-Pointer against the amount of internal garbage in bytes. Ideally a high count for Updated-Pointer should select the car with the greatest amount of internal garbage. So if the policy was working well then it should be selecting the cars in the last column of Table 5.

So why do we get such bad results for Setup and OO1 with these policies? For a policy like Updated-Pointer, the application behaviour must be such that pointer updates are not creating garbage. This result may indeed reflect the behaviour of the Napier88 setup program and OO1 where a significant part of the computation involves adding entries to the front of linked lists and inserting entries into graph-based data structures. So put simply, frequent updates to the head of a list or inserts into a graph will result in Updated-Pointer counts but no garbage. Most likely what we are observing are additions to the Napier88 type-checker hash-table in the setup program and random insertions into the parts database in OO1. Such application behaviour, we claim, is not uncommon and thus questions the efficacy of the Updated-Pointer policy.

Table 5. Updated Pointer vs Bytes of internal garbage after OO1

Internal Garbage in bytes

	0	1	2	4	8	16	32	64	128	256	512	1024	1024+
0	544						2			4	2	1	2
1	12									1	2	1	3
2	21							1		4			11
4	19								2	3			15
8	25									1	1		7
16	19								2	1		2	5
32	69												1
64	22												2
128	6							1	1	40	12		
256										8	9		1
512													
1024													
024+													

(Row labels, read vertically on left: U p d a t e d   p o i n n t e d r / p o i u n t e r / c o u n t e r)

Table 6. Updated pointer vs Bytes of internal garbage after Trees

Internal Garbage in bytes

	0	1	2	4	8	16	32	64	128	256	512	1024	1024+
0	452						2			4	1	1	3
1	13									1	1	1	4
2	19									2	1		28
4	21							1		2			53
8	24									2		1	91
16	15								1			2	125
32	22												62
64	21												1
128	6												1
256													
512													
1024													
024+													

A similar story is true for the Trees program. There is significantly more garbage to find and the Updated-Pointer policy fairs better than in OO1 and Setup but still no better than Random. As shown in Table 6, the pointer policy is still choosing many cars with no garbage.

6   Conclusions and Future Work

Carefully managed simulations, like PSP-S, are very often good predictors of real behaviour. However, our experimental results are surprising and suggest that the winning policies from the simulations are counter-productive in reality. There are probably numerous reasons for the discrepancies.

Primarily, the success of the updated, mutated and weighted policies depends largely on the low connectivity and locality of objects in the store. The assumption is that most garbage is localised and does not span partitions. Clearly this conflicts with the standard Napier88 store that has high connectivity but also suggests investigations into object placement and copying policies may benefit. Secondly, these policies all suffer in situations where there are frequent manipulations to data structures that do not create garbage. The heuristics erroneously suggests local garbage when in fact no new garbage is created. In this scenario the problem is exacerbated over time as partitions containing the real garbage continue to be ignored. We suggest that such updates (linked lists, graphs, queues etc) are very common in database and object stores and certainly indicative of the behaviour of the store setup and OO1.

The use of an object cache (local heap) in the Napier88 system prevents many of the pointer updates from being visible to PMOS#2. Consequently a significant fraction of the non-garbage producing pointer updates are never visible to the selection policies. We would anticipate therefore that, without an object cache, the measured selection policies would have been even less effective. We believe that most persistent object stores and object-oriented databases of a reasonable size generally use an object cache and that our results illustrate typical behaviour.

Our findings suggest then that a more complex policy is needed to find the cars that contain the most garbage. Such a policy should take account of object cache behaviour into its heuristic. Alternatively some form of self-adaptive policy based on the direction of cross-train pointers is worthy of investigation.

Acknowledgements. This work was carried out in this paper is supported in part by Australian Research Council grant A10033014.

References

1. Amsaleg, L., Franklin, M. & Gruber, O. „Efficient Incremental Garbage Collection for Workstation/Server Database Systems". ESPRIT BRA Project 6309 FIDE$_2$ (1994).

2. Brown, A.L., Dearle, A., Morrison, R., Munro, D. & Rosenberg, J. „A Layered Persistent Architecture for Napier88". In *Security and Persistence*, Rosenberg, J. & Keedy, J.L. (ed), Springer-Verlag (1990) pp 155-172.

3. Bishop, P.B. „Computer systems with a very large address space and garbage collection.". Ph.D. Thesis, Massachusetts Institute of Technology (1977).

4. Campin, J. & Atkinson, M.P. „A Persistent Store Garbage Collector with Statistical Facilities". Universities of Glasgow and St Andrews (1986).

5. Cook, J.E., Klauser, A., Wolf, A.L. & Zorn, B.G. „Semi-automatic, Self-adaptive Control of Garbage Collection Rates in Object Databases". In Proc. *ACM SIGMOD International Conference on Management of Data*, Montreal, Canada (1996) pp 377-388.

6. Cattell, R.G.G. & Skeen, J. „Object Operations Benchmark". *ACM Transactions on Database Systems* 17, 1 (1992) pp 1-31.

7. Cook, J.E., Wolf, A.L. & Zorn, B.G. „Partition selection policies in object database garbage collection". In Proc. *ACM SIGMOD International Conference on Management of Data*, Minneapolis, MN (1994) pp 371-382.

8. Cook, J.E., Wolf, A.L. & Zorn, B.G. „A Highly Effective Partition Selection Policy for Object Database Garbage Collection.". *IEEE Transactions on Knowledge and Data Engineering* 10, 1 (1998) pp 153-172.
9. Detlefs, D.L. „Concurrent Atomic Garbage Collection". Ph.D. Thesis, Carnegie-Mellon University (1989).
10. Hosking, A., Moss, J.E.B. & Stefanovic, D. „A Comparative Performance Evaluation of Write Barrier Implementations". In Proc. *Proceedings of the ACM Conference on Object-Oriented Programming Systems, Languages, and Applications (OOPSLA)*, Vancouver, Canada (1992) pp 92-109.
11. Kolodner, E., Liskov, B. & Weihl, W. „Atomic Garbage Collection: Managing a Stable Heap". In Proc. *ACM SIGMOD International Conference on the Management of Data*, Portland, Oregon (1989) pp 15-25.
12. Munro, D.S., Brown, A.L., Morrison, R. & Moss, J.E.B. „Incremental Garbage Collection of a Persistent Object Store using PMOS". In *Advances in Persistent Object Systems*, Morrison, R., Jordan, M. & Atkinson, M.P. (ed), Morgan Kaufmann (1999) pp 78-91.
13. Maheshwari, U. & Liskov, B. „Partitioned Garbage Collection of a Large Object Store". In Proc. *ACM SIGMOD'97*, Phoenix, Arizona (1997) pp 313-323.
14. Moss, J.E.B., Munro, D.S. & Hudson, R.L. „PMOS: A Complete and Coarse-Grained Incremental Garbage Collector for Persistent Object Stores". In Proc. *7th International Workshop on Persistent Object Systems (POS7)*, Cape May, NJ, USA (1996).
15. Unger, D. & Jackson, F. „Tenuring Policies for Generation-Based Storage Reclamation". In Proc. *OOPSLA* (1988) pp 1-17.
16. Ungar, D. „Generation Scavenging: A Non-disruptive High Performance Storage Reclamation Algorithm". *ACM SIGPLAN Notices* 19, 5. Proc. ACM SIGPLAN Notices Software Engineering Symposium on Practical Software Development Environments, Pittsburgh PA (1984) pp 157-167.
17. Wilson, P.R. „Uniprocessor Garbage Collection Techniques". In *Lecture Notes in Computer Science 637*, Springer-Verlag (1992) pp 1-42.
18. Wilson, P.R., Johnstone, M.S., Neely, M. & Boles, D. „Dynamic Storage Allocation: A Survey and Critical Review". In *Lecture Notes in Computer Science 986*, Baker, H.G. (ed), Springer-Verlag (1995) pp 1-116.
19. Yong, V., Naughton, J. & Yu, J. „Storage Reclamation and reorganization in client-server persistent object stores". In Proc. *10th International Conference on Data Engineering* (1994) pp 120-131.
20. Zorn, B.G. „Comparative Performance Evaluation of Garbage Collection Algorithms". Ph.D. Thesis, University of California at Berkeley (1989).

TMOS: A Transactional Garbage Collector

John Zigman[1], Stephen M. Blackburn[2], and J. Eliot B. Moss[2]

[1] Department of Computer Science
Australian National University
Canberra ACT 0200, Australia
John.Zigman@cs.anu.edu.au

[2] Department of Computer Science
University of Massachusetts
Amherst, MA, 01003, USA
{steveb,moss}@cs.umass.edu

Abstract. Defining persistence in terms of reachability is fundamental to achieving orthogonality of persistence. It is implicit to the principles of orthogonal persistence and is a part of the ODMG 3.0 data objects standard. Although space reclamation in the context of persistence by reachability can be achieved automatically using garbage collection, relatively few papers address the problem of implementing garbage collection in a transactional storage system. A transactional GC algorithm must operate correctly in the face of failure, and in particular must deal with the problem of transaction abort, which by undoing changes such as the deletion of references, subverts the GC reachability axiom of 'once garbage always garbage'.

In this paper we make two key contributions. First, we present a generic approach to the design of transactional collectors that promotes clarity, generality, and understandability, and then using this approach, we present a new transactional garbage collection algorithm, TMOS. Our design approach brings together three independent components—a mutator, a transactional store, and a GC algorithm. TMOS represents the application of the Mature Object Space family of GC algorithms to the transactional context through our approach to transactional GC design.

1 Introduction

The practicality and value of abstraction over persistence is increasingly being acknowledged in the mainstream of the database community [Snodgrass 1999; Maier 1999]. While different persistent systems vary in their adherence to the principles of orthogonal persistence, most, including the Java Data Objects (JDO) [Sun Microsystems 1999] and ODMG-3 [Cattell et al. 2000] standards, define persistence in terms of *reachability*. Persistence by reachability (PBR) is a simple corollary of the principle of persistence identification [Atkinson and Morrison 1995] which states that persistent objects are not identified explicitly, but implicitly through transitive reachability from some known persistent root (or roots). With PBR, once an object ceases to be reachable it is by definition not identifiable and is thus garbage. This paper addresses the problem of automatically collecting such garbage in a transactional setting.

Transactions are a means of managing concurrency and recovery in a persistent system. Central to transactions are the notions of atomicity and serializability. While

G.N.C. Kirby, A. Dearle, and D.I.K. Sjøberg (Eds.): POS-9, LNCS 2135, pp. 138–156, 2001.

transactions are ubiquitous in database systems, the rigidity of conventional ACID transactional semantics [Härder and Reuter 1983] and their basis in isolationist rather than cooperative approaches to concurrency control appears to have retarded their integration into programming languages [Blackburn and Zigman 1999]. Nonetheless, transactions represent one important and practical solution to the problem of concurrency control in orthogonally persistent systems, and furthermore are established in persistence standards such as JDO and ODMG-3. Thus the integration of garbage collection into a transactional setting is important.

The argument for space reclamation in *primary* storage is principally based on the relatively high cost of memory. However, for *secondary* storage, the space cost argument is less significant, and the impact of a reclamation mechanism on access characteristics may become the overriding concern. Continued manipulation of a persistent object graph will inevitably result in the store becoming fragmented, and in the limit, each live object will reside on a distinct store page. Garbage collection will improve the clustering of secondary storage, and thus improve retrieval performance. Such clustering can occur either as an explicit function of the garbage collector, or implicitly as a side effect of object reclamation and subsequent space reuse by new objects.

The Problem of Transactional Garbage Collection. A transactional garbage collector must address two fundamental issues, that of safely and efficiently collecting garbage and that of maintaining consistency in the face of concurrency and transactions. The interdependencies between these issues are complex and lead to involved algorithms that are often hard to describe. The resulting algorithms make it hard to distill the issues and choices and separate those that are central to correctness from those are motivated by efficiency. Thus it is often hard to understand such algorithms and have confidence in their correctness. This is the high-level problem which this paper addresses. We do this through the use of an appropriately abstract framework for relating garbage collection and transactions.

In addition to presenting an abstract framework, we identify and address a number of concrete issues common to transactional garbage collector implementations.

Identifying Garbage in the Face of Rollback. The axiom *once garbage always garbage* is key to the correctness of garbage collection algorithms. It says that once a collector has identified some object as unreachable, that object may be *safely* collected—once the object is unreachable it has no means for becoming reconnected to the object graph. However, the introduction of *transactions* demands a re-examination of the axiom.[1] Through *atomicity* transactions exhibit all-or-nothing semantics: either the effects of a transaction are seen completely or not at all. *Isolation* is used to ensure consistency by guaranteeing that other transactions are not exposed to partial results that are subsequently rolled back. A transactional garbage collector must therefore either operate in strict isolation from user transactions (which could place very expensive constraints on

---

[1] For simplicity we specifically address ACID transactions [Härder and Reuter 1983] throughout this paper. Generalization of this approach to include the many flavors of advanced transaction models will in many cases be trivial, but a thorough analysis of the intermix of garbage collection with such models is beyond the scope of this work.

the ordering of user and GC activities), or be aware that partial results may be rolled back, and so the axiom of once garbage always garbage must be carefully reinterpreted. Fortunately, transactions also have the property of *durability*, which means that once a transaction has successfully committed it can't be undone. This, combined with the once garbage always garbage axiom means that it is safe to use any committed image of the store for the identification of garbage, even *stale* (superseded) images.

Additions to the Object Graph. The allocation of new objects poses different problems. If a transaction rolls back, all trace of that transaction must be undone, including the allocation of any objects within the transaction. A second problem relating to allocation is that not all objects created in the course of a transaction will be reachable from persistent roots when the transaction commits. Clearly it would be desirable to avoid the overhead of persistent object allocation for such transient objects.

A simple way of dealing with the first problem is to allocate space in the store for the object during the transaction and then reclaim that space if the transaction is rolled back. A better approach, which addresses both problems, is to defer the allocation of store space until the transaction commit. Any object created by the transaction that is not reachable from a store object modified by the transaction cannot be reachable from the store's root, and is thus garbage. This approach also has a disadvantage, as it raises the question of how newly allocated objects will be identified (i.e., what form an OID or reference to such an object would take) prior to the allocation of a corresponding store object at commit time.

Collecting Both Transient and Persistent Data. When implementing garbage collection for a persistent language, the problems of disk and heap garbage collection can be dealt with either together or separately. On one hand a single mechanism collects a unified persistent space which includes transient heap data, while on the other hand the problems can be seen as distinct and addressed separately.

We take the approach of distinct heap and disk collectors on the basis of two significant observations. The first relates directly to the previously mentioned problem of additions to the object graph—if persistent space is only allocated for objects that are persistently reachable at commit time, the distinction between persistent and transient data is strong. The second hinges on the *substantially* different cost factors for heap and disk collection. The time and space tradeoffs to be made for each are vastly different. Thus a dependence on random access to objects may be quite reasonable for a heap collector, but totally unrealistic for disk-bound objects.

The remainder of this paper is structured as follows. In section 2 we discuss related work. We then discuss our framework for designing transactional garbage collection algorithms in section 3. In section 4 we apply our framework, adapting the MOS [Hudson and Moss 1992] garbage collection algorithm to a transactional context. In section 5 we briefly discuss opportunities for future work and then conclude in section 6.

2   Related Work

Transactional Garbage Collection. The literature records three substantially different approaches to transactional garbage collection. Kolodner and Weihl [1993] adapt a semi-space copying collector to a transactional persistent heap. In their system the mutator and collector are tightly coupled and must synchronize to ensure that the mutator sees a coherent heap image. By using a persistent heap they make no distinction between the collection of transient and persistent data.

Amsaleg, Franklin, and Gruber [1995] tackle the problem of transactional GC in the setting of an orthodox OODB. They examine the interaction of the garbage collector with the store at a detailed level, enumerating cases which cause erroneous behavior in the face of transaction abort and rollback. This leads to a set of invariants that govern the marking mechanism and the object deletion phase of their incremental mark and sweep collector. Although capable of operating over a distributed partitioned object space, their algorithm is unable to detect cycles of garbage which span partitions—a problem which was subsequently addressed by Maheshwari and Liskov [1997].

Skubiszewski and Valduriez [1997] define the concept of *GC-consistent cuts* as a means of establishing a consistent context in which to apply the *three color marking* concurrent collection algorithm [Dijkstra et al. 1978]. Their approach is safe, concurrent and complete, but it is not incremental (no garbage can be reclaimed until the mark phase has completed with respect to the entire database). *GC-consistent cuts* are similar to the incremental coherent snapshot mechanism we describe in section 4.3.

While Amsaleg et al. do highlight key issues for transactional garbage collection, neither theirs nor any of the other papers propose general methodologies for intersecting garbage collection with transactions. Rather, they each present specific solutions based on ad-hoc methodologies for dealing with this complex interaction.

Object Clustering. Yong, Naughton, and Yu [1994] examine a variety of different garbage collection algorithms in the context of a client-server system, and conclude that incremental partitioned garbage collection provides greater scope for reclustering and better scalability than other algorithms. Cook, Wolf, and Zorn [1994] extend this work by examining a range of partition selection policies including: no collection, random, mutated (most pointer updates) and best possible (oracle). Cook, et al. show that a practical and appropriate policy can improve the overall I/O performance of the store. This indicates that incremental partitioned garbage collection can have practical benefits for object store performance, and so motivates further examination and development of such systems.

Lakhamraju, Rastogi, Seshadri, and Sudarshan [2000] discuss the general problem of on-line reorganization in object databases and present IRA, an algorithm which can be applied to copying collectors, online clustering algorithms and other contexts where it is necessary to move objects in the presence of concurrent access to those objects. IRA is able to work when object references are physical (i.e. there is no indirection between user-level and store-level object identification). In TMOS we address this problem through the use of indirection.

Mature Object Space Collector. MOS is a copying collector that is incremental, complete and safe [Hudson and Moss 1992]. PMOS extends MOS to work in the context of a persistent heap [Moss et al. 1996].[2] PMOS is designed to be atomic, but without binding to any particular recovery mechanism. PMOS achieves incrementality and minimizes I/O overheads by delaying the update of partition meta-data and changes to references due to garbage collector activity. It requires a degree of synchronization and co-operation between the mutator and the garbage collector. Munro et al. [1999] explore an initial implementation of PMOS within a system without write barriers. In their implementation the heap is scanned to provide consistent meta-data for the local garbage identification process to operate correctly.

This paper extends the literature by generalizing the problem of transactional collection and developing an abstract framework through which arbitrary collection algorithms can be safely applied to a transactional context. We achieve this generality by providing an abstraction of garbage collection which separates *local* and *global* issues and the problem of *identifying garbage* from that of *removing/reclaiming garbage*. Moreover, we apply this framework to the MOS algorithm, yielding TMOS, which is safe, concurrent, complete and incremental.

3 An Approach to Transactional GC

In this section we present a framework and methodology for the design of garbage collection algorithms for transactional persistent stores. We outline significant issues involved in the design and describe the interrelations between them. Our framework is intentionally abstract and general, and rests upon a simple system model for transactional garbage collection based on a *collection algorithm*, a *store*, and a *mutator*. By raising the level of abstraction we reduce the assumptions made with respect to any particular component, thereby admitting as wide a range of collection algorithms, storage systems, and classes of mutator as possible. Our goal is to facilitate rapid *and correct* design by identifying and addressing the primary issues associated with the intermix of garbage collection and transactions. A strong and safe design provides a good basis for subsequent optimization, at which point the dependencies on each of the system components may be tightened as necessary to minimize impedance between the components as far as possible.

3.1 A System Model for Transactional Garbage Collection

The system has three distinct components: a mutator (of which there may be multiple instances), a transactional store, and a garbage collector. The system model is based on the transactional object cache architecture [Blackburn and Stanton 1999], which while providing strong transactional semantics, allows efficient implementations by virtue of the mutator having direct access to the store's cache. A consequence of this architecture is a clear separation of store and heap collection mechanisms. Indeed, this model does

---

[2] PMOS sacrifices the unidirectional write barrier optimization of the original MOS algorithm in order gain the flexibility of being able to collect cars in any order.

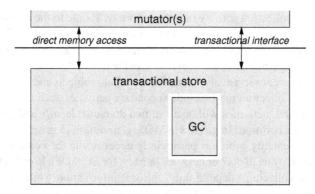

Fig. 1. Generic system model for transactional garbage collection, consisting of a mutator (or mutators), a transactional store, and a garbage collection algorithm.

not preclude the existence of a mutator without a collection mechanism for transient data (a C++ program for example).

Mutator. Each mutator has direct access to store objects cached in main memory. Access to the objects is mediated through a transactional protocol [Blackburn and Stanton 1999]. Before a mutator transaction reads *(updates)* an object for the first time, it informs the store of its read *(write)* intention with respect to that object. The store will guarantee availability and transactional coherency of the object from the time that it acknowledges the mutator's intention until the mutator transaction commits or aborts.[3] A mutator may concurrently execute multiple transactions, however the mutator must ensure transactional isolation is maintained. The protocol is sufficiently abstract to allow the store to employ 'copy-out' or 'in-place' object buffering, and either optimistic or lock-based coherency policies.

Transactional Store. The store must support conventional transactional semantics with respect to a graph of uniquely identifiable objects made available to the mutator as described above. Ideally the store would support multiple concurrent mutator transactions, and implement layered transactions, although neither of these are requirements of the our system model.

Garbage Collection Algorithm. The garbage collection algorithm removes objects that are no longer usable by any mutator. An object that has become permanently unreachable (i.e., as consequence of a committed transaction) from the persistent root is clearly unusable by the mutator and is thus considered garbage. To the extent that the garbage collector performs any operations beyond reclaiming garbage (such as compacting for example), those operations must also be completely transparent with respect to the

---

[3] This does not preclude the use of a store that implements a STEAL policy. However, such a store must use a transparent mechanism such as memory protection to ensure that the page is transparently faulted back into memory upon any attempt by the mutator to access it.

mutator. Garbage collection activity must therefore be visible to the mutator as only as a logical 'no-op' (it consumes resources but does not otherwise visibly affect state).

Conceptually, a garbage collection algorithm must undertake two distinct activities: the *identification* of garbage, and the subsequent *collection* of that garbage. The algorithm must *safely* (perhaps conservatively) identify unreachable objects and conceptually mark them as garbage. Collection may include secondary activities such as compaction and clustering. In general, activities will occur in two domains: *locally* and *globally*. Algorithms typically use partitions (e.g., *cars* in MOS, *generations* in generational collectors) to increase incrementality, which is particularly necessary in the context of significant temporal overheads (due to disk or network latency, for example). Local activities (such as intra-partition collection) depend only on local information while global activities (such as the reclamation of cross-partition cycles) utilize local progress to work towards global properties of completeness. The mapping of the two activities onto these domains is as follows:

- *Local identification* of garbage involves a local (typically intra-partition) reachability analysis of objects with respect to some known (possibly empty) set of references to objects within the local domain.
- *Local collection* of garbage may simply involve deleting those objects not identified as reachable by the local identification phase.
- *Global identification* of garbage involves the identification of garbage not identifiable locally (such as cross-partition cycles).
- *Global collection* of garbage simply involves removing those objects (or partitions) that are not reachable.

3.2   Designing a Transactional GC Algorithm

The design of a transactional garbage collector must address both *correctness* and *performance*. We approach correctness by first establishing the correctness of the collection algorithm on which the transactional collector will be based, and then ensuring that the correctness is not compromised by its introduction into a transactional context. However, correctness alone is not adequate. The reclamation of space (automatically or not) can only be justified by an improvement in long term performance—there is little point in employing a reclamation mechanism if the system will perform better without it.[4] In achieving this, the collection mechanism must impose minimal interference in terms of overall throughput and/or responsiveness of the store operation. We now address the separate concerns of correctness and performance in transactional garbage collector design.

Correctness. We identify the key correctness issues with respect to: *local identification* of garbage, *local collection* of garbage, *global identification* of garbage, and *global collection* of garbage.

---

[4] While the need to reclaim space in an in-memory context is clear, secondary storage is by comparison both very cheap and very expensive to access, making the benefits less clear cut.

Local identification. correctness depends on the *collector* being able to see a consistent and valid view of the object graph and the roots for the region being collected in the face of mutator updates and rollback.

Local collection. correctness depends on the *mutator* being able to see a consistent and valid view of the object graph in the face of the collector deleting (and possibly moving) objects. The deletion of objects identified as garbage raises no significant correctness issues because unreachable objects cannot be seen by the mutator. However, ancillary actions associated with the collection process (such as the movement of live objects to reduce fragmentation) have the potential to impact the mutator. Our system model includes a guarantee of consistency with respect to the objects seen by the mutator for the duration of a transaction, so any change to object addresses must not be visible to a mutator. However, because transactional isolation prevents the mutator from storing object references across transactions, the collector need only be concerned with *intra-transactional* consistency of object addresses seen by the mutator.

Global identification. corrrectness depends on the *collector* being able to see a consistent and valid view of the reachability metadata (e.g. inter-partition reachability information). Such metadata may be changed as a consequence of a mutator updating an object reference.

Global collection. correctness depends on the *mutator* being able to see a consistent and valid view of the object graph in the face of the collector deleting (and possibly moving) objects. Correctness issues for global collection thus mirror those of local collection. For some algorithms this phase is made even simpler because the collection of an unreachable partition and its constituent objects does not lead to the movement of any live objects.

Each of these correctness criteria can be trivially (though inefficiently) addressed by isolating the garbage collector actions from the mutator by performing the collector actions within a user-level transaction.

Performance. Recall that garbage collection should be justified in terms of long-term performance improvement. In the case of persistent data, locality improvements resulting from the positive clustering and defragmentation effects of collection are likely to be the dominant source of performance improvement. We now address issues of performance under the headings of two dimensions which we seek to maximize—*responsiveness* and *throughput*—which correspond to the fundamental temporal dimensions of latency and bandwidth respectively. The relative importance of each of these concerns will depend heavily on the context in which the collector is to be applied. A system with a high degree of user interaction may value responsiveness over throughput. By contrast, an account management system may require high throughput, but have more relaxed responsiveness requirements.

Responsiveness. The problem of maximizing responsiveness is fundamentally one of local optimization (a goal which may run counter to global optimization efforts). Maximizing mutator responsiveness corresponds to minimizing collector disruptiveness.

While the problem of minimizing collector disruptiveness is a goal common to conventional heap collectors, the widely differing cost factors at play and correspondingly different expectations with respect to responsiveness suggest that the issue should be examined freshly for the transactional context. We identify three broad strategies for improving responsiveness: *minimizing the grain of collection increments*, *minimizing mutator/collector resource contention*, and *minimizing collection activity when mutator demand is high*. The first of these strategies will minimize any mutator pause time, but may have the deleterious effect of reducing collection efficiency by shifting the identification/collection efforts from local to the more expensive global domains. Many resources are shared by the mutator and collector, including: CPU, memory, I/O bandwidth, and locks. The computational efficiency of the collection algorithm will impact on CPU contention. An opportunistic algorithm may significantly reduce both memory and I/O bandwidth consumption, and appropriate use of transactions (most notably the use of layered transactions) can dramatically reduce the level of lock contention. The applicability of the third strategy is highly application dependent, but in general, responsiveness will be improved if collections opportunistically exploit lulls in mutator activity.

Throughput. The problem of maximizing throughput is one of global optimization, a goal sometimes at odds with the objective of responsiveness. For example, a clustering policy may yield substantial improvements in *average* performance but might occasionally impact negatively on responsiveness. While a great many aspects of transactional collector implementation will impact on long-term performance, it seems that two relating to I/O are likely to be dominant: *minimizing I/O cost by improving data locality*, and *minimizing I/O overheads through opportunistic collector operation*. Because a collector's capacity to improve object locality through compaction and defragmentation is likely to have a major impact on long term performance, a collector that actively compacts or is able to accommodate a clustering mechanism is likely to yield better throughput improvement. Because it is essential that the collection process does not generate more I/O than it avoids, opportunistic policies, both with respect to reading and writing, are likely to be highly advantageous.

Correctness and Performance. As indicated earlier, each of the four correctness issues can be addressed by isolating collector activity through user-level transactions. This solution is trivially correct because transactional semantics guarantee the coherency of the image seen by any transaction. Unfortunately this approach is heavyweight, requiring read locks to be acquired for each of the objects in the region of collection, leading to strict serialization with any transaction updating objects in that region. Less disruptive approaches exist for each of the four phases.

The correctness of local and global *identification* will be assured if identification occurs with respect to a *snapshot* of some previously committed state of the region of collection (for local identification, the object graph, and for global identification, interpartition meta-data). This approach is trivially correct because the 'once garbage always garbage' axiom ensures that garbage identified with respect to any coherent image of the committed state of the region will always be garbage. While a snapshot could be created by briefly obtaining a read-lock on the region of collection and copying its contents, a coherent 'logical' snapshot can be established cheaply by viewing each object in the region as it is unless a write intention is declared with respect to the object, in which case the 'before-image'[5] of the object is used. The same before-image must continue to be used even if the updating transaction commits (in such a case the before-image will have to be copied by the garbage identification process before the image is removed as part of the commit process).

The primary correctness issue for local and global *collection* is that of ensuring that the mutator is not exposed to the relocation of any live object by the collector. An alternative to encapsulating these phases within a user-level transaction is to use some form of address indirection between the mutator and the collector, which would insulate the mutator from such perturbations. This could be done through the explicit indirection of OIDs, or by using virtual memory techniques.[6]

This section has outlined the elements of a two-step methodology for composing garbage collection algorithms and transactional storage systems. First the candidate algorithm must be decomposed into local and global identification and collection phases. Then for each of the four phases, means must be identified for ensuring the respective correctness criteria outlined above. The simplicity and clarity of this approach allows the bulk of design work to be focused on the efficiency of the particular solution.

4   The TMOS Transactional Garbage Collector

Having outlined a generic design approach, we now apply that approach and develop a new transactional garbage collection algorithm, TMOS. After describing pertinent aspects of the context in which TMOS is developed, we discuss the design of the algorithm by addressing each of the correctness and performance issues outlined in the previous section.

4.1   Implementation Context

The primary design goal for TMOS is that it improve the long term performance of transactional store operation. This objective was a significant factor in our choice of the Mature Object Space (MOS) [Hudson and Moss 1992] collector as the basis for TMOS ('Transactional MOS'). Secondary issues include our desire to be able to integrate clustering algorithms [He et al. 2000] into the collector. We now describe the context in more detail in terms of each of the three components of the system model that underpins our generic design approach.

---

[5] A 'before-image' contains the last committed state of an object, and is typically created by the underlying transaction system as soon as an intention to write to that object is declared. The image is used to re-establish the object state in the event that the transaction is rolled back. This idea is similar to that of *GC-consistent cuts* [Skubiszewski and Valduriez 1997].

[6] Although it would avoid the overhead of an indirection, using virtual memory to achieve this would require each concurrent transaction to execute within a separate address space.

Mutator. The design of TMOS places few preconditions on the mutator beyond the requirement that it interface to the storage layer through a cache and transactional interface according to the transactional object cache architecture. Our implementation of TMOS targets PSI [Blackburn and Stanton 1999], a particular instantiation of such an interface. Beyond compliance to such an interface, we make no presumptions about the mutator. Our specific goals include language run-times for orthogonally persistent Java and Java Data Objects implementations, as well as arbitrary applications such as benchmarking tools written in C and C++.

Transactional Store. The TMOS algorithm in its most general form places no requirements on the store beyond the requirement that it support normal transactional storage semantics. However, significant performance improvements depend on the store supporting (and giving the collector access to) two-level transactions and making before-images of updated objects available to the collector.

Garbage Collection Algorithm. The MOS algorithm was chosen because of its incrementality, completeness, and flexibility. MOS divides the object space into partitions called *cars*, the size of which determines the granularity of collection. The extension of MOS to allow cars to be collected in any order (as long as all cars are eventually collected), greatly facilitates opportunism in TMOS [Moss et al. 1996]. Furthermore, the flexibility of the MOS object allocation and *promotion* (copying) rules is substantial, allowing clustering algorithms to be integrated into the collector. Space constraints preclude a comprehensive account of the MOS algorithm here, so we refer the reader to other publications for details of the algorithm [Hudson and Moss 1992]. Instead we will briefly describe MOS in terms of the various phases of garbage collection identified in section 3.1.

- *Local identification* of garbage depends on identifying the reachability status of each object with respect to external roots and the car's *remembered set* (list of incoming references from other cars).
- *Local collection* of garbage *always* results in the reclamation of an entire car. All externally reachable objects within the car are moved to other cars according to the MOS promotion rules, and dead objects are reclaimed with the car.
- *Global identification* of garbage depends on grouping cars into *trains*, migrating any cycle into a single train, and identifying any trains that are not reachable using reference counting.
- *Global collection* of garbage simply involves the removal of unreachable trains in their entirety, including their constituent cars.

4.2   The Design of TMOS

Following the design approach outlined in section 3.2, we now address correctness and performance issues for the TMOS algorithm.

Correctness. In the following sections we describe how TMOS addresses correctness issues relating to each of the four phases of collection. Our approach to each of these rests directly on the templates for assuring correctness described in section 4. We therefore only elaborate in areas where TMOS extends or otherwise deviates from those templates. The details of *mechanisms* integral to the correctness strategy for TMOS (highlighted below in bold text) are described in section 4.3. The local garbage identification and collection phases of MOS are tightly coupled and would most likely be implemented as a single operation in a TMOS implementation. However, each of the two components raises separate concerns, so for clarity we describe them here separately.

Correctness of Local Identification. The critical issue for the local garbage identification phase is having a coherent image of the target car available for the duration of the identification process, in spite of any mutator attempt to update its contents. In section 4 we describe a **coherent snapshot mechanism**, a means of effectively implementing this approach.

Correctness of Local Collection. MOS moves objects as part of its car collection phase, so the biggest issue for TMOS with respect to the correctness of this phase is that of maintaining coherency of mutator addressing in the face of object movements by the collector. We solve this coherency problem by placing a level of **indirection between mutator and store level addressing** and **deferring the movement of objects** accessed (in either read or write mode) by a mutator transaction.

Correctness of Global Identification. The use of a reference count to detect train isolation in MOS is dependent on identification taking place while the system is in a stable state with respect to the count—i.e., objects are not being moved into or out of the train. MOS uses a *closed* flag to prevent allocation into a train; however, objects can be promoted (copied) into a closed train from older trains. Once a closed train becomes isolated, it will remain isolated, irrespective of mutator activity. The isolation of a closed train can only be undone by the promotion of an object into the train by the collector. Thus in the case of TMOS, correctness of global garbage identification is independent of mutator and transactional activity, but depends solely on the correctness conditions of the MOS algorithm.

Correctness of Global Collection. Once a train (and its constituent cars) have been identified as garbage in the MOS algorithm, the collection process simply involves recovering space associated with the train and its cars. This has no impact on the mutator (as the mutator can have no references to the cars), and is therefore trivial from a correctness standpoint.

Performance. We now address how performance issues impact the design of TMOS.

Responsiveness. Many implementation details impact on responsiveness, but from a design standpoint the dominant concern is minimizing disruptiveness by addressing incrementality and collection opportunism. The first of these indicates minimizing car sizes. The MOS algorithm is flexible in this respect, however local identification is inevitably more efficient than global identification, so reducing car sizes may negatively impact on overall collection efficiency. The second of these indicates the importance of opportunism with respect to I/O by collecting in-memory cars where possible. Together these objectives suggest that a car should be sized to fit into a single *disk page* (the store's unit of transfer between memory and disk). If a car is not contained within a single disk page, opportunistic collection of a car will be conditional on all of the car's pages being memory resident simultaneously. Opportunism with respect to write I/O suggests that pages that have been updated be preferentially targeted for collection.

Throughput. I/O opportunism will also impact significantly on throughput. Thus I/O related operations that do not impact on responsiveness should also occur opportunistically. A significant class of such operations is pointer and remembered set maintenance. An outgoing pointer referring to an object in another car must be updated if the remote object is moved. Similarly a remembered set entry (recording an incoming pointer from a remote object) must be: updated if the referring object moves; created if a new remote reference is created; or deleted if the referring object's reference is deleted. In the MOS algorithm such maintenance would occur at the time of the change to the remote object; however, in the context where much (perhaps most) of the object space is on disk, such an approach is impractical. To this end, PMOS [Moss et al. 1996], which faced the same problem, introduced the concept of buffering Δref and Δloc entries in memory. These entries correspond respectively to mutations of cross-car pointers and movements of objects containing cross-car pointers. Each time a car is brought into memory, unprocessed Δref and Δloc entries are applied to the car's objects and remembered set as necessary. If the number of outstanding entries becomes significant (impacting on memory consumption, for example), cars can be pro-actively brought into memory and updated.

Collector efficiency can also be improved and I/O costs further minimized by collecting multiple cars where possible. Multiple car collections improve clustering opportunities when objects are promoted, and by aggregating multiple updates may reduce the number of I/Os that occur. However, multi-car collection is more disruptive to the mutator and so is at odds with the goal of responsiveness.

4.3 The Implementation of TMOS

We now discuss key implementation details for TMOS. After briefly outlining the system structure we describe three key aspects of the TMOS implementation: the object addressing scheme, actions initiated by mutator behavior, and garbage collection. The three mechanisms identified in section 4.2, *a coherent snapshot mechanism, indirection between mutator and store level addressing*, and *deferring the movement of objects*, are addressed in the following discussion.

System Structure. Figure 2 indicates the basic system model for the TMOS collector. Significant components include the cache shared between the mutator(s) and the transactional store, the OID to PID map, and the log, which is used by the collector to acquire object before-images and Δrefs.

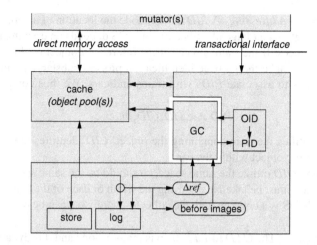

Fig. 2. System model for TMOS, indicating relationship between the collector and key sub-components of the transactional store.

Object Addressing Scheme. As described in section 4.2, decoupling mutator and store level object addressing facilitates transparency of collector-induced object movement. We describe such a scheme in terms of mutator addresses (*OID*s) and store addresses (*PID*s), and mechanisms for maintaining their relationship.

Mutator-Level Object Addresses. The mutator's notion of an OID is that of a value (possibly stored in an object field), which when presented to the transactional interface will uniquely identify a store object for retrieval (or update) through that interface. An OID is only valid within the scope of a single transaction. The size of an OID is implementation dependent, but would usually be 32 or 64 bits.[7] The process of object retrieval within a transaction is bootstrapped by the retrieval of a root object.[8] Assuming the structure of the root object is known to the mutator, traversal of the object graph can begin by accessing any reference field of the root object and using the OID contained within it to retrieve another object. Our means of insulating the mutator from the movement of objects by the collector requires support for a many to one relationship between OIDs and *physical* memory addresses. This can be achieved with *virtual* memory to OID maps being many to one (with indirection via per-transaction maps), or one to one (avoiding indirection). The drawback of hardware address translation is that it depends on each concurrent transaction executing within a separate address space and it constrains object relocation choices to those that preserve the object's intra-page location because it can only re-map the high-order bits of the address.

---

[7] There is a distinct advantage in having the OID the same size as the mutator's reference type, as store objects can be mapped to objects in the mutator space without resizing.

[8] This can be done by using a symbolic OID such as ROOT_OID.

Store-Level Object Addressing. A *PID* must encode the location of an object within the store. Local and global garbage identification in MOS depends on tracking inter-car and inter-train references. If the train and car of the referenced object could be encoded in the *PID*, it would make the garbage identification process substantially more efficient by avoiding maps to associate *PID*s with trains and cars. We thus compose a *PID* as follows:

$$PID =< TID, CID, index >$$

where *TID* identifies the train containing the object, *CID* identifies the car, and *index* identifies a specific object within the car.

The *PID* and *OID* utilize the same space, so should be the same size. If only 32 bits are available, care must be taken in choosing the width of each of the components of the *PID*. Because MOS is a copying garbage collector, addresses can be recycled.

OID, PID Mapping. The OID to PID map is many-to-one and it is dynamic. Because the validity of an OID is limited to the scope of a single transaction, different transactions may have different OID to PID mappings. This makes it possible to manage coherently two images of the same object, seen by different transactions in different parts of memory. Such a feature allows an object to be 'moved' by the collector while a transaction retains a read-lock on that object. The locking transaction and a subsequent reader will see separate identical images of the object (this idea is further motivated below).

Mutator Activity. Aside from the use of address indirection, the existence of the collector impinges on the relationship between the mutator and the store in three principle ways: the faulting of objects into memory, the generation of $\Delta refs$ by the mutator as a result of changes to references, and the flushing of updated objects back to disk.

Car Faulting. Faulting an object into memory in response to a mutator request necessitates the faulting of the car containing that object if the car is not already in memory. This process involves three steps:

1. Fault the appropriate store page from disk into memory.
2. Apply any outstanding Δloc entries to all objects in the car.
3. Swizzle all references from *PID*s to *OID*s.[9]

At this stage the mutator may access the requested object. However, before the car can be subject to garbage identification, one more step must be performed (this need not be performed if the car is not collected):

4. Apply any outstanding Δref entries to the car's remembered set.

Δref Generation. Any changes made by the mutator to object references must be propagated to the collector if those changes are committed. The creation (or deletion) of an inter-car reference will generate an insertion into (deletion from) the target car's remembered set. As described in section 4.2, such changes are applied immediately only if the

---

[9] This process can alternatively be performed lazily, swizzling objects only when they are first accessed by the mutator.

target remembered set is in memory, otherwise a Δref entry is placed on a queue for processing when the target remembered set is faulted in. Because such mutator changes are only relevant when committed, they can be processed as part of the generation of the commit log record (which involves identifying mutator changes and encapsulating them in log Δs).

Car Flushing. Updated cars ultimately must be flushed to disk. Because references are swizzled as part of the faulting process, the flushing process must unswizzle all references from *OIDs* to *PIDs* before writing a car to disk.

Garbage Collection. Finally, and most critically, we now describe the garbage collection process. At both the local (car) and global (train) levels of the algorithm we combine both identification and collection phases in the implementation.

Car Collection. Car collection can be initiated with respect to any car (or cars). However, before collection can proceed, the car must be in memory, be up to date with respect to $\Delta locs$, in a consistent state (transactionally), and closed to allocation of new objects. If a car is in a swizzled state at the time of collection, each reference will be translated from *OID* to *PID* as it is scanned (*PIDs* are used to do reachability analysis). Thus the cost associated with collection will depend on the starting state of the target car.

   If a mutator transaction holds a write lock on any object in the target car when collection commences, then that object's before-image is used in place of the object during the garbage identification phase. For the duration of the collection, mutator transactions are prevented from upgrading read locks on any objects and from committing any updates to objects in the car (new read locks are permitted).

   The reachability status of all objects in the car is then established using the car's remset. The car is then *evacuated* by copying reachable objects to other cars according to the MOS promotion rules (utilizing the flexibility in the rules to maximize clustering where possible). If no mutator locks are held over the car, the car is reclaimed. As long as mutator locks remain on any objects in the car, those objects remain in place in the evacuated car *and* in the car to which they were promoted. In the case of a read lock, new transactions will be given references to the promoted objects (with two images of the same object co-existing in a read-only state). In the case of a write lock, new transactions will be excluded from accessing the object until the lock is released, and if the transaction commits successfully, the new object state is copied to the car to which to object was promoted. As soon as the last mutator lock is released, the car is reclaimed.

   The promotion of each object generates a Δloc for each car referring to the object and a Δref for each object it refers to. The deletion of an object generates a Δref for each object it refers to.

Train Collection. Train collection is substantially simpler than car collection. Train isolation is detected using train reference counts which are trivially maintained as a byproduct of Δref processing (recall that *PIDs* encode train identifiers). Once a train is detected as being isolated, it and its constituent cars can be reclaimed. Isolated cars may be on disk, in which case their reclamation may occur lazily. Correctness of the algorithm will depend on either Δref entries being generated for all objects referred to by reclaimed cars, or by records of car reclamation being kept so that any remembered set entries corresponding to reclaimed cars may be disregarded. The former approach implies a need for all reclaimed cars to be scanned (faulted in from disk if necessary), while the latter may require car reclamation records to be kept for very long periods and may involve relatively expensive lookups when scanning remembered sets.

Recoverability. Collections impact on five aspects of store state: remembered sets (via Δrefs), object pointers (via Δlocs), meta-data describing train membership, meta-data describing car membership, and low-level space allocation meta-data. By maintaining all such data structures (e.g., table of outstanding Δrefs, low-level space allocation map, etc.) as low-level persistent data in the two-level store, the data structures become fully recoverable. By making each collection invocation a single low-level transaction, the effects of each invocation trivially take on transactional recovery properties.

5   Future Work

The TMOS garbage collector is currently being implemented as part of Platypus [He et al. 2000], an object store that has been developed at the Australian National University. Once completed, the TMOS garbage collector implementation will be evaluated. The TMOS collector embodies a high degree of policy flexibility for both allocation and collection. We see the exploration of this policy space and the identification of appropriate heuristics as important research goals. The flexibility of the TMOS collector also provides opportunities for exploring clustering algorithms. We see an implementation of TMOS in Platypus as an excellent vehicle for furthering work on clustering [He et al. 2000].

6   Conclusions

In addition to minimizing disk usage, garbage collection is likely to be an important mechanism for maximizing long term I/O performance of persistent systems. TMOS is a garbage collector that applies the completeness and incrementality of the mature object space (MOS) collector to a transactional storage context. The complexity of designing a garbage collection algorithm for a transactional setting has led us to develop a generic methodology for the design of transactional collectors. The methodology begins with an initial garbage collection algorithm that is known to be correct and a mutator and a store that are strongly separated by a transactional interface. Correctness and performance issues are clearly separated allowing the characteristics of the newly derived transactional garbage collection algorithm to be well understood. This paper thus contributes both a new garbage collection algorithm and a generic methodology for designing transactional garbage collection algorithms.

References

[Amsaleg et al. 1995] AMSALEG, L., FRANKLIN, M. J., AND GRUBER, O. 1995. Efficient incremental garbage collection for client-server object database systems. In U. DAYAL, P. M. D. GRAY, AND S. NISHIO Eds., *VLDB'95, Proceedings of 21th International Conference on Very Large Data Bases, September 11-15, 1995, Zurich, Switzerland* (1995), pp. 42–53. Morgan Kaufmann.

[Atkinson and Morrison 1995] ATKINSON, M. P. AND MORRISON, R. 1995. Orthogonally persistent systems. *The VLDB Journal 4*, 3 (July), 319–402.

[Blackburn and Stanton 1999] BLACKBURN, S. M. AND STANTON, R. B. 1999. The transactional object cache: A foundation for high performance persistent system construction. In R. MORRISON, M. JORDAN, AND M. ATKINSON Eds., *Advances in Persistent Object Systems: Proceedings of the Eighth International Workshop on Persistent Object Systems, Aug. 30–Sept. 1, 1998, Tiburon, CA, U.S.A.* (San Francisco, 1999), pp. 37–50. Morgan Kaufmann.

[Blackburn and Zigman 1999] BLACKBURN, S. M. AND ZIGMAN, J. N. 1999. Concurrency— The fly in the ointment? In R. MORRISON, M. JORDAN, AND M. ATKINSON Eds., *Advances in Persistent Object Systems: Third International Workshop on Persistence and Java, Sept. 1–3, 1998, Tiburon, CA, U.S.A.* (San Francisco, 1999), pp. 250–258. Morgan Kaufmann.

[Cattell et al. 2000] CATTELL, R. G. G., BARRY, D. K., BERLER, M., EASTMAN, J., JORDAN, D., RUSSELL, C., SCHADOW, O., STANIENDA, T., AND VELEZ, F. Eds. 2000. *The Object Data Standard: ODMG 3.0.* Morgan Kaufmann Publishers.

[Cook et al. 1994] COOK, J. E., WOLF, A. L., AND ZORN, B. G. 1994. Partition selection policies in object database garbage collection. In R. T. SNODGRASS AND M. WINSLETT Eds., *Proceedings of the 1994 ACM SIGMOD International Conference on Management of Data, Minneapolis, Minnesota, May 24-27, 1994* (1994), pp. 371–382. ACM Press.

[Dijkstra et al. 1978] DIJKSTRA, E. W., LAMPORT, L., MARTIN, A. J., SCHOLTEN, C. S., AND STEFFENS, E. F. M. 1978. On-the-fly garbage collection: an exercise in cooperation. *Communications of the ACM 21*, 11, 966–975.

[Härder and Reuter 1983] HÄRDER, T. AND REUTER, A. 1983. Principles of transaction-oriented database recovery. *ACM Computing Surveys 15*, 4 (Dec.), 287–317.

[He et al. 2000] HE, Z., BLACKBURN, S. M., KIRBY, L., AND ZIGMAN, J. N. 2000. Platypus: Design and implementation of a flexible high performance object store. In *Proceedings of the Ninth International Workshop on Persistent Object Systems, Lillehammer, Norway September 6–9, 2000* (2000).

[He et al. 2000] HE, Z., MARQUEZ, A., AND BLACKBURN, S. M. 2000. Opportunistic prioritised clustering framework (OPCF). In *ECOOP2000 Symposium on Objects and Databases - Object-Oriented Programming, Sophia Antipolis, France, June 13, 2000, Proceedings*, Lecture Notes in Computer Science (LNCS) (2000). Springer. To appear.

[Hudson and Moss 1992] HUDSON, R. AND MOSS, J. E. B. 1992. Incremental garbage collection of mature objects. In Y. BEKKERS AND J. COHEN Eds., *International Workshop on Memory Management, St. Malo, France Sept. 17–19, 1992*, Volume 637 of *Lecture Notes in Computer Science (LNCS)* (1992, 1992), pp. 388–403. Springer.

[Kolodner and Weihl 1993] KOLODNER, E. K. AND WEIHL, W. E. 1993. Atomic incremental garbage collection and recovery for large stable heap. In P. BUNEMAN AND S. JAJODIA Eds., *SIGMOD 1993, Proceedings ACM SIGMOD International Conference on the Management of Data, May 26-28, Washington, DC*, Volume 22 of *SIGMOD Record* (June 1993), pp. 177–186. ACM Press.

[Lakhamraju et al. 2000] LAKHAMRAJU, M. K., RASTOGI, R., SESHADRI, S., AND SUDARSHAN, S. 2000. On-line reorganization in object databases. In *SIGMOD 2000, Proceedings ACM SIGMOD International Conference on Management of Data, May 14-19, 2000, Dallas, Texas, USA*, Volume 28 of *SIGMOD Record* (May 2000). ACM Press.

[Maheshwari and Liskov 1997] MAHESHWARI, U. AND LISKOV, B. 1997. Partitioned garbage collection of large object store. In J. PECKHAM Ed., *SIGMOD 1997, Proceedings ACM SIGMOD International Conference on Management of Data, May 13-15, 1997, Tucson, Arizona, USA*, Volume 26 of *SIGMOD Record* (June 1997), pp. 313–323. ACM Press.

[Maier 1999] MAIER, D. 1999. Review - An approach to persistent programming. *ACM SIGMOD Digital Review 1*.

[Moss et al. 1996] MOSS, J. E. B., MUNRO, D. S., AND HUDSON, R. L. 1996. PMOS: A complete and coarse-grained incremental garbage collector. In R. CONNOR AND S. NETTLES Eds., *Seventh* (Cape May, NJ, U.S.A., May 29–31 1996), pp. 140–150. Morgan Kaufmann.

[Munro et al. 1999] MUNRO, D. S., BROWN, A. L., MORRISON, R., AND MOSS, J. E. B. 1999. Incremental garbage collection of a persistent object store using PMOS. In R. MORRISON, M. J. JORDAN, AND M. P. ATKINSON Eds., *Advances in Persistent Object Systems: Eigth International Workshop on Persistence Object SystemsSept. 1–3, 1998, Tiburon, CA, U.S.A.* (San Francisco, 1999), pp. 78–91. Morgan Kaufmann.

[Skubiszewski and Valduriez 1997] SKUBISZEWSKI, M. AND VALDURIEZ, P. 1997. Concurrent garbage collection in o2. In M. JARKE, M. J. CAREY, K. R. DITTRICH, F. H. LOCHOVSKY, P. LOUCOPOULOS, AND M. A. JEUSFELD Eds., *VLDB'97, Proceedings of 23rd International Conference on Very Large Data Bases, August 25-29, 1997, Athens, Greece* (1997), pp. 356–365. Morgan Kaufmann.

[Snodgrass 1999] SNODGRASS, R. T. 1999. Review - PM3: An orthogonal persistent systems programming language - design, implementation, performance. *ACM SIGMOD Digital Review 1*.

[Sun Microsystems 1999] SUN MICROSYSTEMS. 1999. Java Data Objects Specification, JSR-12. http://java.sun.com/aboutjava/communityprocess/jsr (July), Sun Microsystems Inc., 2550 Garcia Avenue, Mountain View, CA 94043.

[Yong et al. 1994] YONG, V.-F., NAUGHTON, J., AND YU, J.-B. 1994. Storage reclamation and reorganization in client-server persistent stores. In *Proceedings of the 10th International Conference on Data Engineering*, IEEE Computing Society (Feb. 1994), pp. 120–131.

Session 4: Overview

Antony L. Hosking

Department of Computer Sciences, Purdue University,
West Lafayette, IN 47907-1398, USA
hosking@cs.purdue.edu

The papers in this session both address the behavior of persistent object stores in response to the applications they are intended to support.

The first paper, by Richer and Shapiro, was presented by Nicolas Richer [NR]. It evaluates the behavior of five memory allocation and clustering strategies for the PerDiS persistent distributed object store, when it is used as the underlying storage platform for sites on the World Wide Web. The workloads comprise recorded traces of actual accesses to two different web sites. These are used to drive a simulation of the PerDiS allocation strategies, in which the web sites are modelled as an object graph.

Results of the study include demographics on object size (80% are less than 50K bytes), the fraction of objects participating in cycles (many), and the size of those cycles in bytes and number of objects (small). The simulations show that a large fraction of references cross the boundaries of „bunches", which are regions of clustered objects in the PerDiS store. Inter-bunch references are more expensive than intra-bunch references. Moreover, the bunch is the unit of garbage collection in PerDiS, so cycles that cross bunch boundaries cannot easily be collected. The high number of inter-bunch references is unexpected and negatively impacts performance for all of the PerDiS allocation and clustering strategies. Still, strategies that perform allocation depth-first by graph topology yield marginally better locality of reference overall.

Several questions followed the presentation, paraphrased as follows. Brian Lewis [BL] asked why simulation was used instead of using PerDiS directly. Richer responded that they wanted to work in parallel with the evolution of the PerDiS platform in order to obtain a result. He noted that the simulation included essentially the same allocation strategies as PerDiS.

Malcolm Atkinson [MPA] noted that it is certainly feasible to use the web as an accessible application workload, but wondered if the web can give any real information relating to what goes on in distributed applications. His concern is that the web has no reachability graph that makes much sense, nor update models that are managed in any organized way. He wanted to know how one might transfer knowledge from a Web-based study to other application domains. Richer conceded that this is a difficult point to counter. At the beginning they only wanted to study true persistent applications, but these are not easily available, so they wanted to find something comparable between the Web and some persistent applications. Unfortunately, this comparison is not very encouraging, but a better match might be confirmed by other measurement. He didn't think that the results would transfer

G.N.C. Kirby, A. Dearle, and D.I.K. Sjøberg (Eds.): POS-9, LNCS 2135, pp. 157-160, 2001.

directly, though they can yield some information about widely distributed data; in fact, he could think of nothing more widely distributed than the Web.

Atkinson then made another comment, stating that the talk began by asking how many cycles are not garbage collected by PerDiS since they span the units of garbage collection (i.e., the bunch), but that the paper doesn't seem to address that question directly since it doesn't ask what bunches are going to coincide at any given time while garbage collecting. Again, Richer conceded the difficulty of answering this, since it would require experiments that drive the real behavior of PerDiS with real users from different sites and to measure what is never reclaimed. Currently, the PerDiS platform is not used in this way so there is no real way to measure it yet. They tried in this study to measure the maximum number of cycles that might not be reclaimed; there may be fewer, but they wanted an upper bound. Without real experience of the real platform they cannot say how much for real is not reclaimed.

Alex Wolf [AW] wondered why the study used a simulation·instead of analysis, noting that the workload and data are stable enough for analysis. Richer responded that simulation seemed easier, since it directly encodes the basic policies used in the actual PerDiS platform. He said that they used parts of the real platform in the simulator, so it was simpler to simulate by using the allocation policies directly from PerDiS.

Wolf then made a second observation in that the study took a very traditional programming language approach, worrying about clustering for the particular reason of garbage collection only. He noted that with application to persistent object systems there are so many other reasons to form clusters, such as access patterns, units of transfer between clients and servers, locking granularity, and so on. Looking at things from the one perspective does not give such an interesting result with respect to persistent object systems. In reply, Richer conceded as much, but also stated that they were dealing with PerDiS and wanted to address that alone, in which garbage collection is an important part of the system.

The second paper, by Garratt, Jackson, Burden and Wallis, was presented by Andrea Garratt [AG]. Their study compares two Java-based persistent storage mechanisms and their suitability for implementing the indexing component of an experimental World Wide Web search engine. The platforms compared are PJama and an unnamed commercially available object-oriented database system. The authors were interested in both ease of use and performance, on which scores both systems were judged fairly easy to use, while PJama demonstrates significantly superior performance, though at the cost of more disk space. The following discussion ensued.

Lewis asked what is needed to make a persistent object system successful for a commercial web index. Garratt's answer was that the sheer performance needs to be scalable, and that they did not appear to be getting good scaling from either of the stores they were using, especially regarding response times for very large postings lists. Garratt posited that for sheer performance they would need to implement their own disk management software to get results, but that they were pleased with PJama for what they were doing.

Tony Printezis [TP] commented that with everything in postings lists, sheer performance would be difficult to achieve. Garratt's answer was that compression, and storing the lists contiguously on disk, should improve performance.

Fausto Rabitti [FR] then offered an observation that the work seemed naive from the point of information retrieval, so they cannot compare the results with information retrieval systems for web or for text. There are many things in the literature that could be used here to improve performance. His major point was that the long postings lists must be scanned sequentially, whereas other systems would avoid this by applying techniques to eliminate the post work and get a superset of results which can then be post-processed. He also noted that commercial systems based on basic index strategies go directly to disk, and that indexing in an object-oriented database system is not the same as in PJama, where the B+-tree index must be programmed on top of the system instead of being built-in. Rabitti found it strange that they did not use the internal indexes of the object-oriented database system making the comparison with PJama seem unfair.

Steve Blackburn [SB] followed up by saying that the question is really whether orthogonal persistence can provide a panacea for data management, and that one should not necessarily assume that an orthogonally persistent system will be suitable for all data management tasks. Blackburn felt that one should be asking what the limits are to orthogonal persistence, what it can be applied to, and whether the applications used in these papers are good applications for orthogonal persistence. Garratt answered that her group is pleased with the results for PJama, and that for an experimental search engine such as theirs, PJama offered a good platform in which to try out ideas. They might look for something else for better performance. Bernd Matthiske [BM] asked what scale of application might need to be supported. Garratt indicated that in future they intended to use much larger corpuses (on the order of terabytes).

Tony Hosking [AH] asked if the time measure in the results was wall-clock or CPU time, and if it included the time to access the disk. Garratt responded that the measure was system and user time. Hosking responded that this would not then include disk access time.

Eliot Moss [EM] had a question regarding text indexing, and referred back to work by Eric Brown from the mid-1990s where implementing special access methods and representations for inverted lists inside the Mneme object store seemed to be better than using whatever data structures one gets with a high-level language. Moss asked Garratt to comment on that, in terms of both compactness and speed. Garratt responded that they simply wanted to test out ideas and so did not go down that path. Compression might yield performance improvements.

The whole discussion then took a more general turn. Atkinson commented that he was experiencing a strong sense of *deja vu* from the 1970s, in which he attended lots of meetings about relational database systems and heard many people saying that they made life so much easier, while others claimed they could never go fast enough so one should not pursue them. Atkinson felt that if one takes any technology and tries to map it to disks (which are very complicated beasts), while also supporting a wide range of applications, it takes a very long time and effort in optimization to make it go fast enough. He noted that there are many applications that one can throw at a mature relational database system that will make it crawl. Atkinson felt that it is important to look at the real costs of building applications both in terms of development hours and the number of skilled programmers needed. It would be nice if one could actually measure that. From the Wolverhampton team he was hearing that PJama helped in development time, but he wasn't hearing anything from the PerDiS group on that score.

In response, Richer said it was difficult to quantify. PerDiS was designed from the outset to be easy to use by application programmers, for whom distribution is not familiar, so they wanted to support something that increased productivity and the possibility of new applications without sophisticated knowledge of distributed systems. Richer felt that PerDiS was a success on this count, but that for now performance was a problem. He felt that if the abstractions provided by PerDiS were useful then performance could be enhanced in many ways, but it might take a lot of work.

Ron Morrison [RM] followed with a comment on Atkinson's comment, saying that we might be trying to be far too ambitious. The research space is enormous, but there are a number of valid ways to approach the research. One approach is to build a new computational artefact that has not been built before. In this community persistence and hyper-programming are examples of this. There are many applications that could not have been built without the infrastructure that these technologies provide. Within the Snyder classification these constitute proofs of existence and yield valid science. Alternatively, one can seek performance that is better than prior implementations by showing a new techniques has an edge under certain conditions—proofs of performance. Trying to do that for the whole research space is impossible since it is just too big. Another approach is to demonstrate that a particular configuration of ideas or an approach achieves predefined objectives—this is proof of concept. As a community we must guard against knocking results because they are „not faster" or „not better". There is always an argument that will take away from those results, but that criticism itself must be judged on its pertinence to the issues addressed by the work it criticises.

The last word was had by Blackburn, commenting on orthogonal persistence and the temptation to take it and find direct applications for it. Orthogonal persistence provides an abstraction to help the programming task. He outlined his experience working with some data mining people who were interested in using orthogonal persistence in their domain. Blackburn found that the key people involved were mathematicians devising models using Mathematica, which were then instantiated into code to run data mining systems. He looked at producing Java bytecodes directly from Mathematica and semantically extending those with persistence abstractions. This would have given the data mining people something they could have used: the mathematicians could use the tool they were familiar with, while persistence abstractions sufficient to their needs were incorporated transparently, even though it was not really full-blown orthogonal persistence. Blackburn wondered if applying orthogonal persistence directly is the best way, or whether we should instead take our experiences with orthogonal persistence and extend from them into other domains.

The Memory Behavior of the WWW, or The WWW Considered as a Persistent Store

Nicolas Richer and Marc Shapiro

INRIA - SOR group, BP. 105,
78153 Le Chesnay Cedex, France
{Nicolas.Richer, Marc.Shapiro}@inria.fr
http://www-sor.inria.fr/

Abstract. This paper presents the performance evaluation of five memory allocation strategies for the PerDiS Persistent Distributed Object store in the context of allocating two different web sites in the store. The evaluation was conducted using (i) a web gathering tool, to log the web objects graph, and (ii) a PerDiS memory simulator that implements the different allocation strategies. Our results show that for all the strategies and parameters we have evaluated, reference and cycle locality are quiet poor. The best policy seems to be first sequential fits. Results are linear with the size of the garbage collection Unit (a bunch). There is no clear optimum, but 64K to 128K appear to be good choices.

1 Introduction

PerDiS [FSB+98] is a new technology for sharing information over the Internet: Its abstraction is a Persistent Distributed Object Store. PerDiS provide a simple, efficient and safe abstraction to the application programmer. To attain this goal, it is necessary to understand the way target applications use the persistent store and how the different mechanisms and heuristics perform. This study is the target of task T.C 3 of the PerDiS project. This paper presents the results we have obtained.

The PerDiS persistent store is logically divided into clusters. A cluster is the naming and security unit visible by the programmer. A cluster is attached to a "home" site[1] but can be accessed from any site. From the garbage collection point of view, cluster is further subdivided into bunches, i.e. garbage collection Units. The Garbage Collector always runs on whole bunch and this unit will be completely replicated at one site in order for the GC to run on[2]. This means also that bunches will be stored in a contiguous area in memory. A reference inside a bunch is cheaper than between two bunches (an inter-bunch reference). The latter needs using stubs and scions. The fewer references will be inter-bunch, the better the PerDiS system will perform.

---

[1] The home site ensures data security and reliability.

[2] For latency reasons, bunches could be divided in pages but the page forming a bunch should be fully located at a site for the Garbage Collection to operate on.

G.N.C. Kirby, A. Dearle, and D.I.K. Sjøberg (Eds.): POS-9, LNCS 2135, pp. 161–176, 2001.

1.1   What Are Garbage Collection Components

A Garbage Collection components is a set of objects reclaimed by the garbage collector all at the same time. This could be a single object or several objects link together in a way that they become unreachable all at the same time. Typically, this can be a set of objects with circular references between them.

In this context, Strongly Connected component is an approximation for Garbage Collection component. Rigorously, Garbage Collection components are Strongly Connected component plus all the objects reachable only from this components, but we don't make the difference in this study, because, unfortunately, we are not able to extract real Garbage Collection components from an object graph yet. This approximation may grow up the overall proportion of objects and bytes included in Garbage Collection components. Studying Strongly Connected component provide only minimum proportions, and we don't currently know the maximums.

Note also that Garbage Collection components are often called cycles in this paper because it's shorter.

1.2   The PerDiS Garbage Collector

The PerDiS Garbage Collector use a reference counting algorithm to handle inter-bunches references, this to avoid costly distributed Garbage Collection Algorithms. In consequences, some garbage could not be reclaimed in some situation. This is the case of Garbage Collection components composed by several objects spread between different bunches. This kind of garbage could be reclaimed on the of all the bunch is containing the objects were run located at the same site. This is, unfortunately, the drawback of using reference counting.

The assumption we have made during the design of the PerDiS Garbage Collector is that such kind of unreclaimable components are sufficiently rare to be forgotten and we don't put any kind of global tracing collector for them. Of course, this assumption should be verified in practice and this is precisely why we are interested by Garbage Collection components in this study. Depending of our experimental results, the need for a global tracing collector mechanism will be reconsidered. The important point here is the fewer cycles are inter-bunches, the less garbage will remain unreclaimable. This suggest that object placement strategies (i.e. allocation algorithms) should minimize inter-bunch Garbage Collection components and inter-bunch references. A secondary goal will be to minimize also the number of scions and store fragmentation.

In the current PerDiS implementation, the initial allocator clustering is permanent, because PerDiS support the uncooperative C++ language that does not provide natively all the informations required to perform object relocation. In the future, we plan to implement object relocation in PerDiS using type information extracted by typedesc [Sal99], a tool we have specifically implemented for that.

A complete description of the PerDiS Garbage Collection Algorithm is available in [FS94,FS96]. [BFS98] describe more deeply the implementation.

1.3   Analysis Methodology

Our methodology is to record the persistent object graph during application runs, using a log mechanism. The log subsequently supports simulation of different strategies and parameters. We focus primarily on evaluating memory allocation and clustering strategies. Many studies of memory allocation and clustering strategies already exist [WJNB95,WJ98,ZG92a,ZG92b,DDZ93], but none has been conducted in the context of a persistent distributed garbage collected memory[3]. This is probably related to the very few number of existing persistent store, but even for those that exists, most of them rely on manual memory deallocation. For example, one of the most advanced distributed persistent stores, ObjectStore [LLOW91] is based on manual persistence, in contrast with persistence by reachability [ABC+83] using a distributed garbage collector as in PerDiS.

1.4   Why Study the Web ?

Wilson in [WJNB95] demonstrates the low representativity of synthetically generated allocation requests. Therefore, we chose to evaluate the memory allocation and clustering strategies using inputs from real applications. Consequently, we need some significant persistent applications for our evaluation. Unfortunately, applications that use persistent objects store are rare, and a few that exists are not easily accessible. Furthermore, PerDiS is designed to provide easy access to persistent data over a geographically widely-distributed network. We need applications running in such a large-scale context. The Web application has attracted our attention because it is easily accessible and widely distributed. Hence our decision was to study the behavior of PerDiS as a distributed storage medium for web sites.

Practically, we have not actually stored the full web sites in the PerDiS memory, although it is perfectly feasible to do so[4]. Instead, we have used the PerDiS memory simulator. This simulator has been designed specifically to reproduce the PerDiS memory behavior against several allocation strategies and parameters.

2   Gathering the Web Object Graph

We briefly present in this section how we gather a graph of objects from a web server in order to study it. The basic gathering algorithm is a depth-first top-down traversal implemented using a stack:

---

[3] Data in persistent and transient memory is typically not the same. A lot of data in transient memory (used by graphical library for example), for intermediate results will never be persistent.

[4] QMW, a partner of the PerDiS project, did that for another purpose
(http://www.dcs.qmw.ac.uk/research/distrib/perdis/docs/perdisweb.html).

1. Push some root document URL on the fetch stack.
2. Pop an URL from the fetch stack, retrieve the corresponding document, and parse it to extract the URL it contains.
3. Push all the contained URLs that are in scope on to the fetch stack.
4. Return to step 2 until fetch stack becomes empty.

Starting from an existing mirroring tool seemed a reasonable approach. We chose the w3mir[5] all purpose HTTP copying tool because its source code is freely available and we have good experience with it.

The web objects graph is recorded in the generic log format version 2 of our generic log handling library[6]. Since w3mir is written in PERL[7], we created a PERL interface for the generic log library.

We first integrated the recording of the web objects and references to w3mir by minimizing the modifications in the mirror algorithm in less than three days. The result was not acceptable as is because many processes and fetch was duplicated, so in a second step we have modified the w3mir algorithm to remove this.

The following problems, which are inherent to the World Wide Web, should be noted:

- A document's "last modified date" is often not correctly returned by web servers. When this occurs, we take the current date as the "last modified date".
- Recording the evolution of the Web Objects Graph is difficult in practice. Since there is no reliable protocol for change notification, we need to keep a local full copy of the web site. Furthermore, many web sites are modified rarely; therefore measurements would have to be repeated over very long periods (maybe 6 months or more) in order to see significant modifications. Instead, the results presented in this paper concern a single snapshot of each studied web site.
- The graph that we obtain, using the mirroring method, is different from the real Web graph. Several kinds of document (CGI scripts, Java applets, Netscape Java-script, etc) could not be handled and furthermore, since documents of this types are sometimes used to provide the menu to navigate through the entire web site, a large part of this kind of web sites could not be visible. As far as we know, all existing indexing engines has the same problem with this kind of documents. Nevertheless our partial graph should be sufficient for evaluation purposes and we have to take care of this problem when we choose the web sites to study.

---

[5] http://www.math.uio.no/~janl/w3mir/
[6] The documentation of this library is available from ftp://ftp.inria.fr/INRIA/Projects/SOR/misc/analysis/doc/log_facilities.ps.gz
[7] http://www.perl.com/

3   Characteristics of the Web Sites Studied

This initial study involves the two web sites: http://www.perdis.esprit.ec. org/ and http://www-sor.inria.fr/. This choice was motivated by three criteria:

1. Network connection quality. Since we need to fetch the full web site contents each time we gather the graph, a very fast connection to the servers is crucial.
2. Prior knowledge. Since there are several kinds of documents that our web gathering tool can't handle, having some previous knowledge of the web site content should avoid choosing, for instance, a site where most of the document cannot bet considered because they are all only accessible from a Java applet menu.
3. Total Size. To be able to perform our simulations sufficient memory resources should be available on the simulation machine. In our current setup, this limits the total web site to approximatively 1 Gigabyte.

All the relevant characteristics of the two studied sites are presented in the next two sections.

3.1   Site 1: http://www.perdis.esprit.ec.org/

The PerDiS web site was studied on Thursday September 23 1999. At this date, it contained 3302 objects, with 31408 valid references[8] for a total size of 109 Mbytes.

The smallest object size is 0 byte and the largest 10 Mbytes. The median is 2.4 Kbytes, for an arithmetic mean of 33 Kbytes, and a variation coefficient of 9.7. We present the size frequency distribution in Fig. 1a.

Objects in the PerDiS web site are aged between 6 seconds old to a little more than 3 years. The median age is 1.5 years, for an arithmetic mean of 1.3 years and a variation coefficient of 0.59. We present the age frequency distribution in Fig. 1b.

The average density of references[9] is 9.5 per object and 0.28 per Kbyte.

There are 22 Strongly Connected components that contain 2284 objects (69.2% of total) for a total size of 15 Mbytes (13.5% of total). The smallest S.C component contains 3 objects (7 Kbytes) and the largest 1758 objects (13.6 Mbytes)[10]. Figure 2a shows the size frequency, in number of objects, of strongly connected components. This figure appear quite uniform because there is only 22 components for 19 size ranges, so there is only one component in each size range, except for the seventh bar where there is two and the first bar where there is three. Figure 2b shows strongly connected size frequency in bytes.

---

[8] references that points to documents that exists, not including dangling references that point to unexisting documents (or protected documents that are not available for us).

[9] The density of reference is the number of references contained in one object, respectively in one Kilobyte.

[10] This component is in reality a mail archive with each message as an HTML document and this documents contained each a link to the previous and the next message.

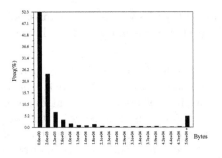

(a) object size class frequency distribution

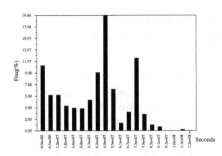

(b) object age class frequency distribution

Fig. 1. PerDiS: size & age of objects

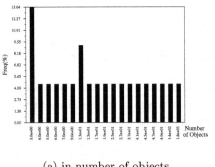

(a) in number of objects

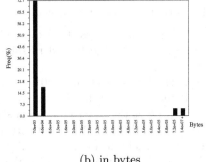

(b) in bytes

Fig. 2. PerDiS: size frequency of strongly connected components

3.2   Site 2: http://www-sor.inria.fr/

The SOR web site was studied on Thursday October 14 1999. At this date, it
contained 8823 objects and 222714 valid references, for a total size of 277 Mbytes.

The smallest object is 8 bytes and the largest one is 8.4 Mbytes. Median is
5.3 Kbytes for an arithmetic mean of 32 Kbytes and a variation coefficient of
5.4. We present the size frequency distribution in Fig. 3a.

Objects in the SOR web site are aged from 10 seconds to 4 years. Median
age is 0.9 years, the arithmetic mean 0.8 years for a variation coefficient of 0.67.
We present the age frequency distribution in Fig. 3b.

The average density of references is 25.2 per object, and 0.78 per Kbyte.

There are 89 Strongly Connected components, containing 2819 objects
(31.9% of total) for a total size of 40 Mbytes (14.56% of total). The smallest

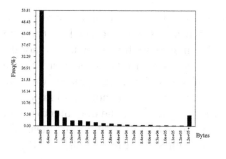

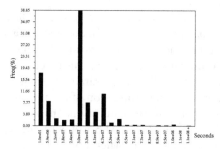

(a) object size class frequency distribution

(b) object age class frequency distribution

Fig. 3. SOR: size & age of objects

S.C component contains 2 objects (1 Kbytes) and the largest 381 objects (16.4 Mbytes). Figure 4a shows sizes frequency in number of objects, of the strongly connected components, whereas Fig. 4b shows their size frequency in bytes.

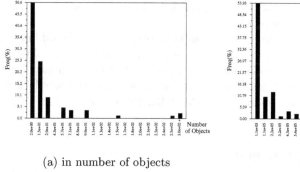

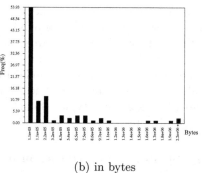

(a) in number of objects

(b) in bytes

Fig. 4. SOR: size frequency of strongly connected components

4 Simulating Memory Allocation in the PerDiS Store

The PerDiS store simulator has been originally implemented to take a graph log, sort the memory allocation to simulate by document last modifications time, replay the allocations using the simulated allocation policy and finally generate a new log with all the old object locations in the heap replaced by the simulated new ones.

Sorting document by "last modifications time" introduced an error in the allocation replaying order because "last modifications time" returned by the web server is not reliable for every documents. Documents with unknown real modification dates exist and in this case, most of the web server return the current date as "last modifications time". To put a bound on the error introduced, we have measured the proportion of documents that have their "last modifications time" younger than the time the snapshot gathering begin. 4% of the documents are in this case in the PerDiS web site and 16% in the SOR web site. Other measurements on several other web sites shows a very high variability (2,3% to 100%) of this proportion.

The PerDiS store simulator is also able to replay the memory allocation in log order. According to the gathering algorithm we currently use (top-down depth-first traversal), log is ordered top-down depth-first.

5   PerDiS Memory Allocation Strategies

The current PerDiS API has applications explicitly place a specific object in a specific cluster. A cluster allocates an object in one of two kinds of bunches, depending on size. Under a certain threshold, it is allocated in a "standard" bunch of fixed size. Any layer object in a "special" bunch, containing only this object. This structure is based on the assumption that big objects are rare. This seems to be confirmed in our measurements (Fig. 1a for site 1 and Fig. 3a for site 2). In our simulations, the maximum proportion of large objects remain under 8% (with standard bunches of 32K).

Bunches are referenced in two doubly linked list, one for the standard bunches and one for the special ones. In the two following sections, we compare different strategies to allocate inside standard bunches and to select the standard bunch to allocate. Since standard bunch have a fixed size, we evaluate the allocation strategies using seven typical bunch size: 32K, 64K, 128K, 256K, 512K, 1024K and 2048Kbytes.

5.1   Strategies for Allocation inside Bunches

In our PerDiS memory simulator, five strategies to allocate an object inside a bunch are currently implemented.

The *fixed size* strategy allows only allocation of object of the same size (or of the same size class) in the bunch. The free list uses a bitmap that keeps track of allocated and free blocks. This strategy is used in the PerDiS memory simulator in conjunction with the segregated bunches selection (see Sect. 5.2).

The other four use an address-ordered free list with deferred coalescing of the free block. The free list is doubly linked. When an allocation request can not be successfully completed because there is no large enough free block, contiguous free blocks in memory are coalesced and the free list is scanned again. There are four strategies to search for a free block in the free list:

- *first fit*: Walk through the free list from the beginning to first large enough free block, and allocate there.
- *best fit*: Walk through the whole list and allocate in the smallest large enough free block.
- *roving pointer*: Walk through the free list from the position where the last allocated object was taken from the free list.
- *linear allocator*: the same as *roving pointer* but never re-use the memory. This kind of allocator could be used only in conjunction with a copying garbage collection algorithm.

5.2   Strategies for Bunch Selection

The five strategies for selecting a standard bunch available in our simulator are all inspired by the strategies for allocating inside bunch:

- *First available bunch*: Bunches are stored in a list and allocation is done in the first satisfactory bunch.
- *Best available bunch*: Bunches are stored in a list and allocation is done in the best satisfactory bunch.
- *Last available bunch*: Bunches are also stored in a list but it is scanned from the last bunch where an allocation has been successfully completed.
- *Linear bunch*: Basically the same than *Last available bunch*, but never re-use the previous bunch in the list, allocate a new one. The same remark than for *linear* inside bunch allocation strategy apply.
- *Segregated bunch*: Use different bunches to allocate object of different size classes. Sizes are rounded up to the nearest power of two.

The first four strategies can be used in conjunction with *first fit*, *best fit*, *roving pointer* or *linear allocator* inside bunch allocation strategies. *Segregated bunch* can be used only with *fixed size* inside bunch allocation strategy.

6   Allocation Simulations Using Significant Strategies

For the simulations presented in this section, five allocation strategies have been selected. They correspond to the five available bunches selection strategies. The inside bunch allocation strategy is not significant in this set of simulations because only one single snapshot is considered and, by the way, there is no memory deallocation.

In the rest of the paper, the five strategies will be referenced using the following names:

1. *cluster_first*: allocate in the clusters using *First available bunch* strategy.
2. *cluster_best*: allocate in the clusters using *Best available bunch* strategy.
3. *cluster_roving*: allocate in the clusters using *Last available bunch* strategy.
4. *cluster_linear*: allocate in the clusters using *linear bunch* strategy.
5. *cluster_segregated*: allocate in the clusters using *segregated bunch* strategy.

6.1   Memory Allocation Simulations in Order of Last Modifications Date

In this section, the simulation results we present has been obtained using the five selected allocation strategies with data allocation ordered by last modifications date.

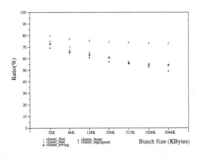
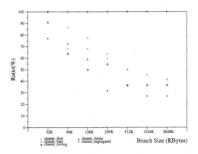

(a) proportion of inter-bunch refer-   (b) proportion of inter-bunches cy-
ences   cles

Fig. 5. PerDiS: simulations in order of last modifications date

Site 1: http://www.perdis.esprit.ec.org/. Figure 5a shows the proportion of inter-bunch references for the five allocation strategies and for seven bunch sizes. Proportion of inter-bunch references is the percentage of all references that are to objects in a different bunch. Clearly *cluster_segregated* is the worse strategy from the point of view of reference locality but this is not a surprise. The best strategies from locality point of view (*cluster_linear* or *cluster_roving*, depending on bunch size) have proportion of inter-bunch references between 50%, for 2048K bunches, to 70%, for 32K ones, that is very high. The good locality results of the *cluster_roving* policy should be taken with care, because there is no freeing in our simulations and unfortunately, the roving policy is known to strew new objects among the old ones whose neighbors have been freed. The inter-bunches cycles proportion is the percentage of cycles which span bunches. Looking at this proportion, in Fig. 5b, it appear that they are not more encouraging. *cluster_segregated* still give the worse results with 100% of inter-bunches cycles but the best strategy gives a proportion between 30% to 78% depends on bunch size. Figure 6a shows the number of scions, i.e. the number of objects that have incoming references from different bunches. This number is comparable to the number of objects for small bunches and go down by only 20% for large bunch and best allocation policy. This signify that, even in the best case, 80% of the objects have incoming references from different bunch, that is a high proportion.

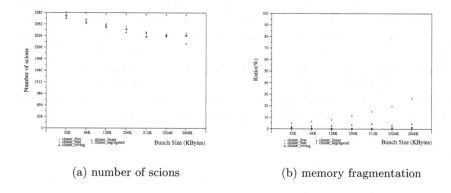

(a) number of scions   (b) memory fragmentation

Fig. 6. PerDiS: simulations in order of last modifications date

Finally, Fig. 6b gives an overview of memory fragmentation (internal and external combined) at the end of a snapshot simulation. This is the moment where the maximum of memory is allocated. Since there is no deallocation in our single snapshot, results about memory fragmentation are not significant, but they show that fragmentation increase with bunch size, as expected. They show also that policy known to be poor on fragmentation, the *cluster_segregated* strategy [WJ98], give the worse fragmentation result, even for small standard bunch sizes. This last result need to be confirmed by other simulations using several snapshots, representing the evolution (including deallocation) of the web site.

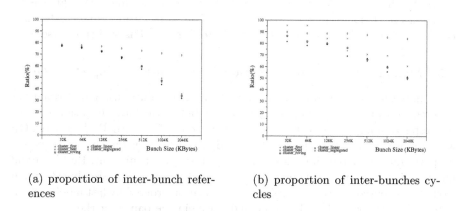

(a) proportion of inter-bunch refer-   (b) proportion of inter-bunches cy-
ences   cles

Fig. 7. SOR: simulations in order of last modifications date

Site 2: http://www-sor.inria.fr/. The second set of simulations, (on the second studied web site) shows many similarities with results for Site 1. Figure 7a shows the proportion of inter-bunches references. *Cluster_segregated* is still the worse strategy. The best proportion is between 30% to 79% for bunches respectively from 2048K to 32K. The inter-bunch cycles proportion, in Fig. 7b, gives mostly the same results as for site 1, *cluster_segregated* is the worse and best proportion vary between 80% for 32K bunches to 50% for 2048K ones. Figure 8a show the number of scions. As for the PerDiS site, this number is comparable to the number of objects for small bunches, but go down more significantly (40%) for large bunch.

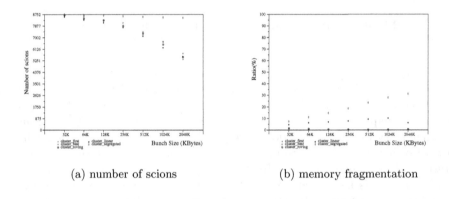

(a) number of scions   (b) memory fragmentation

Fig. 8. SOR: simulations in order of last modifications date

On the fragmentation front (Fig. 8b), the tendency is almost the same as for site 1, except that the *cluster_linear* strategy gives worse results than *cluster_first*, *cluster_best* or *cluster_roving*. However, *cluster_segregated* is still the worse.

6.2   Memory Allocation Simulations in Depth-First Top-down Order

The simulation results presented here has been obtained using the same five selected allocation strategies as in Sect. 6.1 but with data allocation ordered by graph topology, in depth-first top-down order. For both PerDiS and SOR web site, we present only results about proportion of inter-bunch references and proportion of inter-bunch cycles as they are the most significant. Results about number of scions and fragmentation are omitted because they are almost similar to those presented in Sect. 6.1, using data allocation ordered by last modifications date and by the way there is not enough space in the paper for them.

Site 1: http://www.perdis.esprit.ec.org/. Figure 9a and Fig. 9b shows respectively proportion of inter-bunch references and proportion of inter-bunch cycles for the PerDiS web site. The proportion of inter-bunch references is 1% to 7% lower than the proportion we have using the last modifications date order, depend on the bunch size. For proportion of inter-bunch cycles, the difference is between 10% higher for 32K bunches to 10% lower for bunches of 1024K and 2048K.

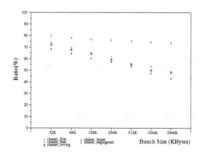 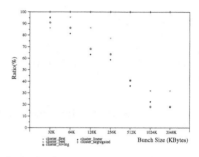

(a) proportion of inter-bunch references

(b) proportion of inter-bunches cycles

Fig. 9. PerDiS: simulations in depth-first top-down order

Site 2: http://www-sor.inria.fr/. Figure 10a and Fig. 10b shows respectively proportion of inter-bunch references and proportion of inter-bunch cycles for the SOR web site. The proportion of inter-bunch references is 0% to 10% lower than the proportion we have using the last modifications date order, depend on the bunch size. For proportion of inter-bunch cycles, the difference is between 3% lower for 32K bunches to 15% lower for 2048K bunches.

7   Conclusion

In this paper, we have analyzed the intrinsic graph characteristics of two web sites (see Sect. 3) and evaluated the respective performance of five memory allocation strategies for a persistent store by simulating their behavior against the two web sites.

From the analysis of graph characteristics, we learned that most of the objects are small (around 80% are less than 50 Kbytes) and reference density is low. This confirms some known results. On the other hand, we learned that a large proportion of the objects is included in cycles (70% for site 1 and 30% for site 2) and the proportion of bytes involved is not negligible (12% to 14%). If we look at the characteristics of the individual cycles, it appears that most cycles are

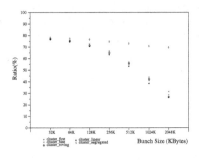

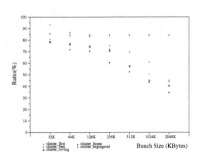

(a) proportion of inter-bunch references

(b) proportion of inter-bunches cycles

Fig. 10. SOR: simulations in depth-first top-down order

relatively small, both in number of objects and in bytes. This result contradict
our assumption of a relatively small proportion of cycles. However, since the
cycles are quiet small, this is not really a problem.

From the memory allocation simulations, we learned that a large proportion
of references are inter-bunch: a large proportion of the cycles are inter-bunches
whatever the bunch size and whatever allocation strategies we choose. This is
not the results we expected. However these results need to be interpreted with
caution because, first, we have studied only two web sites, which are not guaranteed to be representative of other web sites. Second, web application might
not be representative of applications that use a persistent object store.

Finally, the simulation we have done with the allocation sorted by graph
topology in depth-first top-down order shows that this order give always better
locality results than the last modifications date order, but the difference is not so
big. Most often, it stay between 5% to 10% and by the way using the allocation-
order clustering policy seem to be feasible according to this set of simulations.

8   Future Work

This paper presented a first evaluation of the memory allocation strategies for the
PerDiS Persistent Distributed Object Store. Future work direction are numerous.

One is to study the evolution of web sites over a long time period, by recording several snapshot until we are able to see significant graph modifications
and deallocations. This is especially relevant for the measurements of memory
fragmentation. Another direction is to implement more allocation strategies in
our simulator, such as Buddy Systems [Kno65,PN77], Indexed Fits [Ste83], or
Bit-mapped Fits [BDS91]. Extending our measurements on the web to many
other web sites will be also interesting in the future. Another point is to study

applications specifically targeting a persistent objects store and written in an object oriented fashion. More specifically, we plan to study the port to PerDiS of the Atlantis application from IEZ[11]. Comparing many other known dynamic re-clustering strategies (breath-first, depth-first, hierarchical decomposition, type directed, other ?) with our current allocation time placement strategy will be very interesting. In the more distant future, we may design and evaluate a new strategy where the specific target will be to minimize cross-bunches references. Those re-clustering strategies may be used in the PerDiS store if it appears that the static heuristics we have evaluated first are not efficient enough.

References

[ABC+83]   M. P. Atkinson, P. J. Bailey, K. J. Chisholm, P. W. Cockshott, and R. Morrison. An approach to persistent programming. *The Computer Journal*, 26(4):360–365, 1983.

[BDS91]   Hans-J. Boehm, Alan J. Demers, and Scott Shenker. Mostly parallel garbage collection. In *Proc. of the SIGPLAN'91 Conf. on Programming Language Design and Implementation*, pages 157–164, Toronto (Canada), June 1991. ACM.

[BFS98]   Xavier Blondel, Paulo Ferreira, and Marc Shapiro. Implementing garbage collection in the perdis system. In *Proceedings of the Eighth International Workshop on Persistent Object Systems*, August 1998.
`http://www-sor.inria.fr/publi/IGCPS_pos8.html`.

[DDZ93]   David Detlefs, Al Dosser, and Benjamin Zorn. Memory allocation costs in large C and C++ programs. Technical Report CU-CS-665-93, Dept. of Comp. Sc., Colorado University, Boulder, Colorado (USA), August 1993. `ftp://ftp.cs.colorado.edu/pub/cs/techreports/zorn/CU-CS-665-93.ps.Z`.

[FS94]   Paulo Ferreira and Marc Shapiro. Garbage collection and DSM consistency. In *Proc. of the First Symposium on Operating Systems Design and Implementation (OSDI)*, pages 229–241, Monterey CA (USA), November 1994. ACM.
`http://www-sor.inria.fr/publi/GC-DSM-CONSIS_OSDI94.html`.

[FS96]   Paulo Ferreira and Marc Shapiro. Larchant: Persistence by reachability in distributed shared memory through garbage collection. In *Proc. 16th Int. Conf. on Dist. Comp. Syst. (ICDCS)*, Hong Kong, May 1996.
`http://www-sor.inria.fr/publi/LPRDSMGC:icdcs96.html`.

[FSB+98]   Paulo Ferreira, Marc Shapiro, Xavier Blondel, Olivier Fambon, Joâo Garcia, Sytse Kloosterman, Nicolas Richer, Marcus Roberts, Fadi Sandakly, George Coulouris, Jean Dollimore, Paulo Guedes, Daniel Hagimont, and Sacha Krakowiak. PerDiS: design, implementation, and use of a PERsistent DIstributed Store. Technical Report QMW TR 752, CSTB ILC/98-1392, INRIA RR 3525, INESC RT/5/98, QMW, CSTB, INRIA and INESC, October 1998.
`http://www-sor.inria.fr/publi/PDIUPDS_rr3525.html`.

---

[11] IEZ is an industrial partner involved in the PerDiS project, see
`http://www.perdis.esprit.ec.org/members/`.

[Kno65]   Kenneth C. Knowlton. A fast storage allocator. *Communications of the ACM*, 8(10):623–625, October 1965.

[LLOW91]   Charles Lamb, Gordon Landis, Jack Orenstein, and Dan Weinreb. The ObjectStore database system. *Communications of the ACM*, 34(10):50–63, October 1991.

[PN77]   J. L. Peterson and T. A. Norman. Buddy systems. *Communications of the ACM*, 20(6):421–431, June 1977.

[Sal99]   Alexandru Salcianu. Extraction et utilisation des informations de type pour le support des objets répartis. Mémoire de dea, DEA d'Informatique de Lyon, INRIA, Rocquencourt (France), July 1999. `http://www-sor.inria.fr/publi/EUITSOR_dea-salcianu-1999-07.html`.

[Ste83]   C. J. Stephenson. Fast Fits: New methods for dynamic storage allocation. In *Proceedings of the Ninth Symposium on Operating Systems Principles*, pages 30–32, Bretton Woods, New Hampshire, October 1983.

[WJ98]   Paul R. Wilson and Mark S. Johnstone. The memory fragmentation problem: Solved? In *Proc. Int. Symposium on Memory Management (ISMM'98)*, pages 26 – 36, Vancouver, Canada, October 1998. `ftp://ftp.cs.utexas.edu/pub/garbage/malloc/ismm98.ps`.

[WJNB95]   Paul R. Wilson, Mark S. Johnstone, Michael Neely, and David Boles. Dynamic storage allocation: A survey and critical review. In *Proc. Int. Workshop on Memory Management*, Kinross Scotland (UK), September 1995. `ftp://ftp.cs.utexas.edu/pub/garbage/allocscr.ps`.

[ZG92a]   Benjamin Zorn and Dirk Grunwald. Empirical measurements of six allocation-intensive C programs. Technical Report CU-CS-604-92, Dept. of Comp. Sc., Colorado University, Boulder, Colorado (USA), July 1992. `ftp://ftp.cs.colorado.edu/pub/cs/techreports/zorn/CU-CS-604-92.ps.Z`.

[ZG92b]   Benjamin Zorn and Dirk Grunwald. Evaluating models of memory allocation. Technical Report CU-CS-603-92, Dept. of Comp. Sc., Colorado University, Boulder, Colorado (USA), July 1992. `ftp://ftp.cs.colorado.edu/pub/cs/techreports/zorn/CU-CS-603-92.ps.Z`.

A Comparison of Two Persistent Storage Tools for Implementing a Search Engine

Andrea Garratt, Mike Jackson, Peter Burden, and Jon Wallis

School of Computing & IT, University of Wolverhampton, 35-49 Lichfield Street,
Wolverhampton WV1 1EL, UK
{in5969, m.s.jackson, jphb, j.wallis}@wlv.ac.uk

Abstract. This paper compares two Java-based persistent storage mechanisms: a commercially available object-oriented database (OODB) system[1] and the persistent storage tool PJama [1] on the basis of their suitability for implementing the index component of an experimental World Wide Web search engine called WWLib-TNG. Persistence is provided to the builder component of the search engine, which constructs a catalogue of Web pages. The searcher component of the engine searches the catalogue. The implementation of the builder using PJama and using an OODB were compared with respect to time taken to construct a catalogue, efficient use of disk space and scalability. The implementations of the searcher were compared on response time and scalability. The comparison showed that for this application PJama performs better than the OODB. Compared with the OODB, PJama gave 300% better build performance and was more scalable.

1 Introduction

The Wolverhampton Web Library - The Next Generation (WWLib-TNG) is an experimental World Wide Web (Web) search engine currently under development at the University of Wolverhampton [2] [3]. WWLib-TNG attempts to combine the advantages of classified directories with the advantages of automated search engines by providing automatic classification [4] [5] and automatic resource discovery. WWLib-TNG gathers and classifies Web pages from sites in the UK. The Dewey Decimal Classification (DDC) [6] system is used to classify Web pages because it has been used by UK libraries for many years and is therefore well understood.

WWLib-TNG consists of seven software components: the dispatcher, archiver, analyser, filter, classifier, builder and searcher. A description of these components can be found in [2]. The builder analyses Web pages and extracts information from them to build the main database. The searcher, upon receiving a query, interrogates the main database created by the builder and generates results ranked in order of relevance to the query.

This paper briefly describes the design of prototypes representing the builder and searcher components. The builder and searcher prototypes were designed independently of the persistence technologies compared in this paper. The prototypes

---

[1] For licensing reasons it is not possible to name the product.

G.N.C. Kirby, A. Dearle, and D.I.K. Sjøberg (Eds.): POS-9, LNCS 2135, pp. 177-186, 2001.
© Springer-Verlag Berlin Heidelberg 2001

were implemented in Java and the builder prototype implemented using PJama [1] was compared with the builder prototype implemented using a commercially available OODB with respect to build time, disk space usage and scalability. The implementations of the searcher prototype were compared on response time and scalability.

We decided to use a persistent storage tool so that the builder and searcher prototypes could be implemented quickly, allowing more time to investigate result ranking strategies. Initially, an OODB was selected to provide persistent storage for the system. When the performance of an early version of this software proved to be unsuitable even for a prototype system, PJama was evaluated as an alternative. PJama provides persistence via a modification of the Java virtual machine (JVM). The version used in this comparison is 1.6.5 which is based on version 1.2.2 of the Java Development Kit that has the just-in-time (JIT) compiler enabled. The commercially available OODB used in the comparison provides an application programming interface between Java and the OODB, and a post-processor for adding additional byte-codes to application classes so that they can be persistent capable. The version of Java is JDK-1.2.2-001, which has the JIT compiler enabled.

2   The Builder and Searcher

The first stage in the design of the builder and searcher prototypes was to determine what structure the main database should have. We considered three information retrieval storage structures: an inverted file [7], signature file [8] and Pat tree [9] and for each structure, we considered a number of implementations. A theoretical comparison of the structures was done on the following criteria: response time of a query; support for result ranking; support for Boolean, phrase and proximity search techniques; efficient file maintenance; efficient use of disk space; scalability and extensibility. The comparison indicated that an inverted file with a B+tree (a variant of a B-tree [10]) for an index appeared to be the most suitable structure for a Web search engine, unlike the signature file and Pat tree, which would encounter problems with very large corpora.

The inverted file we implemented consists of an index and a number of postings lists. The index contains a list of each distinct word in the corpus. Each distinct word has a pointer to a postings list, which is a list of page accession numbers of Web pages that contain the word. The inverted file consists of word references as opposed to page references and hence performs well because it avoids a sequential scan of the entire structure to discover which Web pages contain the words in the query.

Figure 1 shows an UML class diagram of the main database of WWLib-TNG (an inverted file with a B+tree for an index). The objects that make up the B+tree of the inverted file are B+tree, node, key/pointer, *elem* and term entry. There is a term entry object for each distinct word in the corpus. This includes common words and case-sensitive words. Each term entry object has a pointer reference to a postings list. Accession numbers are stored in posting objects. Each posting object has an array of position objects that hold the location (i.e. title, URL, etc) and word position of the word in the Web page. Word location and position are stored for each word so that phrase and proximity searches are possible and also for result ranking purposes.

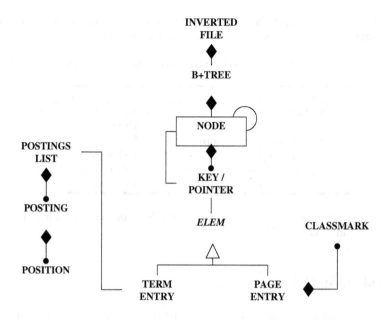

Fig. 1. UML class diagram of the main database of WWLib-TNG

Statistics about each page in the corpus are held for result ranking purposes i.e. page length, DDC class mark(s)[2], etc. It is difficult, however, to hold data about a Web page in the main database because the structure is organised on words and not on page accession numbers. Information about each Web page is therefore held in a second B+tree. The objects that make up the second B+tree are B+tree, node, key/pointer, *elem* and page entry. There is a page entry object for each page in the corpus. Each page entry object has an array of class mark objects that hold DDC class mark(s) for the page.

3   Test Corpus

For the comparison a small corpus was used - The King James Bible, which consists of 4.353MBs of text (future test corpora will be larger, i.e. terabytes in size). The Bible contains 66 books and each book has one or more chapters. For this application, each chapter was judged to be equivalent to a single Web page and assigned a unique accession number. We chose the Bible as test data because we believed that the variable length if its chapters are similar to the variable length characteristic of Web pages. The Bible contains 1,189 chapters, which are treated as 1,189 Web pages. For

---

[2] A DDC class mark is a number from the DDC hierarchy. Example class marks are 781.62 which is *Folk music* and 641.568 which is *Cooking for special occasions including Christmas*.

the remainder of this paper the words page (meaning Web page) and chapter are used interchangeably. Table 1 contains statistics about the corpus.

Table 1. Test corpus statistics

Statistic	King James Bible
Size of raw data	4.353 MB
Number of words[3]	790,881
Number of distinct words[4]	17,471
Number of pages	1,189
Maximum page length	2,445 words
Minimum page length	33 words

The comparison was done on a Sun Ultra 60 workstation with twin 360MHz processors and 512MBs of RAM.

4 Evaluation Criteria

The builder prototype implemented using PJama was compared with the builder prototype implemented using an OODB on the following criteria:

- **Build time**, which is the time taken to index a corpus. Build performance must be efficient because in the Web environment new Web pages will be frequently added to the main database due to the rapid growth of the Web.
- **Efficient use of disk space**. Without the use of compression techniques and with word level indexing an inverted file occupies up to 300% disk space in addition to the raw data [11]. Therefore, the main database built by the builder prototypes should not occupy more than 300% disk space in addition to the raw data.
- **Scalability**, which for both the above should be at least linear.

The two implementations of the searcher prototype were compared on the following criteria:

- **Response time**, which is the time taken by the searcher to produce a result set of accession numbers upon receiving a query. Response time of a query should ideally be no more than 10 seconds. The response time of commercial search engines on average is 3-4 seconds. For a prototype system that is written in Java (as opposed to C) and which uses a persistent storage tool (as opposed to tailored disk management software), a 10-second response time of a query was considered acceptable.
- **Scalability**, which for the above should be linear or better.

---

[3] A word is any word in the Bible (except chapter and verse numbers). For example, *Lord*, *lord* and *Lord's* are all treated as different words.

[4] Distinct words are all the unique words in the corpus, that is, the vocabulary of the corpus. Words, however, lose context when placed in the inverted file and therefore *litter* (as in kittens) and *litter* (as in rubbish) are the same word.

5 The Builder: Build Time and Scalability Comparison

The index of the inverted file is a B+tree. The original concept of a B+tree involves mapping each node of the tree to a page of disk storage. The aim of the WWLib-TNG project, however, was to construct the index quickly. We therefore constructed an index that whilst being self-balancing the same way as a B-tree, did not necessarily map index nodes to disk pages. Since we were not able to guess how either of the implementation platforms would organize tree nodes on disk, the effect of node size on performance was of interest. For both implementations of the builder prototype, we tested a number of node sizes (or branch factors) that ranged from 75 to 200, which gave B+trees that had three and two levels (including the root) for a vocabulary of 17,471 words. Their effect on performance, however, was insignificant.

We also had to decide what class to use to implement the postings lists of the inverted file. We chose a Vector, which is an expandable array. The Vector was chosen over other Java collection classes (i.e. hash table or tree) because postings lists should be stored in ascending page number order so that two postings lists can be efficiently merged for a Boolean AND or OR query. If each postings list was implemented using a hash table or tree then more random disk seeks would be generated by these structures whilst reading a postings list into memory due to traversing the structure in ascending page number order.

On creation a Vector has an initial capacity (IC). When the Vector becomes full it is replaced with a new Vector object that has the additional capacity specified by the growing capacity (GC) value. It was necessary to choose a suitable IC and GC for the vectors. For example, when the Bible is indexed the main database contains 17,471 postings lists (number of distinct words) and the maximum length of a postings list is 1,189 (maximum number of pages) and the minimum length is 1. If the Vector IC was set at 1,189 then no CPU time would be wasted because there would be no need to expand any vectors. Vectors of this size, however, would waste disk space because 81% of postings lists have 10 elements or less when the Bible has been indexed. A small GC (such as 1) produces poor build performance because many vectors will expand frequently, however, no disk space will be wasted. For this corpus an IC and GC of 8, 32 and 64 were tested for each implementation of the builder prototype. An IC and GC of 8 are more efficient in terms of disk space but not build performance. 21.7% of vectors have from 9 to 1,189 elements. An IC and GC of 32 use more disk space but build performance is better. 8.2% of vectors have from 33 to 1,189 elements. An IC and GC of 64 should give the best build performance but use the most disk space. 4.6% of vectors have from 65 to 1,189 elements. After conducting experiments it was found that the optimum IC and GC for the vectors of the PJama prototype was 32 because they gave the best scaling of disk space usage. The optimum IC and GC for the OODB vectors was 8 because they gave the best build performance and disk space usage. A description of the experiments conducted for the OODB implementation of the builder prototype can be found in [12].

The builder prototype implemented using PJama indexed the Bible in a single transaction i.e. for each book in the Bible the pages where analysed and indexed, and after the final book was indexed the data was committed to disk. The analysis phase involved sorting the words in a book into groups of distinct words. The indexing phase was the building of the inverted file structure in memory, and the commit phase was writing data to disk. The size of the object cache was 10MBs and no steps were taken to account for the effects of operating system caching.

The builder prototype implemented using the OODB could not index the Bible in a single transaction in the same way as the builder implemented using PJama. The maximum number of books that the OODB implementation could handle in a transaction was twenty-seven. Twenty-five books per transaction, however, gave the best build time i.e. twenty-five books were read one at a time and for each book the pages were analysed and then indexed, and committed to disk after the twenty-fifth book was indexed. The size of the OODB object cache was unknown and it was not possible to adjust its size. Again, no steps were taken to account for the effects of operating system caching.

The best build time obtained from the builder implemented using PJama was 179.42 seconds. The best build time from the builder implemented using an OODB was 640.62 seconds. The builder implemented using PJama gave approximately 300% better build performance.

CPU time for both implementations of the builder prototype scaled linearly for this corpus. CPU time for the indexing phase of each build, however, for both implementations of the builder prototype scaled slightly worse than linear. The non-linear scaling of CPU time for the indexing phase of the PJama implementation is related to the expansion of vectors which are used to implement each postings list i.e. every time a vector expands data elements from the old vector are copied to the new larger vector. The copying of data elements to a new larger vector is avoided by the OODB platform because OODB vectors have an internal array that links the data arrays together i.e. the first element of the internal array references the initial data array created and the second element of the internal array references the second array created when the vector expanded. The non-linear scaling of CPU time for the indexing phase of the build for the OODB implementation is due to the *addElement* method of the OODB vector class, which is called when a postings list is updated [12]. Before a new posting object is appended to the end of a postings list the *addElement* method performs a sequential search on the OODB vector to locate the end of the vector. This degrades performance of the indexing phase of the build.

6   The Builder: Disk Space Usage and Scalability Comparison

The size of the store built using PJama was 85,209,344 bytes and the store built using the OODB was 67,475,724 bytes. Each figure includes disk space used by the store and log file(s) and they were obtained using the Unix operating system command 'ls - l'. The PJama store uses approximately 1,977% disk space in addition to the raw data and the OODB store uses approximately 1,558% disk space. Both stores use more than 300% disk space, which was the limit set in the evaluation criteria. Disk space usage for each store built using PJama and the OODB, however, scaled linearly.

7 The Searcher: Response Time and Scalability Comparison

Ten queries were used to test the response time and scalability of the searcher prototypes. Figure 2 shows five of the ten queries used. When choosing the queries we tried to reflect: (a) the characteristics of Web user queries which have on average 2.35 terms [13] and (b) the changes that a Web search engine may make to a query, such as using a thesaurus to expand the query (see query 5). We also considered the number of pages that each query term appears in. The first query is a single term query and queries 2 and 3 are Boolean AND type queries. Query 4 is a Boolean OR type query and the last query is a combination of Boolean AND and OR operators.

1	lord
2	the $\wedge$ ten $\wedge$ commandments
3	and $\wedge$ it $\wedge$ was $\wedge$ so
4	Eve $\vee$ tempted $\vee$ serpent $\vee$ garden $\vee$ Eden
5	(forty $\vee$ days $\vee$ nights $\vee$ rain $\vee$ rained $\vee$ storm $\vee$ tempest) $\wedge$ (water $\vee$ waters $\vee$ sea $\vee$ flood) $\wedge$ (animals $\vee$ beasts $\vee$ creatures $\vee$ two $\vee$ by $\vee$ pair $\vee$ pairs) $\wedge$ (Noah $\vee$ ark)

Fig. 2. Five of the ten test queries used to test the searcher prototypes

Table 2 shows the response times for the searcher prototypes implemented using PJama and the OODB after the Bible was indexed. Response time of all ten queries for both implementations of the searcher was well below the 10-second limit set in the evaluation criteria.

Table 2. Response times recorded for test queries in Fig 2

Query	PJama (seconds)	OODB (seconds)
1	1.87	2.11
2	1.02	2.16
3	1.69	3.53
4	0.98	1.56
5	1.22	2.72

Figure 3 shows the scaling of response time for each query in figure 2 for both implementations of the searcher prototype. The scalability of the searcher was tested by indexing approximately 150 pages of the Bible and then processing the ten queries and recording their response time. The next batch of approximately 150 pages were indexed and the queries processed until all the pages in the Bible were indexed. 150 pages were chosen because both builder prototypes read one book at a time and the largest book is Psalms, which has 150 pages. The remaining books in the Bible were grouped together in batches so that the number of pages per batch was approximately 150.

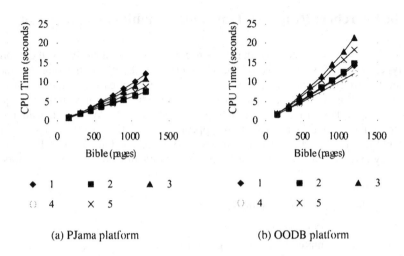

(a) PJama platform   (b) OODB platform

Fig. 3. Scaling of response time for queries in Fig. 2

Response time for query 4 for both implementations scaled reasonably linearly. This query involved the processing of five small postings lists, which were 204 elements in length or less. The scaling of response time for query 2 for the PJama implementation scaled reasonably linearly, however, the scaling of response time for this query for the OODB implementation scaled worse than linear. The scaling of response time for the remaining queries (i.e. 1, 3 and 5) for both implementations is worse than linear. All these queries process large or many postings lists which has affected performance. For example, the term in query 1 appears in 1,007 pages. All the terms in query 3 are common i.e. the term *and* appears in 1,187 pages, *it* appears in 1,039 pages, *was* appears in 821 pages and *so* appears in 753 pages. Query 5 has 20 terms. Response time of the searcher prototype implemented using PJama scaled better than the response time of the searcher prototype implemented using the OODB. This is particularly noticeable for queries 2, 3 and 5. This may be due to memory usage.

8   Conclusions

This paper has compared a Java-based persistent storage tool called PJama with a commercially available OODB on the basis of their suitability for a prototype system of an experimental Web search engine. Prototypes were constructed representing the builder and searcher components of the search engine. The two builder prototypes implemented using PJama and an OODB were compared on build time, efficient use of disk space and scalability. The two implementations of the searcher prototype were compared on response time and scalability. The results of the comparison are summarised below:

- **Build time**. PJama gave approximately 300% better build performance than the OODB. The builder implemented using PJama took 179.42 seconds to index the

Bible (4.353MBs in size) which for a prototype system is sufficient. Build time for both implementations scaled linearly.

- **Disk space usage**. The store built using PJama used more disk space than the store built using the OODB. The store built using PJama used approximately 1,977% disk space in addition to the raw data (4.353MBs in size) and the OODB store used approximately 1,558%. Both stores used more than the 300% disk space limit that was set in the evaluation criteria. Some of the disk space usage is related to the Java language. For example, in Java every object has a 12-byte overhead. For this application, however, performance and scalability are more important than disk space usage. Disk space usage of both stores scaled linearly.

- **Response time** of both implementations of the searcher prototype was well below the 10-second limit set in the evaluation criteria. Response time for both implementations of the searcher scaled reasonably linearly when executing queries that involved the processing of small postings lists. For queries that involved the processing of large postings lists or the processing of many terms (i.e. query 5), response time for both implementations of the searcher scaled worse than linear. Response time for the searcher implemented using PJama, however, scaled better than the response time of the searcher implemented using an OODB.

- **Ease of implementation**. An implementation criterion was to implement the builder and searcher quickly to allow more time to investigate result ranking strategies. By using a persistent storage tool to provide persistence capabilities it was possible to implement the builder and searcher prototypes quickly and meet our implementation criterion. Both PJama and the OODB were easy to incorporate with the builder and searcher code. The incorporation of PJama, however, took less time because fewer classes had to be modified.

The comparison has shown that of the two persistent storage tools studied PJama is the more suitable tool for the prototype system because it gave 300% better build performance, and scaled better than the OODB. Since the experiments conducted in this paper, the builder prototype implemented using PJama has successfully indexed 23,000 Web pages gathered from the University of Wolverhampton web site.

The results received from the builder and searcher implemented using PJama are acceptable for a prototype system, which will be used to test and evaluate result ranking strategies. For the implementation of the actual builder and searcher components of WWLib-TNG, however, neither persistent storage tool is suitable. Neither tool provides the sheer performance that is needed by a Web search engine.

Acknowledgements. The authors would like to thank Sun Microsystems for the donation of the Ultra 60 workstation on which the experiments were carried out.

References

1. Atkinson, M.P., Daynes, L., Jordan, M.J., Printezis, T. and Spence, S., "An Orthogonally Persistent Java", *ACM Sigmod Record*, 24(4), December 1996.

2.   Burden, J. P. H. and Jackson, M. S., "WWLib-TNG - New directions in Search Engine Technology", *IEE Informatics Colloquium: Lost in the Web - Navigation on the Internet*, pp.10/1-10/8, November 1999.
3.   Wallis, J. and Burden, J.P.H., "Towards a Classification-based Approach to Resource Discovery on the Web", *Proceedings of the 4th International W4G Workshop on Design and Electronic Publishing*, Abingdon (near Oxford), England, 20-22 November 1995.
4.   Jenkins, C., Jackson, M., Burden, P. and Wallis, J., "The Wolverhampton Web Library (WWLib) and Automatic Classification", *Proceedings of the First International Workshop on Libraries and WWW*, Brisbane, Queensland, Australia, 14th April 1998.
5.   Jenkins, C., Jackson, M., Burden, P. and Wallis, J., "Automatic Classification of Web Resources using Java and Dewey Decimal Classifications", *Proceedings of the Seventh International World Wide Web Conference*, Brisbane, Queensland, Australia, 14-18 April 1998.
6.   Mai Chan, L., Comaromi, J. P., Mitchell, J. S. and Satija, M. P., Dewey Decimal Classification: A Practical Guide. Forest Press, ISBN 0-910608-55-5, 1996.
7.   Salton, G. and McGill, M. J., Introduction to Modern Information Retrieval. New York: McGraw Hill, 1983.
8.   Faloutsos, C., "Signature Files", in Frakes, W. B. and Baeza-Yates, R. (eds.) Information Retrieval Data Structures and Algorithms. New Jersey: Prentice Hall, pp.44-65, 1992.
9.   Gonnet, G. H., Baeza-Yates, R. A. and Snider, T., "New Indices for Text: PAT trees and PAT arrays", in Frakes, W. B. and Baeza-Yates, R. (eds.) Information Retrieval Data Structures and Algorithms. New Jersey: Prentice Hall, pp.66-82, 1992.
10. Bayer, R. and McCreight, E., "Organisation and Maintenance of Large Ordered Indexes", *Acta Informatica*, 1(3), pp.173-189, 1972.
11. Zobel, J., Moffat, A. and Ramamohanarao, K., "Inverted Files Versus Signature Files for Text Indexing", *ACM Transactions on Database Systems*, 23(4), pp.453-490, December 1998.
12. Garratt, A., Jackson, M., Burden, P. and Wallis, J., "Implementing a search engine using an OODB", To appear in *L'objet*, 6(3), 2000.
13. Jansen, M. B. J., Spink, A., Bateman, J. and Saracevic, T., "Real Life Information Retrieval: A Study Of User Queries On The Web", *SIGIR FORUM*, 32(1), pp.5-17, Spring 1998.

Session 5: Overview

Liuba Shrira

Department of Computer Science, Brandeis University,
Waltham, MA 02154, USA
liuba@cs.brandeis.edu

This session contained three papers loosely centred around low level system support for persistent computation.

The first paper, „An Approach to Implementing Persistent Computations" presented by Ewa Bem [EB], deals with issues of supporting persistent computations in an operating system kernel. The paper identifies the categories of possible process/kernel interactions and describes different solution strategies to the persistent/transient kernel resource issues in each of these categories.

The second paper, „Transparent Orthogonal Checkpointing through User-Level Pagers" presented by Espen Skoglund [ES], considers the design of a transparent orthogonal checkpointer for persistence-unaware programs running on the L4 micro-kernel that works even in the presence of kernel upgrades.

The third paper, „An Overview of Ulisse, a Distributed Single Address Space System" presented by Gianluca Dini [GD], describes a system that implements a distributed single address space. This paper investigates the basic implementation mechanisms to locate, load and manage on a fast local area network a single writeable page copy and many read-only cache copies.

The panel discussion centred around the question of how the low level mechanisms developed to support persistent computation could be gainfully extended to support mobile persistent computation.

Skoglund suggested that since his system supports transparent checkpointing of a Linux process by paging, and since paging over the network would be expensive, his mechanism may be too „heavy weight" to support mobility.

Bem argued that mobile computation architectures often assume that checkpointing happens at well defined states to avoid the complexity of dealing with computation interrupted at arbitrary points, yet support for computation interrupted at arbitrary points is the main difficulty and challenge that her research set out to address.

Dini pointed out that Ulisse - the system he is developing in Pisa, initially had a design for supporting pages following users moving through the network but so far this direction has not received much effort.

Alan Dearle [AD] pointed out that some of his earlier work (reported in POS8) considered support for mobility and argued that „stop the world" persistent checkpointing of all system processes is not a viable approach for mobility support. Instead, what is needed is the ability to isolate the context that a process depends on, to allow checkpointing selectively just this context. This requires checkpointing the mobile process and its closely related cohorts, leaving out the rest of the system

G.N.C. Kirby, A. Dearle, and D.I.K. Sjøberg (Eds.): POS-9, LNCS 2135, pp. 187-188, 2001.
© Springer-Verlag Berlin Heidelberg 2001

processes. Some of the support for this type of process context isolation was present in the original Grasshopper system.

The Chair [LS] observed that mobile computation moving across platforms may need to deal with heterogeneous hardware and so the persistent object abstraction may be helpful in „changing the representations" of computing across platforms. The discussion then moved on to the issue of what platform should a mobile computation assume.

Stephen Blackburn [SB] pointed out that a multi-personality VM such as one from VMware systems already deals with this heterogeneity at the VM level. For example, a user checkpoints his Palm Pilot state at work, and then at home, can restart at exactly the same environment on a different platform, so at least some of the heterogeneity problem is solved at the virtual machine level.

Elliot Moss [EM] argued that VM abstraction may be all that is needed since in many cases, e.g. Palm Pilot the context of the computation is mostly in the head of the owner.

Esklund then argued that locking into a specific VM abstraction is too restrictive because once applications depend on a VM interface, the OS cannot be extensible, e.g. it is easy to replace a network card but not easy to add a different device.

Malcolm Atkinson [MPA] then raised the general question about how the systems discussed by the panel affected the application writers in the new environment: did they make it easier for the programmer to understand the environment or had life got more complicated?

Bem argued that the initial persistent computation goal was certainly to simplify, but the ideal turned out to be very costly in terms of the complexity that the kernel writer has to deal with. Moreover, this approach of forcing a given abstraction on the application writer resulted in strong tensions where users complained that the standard abstraction was either too much or not enough. For example, a database wants to manage the disk itself but the OS is getting in the way.

Dini pointed out that the mechanisms provided by their system provide extra flexibility and performance (e.g. can implement a join directly using user level pagers taking advantage of locality) but this comes at the expense of complexity for the programmer.

Esklund then argued that his group takes a pragmatic approach. Assuming the OS cannot realistically support the model where all data is persistent, neither can the user since, on his own, the task is just too complex. By providing support for orthogonal persistence under Linux for general applications, they let the application writer experiment with this capability so the user can make the tradeoff between the complexity of supporting „better semantics", providing higher performance, and simplicity.

An Approach to Implementing Persistent Computations

Ewa Z. Bem[1] and John Rosenberg[2]

[1] School of Computing and Information Technology
University of Western Sydney Nepean
ewa@cit.nepean.uws.edu.au
[2] Faculty of Information Technology, Monash University
johnr@infotech.monash.edu.au

Abstract. An operating system is persistent if all objects it supports have a lifetime independent of the context in which they were created. This concept, known as orthogonal persistence, extends to data objects and computations (processes and threads). A persistent computation is required to survive system crashes and shutdowns. After the service is restored it is expected to continue with a very small loss of productive activity. Over its lifetime every computation interacts with some transient aspects of its environment, for example I/O devices, network connections etc. The main issue in providing support for persistent computations is how to control such interactions in order to prevent them from becoming a part of the preserved state of a computation. These interactions are mediated by the system kernel; therefore the provision of persistent computations relates directly to the persistence of the kernel itself. In this paper we examine the solutions offered by persistent operating systems constructed to date, and we propose a new approach, implemented in the Grasshopper operating system. We show that this approach is sufficiently flexible to handle all problems identified so far, and sufficiently general to suit any operating system.

Keywords: persistent operating system, persistent computation, persistent kernel

1   Introduction

There is a number of requirements an operating system has to fulfil in order to support orthogonal persistence [2]. One of those requirements stipulates that the computations are to be persistent by encapsulating their state within persistent objects. The support for persistent computations marks the difference between orthogonally persistent systems and systems which merely provide a persistent store.

A persistent computation has the ability to continue despite any breakdown of service, whether planned such as a scheduled shutdown or unexpected such as a system crash. The discontinuity of the execution is transparent to the computation itself just like the discontinuity caused by any pre-emptive scheduling mechanism.

The ability to maintain the state of processes despite crashes and shutdowns is a potential source of performance gains in persistent systems. Not only is the waste of productive activity minimised, but there is no need to rebuild the process environment when the system is restarted after crash or shutdown, as is the case in conventional

G.N.C. Kirby, A. Dearle, and D.I.K. Sjøberg (Eds.): POS-9, LNCS 2135, pp. 189–200, 2001.

systems. These benefits come at a certain cost. Persistent computations introduce an additional level of complexity to the system, because of their interactions with the system kernel where the distinction between volatile and stable data remains visible. Specifically this complexity is caused by the necessity to make the kernel fully persistent, or to make it appear as fully persistent to user processes. In this paper we attempt to define the problems encountered when designing a persistent kernel, and we propose a general solution which is flexible, and has a minimal impact on the system performance.

This paper is organised as follows. Section 2 discusses problems in providing support for persistent computations, known solutions to these problems and their associated cost. Section 3 describes the approaches used in the persistent operating systems built to date. Section 4 presents the new approach developed in the context of the Grasshopper operating system [3, 8]. Section 5 contains a summary of the issues and our conclusions.

2   Persistent Computations

A process in a computing system is represented by some data stored in the kernel of the system and the contents of the architecture's general and special registers. When a process is suspended, the contents of relevant registers are saved as data within the kernel; therefore the process becomes fully defined by a number of kernel data structures. It has been suggested [2] that if the kernel data structures are all made persistent, the computations become persistent implicitly. This statement is true if we assume that it is meaningful to make all such data persistent. As we have already established it is not always so.

In a conventional non-persistent system the kernel data is based on static configuration files available at bootstrap, and on the actual physical configuration of hardware at this time. Such data is entirely ephemeral, and has to be rebuilt every time the system is rebooted. This includes all information related to processes. A persistent kernel has to deal with exactly the same environment, but in such a way that the user processes perceive it as persistent. This implies that all the transient kernel data has to be either hidden from the persistent computations, or rebuilt to match the perception of the persistent computations, or a combination of both.

Another issue in providing support for persistent computations is how to allow for kernel upgrades. In a conventional system an upgrade to any part of the operating system code including the kernel is a fairly straightforward procedure. The first step is to shutdown the system which implies the destruction of all of the existing processes. Even the processes which are routinely restarted as a part of the bootstrap sequence carry no knowledge of the previous state of the kernel other than that contained in the kernel data files. These data files can be easily converted and/or modified if this is required by the upgrade. In an orthogonally persistent system such an approach is not possible. Computations have to persist despite the changes in kernel code. In a sense kernel code is another transient resource, and its volatile nature has to be hidden just like transient kernel data.

2.1   Kernel Data

The state of many of the system resources is inherently transient, and cannot survive the shutdown, for example main memory, processor registers, I/O devices, network connections etc. This transient state is represented by the kernel internal data structures. Any data can be made persistent by copying it to stable media, and there are many known mechanisms [1] which can be applied. The problem is that the state such data represent may in reality no longer exist.

If the data representing the transient state of the kernel is nevertheless made persistent, on every restart it would have to be examined, and most likely reconstructed to reflect the actual state and configuration of the hardware resources, for example to take into account lost network connections or physical resources added or removed while the system was down. This implies that in the general case some of the kernel data structures have to be rebuilt on every restart, just as in a conventional system. The remaining kernel data, presumably persistent, may depend in some ways on the transient data structures built during the previous bootstrap. These persistent structures would also have to be rebuilt to match the new state of the system rebuilt by the current bootstrap, and so on.

Since a core of transient data, however small, always exists in the kernel, it is not possible to construct a fully persistent kernel. With this realisation the main question, when building persistence into the kernel, is where to place the division line between the kernel transient and persistent data. This is one of the fundamental decisions in the design and implementation of a persistent system [10].

The obvious requirement is that no persistent data structure may contain any reference to transient data, as this would result in dangling references and a loss of consistency after restart. There are other design issues apart from integrity of data; these include efficiency, robustness, avoiding unnecessary complexity, flexibility and ease of maintenance. All these may be influenced by the decisions regarding the division line between persistent and transient data in the kernel. Some data is inherently stable, for example information stored on magnetic media, some is inherently volatile, for example data flowing over a network connection, and some although volatile can be made to appear stable from the point of view of persistent computations. To illustrate this point let us examine the problems related to physical memory allocated to a process. Two approaches are possible:

- no attempt is made to preserve the actual contents of main memory, user process working set and any kernel data structures related to it are lost; after restart the process will rebuild its working set by conventional demand paging,
- the contents of memory are preserved between restarts, and the process physical memory allocation is retained, so a user process retains its working set after restart.

The state of the process may be captured by a checkpoint at any point of its execution, for example it may take place while a user process is half way through adding a new page of physical memory to its working set. Such a process interacts with a whole series of kernel data structures representing the current memory allocation, process page tables and working set etc. These structures are not modified simultaneously, so it is conceivable that some are already updated, while some others are not, when the shutdown takes place.

With the first approach the state of the user process in question cannot be meaningfully recreated on restart. If this process was restarted, it would attempt to continue updating the kernel data structures which no longer exist in their previous form. To avoid such problems the memory allocation to a user process has to be performed atomically. Such a requirement may not be reasonable in all cases. If a request is guaranteed always to complete in an acceptably short time it may be so, but for many requests such guarantees cannot be made, for example an I/O operation.

If the second approach is taken, all the kernel data structures in question and the contents of memory persist between restarts, and the user process can continue with its task as if a break in service did not happen. In this case a different set of problems has to be solved. Since all of the physical memory is preserved, we now have to identify those pages in memory which contain transient data representing the ephemeral state of hardware at the time of checkpoint and update these pages to correspond to the current state of hardware. On the other hand the working set of each process is retained in memory, and no processing will be wasted to service all the page fault exceptions as they are triggered by the execution of processes. In general making volatile resources appear as stable increases the complexity of the system recovery, and the time required for system shutdown and reboot, but has a potential to improve run-time performance.

Considering the problems outlined so far it seems that the obvious and safe solution is to provide transient kernel processes to handle all tasks which require access to kernel data and code. Allowing transient processes means that now the system needs to be aware of the existence of two types of processes, so that only the persistent processes are included in the scheduler queues recreated on restart. In addition any interactions between transient and persistent processes have to be formalised strictly to avoid any dependencies between them.

It is evident that every decision, which kernel data structures are to be persistent, and which are to be transient, carries with it a different set of consequences. These consequences should be well understood at the design stage of the system. Otherwise problems are resolved as they arise, often in the implementation stage, which may result in adopting suboptimal ad hoc solutions.

2.2   Kernel Upgrades

Kernel upgrades are more difficult to handle in a system which supports persistent computations. A process captured while executing within the old kernel code cannot simply continue execution within the new code since the return addresses and kernel data addresses saved on its kernel stack will no longer be relevant. There are three broad approaches to handle this situation:

- all kernel space addresses in kernel stacks for all the existing persistent processes are modified to reflect the new locations of the referenced code and data,

- no persistent processes are allowed to execute within the kernel space; if a kernel service is required a request is made to an internal transient kernel server process, while the persistent process waits for the return value outside the kernel.
- persistent processes are allowed into the kernel space, but must leave it before their state is captured.

To succeed, the first approach requires a detailed knowledge of stack usage characteristics. The correct interpretation of the stack contents may be difficult, so numeric data may be interpreted as addresses, or some addresses may be missed. Any later modification of kernel code may easily create unexpected problems so maintainability of the system is affected. For these reasons, although theoretically possible, this approach should be rejected.

The second approach offers a general and reliable solution. The separation between the persistent processes and the kernel is complete, as user processes have no direct access to the kernel code and data. This separation comes at a high cost. Every system call, even as trivial as request for the system time, would require a full context switch. These additional context switches can be a heavy and unavoidable burden on the overall system performance. The need to maintain a number of transient kernel processes in itself also adds to system overheads.

The last approach listed is only possible for those kernel calls, which can be guaranteed to complete in bounded time. Processes may not be allowed to remain in the kernel space for an indefinite time, for example to wait for I/O completion. This could cause deadlocks, and delays in undertaking crucial system activities, for example a shutdown before an impending power supply cut-off. An important implication of this approach is that at any time the kernel has to be aware of how many processes are executing in the kernel space, and it has to have a means of preventing new processes from entering if and when it is required. It appears that a considerable proportion of system calls can be handled in such way, ie. any system call not involving I/O or network devices, and most of the exceptions and interrupts.

The requirement for isolating the persistent and transient kernel data is still in force even when the persistent computations are independent of the kernel code using techniques described above. This is because any persistent computation interacting with kernel data directly or indirectly may not be allowed to become in any way dependent on the kernel transient data.

3   Support for Persistent Computations

Only a small number of operating systems built to date support persistent computations, and it is difficult to draw general conclusions based on their analysis. These systems are:
- the KeyKOS nanokernel – a commercial system designed to run with no support from hardware, and its successor EROS
- the L3/Eumel microkernel – an experimental commercial quality system, succeeded by L4 microkernel, originally without support for persistence

- the MONADS architecture – an experimental system based on custom built hardware, succeeded by Grasshopper – a system with explicit support for persistence.

The KeyKOS system [5] is based on a nanokernel which is declared to be stateless. It requires no dynamic allocation of storage, and any data used by the nanokernel and stored in its cache can be fully reconstructed from the persistent nodes and pages. The system outside the nanokernel is also completely described by the primitive persistent objects, including files, programs, program variables, instruction counters, I/O status etc. If that was indeed the case, the persistence of the KeyKOS kernel would be implicit. As we have already established some of the data any kernel has to deal with is transient, and it is also true for KeyKOS. The designers of this system admit that some state information cannot be saved in persistent objects [6], some ad hoc mechanisms are used in KeyKOS to resynchronise the system after restart. The specifics of these mechanisms were never disclosed. This is an example of the system where the decisions related to dealing with transient aspects of the system are not an inherent part of the design. Each specific interaction with transient resources is handled separately, and no attempt is made to provide a general solution. It is also not clear how kernel upgrades were made possible in KeyKOS. It is not unreasonable to assume that some more ad hoc mechanisms were used.

In the design of EROS [11], the successor to KeyKOS, it has been recognised that the state of processes waiting for service in the kernel (called stalled processes) cannot be adequately captured by the persistent pages and nodes. An additional design rule has been introduced which states that all kernel operations are atomic. The atomicity is achieved by adjusting the program counters of the stalled processes so the kernel invocation is retried automatically if the system restarts from a checkpoint. A similar mechanism is adopted in Fluke [13], which on recovery restarts all system calls transparently. Such an approach requires that all kernel operations are restartable ie. atomic from the user process point of view, or uninterruptible. In these systems a user process restarted from a checkpoint has no means of detecting that it repeats a particular system call.

The MONADS kernel [9] is implemented as a set of cooperating processes each performing a specific kernel task. These processes are transient, and are recreated on every restart. They communicate using kernel message blocks, which can be queued. All user processes reside above the kernel, and are scheduled separately from kernel processes, so there are no mixed queues of transient and persistent processes. User processes make requests to kernel processes by queuing an appropriate message block, and suspending until the request is complete. User processes never interact directly with any kernel data structures, or kernel code. As long as the queue of requests is persistent, the kernel code may change between the system restarts. This is a clean, general solution, which also provides a large degree of freedom to the kernel designer. Unfortunately it is costly in terms of performance, as each system call requires a full context switch.

Persistence in earlier versions of Grasshopper was based on optimistic strategies with user processes initiating their own checkpoint as they deemed necessary. The kernel was responsible for rebuilding a consistent global state of the system on recovery using the available collection of checkpoints. With this mechanism the captured state of the process is always well defined, and the state of other processes is not checkpointed at the same time. With the global checkpointing techniques adopted later such approach is not feasible.

In L3/Eumel system [7] processes are allowed to enter kernel space without any restrictions. The state of processes is captured by stabilising their registers, address spaces and any relevant kernel data. This data, including the stack contents, is manipulated on restart to ensure that no reference is made to the volatile (and no longer available) portion of the process state. We discussed this approach in relation to kernel upgrades. In the general case it is difficult if not impossible to prove that the resulting system state is consistent. This technique was successful in L3, with its small well defined set of system services, and is now proposed for its successor, the L4 microkernel [12] which was originally designed without support for persistence. In addition all incomplete system calls captured by the checkpoint are automatically restarted during recovery by adjusting the program Counter on stack, as in EROS and Fluke. Special provisions are made for the IPC call to avoid repetition of the receive phase. All three systems require that any system call at any point of execution is fully restartable.

Another microkernel of interest is Charm [4], recently developed at the University of St Andrews. The Charm kernel does not provide any thread or process abstraction, so all the problems related to persistent computations have to be handled at user level. Whether this approach will prove to be beneficial remains to be seen.

4   A New Approach to Persistent Computations

All the approaches presented in previous two sections have some merit, but none of them offers the best solution for all cases. Therefore we decided to combine the known methods so that depending on the particular kernel interaction the computation is requesting it is treated in the way most suitable to the request. We have identified three types of user process interactions with the kernel:

- the user process requests access to a peripheral device, the response time of which is outside the control of the system, and as such may take any length of time including infinite time,
- the user process requests some manipulation of kernel data, for example modification of object protection, physical memory allocation etc., where the interaction is fully under kernel control and absolute guarantees can be made about its completion time; this includes exception handling,
- the user process switches to kernel mode to service an interrupt; the process will interact with the kernel on behalf of some other process, or on behalf of the system itself, for example to service the clock interrupt.

Before we can present a meaningful discussion of the above categories let us state the assumptions we make about the kernel as such:

- the kernel is multi-threaded, and there is no limit on the number of computations executing in kernel mode,

- a checkpoint of the kernel data is performed periodically but asynchronously by a dedicated kernel thread; therefore it may capture user processes in an arbitrary state,
- a process synchronisation mechanism exists in the kernel in the form of semaphores or some other mechanism which can be used to implement semaphores.

The approach taken to handle the computations in the first category is shown in figure 1. Such computations may wait for completion of their request indefinitely, for example waiting for keyboard input. To handle this case there is a number of transient kernel threads servicing a common persistent queue of requests. On entry into the kernel a computation places its request block in this queue, and suspends itself. The request block contains space for return values specific to the request. One of the special purpose kernel transient threads collects this request, and performs the specific task on behalf of the suspended computation. If during the time it takes to complete this task there is no intervening checkpoint, the kernel thread will eventually provide the return values in the request block, and wake up the suspended computation. When this happens the only activity this computation may undertake within the kernel is the immediate return to user mode.

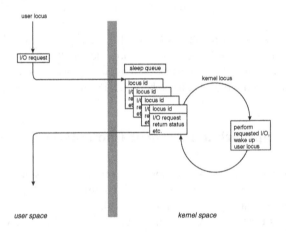

Fig. 1. Handling kernel requests of unbounded time

The state of the persistent computation does not change in any way while it is waiting in the queue. If this state is captured by a checkpoint, it can be used if needed to restore the computation to any point of time between the original request and its completion. Unlike the systems described in section 3 we decided that in general it is safer not to repeat the request automatically because of the possible changes in the hardware configuration, and even the kernel code itself. In case of a broken network connection such automatic reconnection may even constitute a security threat. This also allowed us to avoid manipulations of the stack contents. Therefore on a restart any computation found in the queue is forced to exit the kernel with a return status - "failure due to restart", and it is up to the user code to retry the same request. Requests of this type can fail for many reasons unrelated to checkpointing, so this requirement does not add substantially to the complexity of user level code.

The existence of both persistent and transient processes in the kernel is a source of some complication for the scheduler. All the queues the scheduler maintains i.e. prioritised ready queues, waiting queue and dead queue, may potentially contain both types of processes. These queues are usually implemented as linked lists, and the coherence of the queue after restart depends on the ability to restore the header of the list and all its links. Our solution in Grasshopper is to maintain a global list of all persistent computations in the system, and to use it to recreate scheduler queues on restart. Another approach is to maintain separate queues for persistent and transient computations as in MONADS. In this case the scheduler has to ensure that computations of both types receive a fair share of execution time. An advantage of our approach is that most of the overhead involved affects the system recovery time, not its error-free operation.

Persistent computations in the second category do not need support from dedicated kernel threads, they can be allowed to enter kernel mode, and execute kernel code, if we ensure that all of this activity will complete between two consecutive checkpoints ie. the state of computation will not be captured during that time. This implies that activities of the kernel checkpoint thread and persistent user computations have to be synchronised. This synchronisation is achieved with two semaphores:

- „check-gate" semaphore - stops the controller thread until the last persistent computation leaves the kernel space
- „kernel-gate" semaphore - stops new persistent computations attempting to enter kernel when the checkpoint sequence has started

The activities of the checkpoint thread, and the persistent computations as they enter and leave the kernel space are shown in figure 2. The checkpoint thread wakes up at some interval, dependent on the global checkpoint algorithm used, to determine whether a checkpoint is due. Before the actual checkpoint sequence may commence, the checkpoint thread sets the checkpoint mode flag to stop persistent computations entering kernel via the „kernel-gate" semaphore.

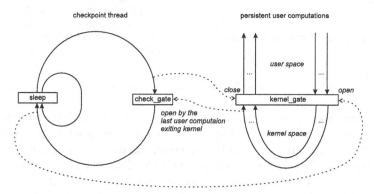

Fig. 2. Synchronisation of the checkpoint cycle

It then waits on the „check-gate" semaphore until the process count in the kernel drops to zero. The last persistent computation leaving the kernel signals the „check-gate" semaphore. From that point on the checkpoint sequence can proceed. When this is complete, the „kernel-gate" semaphore is signalled by the controller thread to release all waiting computations. This sequence of events is repeated for every checkpoint cycle, and it can be implemented as shown by the pseudo code in figure 3.

It is possible that the original reason for entering the kernel mode fits into the second category discussed above, but the kernel code it executes involves waiting for some events which may not occur within the bounded time. To illustrate let us examine the case of a persistent computation which triggered a page fault exception. On entry to the kernel mode this computation executes the kernel_entry procedure, and continues within the kernel code provided to handle page fault exception. If the faulted page is resident in memory then the activities necessary to make the page available, ie. page table and TLB update, will complete in an acceptably short time, and the computation will exit the kernel promptly. If the faulted page has to be copied from hard disk, then obviously this computation has to be forced out of the kernel, and treated as if it requested a disk operation explicitly. This can be achieved by placing the request on the persistent queue to be serviced by a transient kernel thread, invoking the kernel_exit procedure to decrement the count_exec counter, and suspending the faulting process.

```
checkpoint()                              kernel_entry()
begin                                     begin
    count_wait := 0                           if checkpoint_mode then
    checkpoint_mode := true                       wait(kernel_gate)
    if count_exec > 0 then                    else
        wait(check_gate)                          count_exec++
                                          end
... checkpoint activities ...
                                          kernel_exit()
    checkpoint_mode := false              begin
    do                                        count_exec--
        signal(kernel_gate)                   if checkpoint_mode and
    until                                     count_exec=0 then
    sem_count(kernel_gate)=0                      signal(check_gate)
end                                       end
```

Fig. 3. Checkpoint synchronisation

The third category of persistent computations are those which switch to the kernel mode to service an interrupt. The state of such a computation is saved by the conventional mechanisms when it is interrupted, and it cannot be affected in any way while executing the kernel interrupt handling code. Therefore it is of no consequence if such computation is captured by a checkpoint while still in the kernel. If this checkpoint is used to restore the system, all such computations are forced to return to the point in execution where they were originally interrupted. This is similar to the treatment received by the computations in the first category.

Logically all the persistent computations captured by the checkpoint are outside the kernel. In fact all of these computations are in kernel mode, but at the point of execution which involves only a return from system call or return from interrupt/exception. These return instructions are still a part of the kernel code, and their location may change as a result of kernel upgrade. This implies that if recovery is performed after an upgrade the Program Counter value saved on the kernel stacks of all the affected persistent computations has to be updated to correspond to the location in the new code. As the value of PC is stored in a well defined location of the stack we believe that such manipulation is safe, and can be allowed.

5   Conclusions

Many issues related to persistent systems are still basically unresolved, and remain in the domain of research and experimentation. In particular there is no agreement as to which approach is most suitable for constructing a persistent computing environment, and what are the trade-offs involved in selecting any one of them. More research and experimental work is needed before these issues are better understood.

With the exception of Charm, all the persistent operating systems built to date provide some basic abstraction over execution, so they have to deal with the concept of a persistent kernel and resolve the problems related to isolation of transient and persistent kernel resources. Each of the systems discussed solves the issues related to the isolation of transient and persistent state of the kernel in a different way. The KeyKOS solution is the stateless kernel, MONADS provides kernel services exclusively with transient kernel processes, L3, L4, EROS and Fluke rollback the processes to the beginning of the system call by manipulating the stack, and as a consequence require that all system calls are transparently restartable. We believe that each of these methods has some merit, but is not very well suited to handle all types of process/kernel interactions. Therefore we propose an implementation which is a combination of methods, selecting the most appropriate one in each case. We use transient kernel threads only when it cannot be avoided, we permit unrestricted access to kernel code when it can be performed atomically, and the only stack manipulation we allow is very well defined, and not prone to any misinterpretation.

The approach described in this paper has been successfully implemented in the context of the Grasshopper operating system. As we have shown it does not require any features which are not commonly available in other operating systems, and places fewer restrictions on the design and behaviour of the kernel services than other known solutions.

References

1. Bem, E.Z., „Global Stability and Resilience in a Persistent Operating System", PhD Thesis, University of Sydney, 1999
2. Dearle, A., J. Rosenberg, F.A. Henskens, F. Vaughan, K. Maciunas „An Examination of Operating System Support for Persistent Object Systems" Proceedings of the 25th Hawaii International Conference on System Sciences, vol 1 (ed. V. Milutinovic and D.B. Shriver), IEEE Computer Society Press, Hawaii, 1992

3. Dearle, A., R. di Bona, J.M. Farrow, F.A. Henskens, A. Lindström, J. Rosenberg, F.Vaughan „Grasshopper: An Orthogonally Persistent Operating System", Computer Systems, Vol 7(3), Summer 1994
4. Dearle, A., D. Hulse „Operating System Support for Persistent Systems: Past, present and Future", awaiting publication, 2000
5. Hardy, N. „The KeyKOS Architecture" Operating System Review, 1985
6. Landau, C.R., „The Checkpoint Mechanism in KeyKOS" Proceedings of the 2nd International Workshop on Object Orientation in Operating Systems, IEEE, 1992
7. Liedtke, J., „A Persistent System in Real Use – Experiences of the First 13 Years" Proceedings of the 3rd International Workshop on Object-Orientation in Operating Systems, North Carolina, 1993
8. Lindström, A., A. Dearle, R. di Bona, S. Norris, J. Rosenberg, F. Vaughan „Persistence in the Grasshopper Kernel" Proceedings of the Eighteenth Australasian Computer Science Conference, ACSC-18, ed. Ramamohanarao Kotagiri, Glenelg, South Australia, February 1995
9. Rosenberg, J. „The MONADS Architecture: A Layered View" 4th International Workshop on Persistent Object Systems, eds A. Dearle, G.M. Shaw and S.B. Zdonik, Morgan Kaufmann, 1990
10. Rosenberg, J., M.J. Flanagan, S.R. Norris, A. Patterson, Persistent Systems Research Group, Universities of Sydney and Monash, personal communications, Melbourne, July 1998
11. Shapiro, J.S., J.M. Smith, D.J. Farber „EROS: A Fast Capability System" 17th ACM Symposium on Operating Systems Principles, 1999
12. Skoglund E., J. Liedtke „Transparent Orthogonal Checkpointing Through User-Level Pagers" , awaiting publication, 2000
13. Tullmann P., J. Lepreau, B. Ford, M. Hibler „User-Level Checkpointing Through Exportable Kernel State" Proceedings of 5th International Workshop on Object Orientation in Operating Systems, Seattle, 1996

Transparent Orthogonal Checkpointing through User-Level Pagers

Espen Skoglund, Christian Ceelen, and Jochen Liedtke

System Architecture Group
University of Karlsruhe
{skoglund,ceelen,liedtke}@ira.uka.de

Abstract. Orthogonal persistence opens up the possibility for a number of applications. We present an approach for easily enabling transparent orthogonal persistence, basically on top of a modern μ-kernel. Not only are all data objects made persistent. Threads and tasks are also treated as normal data objects, making the threads and tasks persistent between system restarts. As such, the system is fault surviving. Persistence is achieved by the means of a transparent checkpoint server running in user-level. The checkpoint server takes regular snapshots of all user-level memory in the system, and also of the thread control blocks inside the kernel. The execution of the checkpointing itself is completely transparent to the μ-kernel, and only a few recovery mechanisms need to be implemented inside the kernel in order to support checkpointing. During system recovery (after a crash or a controlled shutdown), the consistency of threads is assured by the fact that all their user-level state (user memory) and kernel-level state (thread control blocks) will reside in stable storage. All other kernel state in the system can be reconstructed either upon initial recovery, or by standard page fault mechanisms during runtime.

1   Introduction

Persistent object stores have a long history of active research in computer science. Little research, however, has been targeted at providing orthogonal persistence, and still fewer systems have actually been implemented.

Orthogonal persistence does make sense though, especially with the advent of devices like PDAs. A day planner application would for instance always be running on your machine. Since the application would be persistent, it would transparently survive power failures or system crashes. There would be no need for the application programmer to explicitly store the results of user modifications, effectively saving both development time and program size. Desktop machines and larger servers would also be able to benefit from orthogonal persistence. A long running compute-intensive application would not need to contain complicated (and very likely error-prone) checkpointing code. Researchers could concentrate on algorithm design, and leave the checkpointing to the operating system.

G.N.C. Kirby, A. Dearle, and D.I.K. Sjøberg (Eds.): POS-9, LNCS 2135, pp. 201–214, 2001.

In this paper, we present an approach for easily implementing transparent orthogonal persistence on top of a modern μ-kernel. We hope to prove that implementing orthogonal checkpointing is not inherently difficult, even in a system that was not originally designed for that purpose. One important aspect of the design is that the kernel does not need to collect any kernel data structures into some externalized form (i.e., there is no need to perform the process known as *pickling*).

Before describing the checkpointing design (Sects. 4, 5, and 6), we give a brief overview of the μ-kernel used as a base for the implementation (Sect. 2) and our general approach (Sect. 3). Section 7 lists related work, and finally Sect. 8 concludes.

2   Implementation Basis: The L4 μ-Kernel

The L4 μ-kernel [10] is a lean second generation μ-kernel. The philosophy behind the kernel is that only a minimal set of concepts is implemented within it. A concept is permitted inside the kernel only if moving it outside the kernel would prevent some system functionality to be implemented. In other words, the kernel should not enforce any specific policy on the surrounding system. Following this philosophy, the L4 μ-kernel implements two basic user-level abstractions: threads and address spaces.[1]

2.1   Threads and IPC

A thread is an activity executing inside an address space. Several threads may exist within a single address space, and the collection of threads within an address space is often referred to as a task. Threads (and in particular threads within different address spaces) communicate with each other using inter-process communication (IPC).

The IPC primitive is one of the most fundamental μ-kernel mechanisms. Not only is it the primary means of communication between threads, it is also used as an abstraction for exceptions and interruptions. For instance, if a thread raises a page fault exception, the exception is translated into an IPC message that is sent to another thread which handles the page fault (see Fig. 1). If a hardware interruption occurs, the interrupt is translated into an IPC message and sent to a thread that handles the interruption. This latter example also illustrates an important aspect of the μ-kernel design: device drivers need not be implemented inside the kernel. They may be implemented as threads running in user-level.

2.2   Recursive Address Spaces

Recursive address spaces forms a concept that is relied heavily upon by the checkpointing facility presented in this paper. With recursive address spaces,

---

[1] A rationale for the choice of these basic abstractions and a detailed description of the L4 μ-kernel is given in [10].

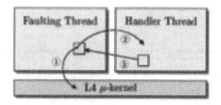

Fig. 1. Page fault IPC. When a page fault occurs in a user level thread; (1) a page fault exception is raised and caught by the μ-kernel, (2) the kernel generates a page fault IPC from the faulting thread to the handler thread, and (3) the handler thread (possibly) maps a page frame to the faulting location.

a task may map parts of its address space to other tasks. These other tasks may in turn map the mapped parts to other tasks, creating a tree of mappings. Upon mapping to another task though, control of the mapped part will not be relinquished. A mapper may at any time revoke its mappings, recursively rendering the mappings in other tasks invalid.

Recursive address spaces enable memory managers to be stacked upon each other. These memory managers are also referred to as pagers. This does not necessarily imply that they swap memory to stable storage (though that may often be the case), but that they handle page faults for threads in their sibling tasks. The top-level pager in the system is backed by physical memory. That is, its address space is mapped idempotently into physical memory. As such, it controls all physical memory in the machine[2] and has no need for pagers backing it.

There has been much concern as to whether μ-kernels suffer a too large performance degradation due to the added number of context switches imposed on the system. It has been argued, however, that this is mostly an artifact of poor kernel implementations, and can be alleviated by properly implemented kernel mechanisms [10].

3   General Approach

This paper focuses on how to implement non-distributed per-machine checkpoints. Cross-machine synchronization and synchronization between persistent and non-persistent objects, threads, and tasks are not topics of this paper.

More precisely, this paper discusses how to implement checkpoints *on top of a microkernel,* i.e., (a) through user-level servers and (b) relatively orthogonal (and thus independent) to other (legacy) system services such as pagers, file systems, network stacks, security servers, and so forth. Figure 2 gives an architectural overview of the system, illustrating the μ-kernel, device drivers, the checkpoint server, and the persistent pagers and applications serviced by the underlying persistence run-time system.

---

[2] Except for some memory which is dedicated to the μ-kernel, for example page tables.

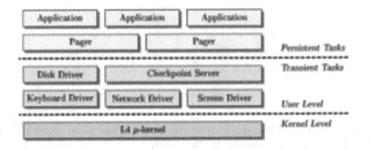

Fig. 2. Architectural overview

3.1 Transient and Explicitly-Persistent Objects

A real system always contains a mixture of transient (non-persistent) and persistent objects. Extreme examples are device drivers that typically can not be made persistent and file systems that are always persistent. So, a persistent application might "use" both persistent and non-persistent objects. Nicely, in an orthogonally persistent system, the applications' address spaces, stacks, registers, and thread states themselves are all persistent objects. Nevertheless, many orthogonally persistent applications will use or contact non-persistent objects and/or servers, e.g., a clock/date service, a remote web site, a phone line, a video camera, a gps receiver, and so on.

Connecting to non-persistent services and using non-persistent objects is a problem that strongly depends on the application and on the nature of the non-persistent servers and objects. A persistent system can only offer basic mechanisms to detect inconsistencies (i.e., the necessity of recovery) and to prevent applications from using unrecovered objects or server connections once a system restart happens or a non-persistent object or server crashes. The general system mechanism for customized user-level recovery in such cases is *to invalidate all connections (including identifiers) to non-persistent objects* once the persistent system restarts (or the non-persistent objects crash or are partitioned from the persistent system).

File systems are well-known members of the class of *explicitly persistent* servers. Such servers implement explicitly persistent objects. If a persistent application uses such servers it has either to deal with a similar synchronization problem as for non-persistent objects, or the system has to synchronize its own checkpoints and the checkpoints of all used explicitly-persistent servers, e.g., through a two-phase-commit protocol. The current paper does not discuss the corresponding problems.

3.2 Implicitly-Persistent Objects

The focus of the current paper is *implicitly persistent* servers (and applications). That is, how do we make servers and applications orthogonally persistent that originally do not include persistence, i.e., that do not include a check-point/recover mechanisms. Implicit persistence should be implemented by a set of system servers that *transparently* add orthogonal persistence to existing non-persistent servers and applications.

For implicit persistence we need to implement transparent checkpointing. Basically, we have to solve three problems:

Kernel Checkpointing. How can we checkpoint the microkernel in such a way that all persistent threads, address spaces, and other kernel objects can be recovered?

Main-Memory Checkpointing. How can we checkpoint those main-memory page frames that are used by persistent applications and implicitly persistent servers?

Backing-Store Checkpointing. How can we checkpoint backing store (disk) blocks that are used by implicitly persistent servers? Or in other words, how can we ensure that transactions made to stable storage by implicitly persistent servers are synchronized with their checkpoints?

4   Kernel Checkpointing

4.1   The Checkpoint Server

The checkpoint server acts as a pager for thread control blocks (TCBs) in the system. This permits it to save the kernel state of the various threads.

Giving control of the thread control blocks to the checkpointer is achieved by not having the kernel own the physical page frames of the TCBs. Instead, when the kernel needs more backing memory for TCBs (whether it be for a persistent or a transient thread), it requests the checkpointer to map a page frame to the kernel (see Fig. 3). The mapped page frame will be owned by the checkpointer, and the checkpointer may at any time access the TCB or unmap it from the kernel. Letting the checkpointer retain full control of the TCBs implies that the checkpointer—just like device drivers—must be a trusted task.

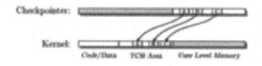

Fig. 3. TCB paging. The checkpointer owns the pages residing in the TCB area of the kernel. Arrows indicate mappings from the checkpointer's address space into the TCB area.

At regular intervals, the checkpointer takes a consistent copy (a *fixpoint*) of all needed system state (i.e., thread control blocks of persistent threads) and writes it to stable storage. A consistent copy could be assured by establishing some causal consistency protocol. Such a protocol, however, would require that the checkpointer has knowledge of all communication between persistent threads. This is not feasible though, since threads can communicate in ways which are not known to the checkpointer, e.g., through IPC or shared memory. The checkpointer therefore implements a simple scheme, taking a snapshot of the system at a single point in time. Since the checkpointer is implemented as a regular user-level task, it is subject to interruptions by the in-kernel scheduler, or by hardware devices. This could cause other persistent tasks to be scheduled before the checkpointer has written their TCBs to stable storage, rendering the fixpoint in an inconsistent state. To cope with this problem, the checkpointer initially makes all persistent thread control blocks copy-on-write (see Fig. 4). Once this is accomplished, the checkpointer can lazily store their contents to stable storage.

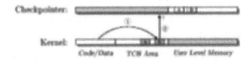

(a) The TCBs in the kernel area have been marked copy-on-write (dark grey). The kernel then tries to, e.g., schedule thread B. This requires access to B's TCB (1), which in turn raises a page fault that is directed to the checkpointer (2).

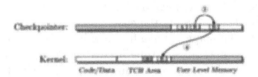

(b) The checkpointer copies the accessed TCB to a new location (3), and maps the copy of the TCB to the kernel with write permissions (4). The kernel may now modify the TCB copy without disturbing the old contents.

Fig. 4. The TCB copy-on-write scheme

During the copy-on-write operation the checkpoint server will not be able to service any page faults for the kernel. As such, the operation does not have to be atomic since no persistent thread which has been marked as copy-on-write will be able to continue until the whole operation has finished. Neither can the TCB of a persistent thread be modified by other threads (e.g., through IPC) while it is marked copy-on-write. Doing so would immediately cause the modifying thread to raise a page fault in the TCB area of the persistent thread, and since the page fault must be served by the checkpointer the modifying thread will also be suspended until the copy-on-write operation has finished. It must be stressed though, that all threads will be able to run while the TCB contents are being written to stable storage. They will only be suspended during the small amount of time it takes to perform the copy-on-write operation.

The checkpointer also contains data structures for keeping track of where the pages in stable storage belong. These data structures must be kept persistent so that the checkpointer can handle page faults correctly after a system restart. Since the checkpointer task itself can not be made persistent (it has to be running in order to take the atomic snapshot), the data structures are written to stable storage as part of the fixpoint.

4.2   Checkpointing Kernel State

For a fixpoint to be consistent, no relevant kernel state other than that contained in the TCBs must be required to be persistent. The design of the L4 kernel easily lends itself to this property.

Ready Queues and Waiting Queues. Persistent applications running on top of L4 can not—due to the nature of time sharing systems—determine how fast they will progress through a sequence of machine instructions. In particular, they can not determine how long it will take them to start executing the next IPC system call. As such, they can make no assumptions about the ordering of in-kernel ready queues and IPC waiting queues. The kernel can therefore upon recovery reconstruct the queues in any order it prefers. It just needs to know in which queues the thread should be residing, and this information is stored within the TCB.

Page Tables and Mapping Database. Page tables are an integral part of the μ-kernel data structures. The mapping database is closely related to the page tables. It includes data structures to keep track of sharing between address spaces. Those data structures enable recursive address spaces to be implemented.

Page tables and the mapping database are not included in the data set that is paged to stable storage during a checkpoint. Upon system restart, the mapping database and page tables will therefore all be empty. Once a persistent task is restarted a page fault will immediately be raised. The page fault is caught by the μ-kernel which redirects it to the faulting task's pager. The pager—whose page tables are also empty—will in turn generate another page fault and subsequently cause its own pager to be invoked. Eventually, the page fault will propagate back to the checkpoint server who loads the saved memory contents from stable storage and maps it to the faulting task. Figure 5 illustrates how the page fault is propagated to the checkpointer task, and how the corresponding page frame is mapped recursively into the faulting task.

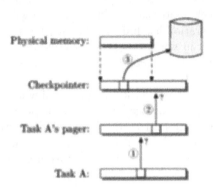
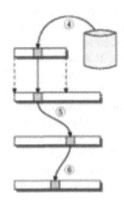

(a) Page faults are propagated up to the checkpoint server which requests the page frame from stable storage.

(b) Once the page frame is retrieved into memory, mappings are propagated down to the faulting task.

Fig. 5. Cascading page faults. The circled numbers indicate the order in which steps are taken. Arrows in Fig. (a) indicate page fault requests/data transfer requests. Arrows in Fig. (b) indicate data transfers/mappings.

Remaining Kernel State. Other data structures than those mentioned above (e.g., list of available dynamic kernel memory) have no relevance to the state of the kernel as a whole. They are usually only visible in the corresponding kernel functionality (e.g., kernel memory allocator) and are initialized when the kernel is restarted.

4.3   TCB Recovery

Ideally, no threads should be inside the kernel during a fixpoint. However, in reality threads may be blocked due to an ongoing IPC operation, or they may be descheduled during a system call. Strictly speaking, due to the fact that only one thread is allowed to run at a single point in time (the checkpointer), all threads will be inside the kernel during a fixpoint. As such, all system calls must either be restartable, or some other mechanism must exist to put the thread into a consistent state during system recovery.

Fortunately, even though L4 was not designed with persistence in mind, all but one system call in L4 can be safely restarted. When a TCB is recovered and is found to be fixpointed in the middle of one of those system calls, the thread is restarted *in user level* at that location where the system call was invoked so that the same system call will be re-invoked.

Only the IPC system call can not unconditionally be restarted. An IPC operation may consist of two phases, a send phase followed by a receive phase. Separately, both phases are restartable, and, indeed, the IPC operation may very well consist of only one of the phases. However, if a send phase has been completed and a fixpoint is taken before the receive phase has been completed, restarting the entire system call would repeat the send phase a second time after restart although the checkpointed receiver has already received the first message. To avoid this message duplication, IPCs are handled as two-phase operations where the leading send phase is skipped on restart if it has been completed at checkpoint time. The restarted IPC then directly enters its receive phase. Uncompleted sends or single-phase IPCs are entirely restarted.

4.4 Kernel Upgrades

An implication of the fact that almost no kernel state is kept during a fixpoint, is that the μ-kernel may easily be upgraded or modified between system restarts. The essential invariant that must be kept between different kernel versions is that the kernel stack layout of interrupted threads must look the same or that the new kernel version knows the layout of the old version and adapts it to the new layout.

5 Main-Memory Checkpointing

We already have a checkpoint server that acts as a pager for TCBs. This server is easily extended to also act as a pager for all physical memory that is used by implicitly persistent servers and applications. Therefore, the checkpoint server is implemented as a pager located directly below the top level pager. Being almost on top of the pager hierarchy, it automatically has access to all user-level memory of its sibling tasks. In particular, it can unmap page frames temporarily from all other tasks (including all other pagers), map page frames read-only, copy them to buffers, write them to backing store, and remap them afterwards. Thus the checkpoint pager can eagerly or lazily (copy-on-write) checkpoint main memory.

The checkpointing mechanism used is heavily influenced by the mechanisms in EROS [14], KeyKOS [7], and L3 [9]. For each physical page frame, we have allocated two disk blocks, an a-block and a b-block, and a status bit that specifies which of both blocks holds the currently valid checkpointed content of the physical page frame.

At regular intervals, the checkpoint server takes a consistent copy of all threads and address spaces, saving the according physical page frames. Dirty page frames are saved into their a/b-blocks: If the according status bit specifies that the a-block is currently valid the new content is saved into the b-block, otherwise into the a-block. Then, the page frame's status bit is toggled so that the newly written block is marked valid. Non-dirty physical page frames are ignored, i.e., their status bits remain unchanged. Once all modified page frames have been written to disk, the location bit-array itself is atomically written (e.g., using Challis' algorithm [1]), and the checkpoint is completed.

An optimization of the presented algorithm uses write logs to minimize seek time (instead of overwriting the a/b-blocks directly) whenever the amount of dirty page frames is low.

6   Backing-Store Checkpointing

Main-memory checkpointing is not sufficient. In addition, pagers, e.g., anonymous-memory servers, have to be modified so that they support persistence, i.e., implement persistent data objects. Servers that are explicitly built to support persistent objects we call *explicitly persistent* servers.

Many servers are not explicitly built to support persistence. Of course, it would be very helpful to also have a general method that easily extends such servers so that they automatically become *implicitly persistent* servers that synchronize their checkpoints with the checkpoint server.

A method of generating implicitly persistent servers combined with the checkpoint server is sufficient to establish orthogonal persistence. Explicitly persistent servers then specialize and customize the system.

6.1   The Implicit-Persistence Problem of Backing Stores

The checkpoint server only takes care of paging thread control blocks and *physically backed* user-level memory to stable storage. Multiplexing the physical memory among user-level tasks, and swapping parts of virtual memory to stable storage must be taken care of by other pagers. Since those pagers deal with stable storage, writing page frames to disk must be synchronized with the checkpoint server in order to avoid inconsistency. Consider, for example, a scenario in which a checkpoint is made at time c_n, and the next checkpoint is to be made at c_{n+1}. Now, the pager writes a page frame to disk at the time w_1 in between the two checkpoints (i.e., $c_n < w_1 < c_{n+1}$). At a time, w_2, in between the next two checkpoints (i.e., $c_{n+1} < w_2 < c_{n+2}$), the pager then replaces the the on-disk page frame with another page frame. If the machine crashes at a time in between w_2 and c_{n+2}, the system will on recovery be rendered inconsistent because the pager will believe that the on-disk page frame is the one that it wrote on time w_1. It has no idea that it changed the contents at time w_2.

For implicit persistence, we need a method to make any pager (or server) that uses the stable backing store persistent; without modifying or extending it. This is achieved by the recoverable-disk driver.

6.2   The Recoverable-Disk Driver

The *recoverable disk* is a user-level server (driver) implementing a logical disk that offers the operations *checkpoint* and *recover* besides normal *read-block* and *write-block*. Disk writes remain fragile until they are committed by a subsequent *checkpoint* operation. The *recover* operation sets the entire disk back to the status of the last successful *checkpoint* operation, i.e. undos all writes after the last completed checkpoint.

All implicitly persistent servers use the recoverable-disk driver instead of the raw disk driver for reading and writing blocks. Furthermore, the checkpoint server synchronizes its main-memory checkpoints with checkpoints in the recoverable-disk driver. As a consequence, all pagers using both memory from the checkpointer and disk blocks from the recoverable-disk become implicitly persistent.

The recoverable-disk implementation uses methods similar to shadow paging [12] and to the algorithms used for main-memory checkpointing (see Sect. 5). It offers n logical blocks; however, physically, it uses $2n$ blocks. Each logical block k is mapped either to physical block a_k or b_k without overlaps.[3] A bitmap *CurrentBlock* specifies for each k whether the a-block or the b-block is currently valid. For a 4 GB recoverable disk and 4 KB blocks, this bitmap requires 128 KB of memory.

A second bitmap of the same size, *CurrentlyWritten*, is used to determine which logical blocks have been written in the current checkpoint interval: Assume that a server/pager writes to logical block k, and a_k is the currently associated physical block. If *CurrentlyWritten$_k$* is not set, then b_k becomes associated to k, and the according *CurrentlyWritten* bit is set. The physical block is then written. If *CurrentlyWritten$_k$* is already set when writing the block, the *CurrentBlock* and *CurrentlyWritten* bitmaps stay as-is, and the block is simply overwritten.

When a checkpoint occurs, the *CurrentBlock* bitmap is atomically saved on stable storage and all *CurrentlyWritten* bits are reset to zero.

Modifications of this algorithm permit multiple valid checkpoints. Furthermore, the number of totally required physical blocks can be reduced to $n + m$ if at maximum m blocks can be written between two checkpoints.

The recoverable-disk driver enables legacy pagers (or other servers accessing disk) to be used in the persistent system without modification. If a pager for efficiency reasons wants to bypass the recoverable-disk driver, it can of course do so. Such pagers, however, should synchronize with the checkpoint server in order to keep the system in a consistent state.

6.3   Device Drivers and File Systems

Device Drivers. As mentioned before, most device drivers can not be made persistent. Care must therefore be taken to not include any state about other threads in the system within the driver. For example, a network interface driver should not include any knowledge about open network connections since this knowledge would be lost during a system reboot. In general, however, this restriction on device drivers does not impose any problems. In the case of the network interface driver for instance, the knowledge of open connections would reside in some network protocol server—a server that would be included in the set of persistent tasks.

---

[3] $a_k \neq b_k$ for all k, and $a_k = a_{k'} \lor b_k = b_{k'} \Rightarrow k = k'$.

File Systems. Having a fully transparent persistent system somewhat obviates the need to support an explicitly persistent file system. There are some cases, however, that point in the direction of having a file system: First of all, many users are simply used to dealing with files and file hierarchies. There is no need to upset users unnecessarily. Moreover, there might be a need to interchange data with other systems. Files are a nice and clean way to handle interchangeability on widely different platforms. Most important though, is that many applications today rely on being backed by some sort of file system. Portability of applications is therefore a key issue.

Since tasks are fully persistent, a UNIX-like file system can easily be implemented as a collection of servers (as in L3 [9] or EROS [14]). In short, a directory or a file is nothing more than a persistent object. As such, a persistent server is used to represent each directory and each file. When another task in the system accesses a file, the requests will be directed to the corresponding file server (or directory server).

Of course, a file system server may also be implemented as a traditional file system explicitly accessing stable storage. If this is the case, they will have to use the recoverable-disk driver.

7   Related Work

The concept of transparent orthogonal persistence is not new. In fact, system-wide persistence was an integral part of L4's predecessor—the L3 μ-kernel [9]. With L4, however, persistence is not an integral part of the kernel. It is an add-on feature that the user may choose to ignore.

Other μ-kernels integrating persistence into the kernel include EROS [14] and its predecessor KeyKOS [7]. With EROS, taking a snapshot of the system also includes performing a consistency check of critical kernel data structures. This catches possible kernel implementation bugs, and prohibits these bugs to stabilize in the system. A checkpoint in L4, on the other hand, does not include any critical kernel data structures. Doing such a consistency check is therefore unnecessary.

In contrast with L3 and EROS, Fluke [15] is a μ-kernel offering transparent checkpointing at user-level. This is achieved by having the kernel export user-visible, partly pickled, kernel objects. The checkpointer pickles the remaining parts of the objects and saves them to stable storage together with the memory-images of the tasks.

Most transparently persistent operating systems are based upon μ-kernels. An exception to this rule is Grasshopper [2]. Grasshopper hopes to achieve persistence through the use of some specially designed kernel abstractions. Based on the experiences learned from Grasshopper, the designers have later created a μ-kernel based operating system, Charm [3], aiming at supporting persistent applications. With Charm, no particular persistence model is enforced upon the applications. The kernel instead provides the application system with mechanisms to construct their own persistence policy. In short, all in-kernel meta-data (such as page tables) are exposed to the application, and the application is itself responsible for making this data persistent.

Several other facilities for user-level checkpointing have been implemented [4, 8,11,13]. Typically, the `fork()` UNIX system call is used to periodically create a snapshot of the task's image, allowing the application to continue execution while the image is being written to stable storage. Such systems, however, can not manage to restore much of the operating system state upon recovery. Neither can they assure that their interaction with the surrounding system will leave the checkpoint in a consistent state. As such, these checkpointing facilities are only usable within a certain type of scientific applications.

8   Conclusions

We have seen that user-level transparent orthogonal checkpointing can readily be implemented in the context of a second-generation L4 μ-kernel. The checkpointing facility relies for the most part on existing kernel abstractions. Only a minimal set of additions to the μ-kernel is needed. The key for implementing persistence on top of the μ-kernel is its concept of recursive address spaces that enables implementation of all main-memory management by user-level servers.

Consequently, orthogonal persistence can be implemented almost entirely through user-level pagers and drivers, particularly through a checkpoint server and a recoverable disk driver. Both are user-level servers and do not depend on the OS personality that runs on top of the μ-kernel. The resulting support of orthogonal persistence is thus widely transparent to and independent from application *and OS*.

The transparent checkpointing design presented here is currently in the process of being implemented. The system will be used in conjunction with L⁴Linux [6] as well as with the multi-server SawMill system [5] on top of L4.

References

1. Michael F. Challis. Database consistency and integrity in a multi-user environment. In *Proceedings of the 1st International Conference on Data and Knowledge Bases*, pages 245–270, Haifa, Israel, August 2–3 1978. Academic Press.
2. Alan Dearle, Rex di Bona, James Farrow, Frans Henskens, Anders Lindström, John Rosenberg, and Francis Vaughan. Grasshopper: an orthogonally persistent operating system. *Computing Systems*, 7(3):289–312, Summer 1994.
3. Alan Dearle and David Hulse. Operating system support for persistent systems: past, present and future. *Software – Practice and Experience, Special Issue on Persistent Object Systems*, 30(4):295–324, 2000.
4. Elmootazbellah N. Elnohazy, David B. Johnson, and Willy Zwaenepoel. The performance of consistent checkpointing. In *Proceedings of the 11th Symposium on Reliable Distributed Systems*, Houston, TX, October 5–7 1992.
5. Alain Gefflaut et al. Building efficient and robust multiserver systems: the SawMill approach. In *Proceedings of the ACM SIGOPS European Workshop 2000*, Kolding, Denmark, September17–20 2000.
6. Hermann Härtig, Michael Hohmuth, Jochen Liedtke, Sebastiann Scönberg, and Jean Wolter. The performance of μ-kernel bases systems. In *Proceeding of the 16th ACM Symposium on Operating System Principles (SOSP)*, Saint-Malo, France, October 5–8 1997.

7. Charles R. Landau. The checkpoint mechanism in KeyKOS. In *Proceedings of the 2nd International Workshop on Persistent Object Systmes (POS2)*, Paris, France, September 24–25 1992.

8. Juan León, Allan L. Fisher, and Peter Steenkist. Fail-safe PVM: a portable package for distributed programming with transparent recovery. Technical Report CMU-CS-93-124, Carnegie Mellon University, February 1993.

9. Jochen Liedtke. A persistent system in real use: experiences of the first 13 years. In *Proceedings of the 3rd International Workshop on Object-Orientation in Operatins Systems (IWOOOS '93)*, Asheville, NC, December 9–10 1993.

10. Jochen Liedtke. On μ-kernel construction. In *Proceedings of the 15th ACM Symposium on Operating System Principles (SOSP '95)*, Copper Mountain Resort, CO, December 3–6 1995.

11. Michael Litzkow, Todd Tannenbaum, Jim Basney, and Miron Livny. Checkpoint and migration of UNIX processes in the Condor distributed processing system. Technical Report #1346, University of Wisconsin-Madison, April 1997.

12. Raymond A. Lorie. Physical integrity in a large segmented database. *ACM Transactions on Database Systems (TODS)*, 2(1):91–104, September 1977.

13. James S. Plank, Micah Beck, Gerry Kingsley, and Kai Li. Libckpt: transparent checkpointing under UNIX. In *Proceeding of the USENIX 1995 Technical Conference*, New Orleans, LA, January 16–20 1995.

14. Jonathan S. Shapiro, Jonathan M. Smith, and David J. Farber. EROS: a fast capability system. In *Proceedings of the 17th ACM Symposium on Operating System Pronciples (SOSP '99)*, Kiawah Island Resort, SC, December 12–15 1999.

15. Patrick Tullmann, Jay Lepreau, Bryan Ford, and Mike Hibler. User-level checkpointing through exportable kernel state. In *Proceedings of the 5th International Workshop on Object-Orientation in Operating System (IWOOOS '96)*, Seattle, WA, October 27–28 1996.

An Overview of Ulisse, a Distributed Single Address Space System

Gianluca Dini, Giuseppe Lettieri, and Lanfranco Lopriore

Dipartimento di Ingegneria dell'Informazione: Elettronica, Informatica, Telecomunicazioni;
Via Diotisalvi, 2; 56126 Pisa, Italy
{dini, lettieri, lopriore}@iet.unipi.it

Abstract. We present Ulisse, a distributed single address space system being developed at the University of Pisa. Ulisse has a symmetric, peer-to-peer architecture, is resilient to certain types of node and network failures, and supports a form of application-controlled approach to memory management. A set of mechanisms make it possible to explicitly control page caching and the page movements across the storage hierarchy, thereby allowing application programs to implement specific memory management strategies, including page replacement, consistency and recovery.

1 Introduction

Let us consider a distributed system composed of a set of computers (*nodes*) interconnected by a fast local area network, featuring a memory management system operating according to a single address space storage paradigm. In a system of this type, threads running on different nodes share access to a single virtual addressing space that is both *persistent* and *uniform*. All these threads can reference any given information item by using the same virtual address. Address space persistence implies that the lifetime of any given information item is independent of the lifetime of the thread that created this information item. Address space uniformity means that the differentiation between primary and secondary storage as well as between local and remote storage disappears. An information item created at a given virtual address maintains this address for its entire lifetime, independently of its position in the primary memory or the secondary memory of any node [7], [16], [6], [24]. Thus, pointers retain their meaning even when they are stored in secondary memory or are transmitted between nodes. Information sharing is facilitated and natural solutions follow for persistent programming [11], [21]. In this respect, the single address space model is particularly attractive for applications manipulating complex, pointer-rich data structures, that may be possibly stored in secondary storage or shared across the network. Examples are integrated software environments such as CAD and CASE [7].

Ulisse is a distributed single address space system being developed at the University of Pisa. Ulisse supports a paged address space, and implements a two-layer storage hierarchy where the secondary memories of the nodes hold the virtual pages and the primary memories are aimed at caching these pages for fast processor access. Ulisse presents a symmetric, peer-to-peer architecture where the secondary memory

G.N.C. Kirby, A. Dearle, and D.I.K. Sjøberg (Eds.): POS-9, LNCS 2135, pp. 215-227, 2001.

of any given node may hold any given page while the primary memory may contain pages from the local disks as well as from remote disks.

Several systems implementing the notion of distributed single address space have been built. Among them, Angel [24], Casper [23], Monads [1], Mungi [15], and Sombrero [21]. These systems implement a traditional, *automatic* approach to memory management. In this approach, the operating system manages memory transparently with respect to applications, and uses memory management policies, e.g. the least-recently-used (LRU) page replacement policy, that are selected according to the expected average behaviour of applications in memory. Of course, an application whose behaviour does not match the operating system expectations will exhibit poor performance [14]. This is the case, for instance, for such memory-intensive applications as database management systems or CAD systems. On the other hand, Ulisse implements an *application-controlled* approach to memory management. A small yet powerful set of primitive operations, called the *page primitives*, allow explicit management of the storage hierarchy. These primitives make it possible to control the residency of a page in the primary memory of any given node, as well as the propagation orderings of pages between primary memory and secondary memory, and the number and the coherence of page copies cached across the network. These primitives implement memory management mechanisms, whereas the policies are delegated to application programs. So doing, we simplify the inner operating system layers, and allow each application program to exploit a knowledge of its own specific memory behaviour to improve storage management. The application-controlled approach to memory management has been proposed for centralized systems [4], [9], [14], [18]. The main aim of Ulisse is to extend the approach to a distributed system.

Ulisse is resilient to certain types of node and network failures. A node may either work correctly or stop working. The network may enter a partitioned state in which one or more nodes become unreachable. Ulisse guarantees consistency of the memory management system in spite of the two types of failures by using a transactional approach. Page primitives are implemented as distributed atomic transactions to preserve atomicity with respect to concurrency and failures. On the other hand, the task of maintaining the consistency of application-level data structures is left to applications themselves, according to the application-controlled memory management paradigm. An application will preserve consistency of its own data structures by using the page primitives to control the order of page propagation to the permanent secondary storage [4], [8]. This has a number of advantages. Only those applications that actually require failure resilience will implement it and pay the related costs in terms of execution times and storage requirements. Furthermore, applications are allowed to integrate failure resilience with specific policies for page replacement and consistency.

The rest of the paper is organised as follows. Section 2 presents our single address space memory model with special reference to the page primitives. Section 3 presents several examples of use of the page primitives. With reference to application programs manipulating objects, we argue that the implementation of a given object may comprise and integrate policies for the management of the memory allocated to the object. In selecting these policies, an object designer may take into account the expected pattern of accesses to the object. Section 4 discusses implementation issues including interpretation of virtual addresses and resilience of the memory

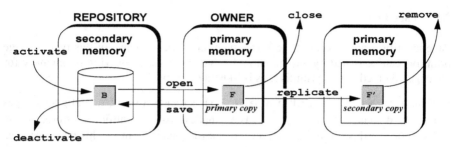

Fig. 1. Page movements in memory.

management system to failures. This section also includes a brief description of prototype efforts carried out by the authors.

2 Single Address Space

In our distributed system, nodes share access to the same unique virtual address space, that is logically split into fixed-sized *pages*. Pages are the unit of memory allocation and management. Every page is named by using a page identifier. A virtual address is logically divided into two components, the page identifier and the offset within the page.

In each node, the primary memory is logically divided into frames and the secondary memory is logically divided into blocks. Pages, frames and blocks have the same size. At any given time, only *active* pages contain meaningful information (Figure 1). Every active page is stored in a secondary memory block. A page is active in a given node if the node reserves a secondary memory block for the page. We call that node the page *repository*. The repository can be changed dynamically. An active page can be *deactivated*. This action releases the block reserved for page storage, thereby losing the page contents.

Programs running on a given node can access an active page if and only if a copy of the page is cached at the node. This means that a frame has been reserved for the page storage in this node. At any given time, a page can be cached at one or more nodes, but at most one cached copy per node is allowed. This means that a page cannot be cached twice at the same node.

Let P be a page and B the block reserved for this page. A *primary* copy of P can be created in a given node N by *opening* the page in this node. This action reserves a frame F for storage of P in N, and copies the contents of block B into F. We call node N the page *owner*. The owner of a given page can be changed dynamically. The primary copy of page P can be *saved*. This action copies the contents of frame F into block B, thereby making these contents persistent. A primary copy can be *closed*. This action releases frame F.

Let node N be the owner of a given page P, and F the frame reserved for P in N. A *secondary* copy of P can be created in a different node M by *replicating* the primary copy of P. This action reserves a frame F' for storage of P in M, and copies the contents of frame F into frame F'. The secondary copy can be *removed*. This action releases frame F'.

2.1   Page Primitives

Page identifiers are objects of the `Page` type. Let P be an object of this type. A page primitive can be issued by any given node, even by a node reserving no memory for the page involved in this primitive, as is illustrated below.

- Primitive `Page P = activate(N, n)` activates a set of n contiguous pages ($n \geq 1$, default value n = 1). The smallest page identifier is stored in P. Execution of this primitive reserves a block for each page in N. This node becomes the page repository of every page in the set.

- Primitive `move(P,N)` changes the repository of page P. The new repository is node N. Let B be the block reserved for page P in the current page repository. Execution of this primitive reserves a block B' for storage of P in N, copies the contents of B into B', and releases B.

- Primitive `open(P,N)` creates a primary copy of page P in node N. This node becomes the new page owner. Let B be the block reserved for P. Execution of this primitive reserves a frame F for P in N and copies the contents of B into F. If a primary copy of P exists in a node, say node M, the contents and the ownership of page P are moved to N. The copy cached at M becomes a secondary copy. If a primary copy already exists in N, the primitive has no effect.

- Primitive `save(P)` saves page P. Let B be the block reserved for P in its current repository, and let F be the frame reserved for P in its current owner. Execution of this primitive copies the contents of frame F into block B.

- Primitive `close(P)` closes page P. Execution of this primitive releases the frame reserved for P in its current owner.

- Primitive `replicate(P,N)` creates a secondary copy of page P in node N. Let F be the frame reserved for page P in its current owner. Execution of this primitive reserves a frame F' for page P in N and copies the contents of frame F into frame F'. If a secondary copy of page P already exists in N, the primitive only copies the contents of F. The primitive fails if a primary copy of page P exists in N, or no primary copy exists at all.

- Primitive `remove(P,N)` removes the secondary copy of page P from node N. Execution of this primitive releases the frame reserved for P in N.

- Finally, primitive `deactivate(P)` deactivates page P. Execution of this primitive releases the block reserved for P in its repository. The primitive fails if a primary copy of P exists.

Every primitive requiring a node name as an argument provides a default argument whose value is `THIS_NODE`. All primitives but `activate` and `deactivate` fail if they involve a page that is not active. Moreover, `activate`, `move`, `open` and `replicate` fail if node N lacks free storage.

Page primitives make it possible to control *when* physical storage resources are allocated and released. On the other hand, these primitives do not allow application programs to specify *which* physical resources are allocated to pages. For instance, a program cannot specify the name of the secondary memory block to be reserved for a given page. This decision is left to the algorithms of `activate()`, that will take advantage of the usual techniques for disk space management, e.g. block clustering, to enhance performance at system level.

3 Structuring Applications

We have conceived our system to support application programs manipulating *objects*. We consider the usual notion of an object type defined in terms of a set of values and a set of operations accessing these values. In the virtual space, a given object X of type T is supported by two memory areas, the *type descriptor* and the *object descriptor*. The type descriptor stores the machine-code representation of the operations of type T, the object descriptor stores the internal representation of object X. Each descriptor may occupy a (portion of) a single page, or may span several pages. In order to execute a given operation on X in node N, the object must be cached at the node. This means that the pages storing the object descriptor and the type descriptor must be cached at N. If the operation does not modify the object, it is sufficient that a secondary copy of X is cached at N. On the other hand, if the operation modifies the object and we want to save the updates, node N must be the owner of the pages storing the object descriptor of X.

Ulisse supports the mechanism of remote operation call, allowing an application program running on a given node to issue a call to an operation of an object presently owned by a different node. Let X be an object of type T, let pX be a pointer to X and let pf be a pointer to a function `f()` implementing an operation of type T. If the object descriptor of X is owned by node N, a call to `f()` involving X issued from a different node C must be accomplished by using the *remote call primitive*. This primitive has the form `remote(pf, pX, arg1, arg2, ...)`, where `arg1`, `arg2`,... denote the arguments of `f()`. Arguments are either of a primitive type or of a pointer type. Execution of `remote()` determines the node N owning the page containing the address specified by pX. Then, the call is transmitted to N, where it generates a local function call of the form `(pX->*pf)(arg1, arg2, ...)`. On termination, the result of the execution of this local call is returned back to node C, where it forms the result of `remote()`.

3.1 Sharing Objects

A set of programs running in different nodes may well share access to object X. To this aim, the object is associated with another object, called the *manager* of X. This object belongs to type `ManagerT` and is responsible for allocation and deallocation of X, coordination of concurrent accesses to X, and implementation of the object sharing policy. A program running on a given node accesses X through an *interface*. This is an object of type `InterfaceT`. The interface object provides the same interface as X, and is essentially conceived to decouple the application from the

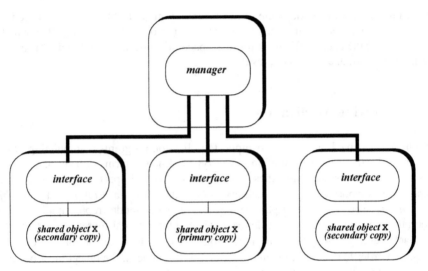

Fig. 2. Configuration of a shared object, its manager, and interfaces in the read replication algorithm. Thick lines between objects indicate interactions through remote calls, whereas thin lines indicate interactions through local calls.

implementation of the object sharing policies. In order to execute a given operation of X, the application program running in a given node executes the corresponding operation of the interface object in the node. This execution gives rise to interactions between the object X, the manager, and the interface.

Suppose now that the pattern of accesses to object X makes it is convenient to share the object according to the *read replication* strategy [10], [22], for instance. According to this strategy, multiple copies of the object may exist (Figure 2). Only the *primary* copy of the object can be modified, whereas the *secondary* copies can only be accessed for read, by those operations that do not modify the object. The primary copy reflects the most recent modifications that have been made to the value of the object. A secondary copy is *valid* if its contents are equal to those of the primary copy.

A program running in a given node N may execute an operation that does not modify object X provided that a valid secondary copy of this object has been cached at N. The interface of X in N is responsible for obtaining the valid copy. To this aim, it will take advantage of the replicate() primitive. On the other hand, if the operation modifies the object value, the requirement is that a primary copy of X is cached at N, and that all the secondary copies are invalidated. The interface object in node N is responsible for obtaining a primary copy (by means of the open() primitive). In addition, the interface remotely calls the object manager requesting invalidation of the secondary copies. The manager maintains a set of pointers to all the interfaces of X and uses these pointers to remotely call an appropriate operation of every interface object.

3.2   Implementing Resilience

The save() primitive can be used to control the propagation order of pages into secondary memory. An application can exploit this opportunity to maintain consistency of its own data structures in spite of failures. Assume that the updates of object X must be atomic with respect to failures (to keep the presentation short, we shall not consider atomicity with respect to concurrent accesses). Assume also that the descriptor of object X spans several pages, and that an update of X may cause write accesses to two or more of those pages. The save() primitive does not support the atomic saving of more than a single page. However, this primitive makes it possible to achieve the same effect through a write-ahead logging technique, as follows.

We associate a *log* object, of type LogT, with object X. For simplicity, let us suppose that the descriptor of this object fits a single page. An update to X is implemented by carrying out the writes, first, and then inserting *redo* records describing the writes into the log. Upon commit, the log page is saved, first, and then the object is made persistent by saving the modified pages of its descriptor. If a crash occurs after the saving of the log page, but before the saving of the descriptor, the updated value of object X will be recovered by re-applying the writes described by records in the log page to those pages.

The interface is responsible for coordination of the actions necessary to commit an operation and recover the object. When a program running on a given node N wants to access object X, a primary or a secondary copy of the object must be obtained at the node following the interactions described in Section 3.1. However, if the program wants to execute an operation that modifies the object value, a primary copy of the log object must also be obtained at node N. This is the only copy of the log object since secondary copies are not necessary. The interface object in node N is responsible for obtaining that copy by means of primitive open().

Moving the implementation of resilience from the kernel up to the application level has several benefits. First of all the kernel structure is simplified with benefits in terms of efficiency. Second, only applications that need resilience implement it, and pay the related costs. Thus the other applications having less stringent requirements are not penalised.

3.3   Implementing Replacement

The page primitives allow an effective control over residency of a page in the primary memory. Consequently, an application has an opportunity to implement an efficient page replacement strategy. Page replacement can be integrated with the order of the page propagation to safeguard recoverability [4], [8]. This overcomes a limitation often encountered in persistent systems [12], i.e. the impossibility of swapping out the dirty pages [17].

Suppose that, while updating object X, a given program needs to access a given page Q, but the page is not resident in primary memory and no free frame is available. It follows that an open page must be evicted from memory in order to free a frame for Q. The program may select the page to be evicted on the basis of the knowledge of its memory access pattern. Assume that the selected page P belongs to the descriptor of object X. In a situation of this type, it is not possible to simply save and close P because the update operation has not yet been committed. A possible solution is to save the log page and then close P. The writes, recorded in the log, will be applied to P again upon bringing it back into primary memory. An alternative is to use undo records [20]. The log pages containing undo records are saved, and then P is saved and closed. If the operation does not commit, the undo records make it possible to restore the original value of the object. These alternative strategies offer a different trade-off between computational overhead and storage overhead.

4 Memory Management System Implementation

The Ulisse memory management system (MMS) is the system component responsible for both virtual to physical address translation and implementation of the page primitives. Translation of a virtual address into the corresponding physical address in the primary memory uses a *frame table* (*FT*) in each node. The frame table of node N features an entry for each page that is cached at N. The entry for a given page P specifies the name F of the frame reserved for this page, and a *mode bit* specifying whether the page is open or replicated in N (Figure 3). FT takes the form of an inverted table. Consequently, the maximum number of entries is equal to the number of frames that form the primary memory of N, and FT can be entirely stored in the primary memory of N [6].

The implementation of any given page primitive requires an ability to determine the present repository and/or owner of the page involved in the execution of this primitive. To this aim, MMS keeps track of the repository of any given active page and the owner of any open page. The result is obtained by following a fully distributed, highly scalable approach, as follows [6].

The address space is logically divided into equal-sized *partitions*. A page identifier consists of a *partition identifier* and a *local identifier* specifying the page within the partition. The i-th partition is associated with the i-th node, which is called the partition *locator*. When a page is made active in a given node, and this node is the locator of a given partition, the new page belongs to this partition. The local identifier of the page will be equal to the present value of a local page counter, that is initialized to 0 at system generation and is incremented by 1 after every page activation.

The locator of a given partition is the starting point of a path determining the network position of the physical resources reserved for any page active in this partition. This result is obtained by asking the locator for the identity of the current page repository (Figure 3). Then, the page repository is asked for the identity of the current page owner. In each given node N, MMS maintains two look-up tables that are indexed by using page identifiers:

- A *location table* (*LT*) featuring one entry for each page that is active in the partition whose locator is node N. The entry for page P specifies the name of the repository of this page.
- A *block table* (*BT*) featuring one entry for each page whose repository is node N. The entry for page P specifies the name B of the block reserved in N for this page. If P is open, the entry also specifies the name of the owner.

Page identifier P

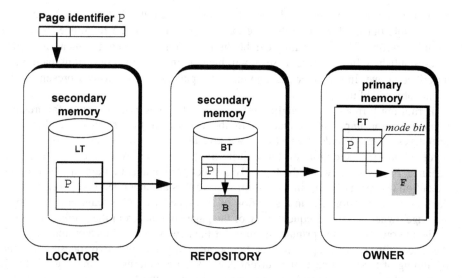

Fig. 3. Configuration of memory management information for a given page *P*.

The location table LT and the block table BT are kept in persistent secondary memory. These tables are updated as part of the actions involved in the execution of the page primitives, which are implemented as distributed atomic transactions according to a two-phase atomic commitment protocol (2PC). Notwithstanding this, system inconsistencies may arise in the case of a node failure as follows. With reference to Figure 3, assume that node W is the owner of a given page P, for instance. Since the frame table FT is volatile, if W crashes, it loses track of both the names and the contents of every page in its own primary memory. Since Ulisse leaves application programs the task of maintaining resiliency of their own data structures, when W recovers Ulisse takes no action to restore the contents of both the pages and the frame table FT. Therefore, after recovery, W is no longer the owner of page P, but the block table of the repository of P continues to indicate W as the current page owner. Of course, this information is erroneous, as the contents of P have been lost in W. This dangling reference problem creates a system inconsistency that should be cleared.

MMS detects and clears the dangling reference as part of the execution of any page primitive that involves both page P and node W, e.g., save(P). With reference to Figure 3, clearing the dangling reference consists of simply clearing the field specifying the page owner in the entry for page P of the block table BT in the page repository. However, detection of the dangling reference is complicated by the fact that a reliable detection can be carried out only if communication with node W is possible. Consider the execution of a page primitive involving page P and node W, and assume that during the execution of that primitive, it is not possible to communicate with W. This fact causes the execution to fail but it is not sufficient to conclude that a dangling reference is present. The impossibility to communicate with node W can be due to either a crash of the node or a network partition. In the former case, a dangling reference is really present and should be cleared. In the latter case, node W is unreachable but no dangling reference exists. Thus clearing the reference to node W would be wrong. This uncertainty can be dissipated only when communication with W is re-established. In the former case, W will have no information concerning page P, as described above. In the latter case, an entry for page P will be instead present in the frame table FT of node W.

Permitting formation of dangling references in the presence of system failures has a potential for important reductions in the latency of the frequently-called page primitives open() and close(), as we save the logging activities in certain nodes involved in the execution of those primitives. Consider primitive open(), for instance. Figure 4 shows all the logically distinct participants that are involved in the execution of open(P, N) in the case that page P is already open in a given node W. As seen in Subsection 2.1, in a situation of this type open() produces a change of the page owner and a consequent copy of the page contents from the primary memory of the old owner W to the primary memory of the new owner N. In accordance to 2PC, the execution of this operation is temporally divided into two phases. At the beginning of the first phase, the current page owner is determined (messages 1 to 3). The initiator sends a control message to the locator, and this message contains the whole information required to start up execution of the primitive (message 1). In turn, the locator forwards the message to the page repository (message 2), which now becomes the *coordinator* responsible for collecting the votes of the participants to 2PC. The repository itself is a participant, as follows from the fact that it must update its own block table by inserting the name of new owner of page P into the table entry reserved for this page. The other participants are the current page owner and the new page owner. The repository sends the current owner a control message requesting the transfer of page contents to node N (message 3). Upon receiving this message, the current owner sends the page contents to node N (message 4). On receipt of these contents, N sends its own vote to the repository (message 6). When all votes have been received (messages 5 and 6), the repository logs a *commit* or an *abort* decision together with the identity of the new owner. The second phase is now started up. A completion message is delivered to the initiator (message 7) and the commit or abort decision is delivered to both the old owner and the new owner (messages 8 and 9). Finally, these participants acknowledge the receipt of the decision (messages 10 and 11). No logging activity is performed on node N, nor on node W. Thus, the minimal latency observed by the initiator is given by the sum of the times necessary to send and receive control messages 1 to 4, 6 and 7, to access the location table in the locator, to access the block table in the repository, and to perform the log in the repository.

The situation illustrated in Figure 4 leads to a worst-case analysis, that may be prone to significant improvements in accordance with the specific configuration of nodes involved in the execution of the page primitive. Consider the case that open(P, N) is issued in node N and this node is the repository of page P. In a situation of this type, node N is both the repository and the new owner of the page involved in the primitive. Consequently, node N may keep the indication that it is the page owner in primary volatile memory and no logging activity is necessary (in addition, the message exchanges between the coordinator and the participants assume the form of local procedure calls).

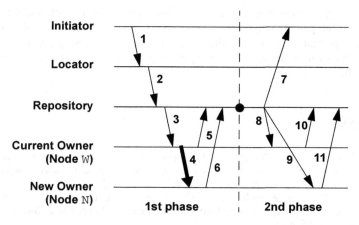

Fig. 4. Message exchange pattern for primitive open(P, N). A thick arrow indicates a page transfer message, a thin arrow indicates a control message, and a dot indicates a logging activity.

Finally, since logging activities are performed only by the repository, significant improvements in terms of the primitive latency can be achieved by taking advantage of a specialized node used as the page repository for commonly accessed data (consequently, this node assumes the functionality of a file server in a classical client/server architecture). For instance, the repository may be equipped with non-volatile RAM or Flash EEPROM modules to speed up the logging activities. We wish to point out that this approach concentrates the hardware cost increase in a single node, and requires no *ad-hoc* hardware in the client nodes.

4.1   Prototypes

An early, fully operational Ulisse prototype has been implemented on a network of personal computers running a variant of the Unix operating system and communicating through the TCP/ IP protocol suite. We have taken advantage of the Unix facilities for system programming, including memory-mapped files and shared memory. The resulting saving in coding effort allowed us to concentrate on the design of the set of the page primitives. In fact, the prototype has been essentially aimed at determining the system requirements for the support of forms of application-controlled memory management, including page replacement [5], page recovery [4], and consistent page caching [10].

At present, we are implementing a second prototype from scratch. The new prototype is aimed at performance measurements and, consequently, it is being built on a bare machine [13]. So doing, we avoid the limitations inherent in the Unix memory-mapping abstraction, that make it difficult to support a large address space together with an efficient failure recovery mechanism [3]. Indeed, part of these limitations could be addressed by taking advantage of external pagers, as is the case in Mach [2] and Chorus [19], for instance. We decided not to rely on external pagers on account of the resulting, limited control over the management of the virtual address space at the application program level. For instance, in both Mach and Chorus the kernel selects the pages to be replaced. In contrast, in Ulisse a decision of this type is left to the application program, that takes advantage of the page primitives to implement its own strategies of memory management by taking its own model of memory behaviour into account.

References

1. D. A. Abramson, J. L. Keedy, "Implementing a large virtual memory in a distributed computing system," *Proceedings of the Eighteenth Annual Hawaii International Conference on System Sciences*, January, 1985, pp. 515–522.
2. M. Acceta, R. Baron, W. Bolosky, D. Golub, R. Rashid, A. Tevanian, M. Young, "Mach: a new kernel foundation for Unix development," *Proceedings, Summer Usenix Conference*, 1986, pp. 93–112.
3. A. Dearle, D. Hulse, "Operating system support for persistent systems: past, present and future," *Software — Practice and Experience*, vol. 30, 2000, pp. 295–324.
4. A. Bartoli, G. Dini, "Mechanisms for application-level recoverable-persistence in a single address space," *Microprocessors and Microsystems*, vol. 22, no. 5, 1998, pp. 247–262.
5. A. Bartoli, G. Dini, L. Lopriore, "Application-controlled memory management in a single address space," *International Journal on Software Tools for Technology Transfer*, to appear.
6. A. Bartoli, G. Dini, L. Lopriore, "Single address space implementation in distributed systems," *Concurrency — Practice and Experience*, vol. 12, 2000, pp. 251–280.
7. J. S. Chase, H. M. Levy, M. J. Feeley, E. D. Lazowska, "Sharing and protection in a single-address-space operating system," *ACM Transactions on Computer Systems*, vol. 12, no. 4, November 1994, pp. 271–307.
8. K.-M. Chew, J. Reddy, T. H. Romer A. Silberschatz, "Kernel Support for recoverable-persistent virtual memory," *Proceedings of the USENIX Mach III Symposium*, Santa Fe, NM, April 1993.
9. P. Corsini, L. Lopriore, "An implementation of storage management in capability environments," *Software— Practice and Experience*, vol. 25, no. 5, 1995, pp. 501–520.
10. G. Dini, L. Lopriore, "Sharing objects in a distributed, single address space environment," *Future Generation Computer Systems*, vol. 17, no. 3, 2000, pp. 247–264.
11. K. Elphinstone, S. Russell, G. Heiser, J. Liedtke, "Supporting persistent object systems in a single address space," *Proceedings of the 7th International Workshop on Persistent Object Systems (POS)*, Cape May, NJ, USA, May 1996.
12. K. Elhardt, R. Bayer, "A Database cache for high performance and fast restart in database systems," *ACM Transactions on Database Systems*, vol. 9, no. 4, 1984, pp. 503–525.
13. B. Ford, G. Back, G. Benson, J. Lepreau, A. Lin, O. Shivers, "The Flux OSKit: A substrate for kernel and language research," *Proceedings of the Sixteenth ACM Symposium on Operating Systems Principles*, October 5–8, 1997, Saint Malo, France, pp. 38–51.
14. K. Harty, D. R. Cheriton, "Application-controlled physical memory using external page-cache management," *Proceedings of the Fifth International Conference on Architectural Support for Programming Languages and Operating Systems*, Boston, Massachusetts, October 1992, pp. 187–197.
15. G. Heiser, K. Elphinstone, S. Russell, J. Vochteloo, "Mungi: a distributed single address space operating system", *Proceedings of the 17th Australasian Computer Science Conference*, Christchurch, New Zealand, January 1994, pp. 271–280.
16. G. Heiser, K. Elphinstone, J. Vochteloo, S. Russell, J. Liedtke, "The Mungi single-address-space operating system," *Software— Practice and Experience*, vol. 28, no. 9, July 1998, pp. 901–928.

17. D. Hulse, A Dearle, "A log-structured persistent store," *Proceedings of the Nineteenth Australasian Computer Science Conference*, February 1996, pp. 563–572.
18. J. Rosemberg, A. Dearle, D. Hulse, A. Lindström, S. Norris, "Operating System Support for Persistent and Recoverable Computations," *Communication of the ACM*, vol. 39, no. 9, September 1996, pp. 62–69.
19. M. Rozier *et al.*, "CHORUS distributed operating systems," *Computing Systems*, vol. 1, no. 4, 1988, pp. 305–367.
20. Y. Saito, B. Bershad, "A transactional memory service in an extensible operating system," *Proceedings of the USENIX 1998 Annual Technical Conference*, USENIX Association, USA, June 1998, Berkeley, pp. 53–64.
21. A. Skousen, D. Miller, "Using a single address space operating system for distributed computing and high performance," *Proceedings of the 1999 IEEE International Performance, Computing and Communications Conference*, Piscataway, NJ, February 1999, pp. 8–14.
22. M. Stumm, S. Zhou, "Algorithms implementing distributed shared memory," *IEEE Computer*, vol. 23, no. 5, May 1990, pp. 54–64.
23. F. Vaughan, T. Lo Basso, A. Dearle, C. Marlin, Chris Barter, "Casper: a cached architecture supporting persistence," *Computing Systems*, vol. 5, no. 3, Summer 1992, pp. 337–359.
24. T. Wilkinson, K. Murray, "Evaluation of a distributed single address space operating system," *Proceedings of the Sixteenth Conference on Distributed Computing Systems*, Honk Kong, May, 1996, pp. 494–501.

Session 6: Overview

Alan Dearle

School of Computer Science, University of St Andrews,
North Haugh, St Andrews, Fife, KY16 9SS, Scotland
al@dcs.st-and.ac.uk

Two papers were presented at this session: „Hyper-Code Revisited: Unifying Program Source, Executable and Data" [1] and „Implementing Orthogonally Persistent Java" [2]. Both these papers proved to be controversial and therefore made for a lively session. As is usual at such sessions, the discussion was not as coherent as this presentation might suggest!

Malcolm Atkinson [MPA] stated his belief that object-oriented languages such as Java encouraged programmers to make many object class definitions. He went on to say that large flat namespaces (which of course we should never have due to the Java package mechanisms) create a presentation problem for programmers, and hyper-code may help with this problem.

Many wanted to compare and contrast hyper-code to Common Lisp [3] or Smalltalk-80 [4]. This charge was lead by Alan Kaplan [AK] who suggested that environments such as those provided by the TI Explorer were similar to hyper-code environments, in that S-expressions were used to encode almost everything.

Olivier Gruber [OG] stated that he liked the hyper-programming approach but wondered if there was any experience in exporting part of an application from one store to another. He gave an example of developing an application in one environment and when you are happy with the result you might want to deploy it in many others.

Vangelis Zirintsis [VZ] stated that he was just finishing the hyper-code system and hadn't looked at these issues.

Graham Kirby [GK] (one of Vangelis' PhD supervisors) responded by saying that in a traditional environment all you have is code and all you care about shipping is code. Consequently you haven't made anything worse with hyper-code systems since you can still ship code. It is only the combination of code and bindings to extant data that makes things more difficult in a hyper-code system.

The Chair [AD] pointed out that Alex Farkas had a paper at DBPL4 in New York [5] addressing that problem and indeed had written a whole thesis related to this issue [6].

Brian Lewis [BL] from Sun Microsystems suggested that the OPJ system was predicated on not being able to make use of lazy swizzling. He claimed that, for example, using object-alignment as a trap mechanism one could lazily swizzle references with Java. Steve Blackburn [SB] retorted that the OPJ system worked above the virtual machine and consequently such techniques could not be used. The Chair notes some five months after the event that this may not be true and exceptions above the VM might be utilised for this purpose.

G.N.C. Kirby, A. Dearle, and D.I.K. Sjøberg (Eds.): POS-9, LNCS 2135, pp. 228-231, 2001.
© Springer-Verlag Berlin Heidelberg 2001

The people from Sun Microsystems were also interested in whether all objects were persistent. Blackburn clarified that the OPJ system implements persistence by reachability in which classes are implicitly persistent and static variables within the classes are persistent.

Predictably, the persistent Java people from Glasgow asked about scalability of the OPJ system from ANU. Blackburn explained that the OPJ system defined a storage API into which many storage architectures could be plugged and the scalability of a configuration depended on the storage architecture. He went on to say that other than the store, scalability depends on the data structures used in the OPJ system which were about as scalable as the data structures used by Sun's.

Not to be outdone Tony Printezis [TP] asked in Blackburn's implementation of the OO7 benchmark [7], how much time is spent in the store and how time is spent moving between the store and the virtual machine? Blackburn replied that this information can be extracted by comparing the cold run to the hot-many run and we can see that there is a big difference. The only difference between the two is the read fault time. This suggests that there was a lot of time spent in the Shore system [8] that was used as the object store. Printezis then asked how much time is spent in the Shore store and how much in the translation code. Blackburn did not have an answer to this, which didn't seem to satisfy Printezis much.

However, this discussion seemed to miss the point somewhat in that it was the new technique pioneered by OPJ that was interesting not the scaling attributes of some particular implementation.

Malcolm Atkinson observed that both the hyper-code system and the OPJ system depend a lot on reflection and introspection over the systems. He asked how good did the panel think the current understanding of reflection interfaces was.

Blackburn clarified by saying that in the OPJ system all user reflection occurs outwith the normal run time and only occurs at class loading time. All the OPJ system requires is a mechanism for examining classes at class load time. Consequently there is no need to use Java's reflection mechanisms much at all.

Zirintsis said that his experience of the (Java) introspection mechanisms with the hypercode system had been positive. However, introspection of code was a problem in the hyper-code system and required the maintenance of a hash-table mapping from Java classes to hypercode representations. It was suggested that some of the newer Byte code reflection systems such as Jikes Byte Code Toolkit [9] might be used to help this problem.

Atkinson asked how easy it was for application programmers to use and understand what was happening in the OPJ system (clearly he hadn't written any PJama programs :). He suggested that if a run time exception occurs, the information might look different to what the programmers expected.

Blackburn replied that with semantic extensions as implemented in the ANU system, it is possible to engineer the exception behaviour so that it is impossible to perceive at run time that any semantic extension has taken place. Many of the problems of this nature identified by Malcolm can be avoided with suitable engineering.

Gruber stated that at IBM with enterprise Java beans and container managed persistence they have experienced many problems with tools displaying trace information from transformed code rather than the source code that is written by the application programmer. This confirmed the problems stated by Malcolm earlier. The problem is that the programmer cannot recognise the code that they have written.

Zirintsis stated that this was not a problem in a hypercode system because the whole point of hypercode systems is that the programmers only perceive a single representation of code and data.

A line of questioning started by the Chair observed that clearly there were problems with working at the Java abstract machine level and problems with working with abstract machine code transformation. Perhaps what was needed was a clean intermediate layer to work with.

Eliot Moss [EM] stated that it was hard to imagine a simpler machine than the Java Abstract Machine that preserved the typing that was required. The discussion focussed on concrete syntaxes for abstract machine code before returning to the old nuggets of Java, the language and its libraries.

Atkinson stated from bitter experience that working with a full Java system causes many problems but we learn things by doing this that we would not have learned otherwise. However, it would be nice to have a nice subset of Java that did not have AWT in it.

Moss pointed out that AWT is not part of the language, it is a library. In his experience the byte code level is relatively clean. It is hard to imagine something simpler than what is encoded in the byte code interpreter that can support the full semantics that you want and with the type safety.

Gruber observed that at IBM they recognise the need to distinguish between the language and the platform because many problems are caused by the combination of the language and platform. In particular with persistence, there is the question of whether we are making the language persistent or the platform persistent? The problem we are faced with with Java is that its success is not due to the language but the widespread adoption of the platform and the write once run everywhere philosophy that it supports. The libraries are part of this contract and therefore cause problems.

Following this exciting discussion we retired to eat more fish and sweet cheese.

References

1. Zirintsis E., Kirby G.N.C., Morrison R. Hyper-Code Revisited: Unifying Program Source, Executable and Data. In: Proc. 9th International Workshop on Persistent Object Systems, Lillehammer, Norway, 2000
2. Marquez A., Blackburn S.M., Mercer G., Zigman J.N. Implementing Orthogonally Persistent Java. In: Proc. 9th International Workshop on Persistent Object Systems, Lillehammer, Norway, 2000
3. McCarthy J., Abrahams P.W., Edwards D.J., Hart T.P., Levin M.I. The Lisp Programmers' Manual. M.I.T. Press, Cambridge, Massachusetts, 1962
4. Goldberg A., Robson D. Smalltalk-80: The Language and its Implementation. Addison Wesley, Reading, Massachusetts, 1983

5. Farkas A., Dearle A. Octopus: A Reflective Language Mechanism for Object Manipulation. In: C. Beeri, A. Ohori and D. E. Shasha (ed) Database Programming Languages, Proc. 4th International Conference on Database Programming Languages (DBPL4), New York City. Springer-Verlag, 1993, pp 50-64
6. Farkas A. Program Construction and Evolution in A Persistent Integrated Programming Environment. PhD thesis, University of University of Adelaide, 1995
7. Carey M.J., DeWitt D.J., Naughton J.F. The OO7 Benchmark. In: Proc. ACM SIGMOD Conference on the Management of Data, 1993
8. Carey M.J., DeWitt D.J., Franklin M.J., Hall N.E., McAuliffe M., Naughton J.F., Schuh D.T., Solomon M.H. Shoring up Persistent Applications. In: Proc. ACM SIGMOD International Conference on Management of Data, Minneapolis, MN, USA, 1994, pp 383-394
9. Laffra C. Jikes Bytecode Toolkit. IBM, 2000

Hyper-Code Revisited: Unifying Program Source, Executable, and Data

E. Zirintsis, Graham N.C. Kirby, and Ron Morrison

School of Computer Science, University of St Andrews,
North Haugh, St Andrews, Fife, KY16 9SS, Scotland
{vangelis,graham,ron}@dcs.st-and.ac.uk

Abstract. The technique of hyper-programming allows program representations held in a persistent store to contain embedded links to persistent code and data. In 1994, Connor *et al* proposed extending this to *hyper-code*, in which program source, executable code and data are all represented to the user in exactly the same form. Here we explore the concept of hyper-code in greater detail and present a set of abstract language-independent operations on which various concrete systems can be based. These operations (*explode*, *implode*, *evaluate*, *root* and *edit*) are provided by a single user interface tool that subsumes the functions of both an object browser and a program editor. We then describe a particular implementation using PJama (persistent Java) and examine the impact of several language features on the resulting system.

1 Introduction

The *hyper-code* abstraction was introduced in [1] as a means of unifying the concepts of source code, executable code and data in a programming system[1]. The motivation is that this may ease the task of the programmer, who is presented with a simpler environment in which the conceptually unnecessary distinction between these forms is removed. In terms of Brooks' *essences* and *accidents* [2], this distinction is an accident resulting from inadequacies in existing programming tools; it is not essential to the construction and understanding of software systems.

Orthogonal persistence [3] brought about several similar simplifications of the programmer's task. One was to unify short-term and long-term data. Another was to unify data and code, in the sense that executable code became first-class (as a procedure or an object) and could be manipulated in the same way as other data. Hyper-code builds on these simplifications by further unifying source code and executable code. The result is that the distinction between them is completely removed: the programmer sees only a single program representation form throughout the software life-cycle, during program construction, execution, debugging, and viewing existing programs and data.

As a consequence, only a single programming tool is required to manipulate this uniform representation form, rather than the various program editors, data browsers,

---

[1] In that paper it was termed *hyper-source*.

G.N.C. Kirby, A. Dearle, and D.I.K. Sjøberg (Eds.): POS-9, LNCS 2135, pp. 232-246, 2001.

debuggers, etc needed otherwise. Various processes such as compilation and linking are also accidental and hidden from the programmer.

In this paper we develop the idea of hyper-code further and attempt to separate the general issues from the language-specific. We describe it in the context of a framework comprising:

- Two abstract domains of *entities* and *representations*, with a set of operations over them. These are intended to be sufficiently general to be applicable to any programming system, and are used to aid description rather than being visible to programmers.
- Criteria to be satisfied by any candidate Hyper-Code Representation form (HCR).
- Criteria to be satisfied by any candidate set of operations over HCRs.
- A particular proposed language-independent HCR.
- A particular proposed set of (broadly) language-independent HCR operations.
- An example implementation of these in a concrete hyper-code system for a particular language (PJama [4]).

We then attempt to draw some conclusions from our experiences in mapping the general concepts to a specific language, and discuss the effect of certain language features on such an exercise.

2 Related Work

A number of programming environments and program editors have attempted to attack accidental complexities. Emacs [5] is a text editing tool that achieves some integration of the programming process, by allowing various operations such as compiling and linking to be invoked from within the editor. However, it does not mask the presence of such accidental operations, and it does not provide any integration of source code, executable code and data.

The Metrowerks CodeWarrior [6] and Microsoft Visual Basic [7] programming environments accelerate the development process by combining an editor, compiler, linker and debugger into a single application. This gathers source code, libraries, graphic resources, and other files into a *project*. An application can be built and executed by pressing a single button, thus the environments largely succeed in hiding accidental operations. They do not, however, integrate source code and data, since these are viewed and manipulated in completely different forms.

Smalltalk-80 is a graphical, interactive object-oriented environment [8] that hides most of the accidents of the traditional programming cycle. However, there are different tools for editing, browsing and debugging, and breakpoints cannot be set interactively. New code being constructed is represented differently from existing objects.

Hyper-programming, as developed in Napier88 [9] and PJama [10], forms the basis for the hyper-code program representation to be introduced in the next section. In those systems, however, there is again a distinction between source code and data, and there is no interactive debugging support.

Finally, the original hyper-code proposal [1] introduced the fundamental idea of hyper-code, that of completely unifying program and data. This paper extends that by developing a general model and describing an implemented system.

3 The Hyper-Code Model

3.1 Design Goals

Software systems may be programmed at various levels of abstraction. The concerns at each level are different, ranging from fine detail such as register values, memory accesses etc, to higher level concepts such as abstract data types, process models etc. The choice of an appropriate level of abstraction depends on the nature of the application. This in turn determines the appropriate tools and software entities to be used to construct the application.

Hyper-code is designed to support programming at a relatively high level of abstraction, which hides the existence of multiple program representations and tools. This requires a single program representation form, and associated tool, that are adequate to support all the activities necessary during the software development cycle. These operations include:

- constructing new programs, which may operate on existing data and programs;
- editing existing programs;
- browsing or viewing existing data structures;
- executing programs, in some cases with debugging and profiling support.

The goal, then, is that the programmer may carry out the entire program development cycle without knowledge of the underlying software tools that support it. The software is viewed in the single consistent hyper-code form in all contexts, whether it is being written for the first time, constructed from existing components, executed, debugged, etc. Where errors occur they are reported in terms of hyper-code; existing persistent data is viewed as hyper-code. This model gives the conceptual simplicity of direct source code interpretation, while retaining the obvious efficiency benefits of standard software tools.

Since hyper-code plays such a large part in the software development environment, two factors are particularly significant to the programmer: the form in which hyper-code is presented, and the operations that may be performed on it.

3.2 Hyper-Code Representations

It is possible to design hyper-code interfaces for various different languages. The precise form of the representation used will depend on the language, as will other aspects of the user interface. We can however identify certain general criteria, derived in part from the design goals listed above:

- To support the construction of new programs that operate on existing data values and programs, the Hyper-Code Representation (HCR) should incorporate denotations for such entities.
- To support browsing or viewing of existing data values, the HCR should allow their structure to be examined interactively.
- Any detailed view of an existing data value should have the same form as that in which an equivalent new value could be defined within a program (since there should only be one single representation form). As a consequence, the representa-

tion of an existing value should be source-code-based and syntactically valid. It may also be desirable, for interoperability, for the HCR to accommodate third-party source code. These factors preclude the use of a graphical data representation.

- It should be possible to initiate execution of a particular HCR instance, and to trace the execution path if desired.

One (and perhaps the only possible) HCR form that fulfils these criteria is the hyper-program [9], with the refinement that hyper-links may themselves have internal structure. A hyper-program may contain both text and hyper-links to existing entities, thus allowing entities to be bound at composition time, rather than the usual restriction to textual specifications that are resolved later at compilation, linking or run-time. For hyper-code, a given link may be expanded interactively to view the structure of the linked entity, without altering the link's meaning—the expanded link continues to denote the same entity. Fig. 1 illustrates this HCR form, containing text, denoted by horizontal lines, and hyper-links, which may or may not be expanded.

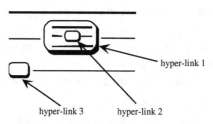

Fig. 1. General Form of an HCR

Here hyper-link 1 has been expanded, so that a representation of the linked entity is displayed within it in the same style. Hyper-links 2 and 3 have not been expanded. Nested links can be expanded to arbitrary degree.

3.3 Hyper-Code Operations

The operations provided by any specific hyper-code interface must support at least the activities identified earlier: editing new and existing programs; browsing data; and executing programs. Clearly there are many possible sets of such operations. In this section we will define one such set which has been designed with simplicity in mind. To aid the description of these hyper-code operations, we first introduce some terminology concerned with programming language entities and representations of those entities.

Domains and Domain Operations
For a given programming language, let E be the domain of language entities, containing all the first class values defined by the language (the Universe of Discourse) together with various denotable non-first-class entities. Depending on the language, the non-first-class entities may include types, classes and executable code.

Let R be the domain of concrete representations of entities in E. These representations could be textual or have some more complex structure. Each entity in E has at least one representation in R. A simple example is the integer value *two* in E and its representation 2 in R. The programmer interacts with the programming system solely by viewing and manipulating representations in R. Entities in E are never dealt with directly, but only through their corresponding representations.

R and E are disjoint. In particular, a representation in R is not itself an entity. Of course, in some circumstances it may be necessary for an executing program to manipulate representations of entities (as is common in reflective programming). To extend the example above, the representation 2 could be manipulated by a program as a string containing the digit 2, and this string could itself be represented as "2". Thus we can distinguish the value, a second value that represents the first (both in E), and the two corresponding representations (in R).

E may be partitioned into a set of executable entities E_{exec} and a set of non-executable entities $E_{no\text{-}exec}$. The former contains programs and program fragments, while the latter contains first class values, types, classes, etc. E_{exec} may be further partitioned into $E_{exec\text{-}res}$, $E_{exec\text{-}no\text{-}res}$ and $E_{exec\text{-}err}$ depending on whether execution generates a result, completes with no result, or fails to complete due to an error. The error may be detected either statically or dynamically.

R may be similarly partitioned, following the structure of E, into R_{exec} (containing $R_{exec\text{-}res}$, $R_{exec\text{-}no\text{-}res}$ and $R_{exec\text{-}err}$) and $R_{no\text{-}exec}$.

We are now in a position to define four *domain operations* over E and R. Our hypothesis is that these domain operations are sufficiently general to describe any set of concrete hyper-code operations for any particular language, and we will illustrate their use in defining our chosen set of hyper-code operations. The domain operations map between and within the domains E and R, as illustrated in Fig. 2.

- *reflect* maps a valid representation to a corresponding entity ($R \Rightarrow E$).
- *reify* performs the reverse operation, mapping an entity to a corresponding representation ($E \Rightarrow R$).
- *execute* executes an executable entity, with potential side effects to the state of the entity domain. This may generate a result ($E_{exec} \Rightarrow E$), complete successfully with no result, or fail due to a static or dynamic error.
- *transform* maps one representation into another ($R \Rightarrow R$).

The rather abstract definitions of the domain operations above may be interpreted in various ways for different concrete hyper-code systems, thus imparting various semantics to the operations. For example, *execute* could involve strict, lazy or partial evaluation of an executable entity, depending on the model of computation supported by the language. The style of representation produced by *reify* could vary. The *transform* operation could be unconstrained, allowing any representation to be produced, or it could limit the possible representations as with a syntax-directed editor.

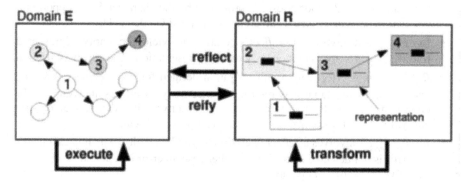

Fig. 2. Domain Operations

Specific Hyper-Code Operations

We now propose a small set of concrete hyper-code operations which is sufficient to fulfil programming requirements, and minimal. Later we will show how these operations may be mapped to a particular example language, together with a specific HCR form. The hyper-code operations are:

- *explode* expands a selected region of a hyper-code representation to show greater detail. This is itself expressed in the form of a hyper-code representation.
- *implode* performs the reverse of *explode*, hiding detail within a hyper-code representation.
- *evaluate* executes a selected hyper-code representation. If there is a result it is expressed as a new hyper-code representation.
- *edit* alters a hyper-code representation.
- *root* returns a selected persistent root as a hyper-code representation.

The actions of these operations can be characterised in terms of the domain operations:

- *explode* and *implode* both replace a selected representation with another, either more or less detailed. They involve a *reflect* operation to yield the entity represented, followed by a *reify* operation to yield a different representation. The result is in R.
- *evaluate* involves various sequences of operations, depending on the particular sub-domain of the representation being evaluated:
  - for $R_{exec\text{-}no\text{-}res}$, it involves a *reflect* operation to yield an executable code entity, followed by an *execute* operation to execute that code, which returns no result. An example is the execution of a traditional „program" such as *gcc*, which is a self-contained sequence of statements that perform some action, with no result being returned directly.
  - for $R_{exec\text{-}res}$, it involves a *reflect* operation to yield an executable code entity, followed by an *execute* operation to execute that code, followed by a *reify* operation to yield a representation of the entity returned as a result of execution. The result is in R. For example, evaluation of the code fragment represented by

the characters *2+3* yields a result represented by the character *5*, as supported in interactive languages such as Smalltalk-80 [8] and Galileo [11].

- for $R_{no\text{-}exec}$, it involves a *reflect* operation to yield the entity represented, followed by a *reify* operation to yield a representation. The result is itself in $R_{no\text{-}exec}$. This is effectively a null operation defined for completeness; since the entity is not executable it is returned immediately as the result. Examples include evaluation of the representation *5* and of a hyper-link denoting an existing entity. Loosely, these correspond to manifest program literals.

- for $R_{exec\text{-}err}$, it involves a *reflect* operation to yield an entity, which is executed if the error is not detected statically. In either case an error is reported.
- *edit* involves a *transform* operation.
- *root* involves a *reify* operation on a persistent entity to yield a representation.

Thus traditional self-contained programs lie in $R_{exec\text{-}no\text{-}res}$, while fragments that return results lie in $R_{exec\text{-}res}$. The *evaluate* operation is defined over both forms.

Tracing Evaluation

The remaining design goal that has not yet been addressed is that of tracing the execution path through an HCR during its evaluation. This requires the HCR to display an indication of the current point of execution at any given time[2], and to provide some means of viewing the current state of any variables. More generally, it should be possible to view the entity bound to any identifier, whether mutable or not.

Since the HCR form supports links that may be exploded to view their structure, the same form can be used for identifiers. This is consistent with the requirement that a single consistent representation should be provided for data and code in all contexts. As a consequence, an HCR being evaluated is changed dynamically as evaluation progresses:

- When evaluation reaches the point at which an identifier is initialised, all subsequent occurrences of that identifier in the HCR, within the identifier's scope, are replaced by links. Depending on the particular language mapping, the links may be to a specific *identifier* entity, or directly to the entity bound to the identifier. In either case, the bound entity may be viewed by *exploding* a link. When evaluation leaves the identifier's scope, the original textual identifier again replaces the links.
- Where an identifier is bound to a mutable location (variable), the corresponding links are updated each time the location is updated.

As a consequence, although the HCR is changed during evaluation, it returns to its original state after evaluation completes. Where an entity is produced as the result of an evaluation, its representation is returned to the programmer. Depending on the interpretation of *reify* chosen for a particular hyper-code system, the result may be a single unexploded hyper-link, an exploded hyper-link, or some other fragment of hyper-code. The programmer chooses whether the result should be returned as a new HCR or inserted into the original HCR being evaluated.

---

[2] Multiple threads can be dealt with by displaying a separate copy of the HCR for each thread.

4 Design and Implementation of a Particular Hyper-Code System

In this section we give a brief overview of the design and implementation[3] of a prototype hyper-code system in PJama [4].

4.1 Mapping of Domains

In Java, and hence PJama, the domain of language entities E contains objects, arrays, primitive values, variables, classes, interfaces, array types and primitive types [12]. We also include code entities, comprising expressions, sequences of statements, or complete class definitions.

Every entity in E has a corresponding representation in the domain R, being a combination of text and hyper-links. We chose to allow hyper-linking to any entity that could be bound to an identifier in a Java program, giving a correspondence between links and identifiers. As a consequence, all entities can be hyper-linked except code entities. This is because the Java model (largely, strict evaluation) does not allow an identifier to be bound to a code expression: an identifier declaration or update causes the expression to be evaluated and the result, rather than the expression, to be bound. For example, evaluating the statement

int i = 1 + 2;

causes the value *3* to be bound to *i*, rather than the expression *1 + 2*.

Although unsatisfying in that not every entity in E can be denoted by a hyper-link, this restriction does not appear to be limiting in practice. Rather, it is intrinsic to the language model of strict evaluation.

Less obviously, we chose to omit methods and fields from E after experimentation with various designs. The fact that they are not first-class made it too awkward to design satisfactory exploded representations for them.

4.2 User Interface

Fig. 3 shows an example of an HCR displayed in a hyper-code window. The first hyper-link is to the class *Person* and the second to an instance of that class (classes and objects are distinguished by different colours).

Fig. 4 shows the effect of performing the *explode* operation on the object link and then again on one of the object links revealed (to the person's address). Each exploded link shows a hyper-code representation of the corresponding object. The representation comprises a call to a newly generated constructor method[4] (*GeneratePerson.newPerson* and *GenerateAddress.newAddress* respectively), taking as parameters links to the object's field values.

This representation fulfils the two main criteria of allowing the structure of the object to be viewed, and being a syntactically valid code-based representation in

---

[3] Details are available at *http://www-ppg.dcs.st-and.ac.uk/Research/HyperCode/*

[4] This is done since there is no guarantee of a suitable constructor being available.

precisely the same form that a programmer might write to construct the object initially. The only difference is that the hyper-code displayed in any exploded link cannot be modified by the programmer, since it is a representation of an entity that already exists. It can of course be copied into another window and the copy modified.

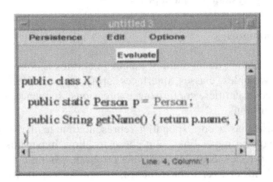

Fig. 3. Example Hyper-Code Representation

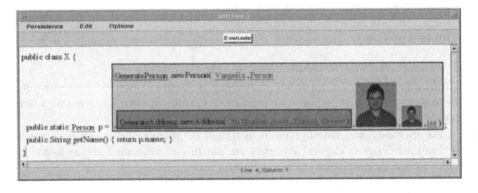

Fig. 4. Effect of Exploding an Object Link

Fig. 5 shows the effect of exploding a class link and several further links within it. Each exploded link displays the class's source code, which itself contains both text and links. This and the previous figure illustrate the unification of code (classes) and data (objects), since exactly the same representation form is used in both.

To write hyper-code operating on existing data, the programmer needs access to the persistent roots. Fig. 6 shows the result of the *root* operation: a window displays a set of hyper-links corresponding to the multiple PJama roots. To operate on one of these, a copy of the hyper-link can be dragged into any other window where it can form part of the hyper-code under construction. In the example, a hyper-link to an array has been exploded so that one of its elements can be dragged to another window.

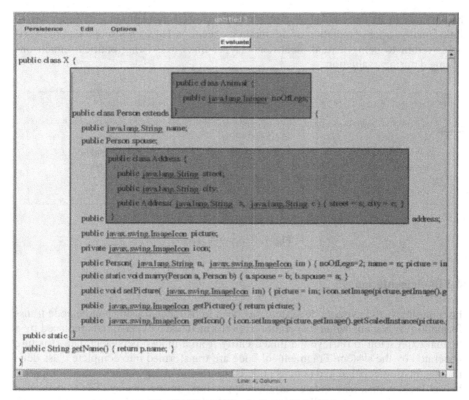

Fig. 5. Effect of Exploding a Class Link

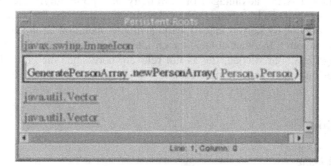

Fig. 6. Persistent Roots Window

At the time of writing (August 2000) the system as described thus far has been implemented. The tracing and control of execution paths using dynamic replacement of variables and links has not yet been completed. However it is possible to give an impression of how this will appear using simulated representations: Fig. 7 shows snapshots at three successive points in the execution of method *m*, indicated by the arrows. In the first, the variable *p* has not yet been initialised and so is represented textually. In the second, after *p*'s initialisation, all uses of the variable are replaced by hyper-links to its current value, which can be viewed by exploding the appropriate link. Finally, after completion of the method execution leaves p's scope and the variables return to being textual identifiers. Hyper-links to existing entities remain unchanged during evaluation.

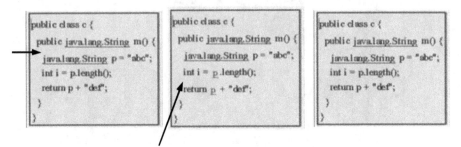

Fig. 7. Execution Tracing

4.3 Implementation

For simplicity, the hyper-code system has been implemented using source code transformation. When an *evaluate* operation is performed, each hyper-link is replaced by a textual expression to retrieve the linked entity from a hidden persistent data structure generated by the system. Fragments of code are transformed into complete class definitions. Instrumentation and control code is inserted in order to track execution paths, halt at breakpoints, and update variables/hyper-links in the display. The transformed code is compiled dynamically using the standard compiler, and the resulting classes loaded and invoked. Full details of the implementation are given in [13].

This scheme has the advantages of simplicity and portability. Alternative techniques such as byte code transformation at class loading time [14, 15] would probably give considerably better performance for the *evaluate* operation, at the cost of greater complexity. Although in other contexts such alternatives also have the advantage of not requiring class source code, this is not relevant here since the entire hyper-code scheme relies on source code being present.

5 Discussion

5.1 General Issues

The paper has described hyper-code in a general framework and given a flavour of a prototype implementation for PJama. Since that is not yet completed, it is not possible to draw any conclusions as to whether the hyper-code model, by removing some of the accidental complexities of programming systems, brings any worthwhile benefits to the programmer. This question could only be answered by conducting a full human factors analysis on target users.

We have claimed that the description of a programming system in terms of abstract entity and representation domains and operations is generally applicable. Similarly, we suggested that a hyper-program form for hyper-code representations is probably the only form possible given the original criteria for hyper-code. These claims need to be tested by designing mappings for other languages.

One obvious problem with the hyper-code representation form is its handling of cyclic data structures: since it imposes a hierarchy on a data structure by displaying each referenced object within the object referring to it, a cyclic structure can be expanded indefinitely without terminating.

5.2 Operation Sets

The set of concrete hyper-code operations described (*explode, implode, evaluate, edit, root*) is just one example of the many possible sets that could support the required activities. It does appear to be simple and minimal, at least in comparison with some of the earlier operation sets from which it evolved during this work. For example, in one version we distinguished between *inspection* of an entity, which generated a read-only representation, and *modification*, in which a representation could be edited and then reflected into a new entity that would replace the original. This scheme turned out to be unnecessarily complex and was too closely coupled with issues of mutability in a particular language. In a later version we defined separate operations for expanding a hyper-link in place and for expanding it to give a new hyper-code fragment. This was unnecessary given the ability to copy the hyper-code within an exploded link, so the two operations were replaced by the single *explode*.

It is not clear whether this operation set is suitable for all languages (without the *root* operation for non-persistent languages); it appears to be suitable for PJama and for another concrete hyper-code system that we have designed for the language ProcessBase [16]. One possibility for further work is to investigate alternative operation sets.

5.3 Language Issues

Focusing on implementation of particular concrete hyper-code systems, two issues may be of interest:

- how do the features of particular languages affect the mapping of those languages to hyper-code?
- what would be the features of a language ideally suited to hyper-code?

We now attempt to relate these issues to the experience of designing the PJama mapping and ProcessBase mappings.

Object Constructors

Since the exploded representation of a Java object takes the form of an expression to construct an equivalent object, it is problematic to decide which of the constructors of that class should be used. There is no way for the system to determine whether a given constructor initialises all of the fields or what other side-effects it causes. This issue is simpler in ProcessBase since a view (i.e. a record, the closest analogue to an object) may be constructed with an anonymous constructor that simply initialises all of the fields. The PJama version attempts to simulate this by generating a new method to construct the object (Fig. 4) but this is rather unwieldy.

Information Hiding

Java's encapsulation model of information hiding, specified by the **protected** and **private** modifiers, does not fit neatly with the desired operation of *explode*, in which exploding an object link should display a full representation of that object. If the object contains hidden members, the choice is to display only a partial representation, in which case the goal of representing the object by a valid expression is not met, or to attempt to subvert the protection using the *AccessibleObject* class available in recent Java versions.

In ProcessBase the only information hiding mechanism is the procedure closure, in which the access path to data used by the procedure may be hidden from general access. This means that the issue described above occurs for procedures rather than objects. The planned system behaviour is that, as with Napier88 [9], the full procedure closure may be viewed when a procedure link is exploded. Thus any data hidden in the closure will be revealed as a link in the hyper-code. This is both a powerful mechanism, and a potential problem since it precludes real information hiding. Clearly, facilities could be provided to apply additional protection mechanisms to the source code.

These are examples of the more general issue of whether a hyper-code system should allow the programmer to achieve anything that could not be achieved by writing conventional programs in the language. In the particular PJama case the system cannot, since it is itself implemented entirely in the language. More generally, where the implementer may have control over aspects of the target language implementation, this is a significant issue.

Mutable Locations

Some complexity is introduced by Java's standard treatment of variables, where an identifier may denote either a location or the current value of that location, depending on its context. For example, a special class of identifier link is required, which behaves differently from all others in that the linked value changes during evaluation on each update. Similarly, the programmer can copy a link to the location of a temporary method variable held on the stack, and paste it in another window. What should be the semantics of that link after the method has returned? The pragmatic but unsatisfactory solution for PJama is that copying the link gives only the corresponding textual identifier.

Both of these problems are avoided if mutable locations are first-class, as in ProcessBase, which provides an explicit location constructor. This simplifies matters—in the first example, the value bound to a link now never changes, although if that value is a location its contents may. In the second example, the location will automatically persist beyond the method invocation, and so the link will continue to denote the same location wherever it is pasted.

Openness

The hyper-code scheme relies on source code being either recorded or generated as required for all entities, so that the *explode* operation can show details. This is feasible in a self-contained persistent system, in which all entities are originally derived from the evaluation of source code. Clearly however it does not work in an open system that has to deal with third-party code for which source is not available. This is true for much of the standard Java class libraries, as well as for most commercial Java software. It is possible to generate approximations to the source code by de-compilation of byte code, but often this will be rendered unusable by deliberate code obfuscation.

Reflection
Java provides good support for introspection over class structure, via the *Reflect* package. It does not, however, provide introspection over method code, even at the byte level, or dynamic access to the compiler. Both of these can be achieved, but implementation of the hyper-code system would be simpler if they were supported directly. Another issue is that current Java compilers work only at the granularity of complete class definitions, so there is considerable overhead involved in processing small expressions since they must be wrapped up into complete classes.

Desirable and Essential Features for Hyper-Code
Although the framework outlined in this paper is intended to be general enough to fit all languages, the following mechanisms, in some form, are essential for hyper-code:

- structural reflection over types
- graphical user interface programming

Several further language features are beneficial when designing a hyper-code system. Some affect the simplicity and elegance of the resulting system, while others impact on the ease of implementation:

- anonymous value constructors (not tightly bound to the value's type)
- information hiding by access path rather than encapsulation
- first-class locations
- dynamic compiler access
- structural reflection over code

The first four items above are provided by ProcessBase, and we intend to implement our hyper-code design as part of our research into compliant architectures [17].

6 Conclusions

This paper has described the following:

- a motivation for providing simpler programming systems;
- a proposed set of criteria to be fulfilled by any candidate system;
- a language-independent program representation form (hyper-code) and a set of operations over it;
- a particular mapping of the above to the Java language.

It is not yet possible to draw any conclusions as to whether hyper-code brings any worthwhile benefits to the programmer, but it appears that it may deliver a valuable simplification of the programming process.

The current status of the PJama hyper-code system, as outlined earlier, is that all of the operations have been implemented, but dynamic evaluation tracing has not (the implementation is currently underway). A design for ProcessBase has been completed and is described in [13].

Acknowledgements. This builds on earlier work carried out with Richard Connor, Vivienne Dunstan and Quintin Cutts. It is supported by EPSRC grant GR/M88938 'Compliant Systems Architecture Phase 2'. We thank the referees for their helpful comments.

References

1. Connor R.C.H., Cutts Q.I., Kirby G.N.C., Moore V.S., Morrison R. Unifying Interaction with Persistent Data and Program. In: P. Sawyer (ed) Interfaces to Database Systems, Proc. 2nd International Workshop on User Interfaces to Databases, Ambleside, Cumbria, 1994. Springer-Verlag, 1994, pp 197-212
2. Brooks F.P. No Silver Bullet – Essence and Accidents of Software Engineering. In: Proc. Information Processing 86, 1986, pp 1069
3. Atkinson M.P., Bailey P.J., Chisholm K.J., Cockshott W.P., Morrison R. An Approach to Persistent Programming. Comp. J. 1983; 26,4:360-365
4. Atkinson M.P., Daynès L., Jordan M.J., Printezis T., Spence S. An Orthogonally Persistent Java™. ACM SIGMOD Record 1996; 25,4:68-75
5. Stallman R. GNU Emacs Manual. Free Software Foundation, 1997
6. Metrowerks Inc. CodeWarrior Pro 5, 1999
7. Microsoft Corporation. Microsoft® Visual Basic® 6.0 Programmer's Guide. Microsoft Press, ISBN 1-57231-863-5, 1998
8. Goldberg A., Robson D. Smalltalk-80: The Language and its Implementation. Addison Wesley, Reading, Massachusetts, 1983
9. Morrison R., Connor R.C.H., Cutts Q.I., Dunstan V.S., Kirby G.N.C. Exploiting Persistent Linkage in Software Engineering Environments. Comp. J. 1995; 38,1:1-16
10. Zirintsis E., Dunstan V.S., Kirby G.N.C., Morrison R. Hyper-Programming in Java. In: R. Morrison, M. Jordan and M. P. Atkinson (ed) Advances in Persistent Object Systems, Proc. 8th International Workshop on Persistent Object Systems (POS8) and 3rd International Workshop on Persistence and Java (PJW3), Tiburon, California, 1998. Morgan Kaufmann, 1999, pp 370-382
11. Albano A., Cardelli L., Orsini R. Galileo: a Strongly Typed, Interactive Conceptual Language. ACM ToDS 1985; 10,2:230-260
12. Gosling J., Joy B., Steele G. The Java™ Language Specification. Addison-Wesley, ISBN 0-201-63451-1, 1996
13. Zirintsis E. Towards Simplification of the Software Development Process: The Hyper-Code Abstraction (PhD Thesis, University of St Andrews). *in preparation.*
14. Marquez A., Zigman J.N., Blackburn S.M. Fast Portable Orthogonally Persistent Java. Software - Practice and Experience, Special Issue on Persistent Object Systems 2000; 30,4:449-479
15. Chiba S. Load-Time Structural Reflection in Java. In: Proc. ECOOP 2000, 2000
16. Morrison R., Balasubramaniam D., Greenwood M., Kirby G.N.C., Mayes K., Munro D.S., Warboys B.C. ProcessBase Reference Manual (Version 1.0.6). Universities of St Andrews and Manchester, 1999
17. Morrison R., Balasubramaniam D., Greenwood R.M., Kirby G.N.C., Mayes K., Munro D.S., Warboys B.C. A Compliant Persistent Architecture. Software - Practice and Experience, Special Issue on Persistent Object Systems 2000; 30,4:363-386

Implementing Orthogonally Persistent Java

Alonso Marquez[1], Stephen M. Blackburn[2], Gavin Mercer[1], and John Zigman[1]

[1] Department of Computer Science
Australian National University
Canberra, ACT, 0200, Australia
{Alonso.Marquez,Gavin.Mercer,John.Zigman}@cs.anu.edu.au
[2] Department of Computer Science
University of Massachusetts
Amherst, MA, 01003-4610, USA
steveb@cs.umass.edu

Abstract. Orthogonally persistent Java combines the power of abstraction over persistence with Java's rich programming environment. In this paper we report our experience in designing and implementing orthogonally persistent Java. Our design approach is anchored by the view that any system that brings together Java and orthogonal persistence should *as far as possible* avoid diluting the strengths of Java or the principles of orthogonal persistence. Our approach is thus distinguished by three features: complete *transparency* of persistence, support for both intra and inter application *concurrency* through ACID transactions, and the preservation of Java's property of *portability*. In addition to discussing design and implementation, we present results that show that our approach performs credibly.

1 Introduction

An orthogonally persistent system provides an abstraction over persistence, enabling programs to execute with respect to transient and persistent data without distinction. This provides a simple programming model, reducing the complexity of the application code, and thereby offering a substantial software engineering advantage. The Java platform is a standard which encompasses a programming language, a virtual machine, and an execution environment. The *'write once run anywhere'* philosophy behind the development of the Java platform is a key to its success and a motivator for our approach to orthogonal persistence for Java (OPJ).[1]

The practicality of orthogonal persistence as a powerful tool for managing complex data is increasingly being recognized by industry. Commercial developments such as GemStone/J [GemStone Systems 1999], PJama [Atkinson et al. 1996] and the Java Data Objects (JDO) standard [Sun Microsystems 1999] indicate the importance of Java as a catalyst for this interest.[2]

---

[1] We use the term *orthogonal persistence for Java* (OPJ) in a generic sense, encompassing any attempt to apply orthogonal persistence to the Java programming language.

[2] GemStone/J is a trademark of GemStone Systems Inc. and Java and PJama are trademarks of Sun Microsystems Inc.

G.N.C. Kirby, A. Dearle, and D.I.K. Sjøberg (Eds.): POS-9, LNCS 2135, pp. 247–261, 2001.

Orthogonally persistent systems are distinguished from other persistent systems such as object databases by an orthogonality between data use and data persistence. This orthogonality comes as a product of the principles of orthogonal persistence [Atkinson and Morrison 1995]:

Persistence Independence. The form of a program is independent of the longevity of the data which it manipulates.

Data Type Orthogonality. All data types should be allowed the full range of persistence, irrespective of their type.

Persistence Identification. The choice of how to identify and provide persistent objects is orthogonal to the universe of discourse of the system.

The impact of these principles on the design and implementation of an orthogonally persistent system is fundamental and pervasive. In this paper we report our experience in applying orthogonal persistence to Java. Our approach is anchored by our view that any system that brings together Java and orthogonal persistence should *as far as possible* avoid diluting the strengths of Java or the principles of orthogonal persistence. As a consequence of this view, our OPJ is marked by three distinguishing features: complete *transparency* of persistence, support for both intra and inter application *concurrency* through ACID transactions, and the preservation of Java's property of *portability*.

After briefly addressing related work, we describe key design issues in section 3, before we discuss major implementation issues in section 4 and conclude with a performance analysis of the three OPJ systems we have built to date.

2 Related Work

Moss and Hosking [1996] present a taxonomy of approaches to developing orthogonal persistence for Java. Their taxonomy explores choices of model, the degree of transparency and the implementation approach. Implementation approaches range from source to byte-code modification, and from compiler modification to runtime system modification. The taxonomy does not explicitly include the key implementation technology used by our approach—user-definable class loaders to transform classes at class loading time.

While there are a number of examples of orthogonally persistent Java implementations, the two most outstanding systems are PJama and GemStone/J, both of which take the approach of modifying the Java virtual machine (JVM).

PJama: The PJama system is a joint project of Glasgow University and Sun Microsystems [Atkinson et al. 1996]. It is based on the Sun JDK platform, where the JVM is modified to extend the system semantics to enable persistence. The system consists of a single JVM with an integrated persistent object store. PJama uses a checkpointing mechanism for flushing updates to the store, although there are proposals for transactional mechanisms for PJama [Daynès 2000].

GemStone/J: GemStone Systems has developed GemStone/J[GemStone Systems 1999], a system targeted at Java server solutions. Multiple JVMs use a transactional mechanism to concurrently operate with respect to a centralized store. To implement the system, Gemstone has developed their own Java compliant JVM which directly supports persistent mechanisms. Technical details of the GemStone/J implementation are not disclosed.

3 Design

Our design was heavily influenced by the ideal of constructing an orthogonally persistent Java system that is true to the principles of orthogonal persistence and yet does not compromise Java's strengths. This objective raised three significant design issues: the method of *persistence identification*, the approach to *concurrency control*, and the preservation of *portability*.

3.1 Persistence Identification

The third principle of orthogonal persistence states that 'the choice of how to identify and provide persistent objects is orthogonal to the universe of discourse of the system' [Atkinson and Morrison 1995]. This is widely interpreted as requiring that the persistence of objects be defined *implicitly* through reachability from some root or roots. We interpret this principle more fully to mean that the roots should also be defined implicitly, an interpretation that is concordant with the first principle of orthogonal persistence, which states that 'the form of a program is independent of the longevity of the data which it manipulates' [Atkinson and Morrison 1995]. We achieve this by making class variables ('static' variables) implicit roots of persistence. Our approach has the significant consequence of making persistence truly transparent, as a Java program requires *no* modification to become orthogonally persistent (see figure 1). By contrast, other systems have required programs to associate explicit textual labels with each root of persistence, which is at odds with the principle of persistence independence.[3]

3.2 Concurrency Control

Strong support for concurrency is crucial to our goals. While non-transactional modes of concurrency control (such as the use of shared variables) provide rich, cooperative programming environments, it is very difficult to effectively intermix such approaches with persistence [Blackburn and Zigman 1999]. For this reason, we use transactions, which are the conventional choice for concurrency control in persistent systems (e.g., databases). Transactions deliver coherency in the face of concurrency through the use of *isolation*, in contrast to the more liberal *cooperative* approach implicit in most non-transactional models of concurrency control. Unfortunately, the combined impact of the principle of persistence independence [Atkinson and Morrison 1995] and

---

[3] Although PJama for a long time depended on explicit roots of persistence [Jordan and Atkinson 1999], it now supports both explicit and implicit modes of reachability.

```
public class Simple {
    static int count    0;
    public static void main(String argv[]) {
        System.out.print(count - " ");
        count++;
    }
}
```

Fig. 1. Depending only on whether it is loaded by a 'persistence-enabled' class loader, this simple program will exhibit either persistent ('0 1 2 . . .') or non-persistent semantics ('0 0 0 . . .').

strict ACID transactional semantics [Haerder and Reuter 1983] means that an orthogonally persistent system that implements only simple ACID transactions will face *extreme* limitations on concurrency (the execution of each application must be confined to a single ACID transaction, thereby curtailing inter-application concurrency) [Blackburn and Zigman 1999].

In order to avoid having to dilute transactional semantics, compromise the principles of persistence, or forgo our goal of strong support for concurrency, we use the *chain-and-spawn* transaction model [Blackburn and Zigman 1999]. This model provides an environment which observes both strict transactional semantics and the principles of orthogonal persistence, while permitting intra and inter application concurrency.

3.3 Portability

Our goal of maintaining Java's 'write once, run anywhere' philosophy has led us to develop a portable design. Portability issues arise in two key aspects of the design: the mechanism by which Java's semantics are extended to include support for persistence, and the portability of the storage layer.

Semantic Extension. The behavior of normal Java programs must be extended in order to incorporate the semantics of orthogonal persistence. Such extensions include: the automatic faulting of objects from storage into memory on demand; the writing of modified objects back to disk when necessary; the transformation of objects between storage and heap formats; and the addition of state information for each object recording whether it has been updated, etc. Moss and Hosking [1996] review some of the wide range of ways of making such semantic extensions to Java. One approach (not explicitly mentioned by Moss and Hosking) is that of using Java's class loader mechanism to semantically extend programs at class loading time. This approach has the advantages of not requiring modification to the Java Virtual Machine (JVM), so it can be used with any JVM, and not depending on compiler modifications or post-processing, so it can be used with any Java class. All that is required for a class to become orthogonally persistent is for it to be loaded by an appropriate class loader.[4] This feature combined

---

[4] Specifically, we create `PersistentClassLoader`, a subclass of `ClassLoader` which implements semantic extension mechanisms for persistence. We then ensure that all user-

with our approach to persistence identification (section 3.1) means that a compiled Java class (such as the one in figure 1) can be orthogonally persistent (or not) depending solely on the class loaders used to load classes for that program—every other aspect of the execution environment, including the class file and the choice of JVM, remains unchanged.

This method of semantic extension introduces a complication relating to Java's reflection mechanism, which provides methods for examining classes and objects and creating or modifying objects. In order to preserve the transparency of persistence, the application's use of the reflection mechanisms should show no trace of the semantic transformations performed by the class loader. Therefore, the transformations must also suitably transform the semantics of the reflection operations.

A similar complication arises with user defined class loaders, which could potentially bypass the bytecode transformation process. Again, a clean solution is provided by the use of semantic extension. The defineClass() method of java.lang. ClassLoader can be semantically extended to apply bytecode transformations just prior to the loading of each class. Thus persistence semantics will be added to all classes, even those semantically extended by other class loaders. Of course this solution only addresses issues relating to our *mechanism* for semantic extension. We do not address the more abstract problem of semantic extensions which may clash with orthogonal persistence (such as other persistence mechanisms). This problem may arise whenever Java's semantics are extended, whether through the use of a class loader, by modifying the VM, or any other by any other means.

Storage Interface. The architecture of our OPJ implementation embodies a clean interface between the Java runtime and the underlying store. By making such a strong separation, we gain portability with respect to the underlying store.[5] We use the PSI storage interface [Blackburn and Stanton 1999], which while providing strong transactional semantics, allows efficient implementations by virtue of the runtime system having direct access to the store's cache.

4   Implementation

The design for OPJ outlined in the previous section raises some challenging implementation issues. We have made three major implementations of such a system and experimented with a number of the many implementation possibilities. Common to all of our systems is a mechanism for performing the semantic extension of classes at class loading time [Marquez et al. 2000]. The specifics of these mechanisms are incidental to the goals of this paper and are omitted for brevity.

---

defined classes are loaded by instances of PersistentClassLoader. A program invoked as 'java Class [args]', would execute with persistence semantics if invoked as 'java PersistentClassLoader [optional store args] Class [args]'.

[5] In fact we have successfully developed bindings to three stores: a major commercial DBMS product, the SHORE object database [Carey et al. 1994], and most recently, to our own object database [He et al. 2000].

The semantic extension of a class to support orthogonal persistence involves a few basic transformations, including: the insertion of 'read barriers', which will ensure that an object has been faulted into memory from storage before it is used; the insertion of 'write barriers', which ensure that updates to heap objects are propagated to storage; and the addition of mechanisms for transforming objects between heap and object store representations. While each of these semantic transformations is fairly simple (such as the insertion of a call to a read barrier method prior to each `getfield`), together they raise major implementation issues.

4.1   Structural Choices: Shells and Façades

In our experience, one of the most important implementation issues is the choice of what structure to use for representing *unfaulted objects*. Unfaulted objects exist as a consequence of our use of eager 'swizzling' strategies.[6] There are a variety of swizzling strategies and the choice of strategy has a significant impact on the design of the system [Moss 1992]. For the purposes of this discussion, four broad options exist: *eager swizzling*, where all references are swizzled as soon as an object is faulted into memory; *lazy swizzling*, where references are swizzled when they are first traversed; *no swizzling*, where references remain in store format and a conversion is made each time such a reference is traversed; and *eager swizzling to handles*, where handles hold OIDs (store-level object identifiers) and an in-memory pointer to the referenced object is established the first time the handle is traversed.

Java's strong typing and our goal of portability severely restrict the approaches that we can take to swizzling. The reference fields in a Java object must contain references of the appropriate type, which precludes the simple overloading of a reference field with an OID—ruling out lazy swizzling and no swizzling. We have therefore experimented with the remaining choices: eager swizzling to objects and eager swizzling to handles. These choices lead to two very different mechanisms for representing unfaulted objects, *shells*, and *façades* , respectively.

Shells. The *shell* approach uses an 'empty'[7] object (which we call a shell) for each unfaulted object. When an OID is swizzled for the first time, an object of the appropriate type is created and the OID is replaced by a reference to that object. All subsequent swizzles of that OID will result in the translation of the OID to a reference to the same Java object. The first time the shell object is accessed, the corresponding object is read from the store and used to initialize the shell. The initialization process will usually involve swizzling references, in which case the process recurses.

The shell approach is relatively easy to implement. An OID field must be added to each object so that the appropriate store object can be read in when the object is first traversed. The same field can serve the purpose of identifying the object's state with respect to initialization and update (the presence of a valid OID in the OID field can be used to indicate that the object remains uninitialized, another value is used to

---

[6] The term 'swizzle' refers to the translation of a reference from persistent to transient forms.

[7] By 'empty' we mean that the object has not been initialized with state from the store.

indicate that the object has been updated). The semantic transformation required for the shell approach is therefore quite trivial—a read barrier is inserted before each `getfield` byte code. The read barrier simply checks to see whether the object to be read has been initialized, and faults it from storage if necessary. Unfortunately shells have one potential drawback—the uninitialized shells may consume a large amount of memory.

Façades. A less memory-intensive alternative to shells is to use *façades,* which have the additional significant advantage of being a mechanism for removing read barriers. A façade is a lightweight representation of an object which masquerades as the real object until such time as the real object is required. The façade must behave like the object that it represents up until the point at which it is first accessed, and once accessed, it must transparently replace itself with the real object. This requires the façade and the real object to be type equivalent and for all classes to be fully 'virtualized' (i.e. all non-private fields made private and external accesses to those fields transformed to use accessor methods such as `getFoo()` and `setFoo()`).

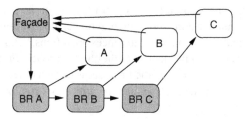

Fig. 2. In order for a façade to be transparently replaced by a real object, all pointers to the façade must be redirected to point to the real object. For this reason, façades must maintain *back references* to all referring objects.

Façades may only be accessed via method invocations (remembering that all classes are fully virtualized), so trapping access to façades simply requires implementing a faulting mechanism in each of the façade's methods. When a façade method is invoked, it creates a corresponding real object, initializes it by faulting in the store object, uses back references to replace all existing references to the façade with references to the real object, and then finally calls the corresponding method on the real object and returns the result. All subsequent method invocations with respect to the object incur no read barrier penalty, as all pointers now refer directly to the real object rather than to the façade.

The semantic transformation required for the façade approach is more complex than that required for shells. Figure 3 illustrates the transformations of a simple two-level class hierarchy. First each class C must undergo a virtualization transformation. Each virtualized class C_v is used to define an interface C_i, and two concrete classes, $C_{v'}$ and C_f, which implement C_i. C_f is the façade class for the 'real' class $C_{v'}$. In the example in figure 3, the implementation $B_{v'}$ of B_i inherits its functionality and fields from the implementation $A_{v'}$ of interface A_i.

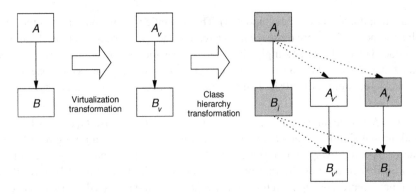

Fig. 3. The use of façades requires a two-stage transformation in order for façades and real objects to be type equivalent. Both transformations occur transparently and automatically at class loading time.

Because a façade is never used to represent the state of the real object, each façade can be much smaller than the corresponding real object, containing only enough state to perform the faulting and replacement of references operations.[8] Thus the façade approach may offer a significant space advantage over the shell approach. Furthermore, the façade approach only incurs a read barrier on the first access to each object. Unfortunately these advantage may be offset by the costs associated with full virtualization.

4.2   Other Implementation Concerns

Object Packing and Unpacking. When an object is faulted into memory, it must be transformed from a store object into a Java heap object. We refer to this process as *unpacking*, and it involves creating a Java object of the appropriate type and then initializing each of its non-transient fields, swizzling references as necessary. The transformation from heap object to store object at commit time is referred to as *packing*, which is simply the reverse transformation. We have experimented with two quite different approaches to packing and unpacking. Our first implementation used C++ pack and unpack methods. We took this approach on account of the perceived performance benefits associated with C++, and in the hope that C++-implemented map structures (used for swizzling) would be faster than Java implementations of the same structures. We quickly found that it was *critical* to minimize the number of traversals of the Java/C boundary, as each traversal is extremely expensive. We also found that the use of Java's reflection mechanism to establish the structure of the transformed object was very expensive.

We have subsequently re-implemented the pack and unpack methods in Java. We did this by including the automatic generation of per-class pack and unpack methods in our semantic extension transformations that occur at class loading time. The major advantages are that this approach minimizes the number of traversals of the Java/C

---

[8] The number of back-references maintained by a façade can be bounded by adopting a policy of eagerly faulting objects once the number of references to the façade reaches some threshold.

boundary, and that it avoids the use of reflection mechanisms at runtime by 'hard-coding' the appropriate instructions into methods at class loading time. We cannot completely avoid the use of JNI, as the calls to read and write objects from the underlying store are necessarily calls to C functions. The use of Java for packing and unpacking depends a great deal on the Java libraries efficiently implementing the map structures which are used in the swizzle process.

Transactional Isolation. The requirement of *isolation* for any ACID transaction means that all transactions concurrently executing within a single JVM must be isolated from each other's uncommitted actions. The implementation of fine-grained locks to ensure isolation between transactions within a single JVM could be very expensive. Fortunately, the Java class loader mechanism provides a powerful feature in this respect—namespace isolation. Namespace isolation ensures that computations running in distinct class loaders are strictly isolated. Class loaders do not share instances or classes (system classes being the exception), so neither instance nor class variables are visible across namespace boundaries. We make use of the class loader mechanism to cheaply implement transactional isolation by binding each transaction to a class loader.[9] To our knowledge, no other OPJ system incorporates a mechanism for enforcing strict isolation semantics.

System Classes. User-defined class loaders, for security and boot strapping reasons, are not able to intercept the loading of system classes. As a consequence, system classes cannot be semantically extended at class loading time. The key impact of this limitation is that we cannot insert read barriers to trap accesses to fields within system classes. The simple (although unsatisfying) solution that we have adopted is to eagerly load objects referred to by system classes. The impact of this is particularly clear in the case of arrays. Because arrays are system classes, we cannot trap accesses to the fields of non-primitive arrays so we eagerly fault *all* unfaulted objects referred to by the array. For a more detailed discussion of this problem, the interested reader is referred to [Marquez et al. 2000].

Thread Persistence. Our current OPJ implementations do not make the execution state of threads persist. Because Java threads are first class objects, this limitation is a violation of the principle of data type orthogonality, which states that 'all data types should be allowed the full range of persistence, irrespective of their type' [Atkinson and Morrison 1995]. However, we believe that it will be possible to implement persistent threads within our OPJ framework by using techniques similar to those used to implement thread migration [Hohlfeld and Yee 1998]. Thread migration depends on thread state being encapsulated and then revived after *transmission*, which has much in common with problem of encapsulating and reviving thread state after *storage*.

---

[9] Note that while we achieve semantic extension by creating a new class loader *class*, we achieve isolation by creating new class loader *instances*. The mechanisms we use for achieving semantic extension and transactional isolation are thus orthogonal.

5   Results

We have used the design outlined in section 3 as the basis for three distinct implementations. In the process, we have explored two major dimensions of the implementation space: the use of shells versus façades for unfaulted objects and the use of C++ versus Java for object packing and unpacking. We will now analyze the performance impacts of these choices and compare our approach to OPJ with two versions of PJama.

5.1   Experimental Setting

OO7 Benchmark. OO7 is an object database benchmark suite [Carey et al. 1993]. The suite consists of a large number of operations including both *traversals*, which are navigational, and *queries*, which are query-like retrievals. The OO7 schema is modeled on that of a CAD application. We have implemented the OO7 benchmark in Java. We used Chain() and Checkpoint() in ANU-OPJ and PJama respectively at OO7's commit points. The non-persistent Java implementation builds the OO7 database in memory before each set of benchmark operations are executed.

Each execution of the benchmark consisted of ten iterations of each operation. The elapsed time for the first iteration is regarded as a *cold* time (the cache was cold), while the times for all subsequent iterations excluding the last are averaged to produce a *hot* time. To help measure transaction initiation and commit costs, OO7 allows the operations to be executed using *many* transactions (i.e., a commit for each iteration), or *one* transaction (i.e., a single commit at the end of the set of iterations). The size of the OO7 database is configurable, but three sizes are commonly used: *small*, *medium*, and *large*. Due to limitations in our OO7 implementation and the underlying systems, it was only possible to use the small configuration, and seven of the operations could not be executed on one or more of the systems (*q4, i, t2b, t2c, t5do,* and *t5undo*). To gain a quantitative impression of the overall performance of each system, we take the geometric mean of the results for each of the operations.

Systems Used. We measured six systems:

label	description
ANU-OPJ-S	ANU OPJ using shells with C++ packing.
ANU-OPJ-S-J	ANU OPJ using shells with Java packing.
ANU-OPJ-F	ANU OPJ using façades with C++ packing.
PJama-1.2	PJama version 1.2.1.
PJama-1.6	PJama version 1.6.4.
Java	Non-persistent Java.

All of the Java systems used JDK 1.2.2, and with the exception of PJama-1.2 and PJama-1.6, all used the Hot Spot just in time compiler (JIT). PJama-1.6 uses a JIT as described in [Lewis et al. 2000]. All of the ANU OPJ systems used version 1.1 of the SHORE object database [Carey et al. 1994]. The benchmarks were executed on a Sun Ultra-170 with 128MB of RAM and separate hard disks for the persistent store and log.

5.2 Performance Analysis

Figure 4 provides a picture of the overall performance of the six systems. We see that all of the ANU OPJ implementations perform worse than PJama-1.6 and PJama-1.2 when cold, which suggests that the cost of starting a transaction in the ANU systems is greater than for either of the PJama systems. The large performance differential in the cold results between the persistent systems and Java is unsurprising as the Java system does not incur the I/O overhead associated with faulting objects into the store. The ANU systems perform much better when hot, with ANU-OPJ-S only slightly lagging PJama-1.6 and performing about five times better than PJama-1.2. The particularly good performance over the shorter operations suggests that fast commit times are a factor in this result. The hot 'one' results (figure 4 (c)) show the performance of four of the systems during normal processing (i.e. excluding startup and commit). This indicates that the performance of PJama-1.6 is close to optimal (*cf* Java). The ANU systems are all appreciably slower, but still significantly faster than PJama-1.2.

Shells versus Façades. A comparison of ANU-OPJ-S and ANU-OPJ-F indicates that the use of façades produces a slow-down in the order of 20%. The success of the façade approach depends heavily on two factors: the ability of the JIT to inline `final` field access methods, and the average size of unfaulted objects being appreciably bigger than façades. These results suggest that the JIT may not be inlining as aggressively as we had hoped, and that the small size of most OO7 objects limits the memory saving that the façade approach can offer over the use of shells.

Java versus C Packing and Unpacking. By comparing ANU-OPJ-S and ANU-OPJ-S-J we see that the use of Java for the management of OID to Java object mappings as well as packing and unpacking operations leads to a performance degredation compared to the case where C++ is used. However, while the hot-one times indicate that there is a significant slowdown in runtime performance, the slowdown is much less for the hot-many times. This is probably because the use of Java leads to more efficient packing and unpacking by avoiding the use of Java's expensive reflection mechanisms.

Overall Performance. These results indicate that our OPJ implementations are lagging the state of the art. However, a number of important factors moderate this result. First, unlike each of the other systems, our OPJ systems are *fully transactional*, implementing fully ACID semantics and supporting inter-transactional concurrency rather than just implementing an atomic checkpoint mechanism. Second, with sufficient resources, we believe that we could make significant improvements to the performance of our systems—the results presented in this paper are the outcome of a very limited implementation effort. Finally, we do not exclude the value of virtual machine modifications—our approach could happily exploit suitably targeted JVM enhancements without sacrificing its portability.

An obvious source of performance improvement for our systems would be the optimization of read and write barriers. Hosking et al. [1998] have demonstrated significant

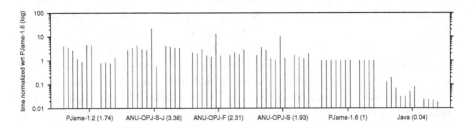

(a) OO7 parameters: *cold* and *many*. Reflected in these results: read IO, transaction startup and commit (including write IO), runtime overheads.

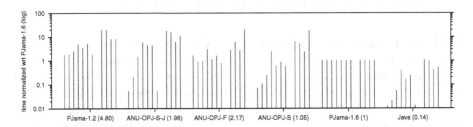

(b) OO7 parameters: *hot* and *many*. Reflected in these results: transaction startup and commit (including write IO), runtime overheads.

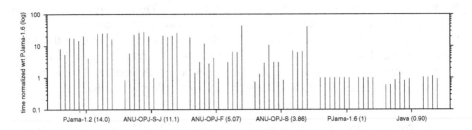

(c) OO7 parameters: *hot* and *one*. Reflected in these results: runtime overheads.

Fig. 4. The performance of each of the six systems. The results are plotted on a log scale, and each impulse reflects the average execution time for a particular operation on a given system *normalized* with respect to the time for PJama-1.6 for the same query. A result lower than one indicates better performance than PJama-1.6. Each set of results is grouped as follows: queries *q1, q2, q3, q5, q6, q7, d* (left) and traversals *t1, t2a, t3a, t6* (right). The geometric means of normalized results for each system appear in brackets.

performance improvements by using code analysis to detect and remove redundant barriers. This approach could be incorporated into the byte code transformations we perform at class loading time.

One of the most difficult constraints that we have had to work with is Java's prohibition of user-defined class loaders modifying system classes (section 4.2). The key impact of this limitation is that we can not insert read or write barriers with respect to field accesses within system classes. A relaxation of this policy would allow us to greatly improve the performance of our systems. A more radical step would be to extend Java with native support for a generic semantic extension language, such as the one we have developed for this project. Our semantic extension language allows extensions to be specified at a very high level, and for the extensions to be applied to classes according to inheritance relationships [Marquez et al. 2000]. Native support for the language would open the possibility of semantic extensions being applicable to system classes. Such an feature would have application well beyond the implementation of OPJ.

Finally, our object faulting mechanisms are expensive because we have no means of directly moving an object image into the Java heap. Instead, a new Java heap object must be created and each of its fields must be separately initialized. An extension to Java that allowed this process to be sped up would improve our 'cold' performance results.

6 Conclusions

We have designed and built an orthogonally persistent Java system, strongly motivated by the desire to remain true to the principles of orthogonal persistence without sacrificing Java's strengths. The product of this effort is a working system with credible performance that is distinguished in three key respects: complete *transparency* of persistence, support for both intra and inter application *concurrency* through ACID transactions, and preservation of Java's property of *portability*. These are achieved by: making class variables implicit roots of persistence, using the chain-and-spawn transaction model, and by making use of Java's provision of a user-definable class loader mechanism.

While performance results indicate that our system is not competitive with the latest release of an OPJ system based on a custom JVM, it seems that much of the performance differential will be susceptible to erosion by improvements in JVM technology and improvements in our implementation approach. The gap might be further narrowed by the provision of suitable hooks in JVMs. We are therefore optimistic that the novel approach to OPJ outlined in this paper will make a genuine contribution to the goal of bringing orthogonal persistence to popular use through Java.

References

[Atkinson et al. 1996] ATKINSON, M. P., JORDAN, M. J., DAYNÈS, L., AND SPENCE, S.   1996. Design issues for Persistent Java: A type-safe, object-oriented, orthogonally persistent system. In R. CONNOR AND S. NETTLES Eds., *Seventh International Workshop on Persistent Object Systems* (Cape May, NJ, U.S.A., May 1996), pp. 33–47. Morgan Kaufmann.
[Atkinson and Morrison 1995] ATKINSON, M. P. AND MORRISON, R.   1995.   Orthogonally persistent systems. *The VLDB Journal 4*, 3 (July), 319–402.

[Blackburn and Stanton 1999] BLACKBURN, S. M. AND STANTON, R. B. 1999. The trans-
actional object cache: A foundation for high performance persistent system construction. In
R. MORRISON, M. JORDAN, AND M. ATKINSON Eds., *Advances in Persistent Object Systems,
Proceedings of the 8th International Workshop on Persistent Object Systems (POS8) and Pro-
ceedings of the 3rd International Workshop on Persistence and Java (PJW3) Sept. 1–3, 1998,
Tiburon, CA, U.S.A.* (San Francisco, 1999), pp. 37–50. Morgan Kaufmann.

[Blackburn and Zigman 1999] BLACKBURN, S. M. AND ZIGMAN, J. N. 1999. Concurrency—
The fly in the ointment? In R. MORRISON, M. JORDAN, AND M. ATKINSON Eds., *Advances in
Persistent Object Systems, Proceedings of the 8th International Workshop on Persistent Object
Systems (POS8) and Proceedings of the 3rd International Workshop on Persistence and Java
(PJW3) Sept. 1–3, 1998, Tiburon, CA, U.S.A.* (San Francisco, 1999), pp. 250–258. Morgan
Kaufmann.

[Carey et al. 1993] CAREY, M. J., DE WITT, D. J., AND NAUGHTON, J. F. 1993. The OO7
benchmark. In P. BUNEMAN AND S. JAJODIA Eds., *Proceedings of the 1993 ACM SIGMOD
International Conference on Management of Data, Washington, D.C., May 26–28, 1993*, Volume 22 of *SIGMOD Record* (June 1993), pp. 12–21. ACM Press.

[Carey et al.] CAREY, M. J., DEWITT, D. J., FRANKLIN, M. J., HALL, N. E., MCAULIFFE, M. L.,
NAUGHTON, J. F., SCHUH, D. T., SOLOMON, M. H., TAN, C. K., TSATALOS, O. G., AND WHITE,
S. J. 1994. Shoring up persistent applications. In R. T. SNODGRASS AND M. WINSLETT Eds.,
Proceedings on the 1994 ACM-SIGMOD Conference on the Management of Data, Volume 23
of *SIGMOD Record* (Minneapolis, MN, U.S.A., May 24–27 1994), pp. 383–394. ACM.

[Daynès 2000] DAYNÈS, L. 2000. Implementation of automated fine-granularity locking in a
persistent programming language. *Software: Practice and Experience 30*, 4 (April), 325–361.

[GemStone Systems 1999] GEMSTONE SYSTEMS. 1999. GemStone/J.
http://www.gemstone.com/.

[Haerder and Reuter 1983] HAERDER, T. AND REUTER, A. 1983. Principles of transaction-
oriented database recovery. *ACM Computing Surveys 15*, 4 (Dec.), 287–317.

[He et al. 2000] HE, Z., BLACKBURN, S. M., KIRBY, L., AND ZIGMAN, J. N. 2000. Platypus:
Design and implementation of a flexible high performance object store. In *Proceedings of the
Ninth International Workshop on Persistent Object Systems, Lillehammer, Norway September
6–9, 2000* (2000).

[Hohlfeld and Yee 1998] HOHLFELD, M. AND YEE, B. 1998. How to migrate agents.
http://www.cs.ucsd.edu/users/bsy/pub/migrate.ps.

[Jordan and Atkinson 1999] JORDAN, M. J. AND ATKINSON, M. P. 1999. Orthogonal persistence for Java? – A mid-term report. In R. MORRISON, M. JORDAN, AND M. ATKINSON
Eds., *Advances in Persistent Object Systems, Proceedings of the 8th International Workshop
on Persistent Object Systems (POS8) and Proceedings of the 3rd International Workshop on
Persistence and Java (PJW3) Sept. 1–3, 1998, Tiburon, CA, U.S.A.* (San Francisco, 1999), pp.
335–352. Morgan Kaufmann.

[Lewis et al.] LEWIS, B., MATHISKE, B., AND GAFTER, N. 2000. Architecture of the PEVM:
A high-performance orthogonally persistent Java virtual machine. In *Proceedings of the Ninth
International Workshop on Persistent Object Systems, Lillehammer, Norway September 6–9,
2000* (2000).

[Marquez et al. 2000] MARQUEZ, A., ZIGMAN, J. N., AND BLACKBURN, S. M. 2000. Fast,
portable orthogonally persistent Java. *Software: Practice and Experience 30*, 4 (April), 449–
479.

[Moss 1992] MOSS, J. E. B. 1992. Working with persistent objects: To swizzle or not to
swizzle. *IEEE Transactions on Software Engineering SE-18*, 8 (August), 657–673.

[Moss and Hosking 1996] MOSS, J. E. B. AND HOSKING, A. L.   1996.   Approaches to adding persistence to Java. In M. JORDAN AND M. ATKINSON Eds., *First International Workshop on Persistence and Java* (Drymen, Scotland, September 16–18 1996). Available online at: http://www.dcs.gla.ac.uk/~carol/Workshops/PJ1Programme.html.

[Sun Microsystems 1999] SUN MICROSYSTEMS.   1999.   Java Data Objects Specification, JSR-12. http://java.sun.com/aboutjava/communityprocess/jsr (July), Sun Microsystems Inc., 2550 Garcia Avenue, Mountain View, CA 94043.

Session 7: Overview

Sonia Berman

Department of Computer Science, University of Cape Town,
Private Bag, Rondebosch 7701, South Africa
sonia@cs.uct.ac.za

The first paper in the final session was „Event Storage and Federation using ODMG" by Jean Bacon, Alexis Hombrecher [AH], Chaoying Ma, Ken Moody and Walt Yao from Cambridge University, and was presented by Alexis. This proposes a way of handling events in a distributed object-oriented environment using the ODMG standard. They advocate storage and query facilities for events to adequately support event-driven applications. ODL is used to keep metadata on event types, stored with events in an object-oriented database. This enables new objects to be discovered dynamically and added to running systems. Hierarchies in event schemas permit translating between different domains in federated semantically heterogeneous event systems. Through stored metadata, contracts between domains can be created and used for event translation. In this way heterogeneous systems can be used together in a federation for tracking and analysing events across multiple application domains.

The second paper was „An Application Model and Environment for Personal Information Devices" by Olivier Gruber [OG] and Ravi Konuru from IBM TJ Watson Research Center in New York. Their Bali project aims at providing a runtime system that enhances application portability over different personal digital devices. It is based on JavaBeans and a Minimal Java Runtime Environment, with persistent beans replicated across devices to permit adaptation to different devices. Links to remote beans and interface navigation introduce little overhead and have proved to be very useful for programmers.

The final workshop paper was „Scalable and Recoverable Implementation of Object Evolution for the PJama Platform" by Malcolm Atkinson [MPA], Misha Dmitriev, Craig Hamilton and Tony Printezis [TP] of Glasgow University. This paper tackles the important problem of object evolution in long-running large-scale persistent application systems. It shows how the partitioned store architecture and the disk garbage collector have been exploited in building an incremental evolution system. Provided with a set of changed classes and code to transform instances from old to new version, the system validates the transformation and creates changed limbo objects in a way that ensures the original state is recoverable in the event of failure. The switch from old to new version is accomplished in a final atomic action. The algorithm requires only two extra partitions and no extra PIDs, and performance grows linearly with the number of evolving objects.

Questions on the first paper focussed on the benefits of using ODMG, which had not previously been mentioned at the workshop. Hombrecher said they had used this because of the rich type system, the ease of connecting to storage and the ability to cross language barriers. There was no overhead for the programmer who simply has

G.N.C. Kirby, A. Dearle, and D.I.K. Sjøberg (Eds.): POS-9, LNCS 2135, pp. 262-264, 2001.
© Springer-Verlag Berlin Heidelberg 2001

to run the ODL stub compiler and use the output skeleton files to program clients/sources. When they chose ODMG it was because it had looked like it would become a widely adopted standard, which in his opinion had in fact not happened.

After Gruber's presentation of Bali, Alan Dearle [AD] asked if there were elements of the Java type system not particularly suitable for the DCOM style of programming. Gruber said this was not what had hindered them, but rather Java's event model. This requires special action when you replicate across different devices—you have to undo connections and redo them appropriately. In answer to a question from Graham Kirby [GK], he confirmed that they still had the concept of a conduit for synchronising with existing applications. He added that he saw only two possibilities, using conduits or connecting to EJB servers that are already persistent. Berndt Mathiske [BM] pointed out similarities with schema evolution where you export in XML format and then take the code back in only after it has been updated. Gruber agreed that you have the same things with models: when you have a new version of a model you write a piece of code that is triggered by the system to translate from one version to the other. XML is one of the candidates for this—the beans export an XML interface or the system generates it, and the code uses the XML. The interface supports self-description and that's what is used to access the internal information.

After the final presentation (of incremental evolution in the Sphere PJama store), Atkinson was asked what would happen if schema evolution required co-ordinated changes to two different classes that were in two different partitions. If the application accesses the objects between upgrading of the first partition but before upgrading of the other, there could be trouble. Atkinson said there was no problem as the application could not run while the evolution was in progress, and all the objects would be evolved. This raised a question of clarification, as to whether the incrementality referred to was with respect to failure rather than with respect to the application. Atkinson responded that you have to cope with two kinds of failure: failure of the supporting systems such as the hardware, and failure of the Java code that's running and throws an exception thereby requiring a return to the pre-evolution state.

Ron Morrison [RM] raised the issue of where you draw the line between what is built into the store and what resides above. If the evolution support was not built into the store technology you could change your evolution mechanism or your store independently without having to change all the components. Atkinson said you could not achieve such evolution support entirely at the Java level, particularly as regards maintaining identities, without doing the equivalent of garbage collection. They believe it is a very sensible thing to combine evolution and garbage collection, since both require a pass over the database. Their decision was motivated by performance gains, but as they haven't built another system they cannot do comparisons. Morrison said the identity problem depends on the increment with which evolution is done; you could evolve the whole store and change identity so that the result is correct; Atkinson maintained that this could not be done entirely in Java.

Dearle raised the problem of running out of PIDs in so doing; Atkinson said you couldn't evolve the whole store in one „increment" because you'd run out of memory. Gruber added that there was still the question of the conversion code, what language you would write that in. Stephen Blackburn [SB] said they had got a long way down the path of working above the VM, and that Marquez had been doing a versioning scheme using a similar sort of technique to that which they used for providing persistence, through the class loader.

Gruber said even with the class loader it is not obvious how to run code normally on the new set of classes and on the old set of classes. At an incremental level it was certainly easier to do in the store than above. Atkinson asked what reflection technology allows you to name two versions of the class and end up with the final version being the same name as the original version, so that your class reference structure and your instance reference structure remain unchanged. That reflection technology may be possible, but does not exist at present. Blackburn responded that it did exist in the class loader. You would know then you had a new class and there was an existing class of the same name, and you could rename both classes to include some version information. You could use the same sort of technique they used to implement façades, and do it incrementally and concurrently. Gruber argued that this wouldn't be evolution, it was completely changing the types and the interface from the user perspective. Evolution should work with the same classes the programmer gave. He added that Blackburn's technology looked very flexible because so much was generated at load time that they were fooling the VM and thus able to do things above it.

Liuba Shrira [LS] changed the subject with a question for Gruber. He had said that if your ISP wanted to upgrade your calendar there was no option to have another version; this was a practical limitation if you wanted to exchange information with others who have not been upgraded yet. Gruber said he had not meant to convey that impression, they wanted to support both. On the one hand if you are happy with the upgrade you don't want to have to look at both; but on the other hand you don't want to get burned that once you have upgraded you can't revert to an earlier version. In their system the server retains a history of the evolution and the different versions, and you can actually force on the device that one bean remains in the old type system (where some other beans are promoted). He added that this assumed that the interface hadn't been changed so dramatically that you'd break all the type systems.

Mathiske asked Atkinson's co-author Printezis if there was a chance to make the conversion technology in the store parallel. Printezis replied that they could parallelise some of the operations, the only problem would be the disk bottleneck. What you could do is support stores residing on different disks, and parallelise the evolution of partitions on different disks. In the final question of the workshop, Ewa Bem [EB] asked Atkinson to talk about his plans to support class versioning. He replied that he didn't believe in version ping-pong—being able to convert in both directions—because it was too hard to manage. And on this somewhat provocative note the discussion was forced to close due to lack of time.

Event Storage and Federation Using ODMG

Jean Bacon, Alexis Hombrecher, Chaoying Ma, Ken Moody, and Walt Yao

Cambridge University Computer Laboratory
New Museum Site, Pembroke Street
Cambridge CB2 3QG, UK
Tel: +44 1223 334600
{Firstname.Lastname}@cl.cam.ac.uk

Abstract. The Cambridge Event Architecture has added events to an object-oriented, distributed programming environment by using a language independent interface definition language to specify and publish event classes. Here we present an extension to CEA using the ODMG standard, which unifies the transmission and storage of events. We extend the existing model with an ODL parser, an event stub generator, a metadata repository and an event library supporting both C++ and Java. The ODMG metadata interface allows clients to interrogate the system at run time to determine the interface specifications for subsequent event registration. This allows new objects to be added to a running system and independently developed components to interwork with minimum prior agreement. Traditional name services and interface traders can be defined more generally using object database schemas. Type hierarchies may be used in schemas. Matching at a higher level in the type hierarchy for different domains is possible even though different specialisations are used in individual domains. Using metadata to describe events provides the basis for establishing contracts between domains. These are used to construct the event translation layer between heterogeneous domains.

1   Introduction

Since the early 1990s we have worked on event-driven distributed applications. The Cambridge Event Architecture (CEA) is compatible with both message passing and object-based middleware. The architecture we describe in this paper is an extension of our previous work. The aim of the extension is to provide an architecture that handles, as well as event transmission, storage and federation of event services. Our previous approaches have tried to tackle event transmission and storage separately [1] [3] [11] [17]. The notion of a federation stems mainly from the database world [16] [15] and has had very little mention in event-based systems. It is our goal to unify these ideas in a single architecture.

We have taken this approach because we have realised that many different application areas exist where events must be stored and/or existing event systems must be linked. For example, a system wishing to make certain guarantees in the face of system failure must store details about event transmission. Events

G.N.C. Kirby, A. Dearle, and D.I.K. Sjøberg (Eds.): POS-9, LNCS 2135, pp. 265–281, 2001.

from banking transactions may need to be stored so that they can be analysed at a later time for fraud detection.

In the past, systems that produce a high frequency of events have stored event occurrences in the form of logs. But retrieval of specific records from a log for analysis is highly inefficient. Also, in an environment where high level queries must be processed to discover useful information, events must be typed. Storing them in a database rather than in a log allows a database query language to be used.

Emerging applications often require intercommunication, while still being autonomous. A loosely coupled federation allows for this. In a federation event occurrences need to be communicated between domains. Since our architecture uses typed events, we can reconcile event occurrences from different, but related domains. In a federated event architecture metadata describing event types is used for event translation.

To support these requirements, we have extended the existing Cambridge Event Architecture by defining events using the Object Data Management Group's (ODMG) Object Definition Language (ODL). For transmission of events we have previously used OMG's IDL as a means of describing events. Using ODL allows us to keep metadata about events, and also store events in an ODMG compliant Object-Oriented Database (OODB) with powerful query support from OQL. The implications for distributed system design of this generality are:

- Application data can be defined in a uniform way for transmission and storage.
- Objects can use the ODMG metadata interface to allow clients to interrogate them at run time to determine their interface specifications.
- Traditional name services and interface traders can be defined more generally using a metadata repository. The ability to use type hierarchies within schemas allows, for example, agreement across domains at a high level with different specialisations within domains.
- Standard database techniques can be used for retrieving event patterns of interest from event stores.

In the rest of this paper we will describe our new architecture. We will focus specifically on event federation as we have described the details of the transmission and storage of events elsewhere. Section 2 explains the motivation and application of our architecture. We will then give some background information to familiarise the reader with the basic terminology and existing research in this area. Following that, we describe our architecture in more detail. In section 5 we describe an instance of a multi-domain event architecture.

2   Motivation and Applications

Our architecture has been motivated by different factors. We feel the world will not restrict itself to using a single programming language or middleware platform. It is essential to support inter-working between heterogeneous systems for wide and long-term impact. Furthermore, persistent data management is a fundamental aspect of system design but a universal persistent programming language is not the answer. It is essential to link components that have been developed in different languages. Our view is that an object model is a realistic basis for software system design including persistent data management. The concepts of types, interfaces and interface references are well established with trader technology for name to location mapping. More novel is that encapsulation of object attributes and methods may be extended to include object management aspects such as concurrency control and other transaction support. A standardisation of data types, such as the Object Data Management Group's ODL [4], forms a minimal basis for interoperability between programming languages and database query languages.

We will begin by discussing applications where integration of distributed entities is done via events. We will then look at applications requiring event storage. Finally, we will discuss environments in which existing notification-based event systems may need to be integrated into a loosely-coupled federation.

2.1 Event-Based Integration

Event-based integration is possibly the most common loose integration approach. Often it is described as a *publish-subscribe* model. The components generating events are *sources*, while the consumers of the events are *sinks*. Sources publish the events they generate, while sinks register interest with particular sources, for certain event types. Upon the occurrence of an event, interested sinks are notified.

Four broad categories of application, which have the requirement for event-driven notification, are described in [18]. This list is not exhaustive.

- composing and building large scalable distributed systems; enterprise application integration; concurrent/parallel programming languages; modelling of information flow; distributed debugging and fault-tolerant distributed systems
- modelling and supporting work practices relating to communication between individuals
- building computer supported cooperative applications
- applications based on monitoring and measurement-taking; real-time applications; active databases; windowing systems and graphical user interfaces

2.2 Event Storage

In the past, events have been mainly transient entities, acting as a glue between distributed components. Increasingly, applications require that events can be made persistent. [18] defines generic application scenarios where event storage is required. These include:

- *Auditing* of event generation, transformation and consumption
- *Identification* of repeating events
- *Analysis* of event registration, notification, and consumption
- *Tracking* of repeating patterns of activity covering one or more event types
- *Checkpointing* of execution for the aid of constructing fault-tolerant distributed systems

Checkpointing is probably the most obvious use for event storage. In an environment where the event system makes an *exactly once* or *at least once* delivery guarantee, events must be stored in case of network or system failure.

Auditing and analysis of event data is useful in applications such as fraud detection, simulation environments and workflow. A bank may want to store all events generated from bank transactions at automated teller machines. This data can then be analysed to discover inconsistencies such as money having been taken out of the same account at different locations at *nearly* the same time. In a workflow environment stored event data can be analysed to determine how work between individuals is being coordinated. This may lead to possible changes, making processes more efficient.

2.3   Event Federation

The term federation denotes a coupling of existing systems. Different degrees of coupling exist, ranging from loosely to tightly coupled federations. The degree of coupling is directly related to the degree of autonomy each member of the federation retains. In a loosely coupled federation, each member retains a greater amount of autonomy, and vice versa.

An example where event federation may be needed is a tracking system, monitoring the whereabouts of objects within a domain. Many different types of tracking system exist. Current systems include electronic badge-based tracking systems [20] [8], login-based systems, or Global Positioning Systems (GPS). Unfortunately, they are all closed domain systems, meaning they can only track individuals within their domain. The electronic badge-based system, for example, can only monitor the location of people within its domain, where hardware for badge location is available. Once an individual leaves the domain, the tracking system can no longer locate the electronic badge. For certain application domains, this type of tracking is sufficient, but we envision a world where different application domains can communicate with each other.

In a global event architecture, a client can register with the tracking service in any given domain. The client is notified according to the local event definition, when events occur at the source, either in the local domain or in a foreign domain. A user can then be tracked world wide (everywhere tracking system domains are installed and can communicate with each other), with registration for tracking events having occurred only in the local domain. Global registration is handled automatically by the system, even though event types and technology may differ.

3   Event Middleware

Distributed middleware can be grouped into different categories. These are *client / server*, *distributed object framework* and *event-driven systems including message oriented middleware*. In many instances there is an overlap between the characteristics of these types of systems.

It is outside the scope of this paper to analyse all existing distributed middleware. Although our architecture is inherently object-oriented through our use of ODMG, we feel that the event paradigm is dominant and will therefore focus on event-driven systems and message-oriented middleware (MOM) in our discussion.

3.1   Event-Driven Systems

Event-driven systems have originated from internal system needs, such as database triggers and graphical windowing. The emphasis is on event sources and clients. Clients register interest with sources, which then notify clients upon the occurrence of the specific event instance. This is somewhat similar to the *publish/subscribe* paradigm used in MOM systems, but event architectures tend to go further by providing a rich type system, template registration, event brokering, and possibly composite event specification.

The Cambridge Event Architecture. CEA uses a *publish-register-notify* paradigm (see Figure 1). Services publish their interfaces, including the typed events they are willing to notify. Clients register interest in events, specifying parameter values and wildcards. Services then notify any events that match their stored registration templates, thus employing source-side filtering. The architecture includes event mediators and composite event services. A standard, language-independent interface definition language (IDL) is used to specify and publish event classes. This allows automatic stub generation to be used for event notification as well as for traditional object invocation. This facility has been implemented in CORBA environments and in a purely message-passing system. For a detailed description of the generic distributed event architecture see [2].

CORBA Event and Notification Service. The CORBA Event Service [12] specification is based on an indirect channel-based event transport within distributed object frameworks. An *EventChannel* interface is defined that decouples the *suppliers* and *consumers* of events. Suppliers generate the events, while consumers obtain events from the channel. The channels are typed, meaning that only a specific type of event can be placed onto it. Events are not objects or entities in themselves. The specification provides for different types of interaction between the *suppliers* and *consumers*, mainly *push* and *pull* interaction. The *push interaction* is *supplier* driven, while the *pull interaction* is *consumer* driven. The CORBA Event Service does not support typed or structured events.

The CORBA Notification Service [14] tries to address the shortcomings of the CORBA Event Service. It supports typed events, content-based filtering and a

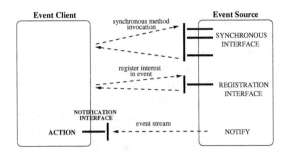

Fig. 1. The Cambridge Event Paradigm

quality-of-service (QoS) interface. Here, an event is similar to an object, having a type defined as a *domain/type/name* triple. The user specified body of an event has two sections. The first allows for the specification of filterable fields, while the second contains additional parameters as defined by the user. Channels support filtering, usually before events come to the consumer. Hence, only events matching the parameters specified in the filter are received by the consumer. Finally, the CORBA Notification Service includes an *Event Type Repository*, which allows for dynamic evolution of events and dynamic adaptation of consumers.

CORBA Persistent State Service. The CORBA Persistent State Service (PSS) introduces PSDL (Persistent State Definition Language), a superset of OMG IDL, that address the problems of persistence [13]. PSDL extends IDL with new constructs to define storage objects and their homes. Like Java and ODMG ODL, it makes distinctions between abstract type specification and concrete type implementation. PSS provides an abstraction layer between a CORBA server and its background storage. This allows a variety of storage architectures to be plugged in and accessed through a set of CORBA-friendly interfaces.

Despite these recent extensions, CORBA does not provide as rich a set of constructors and facilities for data management as the ODMG does. For example, PSS only supports a **find_by_pid** method for access to objects, while ODMG supports OQL. Furthermore, PSS has yet to specify recovery which is well supported by the ODMG standard.

3.2 MOM Systems

MOM systems are the mainstream commercial equivalents of event-based systems. They originated from the need to connect application programs reliably to central database servers. They employ an asynchronous peer-to-peer invocation model, whereby a message is sent to the local middleware before it is sent to its destination. Generally, MOM systems do not have a type system for structuring message data.

IBM MQSeries. MQSeries [6] is not only one of the earliest middleware products commercially available, it is also the most widely used. Its feature set is largely representative of the available solutions.

MQSeries applications place messages on message queues. The receiving queue notifies the application when it is ready to accept a message from the queue. The *Message Queue Interface* is used by applications to manipulate the queues. MQSeries is responsible for moving messages around the network and for handling the relationship between applications and queues. Furthermore, it provides transaction guarantees, either through its built in transaction processing monitor or by an external X/Open compliant TP monitor.

Extensions are available that sit on top of MQSeries, such as IBM Message Broker and MQSeries Integrator. The broker provides *publish/subscribe* facilities, while the latter provides for a limited monitoring of composite events.

MQSeries provides persistence only in so far as it stores events until they have been successfully received by the correct application. Proper provision for storage outside this transactional support is not provided.

Oracle8i AQ. Oracle8i Advanced Queuing [7] is interesting because this architecture is focused around storing messages. Advanced Queues are represented as relational tables and a message is simply a row in the table. The Advanced Queues are an integral part of the database management system. Multiple applications access the database to transfer messages between them, or database systems communicate to move messages between their queues.

Since queues are represented as tables, they can be queried using SQL. This is a very different approach from the usual logging functionality provided by MOM systems.

3.3   Analysis of Existing Systems

None of the systems reviewed provide the functionality required for the scenarios outlined in section 2. Although some systems have support for message storage, these tend to be highly specialised solutions, lacking general applicability. Furthermore, most systems lack the required type system, necessary for event federation. These shortcomings are addressed in our architecture.

4   The Extended Cambridge Event Architecture

We make minimal assumptions on how our world is constructed. In our view, it consists of a set of cooperative domains, possibly federations. A *domain* is a logical scope of a collection of event sources where a single administrative power is exercised. The event sources in a domain are sometimes inter-related, but their relationship is not a requirement for membership of a domain. A domain represents a unit of autonomy. The domain administrator has full control over the event sources and types defined by each source. Domains dramatically reduce the degree of complexity of a distributed system by partitioning it into smaller, more manageable units and allow independent evolution.

Components in our architecture may be *producers* or *consumers* of events, or both. Producers publish their event types, while consumers register interest with producers and receive event occurrences of interest to them. This is no different from other *publish-subscribe* or *publish-register-notify* architectures. Novel is that we view components that store or translate events as consumers. This greatly simplifies the complexity of the system.

We have based our architecture on the Object Data Management Group's standard for object-oriented databases. ODMG has released three standards since the early 1990s, the most recent being ODMG 3.0 [4]. The core of the standard is the ODMG Object Model, which defines a rich type system compatible with major object-oriented programming languages, including the arbitrary nesting of collection types. It defines the Object Query Language (OQL), a powerful superset of SQL. Bindings have been defined for C++, Java and Smalltalk. Types can be specified through the Object Definition Language (ODL) which serves as the data definition language for database schemas. ODMG includes a standard for schema representation by meta-objects, which themselves conform to the object model, thus allowing standard database tools to interrogate metadata as well as data.

4.1   Events

In the extended CEA, events are defined using ODL. Every event is derived from a non-instantiable base type called *BaseEvent*. The *BaseEvent* type is the header of each event occurrence. Amongst other things, it contains a unique ID (consisting of a unique object ID and a source definition for the object), a priority tag and a timestamp.

```
class BaseEvent {
  attribute ID id;
  attribute short priority;
  attribute timestamp signal_time;
};
```

One can construct complex event hierarchies through the use of inheritance (see Figure 2). Grouping related events within a hierarchy can be useful when reconciling different event taxonomies (see Section 4.5).

The event definitions are compiled by an ODL parser and stub generator which translates ODL files into stubs generated as wrappers around event types. The stubs present the application programmers with an intuitive programming interface. *EventSource* and *EventSink* classes have been implemented to allow for a simple connection to the library and to create the service objects.

The example below shows the program code written using the generated stub. In the example we present a simple event, GPSEvent, which is derived from a base event of type LocationEvent. We show both the client-side and server-side code. The client registers with the source for events that signal GPS sightings of any observable subject at 100 degrees longitude.

The ODL definition for the event of type GPSEvent is defined as follows.

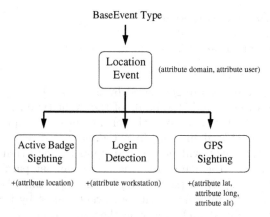

Fig. 2. Event Inheritance

```
class LocationEvent extends BaseEvent {
  attribute string user_name;
};

class GPSEvent extends LocationEvent {
  attribute float longitude;
  attribute float latitude;
  attribute float altitude;
};
```

When registering interest with an event source the client must first initialise an event sink to establish a channel with the source. In the example below, the client constructs a registration template for GPSEvent. Wildcard filtering is the default which, in this example, is deactivated on the parameter "longitude". This allows the client to receive all the event occurrences matching longitude 100. The client can then register with the event source by invoking the method register_event_interest with the prepared template.

```
EventSink sink(argc, argv, "sink", "c1@cl",
               "source", "c2@cl", disconnect);

//construct an event template
templ.longitude = 100;

//construct an event template
GPSEvent_Sink templ;

//set value for parametrised filtering
templ.longitude = 100;

//activate parametrised filtering
```

```
temp.set_longitude_wildcard(false);
...
templ.register_event_interest(sink, gps_callback);
...
```

Classes for event templates are generated by invoking the stub generator. The class name for an event type is the name of the event type as defined in ODL, suffixed by _Sink. In this example, the client constructs an event template for GPSEvent. Parametrised filtering in a template is deactivated by default. This means that the client will be notified upon the occurrence of all events of the type handled by the template. The client can set parameters of interest by explicitly setting the attributes and then activating the filter. Once a template is created, it can register with an event source by invoking the API register_event_interest and supplying the sink object created earlier.

On the server-side, the programming is similar, except for an additional step of activating the source. The source application creates a source by initialising a source object. This binds the source application under the specified name in the domain-wide name service. In order to be able to produce events of a certain type, the type must be made known to the source object. The API method register_new_event is provided for this purpose. Once the event type is known to the source, it can signal events at any time.

4.2   Event Schemas

An event schema is maintained for each event type in a domain. Per domain, many event schemas may exist. As the ODL files are compiled, the metadata is stored in an event repository. We have opted to treat this event repository as a generic event store. Ideally, the repository is ODMG compliant, but this is not a requirement. Mediators must be used to translate from the ODL representation to the internal representation of the store if it is not ODMG compliant. If it is, the ODL compiler of the store can be used and the event metadata is stored as such in the store. This is very useful when the same store is to be used to store event occurrences.

4.3   Naming and Event Brokering

There are a number of options for interface and event publication: an interface trader can be used for the entire service signature including events; event signatures may be published in a separate name service; each service may provide an introspection, or metadata, interface to allow clients to interrogate it at run time to determine its interface specification. The latter approach is the easiest way to allow new services to be added to a running system.

Each domain has a name service, which stores the run-time binding for an event type and an event engine. This information is required by clients so that event sources which are associated with event engines can be located dynamically at runtime. For example, a client wishing to register interest in a particular kind of event must discover whether that event type exists in the domain. To do this, it uses the metadata interface to query the ODMG store. After discovering the appropriate event type, the naming service must be queried to locate the event server. Besides providing a name-to-location mapping, the naming service also provides the client with other information required for registration.

4.4   Event Storage

Event storage can occur at two levels. Firstly, it can be embedded within the event source or client. Secondly, dedicated storage nodes can be used, providing an explicit service. The first is useful for services like buffering at the source or client, while the second is useful for analysis of event histories.

In the latter case, we view event stores as consumers of events. A storage component registers interest with a source when it plans to store event occurrences. Where the object model of the event system is different from the object model of the event store, mediator applications are used to translate between the two. This means that event stores do not directly register interest with the event sources, but rather the mediator handles this task on behalf of the storage system. In instances where events are stored in an ODMG compliant store, this transformation is not necessary, since the object model used at the event source is based on the ODMG standard.

Ideally, the event repository at dedicated nodes of our architecture is an ODMG compliant store. We are currently investigating the use of a commercial product for this. This would provide us with the functionality of a high level query language for event analysis. We are also testing the limitations of such a system in terms of event stream throughput. In systems where thousands of event occurrences need to be stored, special log-like mediators [18] may need to be used before events are actually transferred into the store.

For embedded storage facilities, we have built a lightweight ODMG compliant store. This implementation is used for embedded repositories in either the event consumer or producer. It consists of four major components, a *storage manager*, a *transaction manager*, an ODMG *object layer* and a *parser generator*. These provide the functionality required for storing and retrieving event metadata and event instances.

When constructing event producers or consumers, the application programmer can specify whether event occurrences are to be stored. We have implemented our storage layer as a library that can be embedded within the applications.

4.5   Event Federation

Federating event systems involves schema federation [16] and object translation. Specifically, it involves reconciling semantic differences in schemas for the purpose of constructing a federation. Since the event architecture is based on the ODMG standard, we are limiting the problem to having to reconcile only semantic heterogeneity [9], or more precisely, structural semantic heterogeneity [5].

Structural semantic heterogeneity occurs when the same information occurs in two different domains in structurally different but formally equivalent ways. Different examples of this are:

- the same entity with different attribute names
- the same instance identified differently
- the same conceptual model represented structurally different
- the same universe of discourse represented by different conceptual models
- the same instances aggregated incommensurably in two systems

Structural semantic heterogeneity can be resolved by a series of view definitions which in principle respect the autonomy of the component systems. There are cases in which semantic heterogeneity cannot be resolved by view definitions, even in principle. This more general semantic heterogeneity is referred to as fundamental semantic heterogeneity. Where it occurs between information systems, tight coupling cannot be achieved without changing at least one of the systems, thereby compromising design autonomy.

Fundamental heterogeneity occurs when objects in the two domains under consideration share insufficient attributes to be reliably identified. The metadata in the two domains does not contain sufficient information to determine whether object instances relate to the same entity. This phenomenon has been studied by a number of authors, and has been given several different names. [19] have termed it the instance identification problem, [10] the entity identification problem.

In our architecture we have focused on resolving structural semantic heterogeneity.

Gateways and Contracts. In order to federate event services from different domains, components are needed, which handle the event translation between domains. These components act as a gateway service and must be available within each domain wishing to participate in the federation.

In our architecture, gateway communication is based on contracts. The notion of a contract is derived from real-life examples of how entities interact with each other. Conceptually, a contract is a binding agreement between two or more parties. We employ this idea and apply it to our model. We use the term *contract* to mean an agreement between two or more cooperating domains. From a database federation point of view, a contract is similar to the external schema proposed in the five-level schema architecture put forward by Seth and Larson [16]. A more formal definition of a contract is given below:

> Let T_A be an event type defined by a source S_A of domain A, and T_B be an event type defined by a source S_B of domain B. We can define sets E_A and E_B as the sets of all instances of T_A and T_B respectively. A contract between A and B with respect to T_A and T_B is defined as an event type T, whose set of all instances is denoted as $\mathcal{E}$, and which satisfies the condition that there exists a function $f : E_A \to \mathcal{E}$ for A and $g : E_B \to \mathcal{E}$ for B.

The function that maps a local event to an event of the type defined by a contract is called a *schema translation function*. A schema translation function that translates an event from type T to type S is a translation function from T to S. Schema translation takes place at the intersection of two domains, the gateways. An event which is going to be sent across domains will be translated within its domain of origin. This means the foreign domain always gets events conforming to a contract it has agreed to. One advantage of the elegance and simplicity of this model is that applications are easier to build. Applications only need to handle the types that they are familiar with, so that dynamic handling of foreign types is unnecessary. Another advantage is that this model effectively prevents the details of an event local to a domain being exposed to the foreign domain. This is desirable if an event carries confidential information, such as a credit card number in an `orderMade` event.

Another advantage is that translation only arises at the gateway for events to be exported, with respect to a specific contract. This is entirely demand driven.

5   A Federated E-commerce Example

In this paper we have opted to use an example which focuses on the ability of our architecture to link semantically heterogeneous systems. We leave out event storage here, but the reader should easily be able to see how event stores can be added to the system.

With the recent excitement over dotcoms, we will illustrate the use of our architecture by looking at online travel agents specialising in last minute flights and holidays. Specifically, we will look at two online services, *LastHour.com* and *FirstMinute.com*. Each dotcom represents a domain and allows clients to register interest with event sources available within the domain. For example, customers may want to be notified of last minute travel offers to specific destinations at a specific price. We will illustrate how multiple dotcoms can be joined in a federation to provide a global, highly competitive, holiday shopping environment.

We will first explain event registration, followed a by a more detailed look at event federation.

5.1   Event Registration

As mentioned before, the ODL for the event type definitions will be compiled into header and body files, which implement the event class and interface with the existing event source and sink object implementations. A sample client of *LastHour.com* wishing to register interest in flights with *United Airlines* at that particular price would look as follows (in pseudo C++):

```
Flights fl;
fl.price = 1500;
fl.airline = "United Airlines";

Callback* clb = new Callback(orb, ckfn,
                         sink_host, sink_server,
                         source_host, source_server);

Sink_i *myobj = new Sink_i(clb);
myobj->_obj_is_ready(boa);
```

```
string sink_name = si_server + "@" si_host;
const char* sn = sink_name.c_str();

BaseEventServer::Snk_var myobjRef = myobj->_this();

if(!bindObjectToName(orb, myobjRef, sn))
  ...
boa->impl_is_ready(0,1);
position.register(clb);
```

In the example, the client stub for the *Flights* class has implemented a method
Flight::register(Callback* clb). This method constructs the event body expected
by the *Src::reg_event* operation, and then calls the *Callback::register_interesT*
method. This in turn calls the *Src::reg_event* operation. At the time the callback
object is created, the client binds to a *Src* object and stores the object reference
in the callback object. Thus an invocation to the event registration method
Src::reg_event can be made at a later time via the method *fl.register(clb)*.

5.2   Event Federation

Each domain has event types for which clients can register interest. These event
types are part of an event hierarchy. Figure 3(a) and 3(b) show the event hierarchies for two domains in our example.

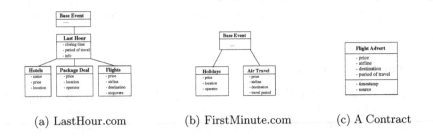

(a) LastHour.com   (b) FirstMinute.com   (c) A Contract

Fig. 3. Event Hierarchies

A contract between *LastHour.com* and *FirstMinute.com* must exist for specific
event types, if the two domains wish to form a federation. The contract specifies
that each domain must be able to translate to and from the type defined in the
contract. Thus, translation functions must be available at the gateway level that
honour the contract.

For the purpose of this example, we will consider a client that wants to register
interest in an event locally and globally. The event of interest is the *Flights* event
from the *FirstHour.com* domain. The client may be interested in a last minute

flight at a price less than $1000 to Sydney with no more than 1 stop-over. The client does not care about the airline.

The client can register interest in the above event by sending the appropriate registration to the event engine for local registration. Alternatively, the client may wish to register interest not only with *LastHour.com*, but also with *First-Minute.com*, or all domains having a contract with LastHour.com for that event type. The registration will be different only in that it must indicate the other domain(s) of interest.

Cross-domain registration has to translate the local registration into a format understood in other domains, in the same way that event types have to be translated between domains. This translation is performed according to the contracts between domains. The translation takes place when the registration leaves the local domain (*LastHour.com*) and when the converted registration enters the foreign domain (*FirstMinute.com*). Upon leaving the local domain, the registration is converted to the contract type and upon entering the foreign domain it is converted into a format understood by that domain. Once translated, the registration is sent to the correct event engine in the foreign domain for the actual event registration.

Event notification in the local domain, *LastHour.com* is trivial. If a flight to Sydney at a price of less than $1000 with no more than 1 stop-over is available, the client is contacted asynchronously by the event engine. On the other hand, when an event of interest occurs in *FirstMinute.com*, a flight to Sydney at a price of less than $1000 (remember the attribute stop-over does not exist in this domain), the appropriate notification is sent from the event engine to the gateway. Here the notification is converted to the contract type. It can then be sent to the gateway of *LastHour.com*. At the gateway of *LastHour.com* the notification gets translated into an event of the local domain. In this instance, the attribute for stop-overs must be given a default value, or left blank (the ODMG *Object Model* supports this through *null-extended* domains). The notification is passed to the event engine, which then notifies all registered clients.

6   Conclusion

We have outlined the functionality and shortcomings of current middleware products with respect to their support for event-driven applications. We argued that such applications require storage and query facilities for events as well as efficient, asynchronous transmission. Also, such applications need to interoperate in an open distributed environment. We have extended our event architecture, CEA, to meet these requirements.

CEA events are specified in ODL, compatible with IDL, and benefit from standard middleware technology such as automatic stub generation. Clients may register interest in events at their source, with specific parameters as well as wildcards, allowing efficient filtering at source before immediate asynchronous notification of occurrences.

Storage of events may be incorporated into the architecture either by embedding persistent storage locally at sources, sinks and mediators, or as separate event stores. The latter may be integrated simply as event clients using the publish, register, notify paradigm.

Using ODMG's ODL and OQL has given us the potential for great flexibility in designing the components of our architecture. All objects have a metadata interface which may be used to interrogate them to determine their schemas; this provides a good way to add new objects to a running system. ODMG data stores may be queried, using OQL, for event patterns of interest in fault or fraud detection.

In this paper we have focussed on the open interoperability of event systems. The use of a type hierarchy for event definition, together with the *publish-register-notify* paradigm, allows for registration at a high level to be specialised in different ways in different domains. We have described our use of gateway servers and contracts; registration is always in the local domain and a local gateway server negotiates contracts with event engines in relevant non-local domains on demand. Parameter values that are not required do not leave the domain in which they occur; this may be important in restricting information flow.

Further work is required in several areas. We must explore the ability of ODMG stores to log large volumes of events for subsequent querying using OQL. Reconciliation of type hierarchies for contract negotiation is a difficult problem in general. We are exploring the role of XML as an alternative interchange format and have built an ODL parser which generates XML.

Although this work is at an early stage we have built demonstrations as proof of concept. We believe that the approach we have taken is more generic than that of existing systems and provides an excellent basis for federation of existing systems as well as incremental evolution.

Acknowledgements. We acknowledge the support of UK EPSRC through the grant GR/M22413 (Global Computation using Events). We would also like to thank past and present members of the OPERA group for their insights and helpful discussions.

References

1. J. Bacon, J. Bates, R. Hayton, and K. Moody. Using Events to Build Distributed Applications. In *7th ACM SIGOPS European Workshop*, Connemara, Ireland, September 1996.
2. J. Bacon, K. Moody, J. Bates, R. Hayton, C. Ma, A. McNeil, O. Seidel, and M. Spiteri. Generic Support for Asynchronous, Secure Distributed Applications. *IEEE Computer*, pages 68–76, March 2000.
3. J. Bates, D. Halls, and J. Bacon. A Framework to Support Mobile Users of Multimedia Applications. In *ACM Mobile Networks and Nomadic Applications (NOMAD)*, pages 409–419, 1996.
4. R. G. G. Cattell, D. Barry, M. Berler, J. Eastman, D.Jordan, C. Russell, O. Schadow, T. Stanienda, and F. Velez. *The Object Database Standard: ODMG 3.0*. Morgan Kaufmann Publishers, San Diego (CA), USA, 1999.
5. R. M. Colomb. Impact of Semantic Heterogeneity on Federating Databases. *The Computer Journal*, 40(5), 1997.

6. IBM Corporation. MQSeries. http://www.ibm.com/software/mqseries/, 1999.
7. Oracle Corporation. Oracle8i Advanced Queuing. http://www.oracle.com/database/features, 1999.
8. A. Harter and A. Hopper. A Distributed Location System for the Active Office. *IEEE Network*, 8(1), January/February 1994.
9. R. Hull. Managing semantic heterogeneity in databases: a theoretical prospective. In ACM, editor, *PODS '97. Proceedings of the Sixteenth ACM SIG-SIGMOD-SIGART Symposium on Principles of Database Systems, May 12–14, 1997, Tucson, Arizona*, pages 51–61, New York, NY 10036, USA, 1997. ACM Press.
10. E. P. Lim, J. Srivastava, S. Prabhakar, and J. Richardson. Entity Identification in Database Integration. In *International Conference on Data Engineering*, pages 294–301, Los Alamitos, CA, USA, April 1993. IEEE Computer Society Press.
11. C. Ma and J. Bacon. COBEA: A CORBA-based Event Architecture. In *Proceedings of the 4th Conference on Object-Oriented Technologies and Systems (COOTS-98)*, pages 117–132, Berkeley, April 1998. USENIX Association.
12. Object Management Group - OMG. Event Service Specification. ftp://www.om.org/pub/docs, 1997.
13. Object Management Group - OMG. CORBA Persistent State Service 2.0. 99-07-07, August 1999.
14. Object Management Group - OMG. *Notification Service Specification*, June 2000.
15. E. Radeke. Extending ODMG for federated database systems. In Roland R. Wagner and Helmut Thoma, editors, *Seventh International Workshop on Database and Expert Systems Applications, DEXA '96, Proceedings*, pages 304–312, Zurich, Switzerland, September 1996. IEEE Computer Society Press, Los Alamitos, California.
16. A. P. Sheth. Federated Database Systems for Managing Distributed, Heterogeneous, and Autonomous Databases. In *International Conference On Very Large Data Bases (VLDB '91)*, pages 489–490, Hove, East Sussex, UK, September 1991. Morgan Kaufmann Publishers, Inc.
17. M. Spiteri and J. Bates. An Architecture to support Storage and Retrieval of Events. In *Proceedings of MIDDLEWARE 1998, IFIP International Conference on Distributed Systems Platforms and Open Distributed Processing*, pages 443–459, Lake District, UK, September 1998.
18. M. D. Spiteri. *An Architecture for the Notification, Storage and Retrieval of Events (TR494)*. PhD Thesis, University of Cambridge Computer Laboratory, Computer Laboratory, New Museum Site, Pembroke Street, Cambridge CB2 3QG, England, July 2000.
19. Y. R. Wang and S. E. Madnick. The Inter-Database Instance Identification Problem in Integrating Autonomous Systems. In *Proc. IEEE Int'l. Conf. on Data Eng.*, page 46, Los Angeles, CA, February 1989.
20. R. Want, A. Hopper, V. Falcao, and J. Gibbons. The Active Badge Location System. *ACM Transactions on Information Systems*, 10(1):91–102, January 1992.

An Application Model and Environment for Personal Information Appliances

Olivier Gruber and Ravi Konuru

IBM T.J. Watson Research Center
30 Saw Mill River Road, Hawthorne, NY 10532
{ogruber, rkonuru}@us.ibm.com

Abstract. Recent years have witnessed a rapid increase in the use of personal information devices such as Palms or smart phones, with some people carrying more than one. Moreover, these devices need to work in disconnected mode and vary widely in their features. How does one provide an information-centric experience, across devices, for the end user? The goal of the Bali project is to provide a run-time platform that improves application portability and adaptability across devices. Bali addresses these issues through a minimal, easily deployable Java Runtime Environment, and a JavaBean-based application model. Beans transparently persist and are the units of replication. Bali provides semi-automated replication where applications only deal with the resolution of conflicting updates across devices. Code deployment is fully automated and coordinated with replication. Bali supports a powerful linking framework between beans allowing hyper-linking applications to be easily developed, even in the presence of cross-device replica. Bali fosters programmers' productivity through transparent object management and leverages a model-view-controller architecture enabling applications to adapt to device features as well as increasing code reuse. This paper describes the Bali application model, the minimal JRE, our partially implemented prototype as well as preliminary experience.

1 Introduction

Recent years have witnessed a rapid increase in the use of personal digital assistant (PDA) devices such as Palms or smart phones, with some people carrying more than one. Moreover, these devices typically need to work in disconnected mode and vary widely in their features and the extent of those features. For instance, two PDAs may both have a screen to display but the resolution can be different. In another instance, a PDA may only be capable of speech input and output. Despite this diversity, we believe that end users want an *information-centric* experience across their devices. First, they want to access the same information across devices. Second, they want the ability to update that information from any of their devices, while being connected or not. Concurrent updates on different devices may naturally occur and need to be dealt with appropriately. Third, they want to be able to relate information as they see fit, adhering to the hyper-linking principles.

G.N.C. Kirby, A. Dearle, and D.I.K. Sjøberg (Eds.): POS-9, LNCS 2135, pp. 282-291, 2001.
© Springer-Verlag Berlin Heidelberg 2001

The number of devices, their diversity, and the end-user requirements represent a challenge for current software technology. First, it is a challenge for programmers who need to write portable and adaptive applications. Ideally, one would like the same code to manipulate the same information across devices; if not possible, one would like to leverage a maximal reuse of code. Moreover, small devices require a fine control over application footprints, which suggests a modular approach to software building. Sharing libraries and leveraging common services are also essential in that regard. Second, it is also a challenge for administrators to centrally manage all these devices, including both automated deployment and update of applications.

The Bali project addresses these challenges through a minimal Java runtime environment (MJRE), and deployable software components based on JavaBeans™, extended with a model-view paradigm. Each device wishing to participate in the Bali universe needs a MJRE. Bali applications are designed as a set of cooperative software components that discover common services at runtime. Some components are models and represent the information that is portable and replicated across devices. Models can be freely hyper-linked even across application boundaries. Other components are views and provide a multi-modal rendering. Multiple views enable application adaptability. For each device, an application has one or more corresponding views, specific to the hardware characteristics of that device. Leveraging orthogonal persistence [2], models are replicated across devices while preserving inter-model hyperlinks and thereby enabling Bali's information-centric experience for end users. During replication, the runtime up calls into the application in the presence of conflicting updates. Support for application deployment and evolution is provided via a service-oriented architecture and a versioning framework.

Although Bali's focus is on the client space, these clients have to integrate with existing web application servers, allowing their information to originate from corporate and legacy information systems. Furthermore, it makes sense to leverage mission-critical scalable storage systems to make the information of millions of devices persist. Consequently, Bali has been designed to inter-operate with the Enterprise JavaBean™[5,6] framework for advanced Java servers.

This paper presents a broad overview of Bali and in particular, describes the core concepts underlying its programming model, and how these are exploited by the runtime to automate replication. The rest of the paper is structured as follows. In Section 2, we provide an overview of the Bali components and frameworks. In Section 3, we discuss how replication is built on top of transparent persistence, describing databases, beans, and bean references. In Section 4, we discuss related work. In Section 5, we present the status of our prototype and in Section 6 we conclude.

2 Bali Overview

To participate in the Bali universe, a client needs the Bali runtime. Some client devices would download it from a server, some other may have it factory-installed; it may even be their only runtime environment. The Bali runtime is essentially a minimal Java runtime environment. Java is the programming language of choice for it has widespread acceptance and useful characteristics. Java is portable and supports incremental loading, both essential features when targeting heterogeneous platforms and automated application deployment from servers. Java is safe (no direct access to memory, no pointer can be forged) and it is garbage collected, providing efficient memory management. Java safety enables security, which is important for better robustness of devices, enabling information privacy and some failure isolation between applications from different providers.

The Bali runtime is a minimal JRE in the sense that it is the minimal set of Java types, classes and interfaces, needed to support the Java language specification. This is actually extremely small, less than a hundred Java types. It also contains a small-footprint support for a service-oriented platform, allowing service registration and discovery. This approach is similar to the OSGI proposal [1]. For a device, the Bali runtime also contains a set of native services corresponding to the hardware capabilities of that device. Examples of such native services are pointing device (mouse or pen), keyboard or speech recognition engine, low-level graphics, etc. These native services will obviously be a mix of Java and C code. The Bali runtime then provides a pervasive runtime foundation to deploy other services, libraries, and applications under a pure Java assumption.

The next step is to determine the device *profiles*. A profile represents a set of libraries and services that a developer can safely program against given that they are certified to be present on any device belonging to that profile. Based on which native services are available on a given device, certain libraries and services are deployable. Consequently, the device will be considered capable of downloading certain profiles. Once potential profiles for a device have been determined, the end user is offered a list of *cabinets* to subscribe to. A cabinet contains applications and *databases* which are collection of persistent objects, called *beans*. Beans are used to implement the models and views of applications. Models are non-visual beans that are pure Java data structures and therefore portable across devices. The views are more traditional visual beans and they render models. Notice the use of the term „render" in order to put the emphasis on the multi-modal nature of views, including viewing, printing, or speaking. Views are device-specific leveraging device-specific characteristics and have limited portability. More about software components, models, and views will be said later.

A cabinet is the unit of subscription, which controls replication and code deployment. On subscription, the cabinet databases are replicated and the Java types (classes and interfaces) in the cabinet are deployed. Cabinets can be subscribed to across multiple devices, thereby enabling the same information to be replicated across multiple devices. Database replication is totally coordinated with code deployment. Replication is fully transparent to programmers. By implementing models as beans, beans are transparently replicated and their updates are automatically tracked by the Bali runtime. Concurrent updates are possible while disconnected. Potential conflicts are automatically detected and are resolved by up calling an application plug-in at a database level. Plug-ins may resolve conflicts automatically or delay it. The database frameworks will keep the multiple conflicting versions until they are merged.

Conflicting versions are replicated to allow application programmers to involve end users in a more manual resolution of conflicts.

Cabinets support type evolution through versioning of immutable types. This allows us to guaranty a loss-free environment across application upgrades. Information is promoted from an older version of an application to a new one by programmer-provided conversion code. Any promotion can be automatically roll-backed if it fails or if, for any reason, the end user is not satisfied with the results. Administrators decide how long end users can wait before rolling back a particular promotion.

We believe that it is important that models can be hyper-linked as end users see fit, therefore, Bali supports references between beans, even across database boundaries. For instance, consider a list of attendee names in the meeting-entry bean in a calendar application. It is desirable to provide seamless navigation from the attendee name to the attendee address bean in an address book application, even if they originate from different data sources and preserve links in the presence of replication. The framework to achieve such a goal is the subject of the next section.

To handle the persistence of beans at servers, especially when considering that most of these beans are probably representing information extracted from legacy and corporate information systems, we have a designed a *conduit* based framework based on ideas adapted from the Palm device. A conduit is a plug-in at a database level. If no plug-in is provided, Bali takes care of bean and database persistence on the server side. If a plug-in is provided for a database, it will be up-called, during device synchronization, with any new bean state that needs to persist. Notice that a plug-in has to expect multiple versions for a bean in case conflicts cannot be resolved automatically. Conduits allow database contents to be stored and managed in external industrial-strength storage systems such as DBMS, CICS, Notes, etc.

The interface between the Bali runtime and the conduit is bean based. When a bean needs to be saved, the conduit is up called with that bean and the bean identity within the Bali world. The bean is passed as a Java object, not as a serialized state.

Ensuring the long-term persistence of beans is actually not enough; bean references may also have a state that requires to persist as well. The principles of the interactions with the conduit are the same. Bean references need to have an identity in the Bali world as beans do so the graph of beans and bean references can be reconstructed.

3 Replication

Bali advocates transparent persistence as the basis for replication. Orthogonal persistence [2] is a simple extension to garbage collection: objects persist as long as they are reachable from persistence roots, some roots being long-term roots and therefore surviving JRE shutdowns.

The Bali registry provides a natural long-term root for persistence. The registry is basically a naming service for supporting a service-oriented architecture. It is simply a well-known place to find what is available in the current JRE: deployed services, available libraries (Java packages), and of course deployed cabinets and their databases.

Replication builds on transparent persistence through the concepts of databases, beans, and bean references. A database is a collection of persistent beans and can be replicated on any devices. The first technical challenge with replication is our optimistic approach to concurrent updates. The rationale for an optimistic approach is the intermittent connectivity between devices and servers. In an optimistic approach, it is impossible to merge unconstrained object graphs that have been concurrently updated.

Databases and beans provide the first necessary structuring concepts, carving out sub-graphs from the total graph of persistent objects. Beans can then be time-stamped and a straightforward protocol for maintaining replicas up to date can be applied. But this is not enough. First, concurrent updates may still conflicts and such conflicts have to be resolved. Secondly, replicating beans may very well break references between these beans. For instance, suppose that a meeting entry in a calendar database refers to the meeting attendees: entries in the address book database. Each entry is a bean, that is, a persistent object. Bean references are therefore Java references between objects. Persistence and replication have to collaborate to allow new versions of beans to be installed during synchronization without breaking referential integrity. Our approach to solve these two problems is presented in the following sections.

3.1 Bean Model

A bean is an object graph and can have cycles. It can be shared and therefore referenced. To implement beans, Bali provides two classes: a Bean and a BeanRef class.

A bean is the graph of reachable objects from an instance of the class Bean, stopping the recursion (non-inclusively) on instances of the class BeanRef. In other words, a bean is a complex object graph whose boundary is defined by BeanRef objects. Note that the bean framework is for carving out sub-graphs for replication purposes, not for persistence. Locally on a device, Bali adheres to orthogonal persistence. Fig. 1 shows two databases with beans and cross-database bean reference.

Designing a bean is a three-step process. First, one has to implement a data structure by sub-classing the class Bean. Second, one has to define the interfaces that will be used to interact with the bean, including the event model if the bean allows listeners to be notified of changes. Third, subclasses of the BeanRef class have to be provided, each implementing one or more interface. These BeanRef subclasses will play the role of „remote" reference to the bean, acting as proxies for the interface they implement.

Let's illustrate beans and bean references with two examples: Swing trees and HTML. In Swing, from JavaSoft, several collection APIs are defined such as list, table, or tree. One may wish to implement a bean that exports a tree API so that a Swing viewer can render it. One will have to choose an implementation and also to design the various bean references for carrying the Tree and TreeNode APIs. Another example is HTML along with its W^3C Java API. A browser designer could choose to implement a bean supporting an HTML document and exporting the corresponding document object model as specified by W^3C. Additionally, it is interesting to remark that an HTML document is a tree, so the HTML bean may want to export a Tree API as well, allowing an authoring tool to display the HTML tree.

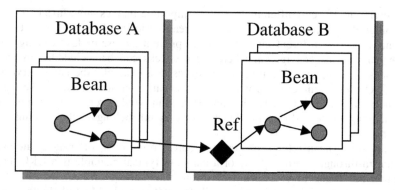

Fig. 1. Beans and Bean references

This example introduces the interesting issue of multiple references carrying multiple interfaces. We need to provide a way of navigating between the different APIs supported by a bean. Java provides a type casting operator allowing interface navigation but on a single object. Unfortunately, this does not work here because a different bean reference object may carry each interface. Having multiple reference objects instead of multiple Java references shatters the Java notion of two objects being equal with respect to their identity.

We therefore introduce a new navigational capability that enables to test for identity equality on beans. We introduce the IBean interface, root of all interfaces on beans. IBean provides interface navigation through the method „QueryInterface" which takes a type as an argument. If the bean is capable of returning a bean reference implementing that requested type, it returns a Java object that can be downcast to the specified interface. If it cannot, it returns null. The returned object must be an instance of the BeanRef class, which implements IBean, allowing interface navigation from any bean reference. Interface navigation actually provides a solution to test if two beans are identity equals. QueryInterface must always return the same bean reference object when requested for an interface of type IBean, thereby allowing Java identity to be used to compare the bean reference objects.

Because bean references are delimiting the boundaries of beans, they entail some marshalling to avoid leaking Java reference on internal objects. Fortunately, this marshalling does not imply any network communication or thread-context switch. Indeed, direct Java references across bean boundaries are forbidden from a replication point of view. In other words, such a cross-bean reference has to be on an instance of the class BeanRef to isolate the states of the two beans. We are conscious of the resulting overhead, both in time and space, as well as the lack of transparency that it entails. While at first, we were concerned about this overhead, it proved quite necessary for most applications and even proved to be quite aligned with Java philosophy. In fact, Java tends to promote a programming style where data structures are accessed through intermediate objects. For instance, hash tables or vectors are accessed through enumeration object. So if we are thinking of a hash table or a vector as a bean, the enumeration object is nothing else than a bean reference.

More importantly, most data structures, especially when considering application interoperability, will want to control reference on their internal structure as well as the kind of access rights. For instance, a name service may want to export a read-only or a read-write interface to different users. It is important that a simple Java cast does not allow upgrading a read-only interface to a read-write interface. By using two bean references, on two different Java objects, we prevent the use of Java casting, forcing to use our interface navigation where extra checks can be included. Having bean references also allows revocation of references. For example, the name service may allow deletion of a directory in which case the name service would revoke the bean references on that directory. Having an indirection would prevent other applications from hanging on to a directory object that does not belong to the naming service anymore.

Additionally, bean references support logical references, offering a late-binding mechanism through a primary key or a name. A typical example is a URL that is a reference but binds to the document through a naming service. Another typical example is a spreadsheet exporting its cells to external tools. Most likely, the goal is a logical naming of relevant cells, that is, through column and row numbers. Having the spreadsheet export a selection API based on row and column numbers can do this. Most likely, an enumeration object, which can be an object reference, will then represent a selection. That object reference would have a strong reference on the spreadsheet and the row and column ranges, allowing logical access the cells.

To summarize, it came to us as a surprise that bean references would prove actually very useful for programmers as opposed to being only a system-driven overhead for supporting replication. Also, it seems that the corresponding overhead is light. Indeed, most method invocations are internal to beans and are consequently using direct Java references, causing no further overhead. Only method invocations for cross-bean interoperability go through bean references, and the ratio has proved to be quite favorable so far.

3.2 Database Concept

A database is simply a collection of beans as far as replication is concerned, the consistency granule being the bean. The Bali JRE keeps track of which beans are modified across replication cycles, allowing to drive and optimize the replication consistency protocol. This obviously requires support at the Java virtual machine (JVM). Without virtual machine support, programmers have to inform the JRE about bean updates, which would be error-prone but possible.

In the absence of concurrent updates on different devices, the consistency protocol is quite simple. Beans carry a replication sequence number (RSN). The server increases the RSN of a bean whenever a client provides a new state for that bean. This happens when the client has modified a bean since the last synchronization. Conversely, a client will acquire the new state of a bean if its locally known RSN is smaller than the one at the server.

Because databases may be replicated on different devices, it may happen that the same beans be updated concurrently on different devices. Such a conflict is not resolved automatically. However, it is detected automatically. In the presence of a conflict, the server keeps the different conflicting states for a bean, as versions, this ensures a loss-free approach. Reconciliation is an application-specific task, and as such, is carried by programmer-provided plug-in at a database level. Upon synchronization, the plug-in is presented with the conflicting beans. Some plug-ins will be able to offer automated reconciliation during synchronization. This is the most effective approach for only one version per bean is kept and therefore replicated on each device. If a fully automated approach is not possible, the reconciliation can be delayed. The server keeps the conflicting versions and replicates them on devices. The applications may then request the end user to re-conciliate the different versions of a bean.

4 Related Work

The Bali work is related to many other works such as other JRE, Java profiles, persistent languages, software component models, model-view paradigms, replication algorithms and protocols, and finally schema evolution support. Quite a vast body of literature exists in these domains and our design is happy to rely on it, not claiming contributions. Indeed, the main contribution of Bali is to define a complete and practical end-to-end solution within the context of orthogonal persistence and model-view paradigm allowing for transparent replication of hyper-linked information.

Bali relates to PalmOS or Lotus Notes on a replication front. PalmOS has a very interesting approach for small devices although it does not promote transparent persistence. PalmOS advocates a database concept similar to ours. A database is a set of records and in-memory construct. Applications are mapping their data structures directly onto database records, mapping C structures on the memory chunks of records, leveraging records references for building linked data structures. Through databases, PalmOS avoids format translation and byte-copy overheads but it suffers from promoting a dialect of C language. The reference framework for records is weak, the approach suffering from a lack of garbage collection. Additionally, mapping C structures does not work across hardware architecture. Records are untyped sequence of bytes from a runtime perspective, preventing the replication engine to apply the necessary format translation (byte order and alignment).

Lotus Notes has been very successful, based on very similar assumptions: databases, replication, forms and views, automated deployment, etc. The two main differences are that Lotus Notes does not support a real programming language such as Java, but supports scripting through LotusScript. The second difference is that databases contain traditional tuples instead of persistent objects. Forms and views are conceptually equivalent to models and views, and Lotus Notes support hyperlinking. Not assuming Java just makes runtime support easier as long as scripting and forms are enough for the targeted applications.

Of course, Bali relates to JavaBean™ and Enterprise JavaBean™. The Bali extensions are mostly around multiple interfaces and references, along with replication based on transparent persistence. In fact, our extensions have been quite inspired by Microsoft COM. The same influence can be seen in the early Sun's proposals for the Glasgow specification, tentatively the new coming JavaBean™ specification. A BeanRef is very similar to Microsoft Monikers. Beans are similar to COM objects, both supporting multiple interfaces with navigation. Beans are also better integrating a model-view paradigm in a very ActiveX way. Although sharing concepts with COM, Bali enjoys accrued robustness and security through Java.

Bali also relates to OSGI in its goal of automated deployment of software components. OSGI is proposing a framework to bundle code and data in JAR files that are the unit of deployment. A JAR file contains services and packages which can be exported. It may also import packages. We differ from OSGI by looking at immutable but versioned types. OSGI has basically no support for evolution, blindly relying on name equivalence. The deployment of new versions of JAR files may lead to failing services and unusable devices.

5 Status

Bali is still in its early prototyping phase. We have completed the design and implementation of the minimal JRE and the framework for databases, beans, and bean references. We have exercised that framework to develop some applications as well as some part of the system itself. For instance, the naming service of our registry is in fact implemented as beans and bean references. The code repository on the Bali server is also coded using databases, beans, and bean references. Bean references have proven to be quite powerful and easy to use, although a bit fragile from a consistent marshalling point of view without tools to generate them.

Transparent persistence is supported by an underlying object store using a single-level store technology. It is plugged under the J9 JVM from IBM OTI, specialized in Java for embedded systems. Although J9 runs on many hardware and operating systems, our prototype runs only on Windows so far. We are currently porting it to Palm and are looking at embedded Linux. Replication and automated code deployment are both fully designed and coding is underway.

6 Conclusion

The Bali project is exploring how the qualities and success of the Java language can be leveraged in order to provide a pervasive runtime environment suited to pervasive devices. We are interested in allowing an information-centric experience for end users on replicated data across devices.

We have chosen the cornerstone of orthogonal persistence associated with a software component model that adheres to a model-view paradigm. We believe orthogonal persistence is best suited for small devices for it best benefits from their persistent main memories. This model-view paradigm, along with a transparent persistence assumption, enables automated replication with optimistic consistency, across different hardware architectures. We plan to demonstrate it is a more viable long-term approach than approaches based on markup languages such as WAP.

Bali's main contribution is in exploring a Java-based platform as a practical solution by assembling a complete, end-to-end solution for server-based businesses to deploy information, applications, and services onto pervasive devices. Our approach nicely integrates with Enterprise JavaBeans™ servers, opening our approach to legacy and corporate information systems.

Bali is still in its in infancy and experience is needed to evaluate the usability and practicability of the approach. This is especially true regarding type evolution. The design is complete and the prototyping well underway. This summer, programmers outside our group will be programming against the model, and we plan to present their experience at the workshop.

Acknowledgments. The authors are indebted to Robert D. Johnson, at IBM Watson Research Center, for making this research possible, refining its scope and providing valuable contributions to the definition of its corresponding business case.

References

1. Open Services Gateway Initiative, Specification V1.0, see http://www.osgi.org
2. M.P. Atkinson, L. Daynès, M. Jordan, T. Printezis, and S. Spence, „*An Orthogonally Persistent Java*", ACM SIGMOD Record, Volume 25, Number 4, December 1996.
3. M. Dmitriev: „*The First Experience of Class Evolution Support in PJama*", The Third International Workshop on Persistence and Java, Tiburon, California, September 1998.
4. M. Dmitriev, M. Atkinson, „*Evolutionary Data Conversion in the PJama Persistent Language*", In the Proceedings of the 1rst ECOOP Workshop on Object-Oriented Databases". In Association with 13th European Conference on Object-Oriented Programming, Lisbon, Portugal, June 1999.
5. *JavaBeans*™ *Specification*, see http://www.javasoft.com
6. *Enterprise JavaBeans*™ *Specification*, see http://www.javasoft.com

Scalable and Recoverable Implementation of Object Evolution for the PJama₁ Platform

M.P. Atkinson, M. Dmitriev, C. Hamilton, and T. Printezis

{mpa,misha,craig,tony}@dcs.gla.ac.uk
Department of Computing Science, University of Glasgow,
17 Lilybank Gardens, G12 8RZ, Scotland

Abstract. PJama₁ is the latest version of an orthogonally persistent platform for Java. It depends on a new persistent object store, Sphere, and provides facilities for class evolution. This evolution technology supports an arbitrary set of changes to the classes, which may have arbitrarily large populations of persistent objects. We verify that the changes are safe. When there are format changes, we also *convert* all of the instances, while leaving their identities unchanged. We aspire to both very large persistent object stores and freedom for developers to specify arbitrary conversion methods in Java to convey information from old to new formats.

Evolution operations must be safe and the evolution cost should be approximately linear in the number of objects that must be reformatted. In order that these conversion methods can be written easily, we continue to present the pre-evolution state consistently to Java executions throughout an evolution. At the completion of applying all of these transformations, we must switch the store state to present only the post-evolution state, with object identity preserved. We present an algorithm that meets these requirements for eager, total conversion.

This paper focuses on the mechanisms built into Sphere to support safe, atomic and scalable evolution. We report our experiences in using this technology and include a preliminary set of performance measurements.

1   Introduction

An effective schema evolution technology is essential for any persistent platform. One of the dominant effects of time is change, and in enterprise applications[1], this manifests as changes in requirements, changes in understanding of the application, and changes to correct mistakes [38]. In the case of an object-oriented persistent platform, these changes result in a requirement to change the descriptions of existing objects, both their content and behaviour, to change their instances to conform with the new descriptions, and to introduce new descriptions that will later generate new objects.

---

[1] Applications that are typically long-lived, complex and large scale, referred to as "Persistent Application Systems" in [7].

G.N.C. Kirby, A. Dearle, and D.I.K. Sjøberg (Eds.): POS-9, LNCS 2135, pp. 292–314, 2001.

Zicari explored this issue in the context of O_2 [44,10]. Odberg identified a classification of object-oriented schema evolution techniques [36] and Wegner and Zdonik have examined the issues of schema edits in OODBs [43,40]. Our work contrasts with theirs, as for orthogonality and consistency PJama$_1$ stores the methods in the store [25,26,5], which provides us with the opportunity of supporting developers by verifying the mutual consistency of the new classes *including the code in methods.* As far as we know, commercial (O)RDBMs and OODBMs that support schema edit, such as GemStone [20], do not attempt such consistency checking. We describe our approach to schema editing covering:

❶ the way that changes are specified,
❷ the set of changes supported,
❸ the consistency checking undertaken, and
❹ the set of object population reformattings that may ensue from such a change.

In previous papers [15,17] we reported our rules for verifying that a set of changes were consistent and our evaluation of that approach using an algorithm that was not scalable, as it depended on building the new store state in main memory. The new contribution of this paper is an algorithm that safely, i.e. after validation checks and atomically, carries out eager evolution. We believe that it has good scalability properties. The algorithm depends on particular properties of our new store technology, Sphere, and is a partial validation of their value.

The challenge that we sought to overcome is presented by the combination of three factors. The algorithm has to be safe, that is any failure must leave the store in its original or final state. It has to be scalable, which means that it cannot rely on major data structures or evolved object collections fitting into main memory. And it has to be complete and general purpose. By this we mean that it has to accommodate any changes to any population of objects. That in turn requires that we must be able to run conversion code developed by application developers during evolution. In order that this code is tractable for application developers, the initial state of the store must remain stable and visible throughout the evolution. The new state appears atomically after all of their code has been executed.

The principal topics of this paper, are the algorithm and the support it obtains from Sphere and measurements demonstrating scalability. This support from Sphere includes incremental scanning, atomicity and durability. We provide a discussion of evolution models and a summary of our previous work ($\leadsto$2). We present PJama$_1$, an orthogonally persistent platform ($\leadsto$3), followed by an introduction to Sphere ($\leadsto$4). This is followed by a description of our *eager* evolution algorithm ($\leadsto$5). We present initial performance measurements ($\leadsto$6) before reviewing related work ($\leadsto$7) and offering our conclusions ($\leadsto$8).

2   Categories of Evolution

There are two important contexts in which evolution is required: *development evolution* ($\leadsto$2.1) and *deployed evolution* ($\leadsto$2.2).

2.1   Development Evolution

When developers are working on a persistent application they will frequently want to test it against persistent data. They therefore work on a collection of data and classes that represents the currently relevant aspects of the eventual enterprise application. At this time, they usually require up to a few hundred megabytes of data to achieve representative behaviour and run trials. For example, when testing the geographic application of persistence (GAP, ↝6.3) we use a few counties of the UK or California, rather than the whole UK or USA data.

It is typical of this phase of use, which may include user trials, that changes occur very frequently. The developer then needs to change classes and install them and the consequential changes in the experimental store. As any users involved are aware that this is a development system, it is acceptable to interrupt the prototype service if one exists. Normally, using the evolution technology proves much faster than rebuilding the store. However, we have observed developers still rebuilding the store as opposed to using the evolution technology, and conclude that convenience is crucial to the use of evolution technology in this context. We are therefore working on making the evolution technology easier to use e.g. integrating it with build and compilation technology [16].

2.2   Deployed Evolution

Once developers ship a version of an enterprise system we expect it to be in constant use at a large number of customer sites. These customers, or other bespoke software vendors, will develop their own software (classes) and populate their stores with the shipped classes, their own classes and instances of both sets of classes. Meanwhile, the original developers will have fixed bugs or provided new facilities, and will need to ship the revised classes to the stores of customers that want to obtain bug fixes or a new release. This requires a different treatment from development evolution.

❶ *Validation and Preparation*: As much as possible of the validation and preparation must be completed at the developer's site, based on configuration management information recording the exact versions of classes shipped to each customer.

❷ *Defining the Transformations*: Some optimised "pre-compiled" form of all of the transformations of previously shipped classes would be assembled at the developer's site. The developer would take responsibility for information migrating to the new forms, just as an office-tool or CAD-tool vendor does today.

❸ *Packaging the Change*: The results of the previous two steps have to be packaged into a "self-installing" unit, that can be shipped to a customer site and activated by the customer.

❹ *Installing the Change*: Once activated, the change must install against very large collections of data, without excessive disruption of a customer's workload. That is, the evolution must operate safely and concurrently with the existing workload and the customer must be able to meet an urgent requirement by limiting evolution's resource consumption, interrupting or terminating the evolution if necessary.

As far as we know, it is not yet possible to perform *validated, safe and non-disruptive, deployed* evolution in any system. It would, of course, need to be incremental, to limit disruption, and in most cases would need to be partial, so that some code can continue to work with earlier versions. This paper is concerned only with *development* evolution, which we believe can usefully be eager and total, provided that it is scalable and safe.

2.3   Development Evolution Requirements

The goals for development evolution technology have been described [15,17]. Here we present a summary.

❶ *Durability*: A primary aspect of safety is that evolution should never leave a persistent object store (POS) in an inconsistent state. That is, any failure must either leave the POS unchanged or an evolution must complete i.e. evolution should be treated as atomic. Either of these may utilise recovery on restart.

❷ *Validity*: Best efforts must be made to detect developers' mistakes as early as possible, in order that preventable errors are not propagated into the POS. In particular, the classes in a PJama$_1$ store after an evolution must be completely *source compatible* [21], and all instances must conform to their class's definition.

❸ *Scalability*: Any evolution step should be completed in a reasonable time, and with reasonable space requirements, taking into account the nature of the changes requested. For example, the resources used should, at worst, be approximately proportional to the volume of data that must be updated in the POS.

❹ *Generality*: Whatever change developers discover they need, they should be able to achieve it. This includes any transfer of information between the pre-evolution and post-evolution state that they require, even if its representation is fundamentally different.

❺ *Convenience*: Developers should be able to achieve evolution of a POS using tools and procedures that are as close as possible to their normal methods of working. The amount of additional concepts that they have to understand and the number of additional steps they have to take, should both be minimal.

Durability (❶) is achieved using logging ($\rightsquigarrow$4); but excessive logging has to be avoided as it would impact scalability (❸). Generality (❹) and convenience (❺) are achieved by allowing developers to present new or redefined classes that have been obtained in any way they wish, either as source Java or classes in bytecode form, e.g. obtained from a third party. They can also explicitly change the class hierarchy.

General transport of information from the pre-evolution to post-evolution state is supported by allowing developers to write *conversion methods* in Java. This requirement to execute arbitrary, developer-supplied code during evolution imposes three technical requirements on our implementation:

- A Java Virtual Machine (JVM) [28] must be available to execute this code (at present we use PJama₁, $\rightsquigarrow$3). It must support all of the normal PJama₁ semantics — particularly, the creation of **new** objects that then become persistent because they are reachable in the post-evolution state.
- Failures, e.g. uncaught exceptions, in this code must result in the whole evolution step being rolled back (requirement ❶).
- This code must have understandable semantics. We choose to guarantee that the pre-evolution data state remains visible and unchanged throughout the evolution transaction, so that algorithms that scan data structures do not encounter partially transformed data. We also allow access to the post-evolution state, selected via a class naming scheme.

2.4   Lessons from Version 1

The previously-reported work [15,17] emphasised the opportunity and need to verify an evolution before applying it. In order that developers can use their usual tools, we allow them to edit and recompile classes (or replace classfiles) in the usual way. The change involved in an evolution step is then defined by the difference between these new class definitions and the old definitions[2].

For any case where the default transformation between the old and new instance format is not satisfactory, a developer can provide a conversion method written in Java. During evolution, for each instance of the specified class in the old state, this method is called and supplied with that instance in its original state, and the new instance after default transformation[3]. While these methods are executing, they may traverse structures reachable from the old version of the instance and they may build arbitrary new structures reachable from the new version of the instance.

Before proceeding with any changes to the store, a verification step analyses all of these classes and methods (and explicit changes) to make certain that they are compatible. For example, it checks that there aren't still methods in the new definitions (or in the classes that are unchanged) that potentially use a discontinued member of a class. Only when it is clear that no predictable inconsistencies will be created between classes or between classes and data in the store, do we proceed with evolution. All of these changes we retain and reinforce.

The previous and current algorithm, identify the subset of changed classes whose instances need to be visited, and then they perform a scan of the store,

---

[2] In addition, the developer can specify explict class removals, class insertions and class renaming.

[3] There are actually variants, for example to allow the developer's method to choose which subclass to construct.

visiting those instances and supplying them to conversion methods if necessary. The previous algorithm simply faulted each old object into main memory, allocated a new object and performed the transformation. It kept all of the new objects in main-memory until the scan was complete, and then committed them to the store in a single checkpoint, fixing any references that were once to the old versions to refer to the new versions. This had two non-scalable features. The whole of the set of new versions and their dependent structures, and the fix-up table had to fit in main memory. The whole of the set of old versions and the whole of the set of new versions and the dependent structures of both sets had to fit in the persistent object store simultaneously.

3   Aspects of PJama$_1$

A full description, rationale and review of PJama is available [5], which also summarises progress since the original proposal [6,3][4]. Here we select a few aspects of the latest version, PJama$_1$.

PJama is an attempt to deliver the benefits of orthogonal persistence [7] to the Java programming language [21]. It attempts to capitalise on the established experience of persistence [9] and on the popularity and commercial support for Java.

PJama$_1$'s aims to provide: orthogonality, persistence independence, durability, scalability, class evolution, platform migration, endurance, openness, transactions and performance. Evolution inherits requirements from these general requirements, in particular: orthogonality, persistence independence and openness lead to generality (❹) and validity (❷). Durability, scalability and performance are directly inherited.

PJama$_1$ was constructed by combining the Sunlabs Virtual Machine for Research (previously known as ExactVM or EVM) [41] with Sphere. This architecture is illustrated in figure 1 and further described in [30,27]. Much of the evolution code is written in Java and uses reflection facilities over the POS.

4   Sphere's Support for Evolution

Sphere is definitively described in [37]. We refer to the application that is using Sphere as the *mutator*, which may be some C or C++ application, or an application in some other language and its virtual machine. The latter is the case when we consider PJama$_1$. The code, written in Java, that organises evolution, is an example of a mutator, from Sphere's point of view.

4.1   Overview of Sphere's Organisation

Sphere permits an object to be any sequence of fields, where a field can be a scalar of 1, 2, 4 or 8 bytes or a pointer of 4 bytes[5].

---

[4] An intermediate review appeared as [25,4]

[5] Sphere can be recompiled for 64-bit pointers, but cannot operate with a mixture of address sizes.

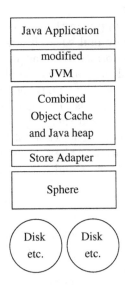

Fig. 1. PJama₁ Architecture — Sphere supports PJama

Objects are grouped into *partitions*. Each partition contains a data structure, called the *indirectory entry*, for each object that it holds. This provides one level of indirection to each object. The indirectory entries in a partition are grouped in a table called the *indirectory*.

Each partition is managed by a *regime*. This regime determines how space is administered. Objects are allocated in partitions that are appropriate for their size, number of pointers, etc.

Each object is identified by a unique *persistent identifier* (PID). A PID consists of a pair ⟨LP#, IEI#⟩ where LP# is a *logical partition identifier* and IEI# is an *indirectory entry index* used to address the entry in the indirectory.

When necessary, an object holds a reference to a *descriptor*. Descriptors are auxiliary objects that describe the layout (e.g. location of reference fields) of objects of the same type (i.e. in the case of PJama, instances of the same class). A descriptor is lazily replicated in each partition that contains objects that need to be described by it and is then shared by these objects. A descriptor is eliminated automatically from a partition when the garbage collector removes the last object that it describes. Hence the presence of a descriptor implies instances in this partition and its absence implies that there are none of its instances here. A descriptor index in each partition supports a rapid test for the presence of a particular descriptor.

Partitions are introduced to permit incremental store management algorithms, such as evolution and disk garbage collection. The partition's regime selects particular versions of their increments to apply. A mapping between physical and logical partitions is used to permit simple atomic transitions, as in Challis' algorithm [11,12] or in shadow paging [1,13,35].

4.2   Recovery Mechanisms

The recovery mechanism is based on the ARIES write-ahead logging algorithms [33,32,31] so that we can exploit logical logging and other techniques for using relatively small amounts of data to support durability [22].

4.3   Sphere's Support for Evolution

The technology to support evolution is described in [23] and can be summarised as follows.

- The use of a partition and regime structure to selectively scan the store linearly and incrementally.
- The use of the *descriptor invariant* to rapidly discover whether any instances of a class exist within a partition and hence to rapidly identify the extent of the classes to be transformed, without having to maintain exact class extents during other computations, which are presumed to dominate processing.
- The use of the disk garbage collector's algorithms to manage identity and copying.
- The use of the logical to physical partition number mapping to achieve durable atomic transitions without excessive log traffic.
- The use of hidden *limbo* versions of objects ($\leadsto$5) to
  - avoid log traffic,
  - avoid PID allocation,
  - hold the old and new state simultaneously at a cost proportional to the actual changes, and
  - to reveal the new state atomically at the conclusion of evolution.

5   An Eager Evolution Algorithm

We will use the following terminology. We refer to objects that are undergoing evolution as *evolving objects*. During the execution of the conversion methods and for some period thereafter, these objects exist simultaneously in their old form, *old object*, and in their new form, *new object*. During part of this co-existance, they are both referred to by the same *PID*, to avoid the costs of allocating additional *PID*s, and in the post-evolution state the new object has the identity previously owned by the old object, which has now disappeared. While they share the same *PID*, the hidden new state is referred to as a *limbo object*.

The main steps in an evolution are the following (see [23]).

❶ *Specify the Set of Class Changes and Instance Transformations*: Developers generate, or obtain in the case of third-party code, a set of revised classes and ask the evolution tool to install them in a specified store. They must also define methods to take information from old instances of a class to new instances of that class, or some related class, whenever the default transformations will not suffice.

❷ *Analyse and Validate the Set of Changes*: The PJama₁ *build tool*, which includes a specialised version of the standard Java source compiler[6] is used to verify the consistency of the new set of classes. We define consistency as follows: the classes should be mutually *source compatible* [21]. This means that it must be possible to compile their source files together without problems. The tool maintains records of the classes used with and contained in the store, and compares those with the classes presented and reachable through the current CLASSPATH. It then selectively recompiles those classes for which the source has changed. If a class does not have source code (e.g. it belongs to a third-party library), this should be explicitly confirmed by the developer. After recompilation, the build tool compares the resulting classes with their original versions saved in the store. If a class has changed in a potentially incompatible way (e.g. a public method has been deleted), the tool forces recompilation of all of the classes that might be affected by this change. In the above case that would be all of the classes whose old versions called the deleted method, and which haven't yet been recompiled. If recompilation fails, the whole evolution is aborted. Therefore an inconsistent set of changes can never be propagated into the store.

Changes to the class hierarchy are performed implicitly, by changing the **extends** phrase of the classes definition. However, if the developer wishes to delete a class, say D, completely, they have to explicitly specify this operation. An outcome of this analysis will be a set of class replacements, $\mathcal{R}$, of the form C ↦ C', a set of new classes, $\mathcal{N}$, a set of classes to be deleted, $\mathcal{D}$, and a set of transformations, $\mathcal{T}$, (developer-supplied or default). For each member of $\mathcal{R}$ modified such that the format of its instances is changed, there must be a corresponding member of $\mathcal{T}$ or there must be no instances of the class currently in the store. This latter property is verified immediately, since Sphere performs that check very quickly. Similarly, for each class in $\mathcal{D}$, there must either be no instances of that class in the store, or a method must be specified in $\mathcal{T}$ to *migrate* all of its "orphan" instances to other classes.

We enter the next phase with a set, $\mathcal{CV}$, which is all of the classes whose instances must be visited during store traversal. These are the classes for which there exists a default or developer-defined transformation in $\mathcal{T}$. If $\mathcal{CV}$ is empty, skip steps ❸, ❹ and ❺.

❸ *Prepare for Evolution*: Carry out the *marking phase* of Sphere's off-line cyclic garbage collector for the whole store (SGGC, see [37]). This ensures that all of the garbage objects are marked so that they will not participate in evolution and hence be resuscitated by being made reachable.

❹ *Perform all of the Instance Substitutions*: Traverse the store, one populated partition, p, at a time, visiting only partitions with relevant regimes, e.g. partitions containing only scalar arrays need not be visited. For each class, C, in $\mathcal{CV}$ lookup C in p's descriptor table. If no descriptors are found, skip to the next partition. Conversely, if a descriptor for any C is found, scan the objects

---

[6] Specialised to enable it to deal with old and new definitions of classes simultaneously in conversion methods, and to access class information kept in the store.

in p. For each non-garbage object that has a descriptor that refers to a class in $\mathcal{CV}$, create a new instance in the format C' in a new partition, record the ⟨old-PID, new-PID⟩ pair[7], move data into the new object using the default transformation, and then apply any developer-supplied transformation.

When all of the evolving objects in p have been converted, the old and new worlds are co-located into one new partition using a slightly customised partition garbage collector. In the resulting partition, the old form of each instance is directly referenced by its PID but the *limbo* form lies in the following bytes, no longer directly referenced by a PID[8]. The change in logical to physical mapping is recorded in the log, as is the allocation and de-allocation of partitions, as usual for a garbage collection. If phase ❺ does not occur, e.g. due to a crash, the limbo objects are reclaimed by the next garbage collection. Hence the reachable store currently hasn't changed, it has only expanded to hold unreachable limbo objects and new instances reachable only from them.

❺ *Switch from Old World to New World*: At the end of the previous phase all of the new format data and classes are in the store but unreachable. Up to this point recovery from failure, e.g. due to an unhandled Exception thrown by a developer-supplied transformation, would have rolled back the store to its original state. We now switch to a state where recovery will roll forward to complete the evolution, as, once we have started exposing the new-world we must expose all of it and hide the replaced parts of the old-world.

A small internal data set is written to the log, so that in the event of system or application failure, there is enough information to roll forward, thus completing evolution. This set essentially records all partitions that contain limbo objects. Each partition in this set is visited and all evolving object/limbo object pairs are swapped i.e. the evolving object is made limbo and the evolved limbo object is made live. The now limbo old objects can then be reclaimed at the next partition garbage collection.

Once this scan has completed, the new world has been merged with the unchanged parts of the old world.

❻ *Complete the Manipulation of Persistent Classes*: The classes that have fallen into disuse are removed.

❼ *Commit Evolution*: Release the locks taken to inhibit other use of this store and write an end-of-evolution record in the log.

The evolution technology is complex, but all aspects of it are necessary. For example, the new versions of instances have to be allocated away from the instances

---

[7] To permit references to new objects to be fixed up to the corresponding old-object's *PID*.

[8] This has the advantage that no extra PIDs are needed in the new partition and that extra space is only needed for the normally small proportion of instances that have evolved in each partition. There is a slight problem as developer-supplied transformation code may try to revisit these limbo new objects while transforming some other instance, e.g. to form a forward chain. A solution to this, which complicates the Sphere interface, is being considered.

they replace so that they can both be referenced in the developer-supplied Java transformation code. They then have to be moved, so that *only two extra partitions* are needed to complete the evolution, and no extra PIDs are needed in fully populated partitions. The garbage collector expands or contracts partitions as appropriate, when it allocates the destination partition, but it cannot expand a full indirectory. Use of limbo objects to arrange that both old and new objects and their dependent data structures can co-exist in the store avoids writing images of evolving objects to the log. A prepass of the cyclic garbage collection mark phase ❸ is necessary attempts are made to evolve unreachable instances. Occasionally these caused the developer's conversion methods to fail because they contained obsolete data. A beneficial side-effect is that evolution also performs a complete disk garbage collection and the recovered space is available to use during the process.

6   Initial Measurements

We have measured the time that it takes for our system to evolve a store with a certain number of evolving objects. The number of factors on which this depends is large, so we concentrated on the following issues:

- Verify that the time grows linearly with the number of evolving objects.
- Explore the impact of non-evolving objects in the store on the performance, particularly when their number is much greater than that of those evolving.
- Explore how the complexity of the objects and of the conversion code affects the evolution time.
- Validate synthetic tests with some real-life applications.

6.1   Benchmark Organisation

Our benchmark consisted of three synthetic tests, which are summarised in the following table:

Test No.	Description	Objects	Change
1	Simple class	simple	simple
2	001 benchmark	complex	simple
3	001 benchmark	complex	complex

In all three tests we varied the number of evolving objects (denoted n) in the store between 20,000 and 200,000. The second varying parameter was the number of non-evolving objects per evolving object, denoted by g for *Gap*. This varied between 0 (all of the objects in the store are evolving) and 9 (9 non-evolving objects per one evolving object). The objects were physically placed in the store such that evolving and non-evolving objects were interleaved. This is illustrated in figure 2. From the evolution point of view, this is the worst possible store layout, since we have to scan and evolve all of the partitions.

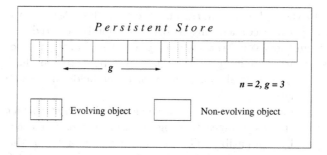

Fig. 2. Test store layout example

All of the tests were run with a constant Java heap size of 24MB (that is the default size for PJama$_1$), which, in the worst case, is an order of magnitude less than the space occupied by all the evolving objects. The sphere disk-cache size was set to the default value of 8MB.

In test 1 the old and the new versions of the evolving class were defined as follows:

```
// Old version          // New version
public class C {        public class C {
   int i, j;               int i, j;
                           int k;


...                     ...
}                       }
```

Default conversion (a simple method used by PJama if no custom conversion code is supplied) was applied to instances of C. According to the rules of default conversion, the values of fields i and j were automatically copied between the old and the new object, and the k field was initialized to 0.

Tests 2 and 3 were performed over stores populated with instances of the class from the adapted version of 001 benchmark, which we have taken from Chapter 19 of [42]. The initial Java version of this class looks as follows:

```
import java.util.LinkedList;

public class Part {
   int id;
   String type;
   int x,y;
   long build;
   LinkedList to;
   LinkedList from;

   // Methods to set/get fields, etc.
}
```

As defined in the 001 benchmark, an object of class `Part` contains a unique id and exactly three connections to other randomly selected parts. Instances referenced from the given `Part` instance p are stored in the p's `to` list. In turn, all instances that reference p in their `to` lists are stored in the p's `from` list, allowing a reverse traversal. The values of other fields are selected randomly from a given range.

In test 2 the only change in the new version of class `Part` was a different type of its `id` field — it was changed to `long`. Java types `int` and `long` are logically, but not physically compatible. This means that the values of the former type can be safely assigned to the fields of the latter, but the size of fields of these types are different (32 bits and 64 bits respectively). So object conversion is required in this case, but default conversion is enough to handle information transfer correctly.

In test 3 a more complex change was applied: the type of `to` and `from` fields was changed to `java.util.Vector`. The objects contained in the list can't be copied into another data structure automatically, so the following conversion class was written:

```
import java.util.LinkedList;
import java.util.Vector;

public class ConvertPart {
  public static void convertInstance(
                Part$$_old_ver_ partOld,
                Part partNew) {
    int toSize = partOld.to.size();
    partNew.to = new Vector(toSize);
    for (int i = 0; i < toSize; i++)
      partNew.to.add(partOld.to.get(i));

    int fromSize = partOld.from.size();
    partNew.from = new Vector(fromSize);
    for (int i = 0; i < fromSize; i++)
      partNew.from.add(partOld.from.get(i));
  }
}
```

As a result of conversion, for each `Part` instance two new objects are created, and six objects are discarded.

In each test run we were invoking our standard build tool that analyses and recompiles classes and then initiates instance conversion. It was only the instance conversion phase which we measured. In each test we measured the *Total Time*, defined as the time elapsed between the start and the end of conversion. We also measured the *Sphere Time*, defined as the time spent within the Sphere calls corresponding to step ❹, part 2 and step ❺ of the evolution algorithm. The difference between these two times was called the *Mutator Time*.

Every test run with the same values of n and g parameters was repeated ten times, and the average time value was calculated after discarding the worst case. All experiments were run on a lightly-loaded Sun Enterprise 450 server with four[9] 300MHz UltraSPARC-II CPUs [39], an UltraSCSI disk controller, and 2GB of main memory. The machine runs the Sun Solaris 7 operating system. The Sphere configuration included a single 1GB segment and a 150MB log. The store segment and the log resided on the same physical disk[10] (9.1GB Fujitsu MAB3091, 7,200rpm [29]).

6.2   The Experimental Results

In tests 1 and 2 we observe completely uniform behaviour, characterised by almost perfectly linear growth of the evolution time with both n and g. In test 1 the minimum and maximum total time values were 1.25 and 57.38 sec, whereas in test 2 they were 2.42 and 75.10 sec, respectively.

These figures show the total time taken during the evolution phase, with a further breakdown indicated at the extremes of both axes. Figure 4 shows the breakdown in more detail for a fixed $g = 0$, varying n. Figure 5 shows the same breakdown, this time for a fixed $n = 200,000$, varying g.

Graphs for all experiments at each value of n and g were generated, yielding the same typical set of results, namely that as the number of evolving objects increases, more of the total time is spent within the Sphere kernel, than within the Mutator.

Linear growth of the time with n means that the scalability requirement for evolution technology is satisfied at this scale. Despite the fixed Java heap size, the time grows proportionally with the number of evolving objects.

The growth of evolution time proportionally with the object gap (this parameter can also be interpreted as the total number of objects in the store), illustrates a trade-off we have made. When a partition is evolved, all of the objects contained in it are transferred into a new partition, thus a comparable amount of time is spent handling both evolving and non-evolving objects. The alternatives are to explicitly maintain exact extents or to segregate classes. Either would impact normal executions, we believe significantly[11].

On the other hand, the current implementation's results are quite acceptable: the time it takes to convert a store in which only 1/10th of objects are actually evolving is only about 4 times greater than the time it takes to evolve the store containing only evolving objects. We also performed experiments with the stores where evolving and non-evolving objects were laid out in the store in two solid

---

[9] The evolution code makes very little use of multi-threading.

[10] A pessimal arrangement to accentuate effects due to log writes.

[11] With an explicit extent, every object creation has to perform an insert and additional space is required. Such extents increase the complexity of garbage collection, which has to remove entries. Our regime scheme already provides as much segregation as the mutator chooses. We currently segregate into four regimes: large scalar arrays, large reference arrays, large instances and small instances. As segregation is increased, clustering matching access patterns is reduced.

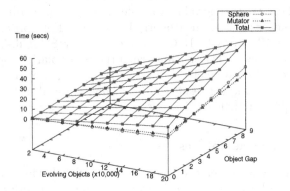

Fig. 3. Test 1 results

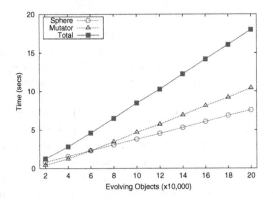

Fig. 4. Test 1 results – fixed $g = 0$

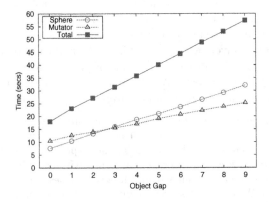

Fig. 5. Test 1 results – fixed $n = 200,000$

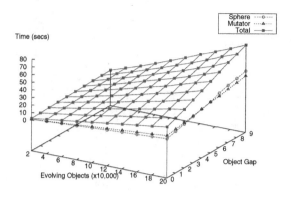

Fig. 6. Test 2 results

blocks, i.e. optimally clustered. On average, the slowdown for the store with $g = 9$ compared to the store with $g = 0$ was only about 5%.

In test 3 (figure 7) we observe the same linear behaviour of Sphere however the total time demonstrates a strange "quirk" in the part of the graph, where the number of objects is the greatest and they are packed densely. The cross-section of this graph at the constant value of $n = 200,000$ is presented in figure 8. The behaviour is clearly caused by some pathology in the upper software layer, i.e. JVM and Object Cache. At present we are investigating this problem.

To verify the linearity of our system's behaviour for much larger number of objects, we have performed the same evolution as in test 1, but with fixed $g = 5$ and with the number of objects varying between 100,000 and 2,000,000. The results are presented in figure 9. At the highest point in the graph, the store contains approximately 12,000,000 objects of which 2,000,000 interleaved objects are evolved.

In all of our tests we measured the amount of log traffic generated as part of evolution. Building limbo evolved objects generates no additional log traffic, as this step is performed as part of disk garbage collection, which itself has been optimised for very low log traffic (see [23,37]). Evolution only requires the generation of a log record for every evolving object at commit time i.e. when swapping the state of limbo objects to make them live (step ❺). Each log record is of a fixed size of 64 bytes (of which 40 bytes are system overhead), regardless of object size. In real terms 200,000 evolving objects generates approximately 16MB of log traffic[12].

---

[12] We anticipate that a further reduction in log traffic is possible by optimising the log records associated with swapping the limbo states. We believe we can cache the information, generating log records which represent a vector of swapped states, rather than the current one-per-object.

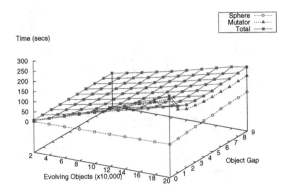

Fig. 7. Test 3 results

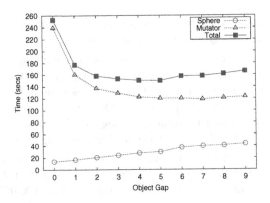

Fig. 8. Test 3 graph cross-section at $n = 200000$

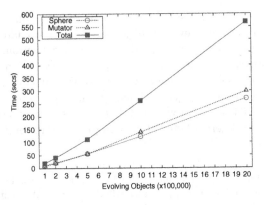

Fig. 9. Test 1 with large number of objects, fixed $g = 5$

We observed the time per evolving object. For each test we have calculated average total and average Sphere time per object (in test 3 not taking into account the pathologically behaving part of the graph). The results are summarised in the following table:

Test	Test 1	Test 2	Test 3
Object size (words)	2 − 3	7 − 8	7 − 7
Average total time per object (ms)	0.174	0.182	0.624
Average Sphere time per object (ms)	0.102	0.130	0.143

Comparing the time for test 1 and test 2, we observe relatively small change of time (30% for Sphere and almost 0% for total time), whereas the object size has grown about three times. We can conclude that at least for small objects and simple conversions the number of evolving objects matters much more than their size. Consequently, effects such as significant difference in conversion time for same size stores are possible. However, this might be different for larger objects. We plan to measure this in the near future.

6.3   A Real-Life Application

To validate these synthetic tests with a real-life application, we performed several experiments with GAP (Geographical Application of Persistence), an application which is being developed at the University of Glasgow by a succession of student projects. User map edits and and cartographic generalisation were added this year [24]. GAP is a relatively large system consisting of more than 100 classes, of which about 25 are persistent. The size of the main persistent store containing the map of the UK as poly-lines composed into geographic features, is nearly 700MB. So far the application's facilities focus mainly on displaying maps at various scales (with user-controlled presentation) and finding requested objects. In our evolution experiments we were changing persistent instances of "geographical line" class, subclasses of which represent such geographic features as roads and rivers. The form of vector data storage for such a feature can be in two forms shown on figure 10.

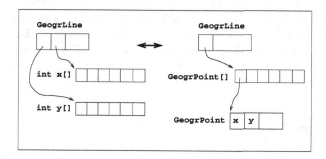

Fig. 10. Representations of Geographical Lines

During GAP development, both of these representations were tried, so we decided that conversion between them is a good example of a "real-world" schema change. We converted successfully about 900,000 line objects (complete UK data store), which took about 30 minutes. We also performed several experiments with smaller numbers of objects and observed practically linear time growth.

7   Related Work

To our surprise, we have managed to find very few works that deal with scalability and recoverability of evolution and its performance. There is one work where the O_2 system is benchmarked, which was published in 1994 [19]. Its extended variant was then included into [42]. In that work the authors concentrate on measuring and comparing the performance of immediate and deferred updates to variable size object databases. Since in PJama$_1$ we have currently implemented only immediate (eager) conversion facilities, this work is of no direct relevance to us. It is also not clear, whether the requirements of scalability and safety were considered in O_2. Furthermore, it is hard to compare the performance results, since in this work the authors didn't specify the changes they were making, and the hardware they used would be considered almost obsolete these days.

The RD45 project at CERN has focussed on the problems of providing persistent storage for vast quantities of data generated in physical experiments since 1995. At present the main system selected for use in this project is Objectivity/DB. Its evolution facilities are quite sophisticated. For example, it supports three kinds of object conversion: eager (immediate in their terminology), lazy (deferred) and what is called on-demand, which is eager conversion applied at the convenient time to the selected parts of the database. It also supports both default conversion and programmer-defined functions. A CERN internal report [18] contains some performance measurements for evolutionary object conversion with this system. Unfortunately, they mainly cover lazy conversion performance. And again, the hardware configuration used in the experiments (90MHz Pentium PC with 64MB memory and 1GB hard disk), does not allow us to compare absolute performance values. They also showed that the time was linear in the number of objects evolving, and not particularly sensitive to object size.

As for the scalability and recoverability requirements, it looks as if Objectivity/DB satisfies the latter but does not satisfy the former, at least when eager conversion is used. According to the report, during evolution this system gradually loads all the evolving objects into RAM and keeps them there until the end of the transaction.

8   Conclusions

In this paper we have identified the need for scheme evolution in persistent object systems and discriminated between two categories of evolution. We focus on providing *development* evolution using an eager algorithm that exploits the potential for incremental algorithms which we designed into Sphere. This algorithm makes only moderate demands on the logging system, yet provides tolerance to crashes and a separation of co-existing before and after states. It utilises algorithms already developed for disk garbage collection and allows application developers to supply methods written in Java to migrate information from the old instances to their new versions. It is incremental, proceeding a partition at a time, and only needs two additional partitions, plus space for completely new data structures made reachable by the developers' conversion code. Yet the transition from the old to new state is atomic. Although illustrated for classes defined in Java, it is general purpose and could be used for any other collection of persistent classes and their instances.

The steps in the algorithm are:

❶ Identify the changes as the difference between old and new class definitions.
❷ Verify that the changes are complete, mutually consistent and will leave the store in a consistent state.
❸ Prepare the store by carrying out the marking phase of a cycle-collecting disk garbage collector.
❹ Scan the store, one partition at a time, calling conversion code for reformatted instances. Create new versions and their newly-reachable data structures in a new partition.
❺ Merge new and old versions of instances in a partition, using a modified garbage collector. Repeat from ❹ until all partitions that may contain instances have been processed.
❻ Fix up pointers in new objects to new versions of evolving objects.
❼ Atomically flip from exposing the old versions to exposing the new versions.

We have developed this algorithm to be scalable after experience with versions that we have reported previously [15,17], which required the complete evolved state to be resident in main memory. Proceeding one partition at a time limits the total space requirement, but still delivers linear performance and an atomic switch from the pre-evolution to post-evolution state. Our initial measurements, reported in this paper, indicate that we have met the target of linear performance with modest space and log requirements.

Further analysis, particularly with real work-loads, will be needed to confirm this. We have uncovered one anomaly which occurs when conversion methods try to revisit new objects that were created by earlier conversion method calls in a different partition. This requires a solution.

We are aware of several factors that will accelerate these algorithms, particularly the use of larger transfer units [37] and compression of the few log records that we write.

A feature of the evolution algorithms that we are developing is that they carry out extensive checks before proceeding as a "best effort" at catching developers' mistakes and inconsistencies, rather than letting them become persistent structural defects in a persistent object store. This line of development is also closely integrated with our work on making evolution more convenient by integrating it with the build and compilation processes. Whilst we have mentioned it here, that work is still under development, and we expect to report it in a future paper.

We have noted that established software requires incremental background evolution, *deployed evolution* rather than the eager interruption of normal operations inherent in the work reported in this paper. We plan to investigate lazy and class versioning algorithms that meet such deployed evolution in our future work.

References

1. M.M. Astrahan, M.W. Blasgen, D.D. Chamberlin, K.P. Eswaran, J.N. Gray, P.P. Griffiths, W.F. King, R.A. Lorie, P.R. McJones, J.W. Mehl, G.R. Putzolu, I.L. Traiger, B.W. Wade, and V. Watson. System R: A relational approach to database management. *ACM Transactions on Database Systems*, 1(2):97–137, June 1976.
2. M.P. Atkinson, V. Benzaken, and D. Maier, editors. *Persistent Object Systems (Proc. of the 6th Int. W'shop on Persistent Object Systems)*, Workshops in Computing, Tarascon, Provence, France, September 1994. Springer-Verlag.
3. M.P. Atkinson, L. Daynès, M.J. Jordan, T. Printezis, and S. Spence. An Orthogonally Persistent Java™. *ACM SIGMOD Record*, 25(4), December 1996.
4. M.P. Atkinson and M.J. Jordan. Issues raised by three years of developing PJama. In C. Beeri and O.P. Buneman, editors, *Database Theory — ICDT'99*, number 1540 in Lecture Notes in Computer Science, pages 1–30. Springer-Verlag, 1999.
5. M.P. Atkinson and M.J. Jordan. A Review of the Rationale and Architectures of PJama: a Durable, Flexible, Evolvable and Scalable Orthogonally Persistent Programming Platform. Technical Report TR-2000-90, Sun Microsystems Laboratories Inc, 901, San Antonio Road, Palo Alto, CA 94303, USA, 2000.
6. M.P. Atkinson, M.J. Jordan, L. Daynès, and S. Spence. Design issues for persistent Java: A type-safe, object-oriented, orthogonally persistent system. In Connor and Nettles [14], pages 33–47.
7. M.P. Atkinson and R. Morrison. Orthogonal Persistent Object Systems. *VLDB Journal*, 4(3):309–401, 1995.
8. M.P. Atkinson, M.E. Orlowska, P. Valduriez, S. Zdonik, and M. Brodie, editors. *Proc. of the 25th Int. Conf. on Very Large Data Bases*. Morgan Kaufmann, Edinburgh, Scotland, UK, September 1999.
9. M.P. Atkinson and R. Welland, editors. *Fully Integrated Data Environments*. Springer-Verlag, 1999.
10. F. Cattaneo, A. Coen-Porsini, L. Lavazza, and R. Zicari. Overview and Progress Report of the ESSE Project: Supporting Object-Oriented Database Schema Analysis and Evolution. In B. Magnusson, B. Meyer, and J-F. Perrot, editors, *Proc. 10th Intl. Conf. on Technology of Object-Oriented Languages and Systems (TOOLS 10)*, pages 63–74. Prentice Hall, 1993.
11. M.F. Challis. The JACKDAW database package. In *Proc. of the SEAS Spring Technical Meeting (St Andrews, Scotland)*, 1974.
12. M.F. Challis. Database consistency and integrity in a multi-user environment. In B. Shneiderman, editor, *Databases: Improving Usability and Responsiveness*, pages 245–270. Academic Press, 1978.

13. D.D. Chamberlin, M.M. Astrahan, M.W. Blasgen, J.N. Gray, W.F. King, B G. Lindsay, R. Lorie, J.W. Mehl, T.G. Price, F. Putzolo, P.G. Selinger, M. Schkolnick, D.R. Slutz, I.L. Traiger, B.W. Wade, and R.A. Yost. A history and evaluation of system R. *Communications of the ACM*, 24(10):632, October 1981. Reprinted in M. Stonebraker, Readings in Database Systems, Morgan Kaufmann, San Mateo, CA, 1988.

14. R. Connor and S. Nettles, editors. *Persistent Object Systems: Principles and Practice*. Morgan Kaufmann, 1996.

15. M. Dmitriev. The First Experience of Class Evolution Support in PJama. In Morrison et al. [34], pages 279–296.

16. M. Dmitriev. Class and Data Evolution Support in the PJama Persistent Platform. Technical Report TR-2000-57, Department of Computing Science, University of Glasgow, Glasgow G12 8QQ, Scotland, 2000.

17. M. Dmitriev and M.P. Atkinson. Evolutionary Data conversion in the PJama Persistent Language. In *Proc. of the 1st ECOOP W'shop on Object-Oriented Databases*, 1999.

18. European Organization for Nuclear Research (CERN). Using an Object Database and Mass Storage System for Physics Analysis.
http://wwwinfo.cern.ch/asd/rd45/reports/m3_96/milestone_3.htm [May 9, 2000].

19. F. Ferrandina, T. Meyer, and R. Zicari. Schema Evolution in Object Databases: Measuring the Performance of Immediate and Deferred Updates. In *Proc. of the 20th Int. Conf. on Very Large Data Bases, Santiago, Chile*, 1994.

20. GemStone Systems Inc. The GemStone/J iCommerce Platform.
http://www.gemstone.com/products/j/main.html [May 9, 2000].

21. J. Gosling, B. Joy, and G. Steele. *The Java Language Specification*. Addison-Wesley, December 1996.

22. C.G. Hamilton. Recovery Management for Sphere: Recovering a Persistent Object Store. Technical Report TR-1999-51, Department of Computing Science, University of Glasgow, Glasgow G12 8QQ, Scotland, December 1999.

23. C.G. Hamilton, M.P. Atkinson, and M. Dmitriev. Providing Evolution Support for PJama₁ within Sphere. Technical Report TR-1999-50, Department of Computing Science, University of Glasgow, Glasgow G12 8QQ, Scotland, December 1999.

24. R.P. Japp. Adding Support for Cartographic Generalisation to a Persistent GIS. BSc Dissertation, University of Glasgow, Department of Computing Science, 2000.

25. M.J. Jordan and M.P. Atkinson. Orthogonal Persistence for Java — A Mid-term Report. In Morrison et al. [34], pages 335–352.

26. M.J. Jordan and M.P. Atkinson. Orthogonal Persistence for the Java Platform — Specification. Technical report, Sun Microsystems Laboratories Inc, 901, San Antonio Road, Palo Alto, CA 94303, USA, 2000.

27. B. Lewis and B. Mathiske. Efficient Barriers for Persistent Object Caching in a High-Performance Java Virtual Machine. In *Proc. of the OOPSLA'99 w'shop "Simplicity, Performance and Portability in Virtual Machine Design"*, 1999.

28. T. Lindholm and F. Yellin. *The Java Virtual Machine Specification*. Addison-Wesley, 1996.

29. Fujitsu Ltd. 3.5-inch Magnetic Disk Drives MAB3045/MAB3091.
http://www.fujitsu.co.jp/hypertext/hdd/drive/overseas/mab30xx/mab30xx.html [January 5, 2000].

30. B. Mathiske, B. Lewis, and N. Gafter. Architecture of the PEVM: A High-Performance Orthogonally Persistent Java Virtual Machine, March 2000. These proceedings.

31. C. Mohan. Repeating History beyond ARIES. In Atkinson et al. [8], pages 1–17.

32. C. Mohan, D. Haderle, B. Lindsay, H. Pirashesh, and P. Schwarz. ARIES : A Transaction Recovery Method supporting Fine-granularity Locking and Partial Rollbacks using Write-Ahead Logging. *ACM Transactions on Database Systems*, 17(1):94–162, March 1992.

33. C. Mohan, B. Lindsay, and R. Obermarck. Transaction Management in the R* Distributed Database Management System. *ACM Transactions on Database Systems*, 11(4):378–396, December 1986.

34. R. Morrison, M.J. Jordan, and M.P. Atkinson, editors. *Advances in Persistent Object Systems — Proc. of the 8th Int. W'shop on Persistent Object Systems (POS8) and the 3rd Int. W'shop on Persistence and Java (PJW3)*. Morgan Kaufmann, August 1998.

35. D.S. Munro, R.C.H. Connor, R. Morrison, S. Scheuerl, and D. Stemple. Concurrent shadow paging in the flask architecture. In Atkinson et al. [2], pages 16–42.

36. E. Odberg. Category classes: Flexible classification and evolution in object-oriented databases. *Lecture Notes in Computer Science*, 811:406–419, 1994.

37. T. Printezis. *Management of Long-Running, High-Performance Persistent Object Stores*. PhD thesis, Department of Computing Science, University of Glasgow, Glasgow G12 8QQ, Scotland, 2000.

38. D.I.K. Sjøberg. *Thesaurus-Based Methodologies and Tools for Maintaining Persistent Application Systems*. PhD thesis, Department of Computing Science, University of Glasgow, Glasgow G12 8QQ, Scotland, 1993.

39. Sun Microsystems Inc. Workgroup Servers, Sun Enterprise™ 450. http://www.sun.com/servers/workgroup/450/ [January 5, 2000].

40. P. Wegner and S.B. Zdonik. Inheritance as an incremental modification mechanism or what like is and isn't like. In S. Gjessing and K. Nygaard, editors, *ECOOP '88, European Conf. on Object-Oriented Programming, Oslo, Norway*, volume 322 of *LNCS*, pages 55–77. Springer-Verlag, August 1988.

41. D. White and A. Garthwaite. The GC interface in the EVM. Technical Report TR-98-67, Sun Microsystems Laboratories Inc, 901, San Antonio Road, Palo Alto, CA 94303, USA, 1998.

42. C. Zaniolo, S. Ceri, C. Faloutsos, R.T. Snodgrass, V.S. Subrahmanian, and R.Zicari. *Advanced Database Systems*. Morgan Kaufmann, 1997.

43. S.B. Zdonik. Version management in an object-oriented database. In *Proc. of the IFIP Int. W'shop on Advanced Programming Environments*, pages 405–422, Trondheim, Norway, June 1987.

44. R. Zicari. A Framework for Schema Updates in an Object-Oriented Database System. In F. Bancilhon, C. Delobel, and P. Kanellakis, editors, *Building an Object-Oriented Database System: The story of O_2*. Morgan Kaufmann, 1992.

Epilogue

Ron Morrison

School of Computer Science, University of St Andrews,
North Haugh, St Andrews, Fife, KY16 9SS, Scotland
ron@dcs.st-and.ac.uk

1 Congratulations

There are a number of components that must seamlessly gel to ensure a successful POS Workshop. The first component is the environment and we are indebted to Dag Sjøberg and his team for inviting us to this beautiful part of the world, organising excellent accommodation and preparing a memorable social programme. The excitement of the 120 metre ski jump and the bobsleigh run (even if only simulated) at the Olympic stadium was neatly balanced by the peaceful serenity of the paddle steamer Skibladner on Lake Mjøsa.

The second essential component is the technical programme. To some extent this is out of the control of the organisers since it depends on the papers that are submitted to them. Graham Kirby and Al Dearle took our offerings and moulded them into a stimulating, well-balanced programme. The format provided for traditional paper presentation and most notably a platform for extensive and healthy challenge and debate. Our thanks are due to them and the Programme Committee for undertaking this difficult task.

The final component of a successful Workshop is the participants themselves. The 9th POS Workshop will be remembered for the high-quality engagement and interaction of the attendees (and not just on the dance floor). While the exchanges were challenging they were also tolerant and well argued, particularly when it involved our younger researchers. This was the mood of the Workshop and it is hard to escape the conclusion that it was, in no small way, a consequence of the Norwegian environment and superb technical programme.

2 Innovation in the Workshop

Since 1985 the POS Workshop series has continuously changed its methods to meet the needs of the community. If there is another POS (POS X) I would like to suggest three areas we might tackle to keep the Workshop, and our research, at the leading edge. These are:

- the reviewing process
- the demonstration of working systems
- the presentation of experimental results

G.N.C. Kirby, A. Dearle, and D.I.K. Sjøberg (Eds.): POS-9, LNCS 2135, pp. 315-319, 2001.
© Springer-Verlag Berlin Heidelberg 2001

We should remember that the POS Workshop series was originally set up to cater for both theory and experimentation but has always encouraged theory that is firmly placed in practice.

2.1 The Reviewing Process

There was a lot of discussion before and during the Workshop on the subject of reviewing and how we could maintain the high-quality feedback we require for our research. Reviewing is a growing problem in Computer Science as the subject becomes more diverse and reviewers have less and less time to donate to the process. I would therefore like to make a suggestion for good practice to the organisers of POS X that may give a lead for the whole of Computer Science.

The suggestion is that we adopt a system of open reviewing where reviewers names are made known to the authors after the decision making process. For accepted papers the reviewers' names are published, as having reviewed the particular paper, in the proceedings. By this, reviewers take some responsibility for the quality of the papers presented at the Workshop, as well as for the feedback they give on rejected work.

While open reviewing is more difficult for Programme Committee members, I believe that it is how we would all wish to be reviewed ourselves. I look forward to its implementation and the response of the Computer Science community.

2.2 Demonstration of Working Systems

The POS Workshop series has always recognised the importance of experimental systems, and it is on this theme that I would like to suggest a second innovation. This is that wherever possible a paper presentation should include, or indeed may be replaced by, a demonstration of a working system.

Given that the paper is published in the proceedings of the Workshop, the demonstration can be used to illustrate the claimed results, and may even seduce some sceptics into reading the paper. With the advent of very powerful lightweight portable computers, demonstrations should not pose insurmountable technological problems.

2.3 Presentation of Experimental Results

Many scientific subjects have well proscribed ways of presenting results. Computer Science, being so young, has not yet developed these techniques and it is left to the ingenuity of the presenter to set the work in context. We often use the well-known technique of presenting a hypothesis and illustrating how the work meets the hypothesis. I would like to suggest that wherever possible we take a lead, and ask authors to use the categorisation developed by Larry Snyder [3] to highlight their results. The Snyder categorisation uses three themes in presenting work. These are:

- proof of existence
- proof of performance
- proof of concept

I have tried to use this categorisation for the papers in POS 9 and include it here. Some papers overlap, and I leave as a challenge to the authors to either show my error or sharpen up the claim made in the category.

2.4 Proof of Existence

Proof of existence gives evidence of the establishment of a new computational artefact. In a sense the persistence concept is our theory and some examples of existence are:

Computational Artefact	Proof of Existence
Can we build a persistent language?	PS-algol
Can we express all the computation in a persistent environment?	Napier88
Can we build a commercial system?	PJama
Can we build a persistent operating system?	Grasshopper
Can we unify code and data in a system?	Hyper-code
Can we build a poly-lingual environment?	PolySPIN, P^3
Can we build object stores?	Nmeme, Sphere

POS 9 papers in this category are:

- *A Framework for Persistence-Enabled Optimization of Java Applications*
- *Architecture of the PEVM: A High-Performance Orthogonally Persistent Java Virtual Machine*
- *SiteCache: a Transactional Group Coherence Protocol for Object Storage System*
- *Platypus: Design and Implementation of a Flexible High Performance Object Store*
- *TMOS: A Transactional Garbage Collector*
- *The Memory Behavior of the WWW, or The WWW Considered as a Persistent Store*
- *An Approach to Implementing Persistent Computations*
- *Transparent Orthogonal Checkpointing through User-Level Pagers*
- *An Overview of Ulisse, a Distributed Single Address Space System*
- *Hyper-Code Revisited: Unifying Program Source, Executable and Data*

2.5 Proof of Performance

Proof of performance gives evidence of an improvement on previous implementations. It may compare a new implementation to previous ones or it may compare competing systems. In the database world, papers based on the 001 [2] and 007 [1] benchmark fall into this category. Furthermore work on measurement, analytical modelling and simulation can often be reported in this style.

The main difficulty with proof of performance papers is ensuring that the measurements are accurate and not subject to undue disturbance factors. Measurements performed by more than one team are often more convincing.

POS 9 papers in this category are:

- *Evaluating Partition Selection Policies using the PMOS Garbage Collector*
- *A Comparison of Two Persistent Storage Tools for Implementing a Search Engine*
- *Implementing Orthogonally Persistent Java*
- *Event Storage and Federation using ODMG*

2.6 Proof of Concept

Proof of concept is a demonstration of how a particular set of ideas achieves its objectives. For example:

- what are we looking for a system to do?
- can we build it for such a cost?
- can we build it to run in a certain space or time?

Quite often a proof of concept investigation will involve a Human Factors analysis. POS 9 papers in this category are:

- *A Spatiotemporal Model as the Basis for a Persistent GIS*
- *Experience with the PerDiS Large Scale Data Sharing Middleware*
- *Toward Pure Polylingual Persistence*
- *An Application Model and Environment for Personal Information Devices*
- *Scalable and Recoverable Implementation of Object Evolution for the PJama Platform*

3 Epilogue to the Epilogue

Given the excellent quality of the food and scientific discussion at the Workshop, it is appropriate to conclude with a quote from The Hitchhiker's Guide to the Galaxy by Douglas Adams—„Thanks for all the fish". I look forward to the reassembly of our group at POS X. See you there …

Ron Morrison

References

1. Carey, M.J., DeWitt, D.J. & Naughton, J.F. „The OO7 Benchmark". In Proc. ACM SIGMOD Conference on the Management of Data (1993)
2. Cattell, R.G.G. & Skeen, J. „Object Operations Benchmark". ACM Transactions on Database Systems 17, 1 (1992) pp 1-31.
3. Snyder, L. „Academic Careers for Experimental Computer Scientists and Engineers". National Academy Press, USA (1994).

Author Index

Lecture Notes in Computer Science

For information about Vols. 1–2126
please contact your bookseller or Springer-Verlag

Vol. 2168: L. De Raedt, A. Siebes (Eds.), Principles of Data Mining and Knowledge Discovery. Proceedings, 2001. XVII, 510 pages. 2001. (Subseries LNAI).

Vol. 2170: S. Palazzo (Ed.), Evolutionary Trends of the Internet. Proceedings, 2001. XIII, 722 pages. 2001.

Vol. 2172: C. Batini, F. Giunchiglia, P. Giorgini, M. Mecella (Eds.), Cooperative Information Systems. Proceedings, 2001. XI, 450 pages. 2001.

Vol. 2173: T. Eiter, W. Faber, M. Truszczynski (Eds.), Logic Programming and Nonmonotonic Reasoning. Proceedings, 2001. XI, 444 pages. 2001. (Subseries LNAI).

Vol. 2174: F. Baader, G. Brewka, T. Eiter (Eds.), KI 2001: Advances in Artificial Intelligence. Proceedings, 2001. XIII, 471 pages. 2001. (Subseries LNAI).

Vol. 2175: F. Esposito (Ed.), AI*IA 2001: Advances in Artificial Intelligence. Proceedings, 2001. XII, 396 pages. 2001. (Subseries LNAI).

Vol. 2176: K.-D. Althoff, R.L. Feldmann, W. Müller (Eds.), Advances in Learning Software Organizations. Proceedings, 2001. XI, 241 pages. 2001.

Vol. 2177: G. Butler, S. Jarzabek (Eds.), Generative and Component-Based Software Engineering. Proceedings, 2001. X, 203 pages. 2001.

Vol. 2180: J. Welch (Ed.), Distributed Computing. Proceedings, 2001. X, 343 pages. 2001.

Vol. 2181: C. Y. Westort (Ed.), Digital Earth Moving. Proceedings, 2001. XII, 117 pages. 2001.

Vol. 2182: M. Klusch, F. Zambonelli (Eds.), Cooperative Information Agents V. Proceedings, 2001. XII, 288 pages. 2001. (Subseries LNAI).

Vol. 2183: R. Kahle, P. Schroeder-Heister, R. Stärk (Eds.), Proof Theory in Computer Science. Proceedings, 2001. IX, 239 pages. 2001.

Vol. 2184: M. Tucci (Ed.), Multimedia Databases and Image Communication. Proceedings, 2001. X, 225 pages. 2001.

Vol. 2185: M. Gogolla, C. Kobryn (Eds.), «UML» 2001 – The Unified Modeling Language. Proceedings, 2001. XIV, 510 pages. 2001.

Vol. 2186: J. Bosch (Ed.), Generative and Component-Based Software Engineering. Proceedings, 2001. VIII, 177 pages. 2001.

Vol. 2187: U. Voges (Ed.), Computer Safety, Reliability and Security. Proceedings, 2001. XVI, 261 pages. 2001.

Vol. 2188: F. Bomarius, S. Komi-Sirviö (Eds.), Product Focused Software Process Improvement. Proceedings, 2001. XI, 382 pages. 2001.

Vol. 2189: F. Hoffmann, D.J. Hand, N. Adams, D. Fisher, G. Guimaraes (Eds.), Advances in Intelligent Data Analysis. Proceedings, 2001. XII, 384 pages. 2001.

Vol. 2190: A. de Antonio, R. Aylett, D. Ballin (Eds.), Intelligent Virtual Agents. Proceedings, 2001. VIII, 245 pages. 2001. (Subseries LNAI).

Vol. 2191: B. Radig, S. Florczyk (Eds.), Pattern Recognition. Proceedings, 2001. XVI, 452 pages. 2001.

Vol. 2192: A. Yonezawa, S. Matsuoka (Eds.), Metalevel Architectures and Separation of Crosscutting Concerns. Proceedings, 2001. XI, 283 pages. 2001.

Vol. 2193: F. Casati, D. Georgakopoulos, M.-C. Shan (Eds.), Technologies for E-Services. Proceedings, 2001. X, 213 pages. 2001.

Vol. 2194: A.K. Datta, T. Herman (Eds.), Self-Stabilizing Systems. Proceedings, 2001. VII, 229 pages. 2001.

Vol. 2195: H.-Y. Shum, M. Liao, S.-F. Chang (Eds.), Advances in Multimedia Information Processing – PCM 2001. Proceedings, 2001. XX, 1149 pages. 2001.

Vol. 2196: W. Taha (Ed.), Semantics, Applications, and Implementation of Program Generation. Proceedings, 2001. X, 219 pages. 2001.

Vol. 2197: O. Balet, G. Subsol, P. Torguet (Eds.), Virtual Storytelling. Proceedings, 2001. XI, 213 pages. 2001.

Vol. 2198: N. Zhong, Y. Yao, J. Liu, S. Ohsuga (Eds.), Web Intelligence: Research and Development. Proceedings, 2001. XVI, 615 pages. 2001. (Subseries LNAI).

Vol. 2199: J. Crespo, V. Maojo, F. Martin (Eds.), Medical Data Analysis. Proceedings, 2001. X, 311 pages. 2001.

Vol. 2200: G.I. Davida, Y. Frankel (Eds.), Information Security. Proceedings, 2001. XIII, 554 pages. 2001.

Vol. 2201: G.D. Abowd, B. Brumitt, S. Shafer (Eds.), Ubicomp 2001: Ubiquitous Computing. Proceedings, 2001. XIII, 372 pages. 2001.

Vol. 2202: A. Restivo, S. Ronchi Della Rocca, L. Roversi (Eds.), Theoretical Computer Science. Proceedings, 2001. XI, 440 pages. 2001.

Vol. 2204: A. Brandstädt, V.B. Le (Eds.), Graph-Theoretic Concepts in Computer Science. Proceedings, 2001. X, 329 pages. 2001.

Vol. 2205: D.R. Montello (Ed.), Spatial Information Theory. Proceedings, 2001. XIV, 503 pages. 2001.

Vol. 2206: B. Reusch (Ed.), Computational Intelligence. Proceedings, 2001. XVII, 1003 pages. 2001.

Vol. 2207: I.W. Marshall, S. Nettles, N. Wakamiya (Eds.), Active Networks. Proceedings, 2001. IX, 165 pages. 2001.

Vol. 2208: W.J. Niessen, M.A. Viergever (Eds.), Medical Image Computing and Computer-Assisted Intervention – MICCAI 2001. Proceedings, 2001. XXXV, 1446 pages. 2001.

Vol. 2209: W. Jonker (Ed.), Databases in Telecommunications II. Proceedings, 2001. VII, 179 pages. 2001.

Vol. 2210: Y. Liu, K. Tanaka, M. Iwata, T. Higuchi, M. Yasunaga (Eds.), Evolvable Systems: From Biology to Hardware. Proceedings, 2001. XI, 341 pages. 2001.

Vol. 2211: T.A. Henzinger, C.M. Kirsch (Eds.), Embedded Software. Proceedings, 2001. IX, 504 pages. 2001.

Vol. 2212: W. Lee, L. Mé, A. Wespi (Eds.), Recent Advances in Intrusion Detection. Proceedings, 2001. X, 205 pages. 2001.

Vol. 2213: M.J. van Sinderen, L.J.M. Nieuwenhuis (Eds.), Protocols for Multimedia Systems. Proceedings, 2001. XII, 239 pages. 2001.

Vol. 2215: N. Kobayashi, B.C. Pierce (Eds.), Theoretical Aspects of Computer Software. Proceedings, 2001. XV, 561 pages. 2001.

Vol. 2217: T. Gomi (Ed.), Evolutionary Robotics. Proceedings, 2001. XI, 139 pages. 2001.